The Lawyers' Committee for Civil Rights Under Law

The Making of a Public Interest Law Group

Ann Garity Connell, Ph.D.

LAWYERS' COMMITTEE FOR
CIVIL RIGHTS
UNDER LAW

Cover design by Kelly Rebb, ABA Publishing

ISBN: 0-9742466-0-3

www.lawyerscommittee.org

CONTENTS

Dedication

This work is dedicated to those whose moral leadership made possible the founding of the Lawyers' Committee for Civil Rights Under Law: President John F. Kennedy and Attorney General Robert F. Kennedy, whose sponsorship of civil rights legislation, bearing great political risk, gave rise to the convocation of lawyers at the White House; to the civil rights workers and advocates of the period whose dignity, courage, and perseverance inspired a President and induced a nation to honor its principles; and to the lawyers whose response to the President and to the moral imperatives of their day led to the creation of an institution which has served to ennoble their profession over the ensuing decades.

Foreword

All three of us were deeply involved with the Lawyers' Committee for Civil Rights Under Law during its early years, and one of us was "present at the creation" in 1963. We thought we knew a lot about the Lawyers' Committee. In this authoritative and deeply researched book, however, a strong historian shines her searching lamp into dusty corners that we had forgotten, or never visited, and teaches us much that we never knew about a significant American legal institution. Just as important, Ann Garity Connell shows us the broad historical context from which the Lawyers' Committee emerged and in which it has functioned.

Until this book was written, the Lawyers' Committee's own institutional memory of its origins and its early history had been distilled over the years to a simplistic myth: Robert Kennedy, the Attorney General, frustrated by the treatment of civil rights workers in the South and the intransigence of Governor George Wallace, wondered out loud, "Where are the lawyers?" His brother, the President of the United States, then summoned leaders of the bar to the White House, where the Lawyers' Committee was born, like Venus on the half-shell.

As Dr. Connell shows us, the full story is far more complex, far more interesting, and far more important. It is, as she says, "fundamentally the story of a civil rights organization," but it is also a story about leadership, and about how that leadership, working from within the deeply conservative American legal establishment of the time, brought about the awakening of the American Bar to its responsibilities.

The word "establishment" has an archaic sound in today's disaggregated world of instant and constant communication, where entire industries (not to mention law firms!) appear like mushrooms and disappear overnight, and where politicians live by the 24-hour news cycle, tracking polls and Internet coalitions. But in 1963 there was an "establishment" in America, and there was emphatically a "legal establishment," dominated by the American Bar Association and perhaps two dozen big Wall Street firms, devoted to business and finance, that were, to use Dr. Connell's word, "reactive." In retrospect, it is amazing that the Lawyers' Committee could have been convened and its strong action-oriented agenda shaped from within that legal establishment, but it was.[1] The Lawyers' Committee was very careful to establish and maintain strong ties with the ABA.

The first co-chairmen, who served at the request of President Kennedy, were Harrison Tweed, then president of the American Law Institute, and Bernard Segal, later president of the ABA itself. Among the members of the Committee's initial executive committee were Lloyd N. Cutler, Judge Samuel Rosenman, William T. Coleman, Jr., William P. Rogers, William L. Marbury, and Dean John Wade. For the first 20 years of its existence (at least), the Committee's annual meeting was held "in conjunction with" the ABA's annual convention and literally under the same roof. The Committee was also determinedly nonpartisan: For many years, and perhaps still today, it was doctrinally required that one of the co-chairs be a Republican and the other a Democrat.

Dr. Connell's evidence suggests, disturbingly, that had it not been for the formation of the Lawyers' Committee and the leadership it asserted, the American Bar Association might well have traveled down a much different road in response to the civil rights marches and protests of the 1960s. The ABA's first reaction to President Kennedy's invitation to a White House meeting was to form an ad hoc Committee on Civil Rights and Civil Unrest, with a number of avowed racists as members. Its chairman did not believe that people involved in unpopular causes had trouble getting counsel and was on record for the proposition that the Executive Branch of government had no authority to enforce judicial decrees. Ultimately, however, the ABA took the other road: In 1966, instructed by the Lawyers' Committee's example, it disbanded the Civil Rights and Civil Unrest Committee and established in its stead the Section of Individual Rights and Responsibilities.

The rest, as they say, is history. The Lawyers' Committee went on to establish a litigation office in Mississippi; to advocate, and to litigate all the way to the Supreme Court for, the enforcement of controversial court decrees; to organize local committees in 15 cities, in the wake of the urban riots that swept the nation in the late 1960s; and to launch action projects in its National Office directed to voting rights, employment, education, and housing, as well as a Southern Africa project that gave enormous support to opponents of apartheid. All of these developments, and more, are recounted in the following pages.

---

1. Cognoscenti will appreciate Appendix A, which lists the names and affiliations of most of the 244 lawyers who attended the White House meeting.

This book returns value to the reader at several levels. For those who, like us, were alive and awake during the 1960s and 1970s, and especially for those who participated in the events chronicled in this book, this is a fascinating and detailed reminder of what happened, when, and who was involved. At another level, professional historians and students of the period will find this a valuable source, for Dr. Connell has collected and recorded the recollections of many people who were directly involved in these events, and she has been given access to private memoranda and other materials that have not been publicly available before now. At yet another level, Dr. Connell's book locates the Lawyers' Committee in the history of law and lawyers in America, from before the beginning of the Republic, through the origins of legal aid and public advocacy, to the early 1970s—a time when the Lawyers' Committee was a major force in bringing about a sea change in the way lawyers think about themselves, their work, and their obligations to a free society,

In the nearly 30 years that have passed since the period covered by this book, the Lawyers' Committee, no longer primarily focused on the South or the enforcement of desegregation decrees, has grown into a major national civil rights and minority advocacy group (www.lawyerscommittee.org). It has also evolved, as historical context has evolved. The Committee is today essentially a staff lawyer organization, no longer so dependent upon or representative of the private bar. The leading lawyers who are the co-chairs, directors, and trustees of the Lawyers' Committee today no longer need to have monthly meetings in New York to review developments and set the agenda. But we like to think they are a "fleet in being," ready to mobilize again when, if, and where our nation needs them.

> Louis F. Oberdorfer, Senior United States District Judge
> David S. Tatel, United States Circuit Judge
> James Robertson, United States District Judge

> February 2003

Acknowledgments

I want to express my deepest appreciation to Professor Herman Belz, without whose faith, guidance, and constant encouragement this work would not have been possible. I also owe a great deal of gratitude to all those men and women who were so generous in sharing with me their experiences from the early days of the Lawyers' Committee, and particularly to Jerome Shestack, who gave freely from his voluminous contemporary records on the founding of the committee. Finally, I am deeply gratified that the American Bar Association chose to publish this work, which memorializes the important place of the Lawyers' Committee in pioneering the public interest role of the American bar.

—Ann Garity Connell

Lawyers' Committee Acknowledgments

The Lawyers' Committee for Civil Rights Under Law thanks Ann Connell for this remarkable scholarly work, which shares the story of our early years and the permanent impact of our institution in making civil rights and racial equality a commanding priority in both the private and public interest bars and in other sectors of our society. We also commend the giants of our profession without whom the visionary efforts of President John F. Kennedy and Attorney General Robert F. Kennedy would never have borne fruit—Bernard G. Segal, Harrison Tweed, Louis F. Oberdorfer, Jerome J. Shestack, Berl I. Bernhard, Lloyd N. Cutler, John E. Nolan, John Doar, Nicholas deB. Katzenbach, Burke Marshall, Wiley A. Branton, Goler Teal Butcher, Whitney North Seymour, John Doyle, Paul Dimond, Milan C. Miskovsky, George N. Lindsay, David S. Tatel, John W. Douglas, James Robertson, Dennison Ray, Chesterfield Smith, Edwin Wolf, Frederick M. Nicholas, Frank R. Parker, J. Harold Flannery, Stephen J. Pollak, Norman Redlich, Thomas D. Barr, Robert F. Mullen, William L. Robinson, Robert A. Murphy, George Peach Taylor, Herman "Tex" Wilson, and so many others. In this book Ms. Connell also speaks about the critical leadership provided by the Board of the Lawyers' Committee and introduces the reader to the remarkable staff and legal volunteers whose dedicated and inspired advocacy added a new dimension to the term public interest law firm. Of course, this book is given life each day by the incredible, unceasing efforts of our present officers, board of directors and trustees, talented staff, local Lawyers' Committees, law firm volunteers and courageous clients.

Introduction

"If we are to keep our democracy, there must be one commandment: Thou shalt not ration justice."

Learned Hand
February 16, 1951
75th Anniversary Dinner of the
Legal Aid Society in New York

A perceived responsibility of the American Bar is the provision of competent legal advocates, including to poor and minority clients. In the early 1960s, neither the organized bar nor practicing attorneys in the South recognized or accepted responsibility for defending the civil rights of black citizens in that segregated society. As civil rights workers sought to change the discriminatory laws and practices in the South, the law was used against them. In an effort to empower them to defend their rights in an adversarial system, President Kennedy convened a meeting in the White House on June 21, 1963, of 244 of the nation's leading lawyers. He asked them to help move the civil rights crisis back into the courts, where blacks could find justice. They responded by forming the Lawyers' Committee for Civil Rights Under Law, which, in the period covered by this dissertation, 1963-1974, radically changed the bar's perception of its responsibility to advocate for minority rights pro bono publico by engaging major law firms around the country to provide, on a sustained basis, legal services in cutting-edge civil rights litigation.

The Lawyers' Committee also worked to foster the rights of black South Africans through legal work in the United States and in South Africa. Its leading members played a major role in institutionalizing within the American Bar Association a responsibility of the organized bar to work to protect American citizens' rights, and in incorporating in the ABA's Code of Professional Responsibility the renewed perception of each lawyer's duty to serve the public interest. The small ad hoc group evolved into one of the foremost public-interest law groups that appeared in the latter half of the twentieth century.

This essay examines that process. The Committee's records and personal interviews are the significant research component of this dissertation. Interviews with the founding members and leaders of the organization provided facts that are missing from the official record, as well as firsthand testimony concerning the group's motivation. Secondary sources are an important element in the research for the study of the bar and the history of legal aid.

Dissertation submitted to the Faculty of the Graduate School of the University of Maryland at College Park in partial fulfillment of the requirements for the degree of Doctor of Philosophy, 1997.

Advisory Committee

Professor Herman Belz, Chair/Advisor
Dr. Mark Graber
Professor James Henretta
Dr. Alfred Moss
Professor Keith Olson

CHAPTER 1

The Lawyers' Committee: A Historical and Professional Context

The Essentiality of Legal Advocacy in the American System of Justice

For more than 350 years, Americans have struggled with the dilemma of maintaining equity between public and private needs. This fundamental tension between the desire for personal freedom and the need to protect the public interest[1] is key to the development of American law and legal institutions.[2]

In the eighteenth century, when the American people won the right to govern themselves, they established a written constitution. The Constitution of the United States instituted a neutral legal system to balance the conflicting interests in society and to provide for liberty and justice.[3] Fundamental to the impartiality of the constitutional system is the "due process of law," given affect through the adversarial legal process.[4]

---

1. For a discussion of this concept, see KERMIT L. HALL, WILLIAM M. WIECEK & PAUL FINKELMAN, AMERICAN LEGAL HISTORY: CASES AND MATERIALS (Oxford Univ. Press 1991), ch. 1, *Law in the Morning of America*, 3-54.
2. *See* GEORGE L. HASKINS, LAW AND AUTHORITY IN EARLY MASSACHUSETTS: A STUDY IN TRADITION AND DESIGN (Macmillan 1960).
3. *The Constitution of the United States, The Preamble*, as in CHARLES C. TANSILL, DOCUMENTS ILLUSTRATIVE OF THE FORMATION OF THE UNION OF AMERICAN STATES (Washington: Government Printing Office 1927) 989.
4. Edmund Cahn, *Justice*, in INTERNATIONAL ENCYCLOPEDIA OF THE SOCIAL SCIENCES vol. 9 David L. Sills ed. (Macmillan & The Free Press 1968) 343: "In the law courts, the main requirements of due process, or procedural justice, are the following: No one must be

In the adversarial process competing litigants—rather than court officials—have responsibility for gathering evidence, formulating legal theories, and presenting evidence and theories at trial to a judge or jury.[5] Advocates act not as judge or jury, or even as social conscience, but as defenders of a single issue whose duty it is to present the strongest legal arguments possible to advance the cause represented by them. The decision maker—the judge or jury—is expected to be neutral and to approach the case with an open mind.[6] Fairness requires competent advocates on both sides of a dispute.[7] In grave matters, lawyers, or legal advocates, are indispensable for justice in the United States.

---

accused of behavior unless he could have ascertained the existence and meaning of the rule before he committed the challenged act. When accused, a person is entitled to know the charge against him, to know the evidence adduced in support of the charge, and to have a fair opportunity to collect and present his own evidence. The judge or other arbiter must be disinterested, unbiased, and attentive. If the accusation is grave, the accused is entitled to the assistance of counsel and advocate. . . . Moreover, even if a person has been found guilty, procedural justice requires that some way be afforded to reconsider the case later and correct any serious error that comes to light."

5. Stephen A. Saltzburg, *Adversary System*, in INTERNATIONAL ENCYCLOPEDIA OF THE SOCIAL SCIENCES vol. 9 David L. Sills ed. (Macmillan & The Free Press 1968), 108.

6. "In democratic societies adjudication is based on an entirely different set of expectations than those that underlie the legislative and executive functions. What the majority wishes is what the legislators should decide. But adjudication calls for decisions in accord with standards of right, to be made by persons who are free to apply these standards without concern for the popularity of their decisions . . . . the judicial process is deliberately organized to 'disconnect' it from the rest of the community." J.W. Peltason, JUDICIAL PROCESS, in Sills *supra* note 5, at 8:286,

7. RAYMOND MARKS, KIRK LESWING & BARBARA A. FORTINSKY, THE LAWYER. THE PUBLIC AND PROFESSIONAL RESPONSIBILITY (American Bar Foundation 1972), 9-10: "The traditional view of a lawyer's role in a society with a legal system based on the common law relies heavily on the adversary method. A single interest—a single side of any conflict—is represented by the lawyer. He is an advocate in the true sense of the word. He is neither judge nor jury; he is not even a social conscience. He is simply the advocate. Accordingly, he does not relate his conduct to the social rules produced by the cases he handles. He is interested solely in seeing to it that the interest of the party he represents is as ably advanced as is humanly and professionally possible. If it is done—on both sides of any adversary conflict—it follows, according to the central assumption of the traditional view, that the result will be both acceptable and just. . . . The traditional lawyer has seen himself as serving the public interest by simply doing his daily job of representing only one side of a controversy. In fact, he reasons that if he does anything but serve the singular interest of his client, he is deserting the public interest."

Roscoe Pound, the dean of American jurisprudence, judged lawyers indispensable. He wrote, "Our constitutional polity is so legal as to be dependent upon lawyers for interpretation, application, and maintenance."[8] Unfortunately, by the middle of the twentieth century, the bar in the United States had lost sight of the essentiality of legal advocacy for all classes. In 1963, the failure of the legal profession to assume any responsibility for the defense of the constitutional rights of black citizens in the South had resulted in a racial conflict that threatened the very fabric of American life, the constitutional system. To its dishonor, the legal profession in the United States watched in silence as the southern bar turned its back on the judicial process and on legally mandated change.

As the divide between the races grew more menacing, a movement to reform professional practices, particularly in the South, took shape in the heart of the legal establishment. Leaders of the corporate bar, the "barons of the bar," successfully called for the formation of a national Lawyers' Committee for Civil Rights Under Law. Its purpose was to marshal the advocacy of the private bar to help mediate the civil rights crisis. The activities of the Lawyers' Committee helped change the administration of justice in the United States. It is impossible to appreciate its impact without an understanding of the professional and historical context out of which it emerged.

The Evolution of Lawyering in America

The right to legal aid in America is rooted in the fifteenth-century statutory right of the poor in England to legal counsel.[9] It is clear that the colonists did

---

8. ROSCOE POUND, THE LAWYER FROM ANTIQUITY TO MODERN TIMES: WITH PARTICULAR REFERENCE TO THE DEVELOPMENT OF BAR ASSOCIATIONS IN THE UNITED STATES (American Bar Association 1953), xxvi.

9. *The Right to Counsel in Civil Litigation*, 66 COLUM. L. REV. (Nov. 1966), 7:1326. This article states that the right to sue for and defend his Right in court—the right to due process of law—and the obligation of the courts to assign counsel to protect the rights of indigents, were some of the prerogatives of English citizenry that were assumed into the legal system of the New World. The article quotes from English law: "And after the said Writ or Writs be returned, if it be afore the King in his Bench, the Justices there shall assign to the same poor Person or Persons Counsel learned, by their discretions, which shall give their Counsel, nothing taking for the same; and likewise, the Justices shall appoint Attorney and Attorneys for the same poor Person or Persons, and all other Officers requisite and necessary to be had for the Speed of the said Suits to be had and made, which shall do their Duties without any Reward for the Counsel, Help, and business. . . . " Statute of Henry VII, 1405, 11 Hen. 7, c. 12 (repealed).

not import the whole of the British legal tradition but adapted it to suit their experiences.[10] From the earliest days, they recognized the necessity for the accused to bring a competent advocate to legal proceedings.[11] At the same time, they rejected the English common law[12] and its auxiliary, an organized legal profession.[13] In place of the formalistic bar of the old country, they

---

Also, KERMIT HALL, ET AL., *supra* note 1, at 5, quote chapter 39 of the English Magna Charta, 1215, as the source of modern procedural and substantive due process. Two British parliamentary enactments of the Middle Ages supplemented chapter 39 by extending the benefits of Magna Charta beyond the nobility to all subjects of the realm. The first provided that "every Man may be free to sue for and defend his Right in our Courts and elsewhere, according to the Law" (20 Edw. III, c.4). The second introduced the phrase "due process of law" for the first time into English law: "no Man, of what Estate or Condition that he be, shall be put out of Land of Tenement, nor taken, nor imprisoned, nor put to Death, without being brought in answer by due Process of Law" (28 Edw. III, c.3).

10. Donald P. Kommers, *Reflections on Professor Chroust's "The Rise of the Legal Profession in America,"* 10 THE AMERICAN JOURNAL OF LEGAL HISTORY (Philadelphia) 202: "Lawyers were a fundamental necessity given the general adoption of English legal traditions and institutions."

11. CHARLES & MARY BEARD, THE RISE OF AMERICAN CIVILIZATION (Macmillan Co. 1930), vol. 1, 100. The right to counsel was incorporated into the Massachusetts Body of Liberties adopted in 1641. It formalized the colonial practice of allowing everyone to plead his own case, and if he could not do so, he should get someone else to help him whom he was to give "noe fee or reward for his paines."

12. Paul Samuel Reinsch, *English Common Law in the Early American Colonies*, vol. I, (1899), reproduced in SELECTED ESSAYS IN ANGLO-AMERICAN LEGAL HISTORY, 3 vols., by Various Authors (Little, Brown & Co. 1907), at 8: "It is generally agreed by students of the period that in the early American colonies there was a period of rude, untechnical popular law, followed, as lawyers became numerous and the study of law prominent, by the gradual reception of most of the rules of English common law." At 9: "Even after the common law had been generally received, still marks of the old popular law remain strong." At 53: "Most of the original departures in American jurisprudence . . . (can be traced) back to the earliest times." Also, for a discussion on English customary law in the colonies, see Julius Goebel, Jr. & T. Raymond Naughton, *Law Enforcement in Colonial New York: A Study in Criminal Procedure, 1664-1776,* 31 COLUM L. REV. 416 (1931), 420.

13. POUND, *supra*, note 8, 130-31. The first English settlers rejected the British Common Law along with is concordant institution, the highly trained and professionally organized common law bar, whose "records were in Latin and reports in Law French." The British common law with its "formalism" and "strict laws," and ideals "of the relationally organized society of the Middle Ages," was not in accord with those of pioneers opening up the wilderness.

established a tradition of democratic legal advocacy.[14] In America, anybody with the wit or talent for argument could act as a legal advocate.[15] This system of legal counsel thrived in the frontier,[16] but as commerce became more established in the colonies, some Americans returned to the protections afforded them as British citizens under the common law.[17]

---

14. MAXWELL BLOOMFIELD, AMERICAN LAWYERS IN A CHANGING SOCIETY, 1776-1876 (Harvard Univ. Press 1976), 33.

15. ANTON-HERMAN CHROUST, THE RISE OF THE LEGAL PROFESSION IN AMERICA, 2 vols. (Univ. of Oklahoma Press 1965). Chroust finds several factors inhibited the development of a legal profession in America before the Revolutionary War. The most important among these were the influence of the Puritans, who enforced decisions based on the 'word of God' as they understood it, rather than on English law; a hostile public attitude toward a profession associated with the arbitrary behavior of the Crown; a poorly trained bar due in part to the almost total absence of formal legal education; and the fact that the power structures of the community, dominated in the southern colonies by the religious leaders, refused to admit the lawyer into their ruling circles.

16. CHARLES WARREN, A HISTORY OF THE AMERICAN BAR (Howard Fertig 1966), 3-5: "In all the colonies, the General Assembly was the sole court of law. It was not until half a century after settlement that separate and independent courts were instituted. In all the colonies the courts were composed of laymen, with the possible exception of the Chief Justice." The word *attorney* was frequently used in early records, but it did not imply a man bred to the law or who made its practice an exclusive employment. These 'attorneys' were very largely traders, factors, land speculators, and laymen of clever penmanship and easy volubility, whom parties employed to appear and talk for them in court. The few persons who acted as professional attorneys were at first mostly "pettifoggers, or minor court officers such as deputy sheriffs, clerks and justices, who stirred up litigation for the sake of the petty court fees. In most of the Colonies statutes were passed prohibiting such persons from acting as attorneys." *Also see* Joseph Storey, *The Dilemma of the American Lawyer in the Post Revolutionary Era*, 35 NOTRE DAME LAWYER (1959), 49: "Before the Revolution . . . our progress in the law was slow . . . The resources of the country were small, the population scattered, the business of the courts was limited, the compensation for professional services was moderate, and the judges were not generally selected from those who were learned in the law . . . . From the nature of the business, which occupied the courts, the knowledge required for common use was neither very ample, nor very difficult."

17. BLOOMFIELD, *supra* note 14, at 34: "In the early colonial period, untrained men were the first to interpret and apply the new rules. Lay judges attempted to render substantial justice to both parties, regardless of common-law niceties. They avoided unnecessary formality, employing straightforward inquisitorial methods to uncover the moral factors involved in each case. Such rough-and-ready tactics, which mirrored the practices of certain English courts, worked well enough so long as communities remained small and economically self-contained. Every man might safely act as his own lawyer while

At the beginning of the eighteenth century, an organized bar that studied and practiced the British common law developed in the colonies. It represented the interests of the commercial classes.[18] Its members were learned in British law;[19] some even studied at the Inns of Court in England.[20] The colonial bar was a prominent force in the thinking of the Revolutionary period.[21]

---

society stood ready to protect his moral as well as his legal rights. The utopian image of man—stressing his corporate nature, subordinating his total behavior to community norms, and judging his transgressions by absolute moral standards—provided an essential foundation for early American jurisprudence."

18. RICHARD B. MORRIS, STUDIES IN THE HISTORY OF AMERICAN LAW: WITH SPECIAL REFERENCE TO THE SEVENTEENTH AND EIGHTEENTH CENTURIES, Second Edition (Octagon Books 1964). Morris finds that at the end of the seventeenth century the new British policy of constructive imperialism was introduced. It proposed the supplanting of chartered colonies by royal governments, the combination of smaller self-governing or proprietary units into large units of administration, and the strengthening of the executive power at the expense of the colonial representative assemblies. The new colonial charters reserved the King in Council the right to disallow colonial legislation and the right to hear cases on appeal from provincial courts. At the same time, wealth and the accumulation of property was growing in the colonies. On page 62, he writes, "The close of the seventeenth century was marked by a conflict in the law between the forces making for change and progress and the forces making for static security and conservatism. The compromise which was effected in the eighteenth century was largely a victory for the forces of reaction and brought about the widespread adoption of common-law."

19. Alan Day, *Lawyers in Colonial Maryland, 1660-1715*, 17 AM. J. LEGAL HIST. (1973) 145-63. Day argues that the professionalization of the bar can be attributed to the economic development in the late seventeenth century.

20. John M. Murrin, *The Legal Transformation: The Bench and Bar of Eighteenth Century Massachusetts*, in COLONIAL AMERICA: ESSAYS IN POLITICS AND SOCIAL DEVELOPMENT (Boston 1983), Stanley N. Katz & John M. Murrin, eds. Murrin states, "In the colonies British law and constitutional thought remained the only common denominator among Americans, who in other respects differed from each other far more radically than they differed from Great Britain."

21. CHARLES WARREN, *supra* note 16, at 187, found that only 25-50 American-born lawyers had been educated in England prior to 1760, and from 1760 to 1789, 115 Americans were admitted to the British Inns of Court. Warren thinks that the influence on the American Bar of these lawyers was "most potent," particularly in the southerly colonies. Their training was confined "almost exclusively" to the Common Law, based as it was on historical precedent and customary law. The habits that they formed there of solving all legal questions by the standards of English liberties and rights of English subjects proved of immense value to them when they later became leaders of the American Revolution.

Also see KERMIT HALL ET AL., *supra* note 1, at 53: 25 of the 56 signers of the

The American common law bar incorporated the British tradition of providing voluntary legal assistance to the poor at the request of the court. The right to pro bono legal assistance was not granted to criminals in England. However, in eighteenth-century America, pro bono legal assistance in both civil and criminal cases was a common practice.[22] The Americans deemed the right to counsel in criminal cases a necessity, and in the United States Constitution it was included in the Bill of Rights.[23]

Despite the influence of the Revolutionary bar, the continuance of a restrictive, elite, professional class[24] was resoundingly rejected by the new Republic. At the end of the eighteenth century, Americans reopened the calling to practically all comers,[25] and legal counsel continued to be affordable and

---

Declaration of Independence and 31 of the 55 delegates to the Constitutional Convention in 1787 were lawyers. Hall believes, "The colonies might well have revolted in any case, although it is doubtful that they would have without the presence of the bar. Lawyers did not cause the American Revolution, but they did define its intellectual boundaries and its essentially conservative cast. This was so because they were essentially attempting to define the nature of the rule of law as it applied under colonial circumstances."

22. *The Right to Counsel in Civil Litigation*, 7 COLUM. L. REV. (1966), 1326-29. The author states, "in the United States Constitution, the sixth amendment was designed to accord a right to retain counsel in criminal prosecutions; yet there is every indication that counsel was equally prevalent in civil proceedings at the time of the Constitution." "In 1836, Parliament provided that accused felons should be permitted to answer and defend by counsel, yet it was not until 1903 that provision was made for appointing counsel in felony cases, and not until 1949 that the extent of the right to counsel was finally clarified." This article argues that "because English practice had recognized the right to retain civil counsel, there was no need to reaffirm the prerogative" in the Constitution of the United States, but that "in view of the anomalous procedures in British criminal courts, it is not surprising that the framers of the American Constitution specifically provided for a right to retain counsel in criminal prosecutions."

23. Tansill, *supra* note 3, *Article VI of the Constitution of the United States*, at 1067.

24. POUND, *supra*, note 8, at xxvii: "after developing a strong profession by the time of the American Revolution and setting up a legal constitutional government . . . at the outset of our formative era, the people . . . all but destroyed the profession while permitting the calling." Also CHROUST, *supra* note 15, vol. 2, *The Revolution and the Post-Revolutionary Era,* at 5: "the profession lost a considerable number of its most prominent members; second, a particularly bitter antipathy against the lawyers as a class . . . soon made itself felt . . . ; this, a strong and at times unreasonable dislike of everything English, the Common Law, the English statutes, and the English way of administering justice, became widespread; and fourth, the lack of a distinct body of American law . . . made the . . . practice of law extremely difficult and haphazard."

25. M. LOUISE RUTHERFORD, THE INFLUENCE OF THE AMERICAN BAR ASSOCIATION ON PUBLIC OPINION AND LEGISLATION (Univ. of Pennsylvania 1937) 8: "With the rise of Jeffersonian

readily available to most white Americans.[26] The simplicity of the legal process allowed a wide cross-section of the male population to use their talents as courtroom advocates. For the study of jurisprudence, the early nineteenth century has been called the golden age of American law.[27]

The Civil War and its aftermath mark a watershed in American life[28] and law.[29] Urbanization, immigration, and industrialization created a whirlwind of change. It was also a period of unprecedented corruption in the social order.[30] The exigencies of legal practice in industrialized America affected

---

and Jacksonian Democracy in the early nineteenth century, the idea of a government of experts was repudiated and a narrow, elitist profession was rebuffed." GERARD W. GERWALT, MASSACHUSETTS LAWYERS: A HISTORICAL ANALYSIS OF THE PROCESS OF PROFESSIONALIZATION, 1760-1840 (Clark Univ. 1969), *quoted in* BLOOMFIELD, *supra* note 14, at 139: "By 1806 the major county bar associations had been transformed into quasi-social clubs and that the subsequent dissolution of these agencies in the 1830s was due less to outside pressure than to apathy among the members themselves."

26. JAMES WILLARD HURST, THE GROWTH OF AMERICAN LAW: THE LAW MAKERS (Little, Brown & Co. 1950) 299: "Through most of the nineteenth century the average practitioner took his quota of cases in defense of persons accused of crime, even lawyers most occupied with large affairs appeared for the defense in criminal cases."

27. THE GOLDEN AGE OF AMERICAN LAW, Charles Haar ed. (George Braziller 1965).

28. KERMIT HALL ET AL., *supra* note 1, 353-56: "The Civil War period and its aftermath was a watershed period in American law and culture, and legal practice in the United States adjusted accordingly. Post–Civil War America saw the emergence of large-scale enterprises and undreamed of aggregates of capital. During this period the role of government changed profoundly. It went from the giver of benefits, such as land grants, patents, charters, etc. that is distributive and promotional, to restrictive and regulatory."

29. G. Edward White, *John Marshall Harlan 1: The Precursor,* XIX AM. J.LEGAL HIST. (1975) 2. Two issues of immense legal significance dominated the post-Civil War era. "First was the impact of the Reconstruction Amendments, which augured two substantial changes in American law, a new orientation of the relationship between the federal government and the states and an expanded meaning of the rights of American citizenship. Second was the growth and consolidation of large scale industrial enterprise, lending a new dimension to the conflicts between individual property rights and the state."

30. Howard C. Westwood, *Getting Justice for the Freedman,* 16 HOWARD L. J. (1971) 492-537. *Also see* BLOOMFIELD, *supra* note 14 at 344-46. One notable footnote to the work of the bar of this era was an attempt by some lawyers to secure a modicum of progress in civil rights. On March 3, 1865, Congress created the Freedman's Bureau in the War Department to help former slaves adjust to the conditions of life in the new South. The bureau was effectively dismantled by 1868, but it is a noteworthy exception to the general professional trend of the era. For a time, the bureau maintained a network of courts throughout the South to adjudicate minor civil and criminal disputes involving

the bar most fundamentally by rotating the focus of lawyering away from the courtroom,

In the 1870s, lawyers once again began to form selective, restrictive bar associations, in part because of the rampant corruption of the bench and bar, and, in part, because of the cultural changes wrought by immigration and urbanization. After almost a century of an open, democratic bar in the United States, these new local, state, and national associations—predominantly Protestant, Anglo-Saxon, white male—took control of the standards for professional character and behavior.[31] They became the self-appointed stewards of American legal education, professional discipline, and admittance to practice.[32] The modern elite class of legal professionals were groomed, as in the eighteenth century, to serve the interests of the rich and the commercial classes.[33]

---

blacks. As the regular civil courts were reestablished, the bureau continued to recognize a need to provide legal services for indigent freemen. A pioneer legal aid program, the earliest attempt by Americans to respond in a systematic way to the legal problems of the poor, was established. For the first time the poor were recognized as having a right to legal services, and the power of the federal government was used to help them gain access to the courts and lawyers. Unfortunately, the Freedman's Bureau had little impact upon the mass of practitioners who preferred private profit to social justice.

31. KERMIT L. HALL, THE MAGIC MIRROR: LAW IN AMERICAN HISTORY (Oxford Univ. Press 1989), 224-25: "Lawyers accommodated and accepted the changes in American life, they did not resist them. The elite of the bar, through law associations and influential law schools, turned toward a professional model that made legal culture in the United States more impersonal, scientific, and lucrative. Lawyers joined with the business community on many levels and consequently shared in both its socioeconomic advances and its national outlook, emerging as the 'new high priests' of an increasingly legalistic, industrialized society." *Also see* LAWRENCE M. FRIEDMAN, A HISTORY OF AMERICAN LAW (Simon & Schuster 1973) 551, who says that the pre-Civil War lawyers "who argued great cases before great courts, who went into politics, and, above all, were skilled in the arts of advocacy," never went out of style. Their direct descendants are "the great civil-rights lawyers, on the one hand, and, on the other, the criminal lawyer."

32. THE NEW HIGH PRIESTS: LAWYERS IN POST CIVIL WAR AMERICA, Gerard W. Gerwalt ed. (Greenwood Publishing Group 1984). Also, KERMIT HALL, ET AL., *supra* note 1 at 216.

33. A.A. Berle, *The Modern Legal Profession*, 9 THE ENCYCLOPEDIA OF SOCIAL SCIENCES, 344. Berle contends that the effect of regularizing the practice of law with standards set by an elite class tended to neutralize the natural vitality of the institution and that during this period lawyers turned over their traditional leadership in social affairs to entrepreneurs. "Traditions of public service, such as are found in the medical profession, insensibly disappeared . . . intellectually the profession commanded and still commands respect, but it is respect for an intellectual jobber and contractor rather than for a moral force."

The most prominent of the new legal organizations was the American Bar Association (ABA), the first national bar association. Its membership represented the interests of business and finance in the United States. According to one historian, "The creation of the ABA was an effort on the part of the most prestigious element of the bar to differentiate itself from other professional groups, while fostering a sense of professional consciousness all its own."[34] It was established in 1878 "to advance the science of jurisprudence, promote the administration of justice and uniformity in legislation . . . uphold the honor of the profession . . . and encourage cordial intercourse among the members of the American Bar."[35] In 1908 the ABA adopted a set of ethical requirements for lawyers known as the Code of Professional Responsibility. The code was a set of "eight duties," or rules of behavior, developed in 1887 by Judge Thomas Goode Jones of Alabama. The code was concerned with the internal character of the ABA and its professional reputation.[36] Bar associations never quite succeeded in monopolizing entry into the institution, but their reappearance did much to limit the unfettered character of the calling.

Lawyers in the first half of the nineteenth century and before were generalists, but the scale of commerce and capital in the post–Civil War period began to alter this attribute, particularly in the largest urban centers. Up to this period, the natural locus of lawyers was the courtroom, where the poor went for justice and where lawyers acted as defenders of past actions.[37] Now the tendency of the profession was toward the protection of business interests. Lawyers became counselors, masters of facts that equipped them to

---

34. Joel Auerbach, as quoted in KERMIT HALL, ET AL., *supra* note 1 at 216.
35. *Id.* at 651.
36. RUTHERFORD, *supra* note 25 at 86-89.
37. HURST, *supra*, note 26 at 336: The lawyer "before 1850, in his then most prominent role as special pleader and advocate, the lawyer—and the courts also—dealt with situations that were rather simple . . . . in the early nineteenth century men still saw their relationships largely on a one-to-one basis . . . they had little familiarity with multicornered dealings; they had little sense of individual helplessness in the face of great impersonal social currents; they felt little awareness that the public might have concern with matters wholly 'private' in origin . . . after 1850 the handling of facts took on a new importance both in advocacy and counseling. By the 1890s the complex facts of the economy in particular offered both the setting and the pressure for the lawyer to take on a new role— as a specialist in incisive, accurate, fast appraisal of snarled or complicated situations . . . there now came a change in emphasis that amounted to a change in function. As advocate, the lawyer was typically called in after trouble was full-blown . . . his job then was to cull from past events those aspects which would support his clients' position. . . . As counselor . . . the activities were usually done according to the simple dominant criterion of meeting a possible challenge in court."

advise their clients on the protection of their long-term interests, financial and otherwise.[38] Large, impersonal corporate law firms appeared. Firm lawyers became legal specialists, masters of the details on which the new multi-faceted commercial world turned. In the first half of the nineteenth century, even the most prominent members of the bar took their quota of court-appointed cases, but, with the distancing of the lawyer from the courtroom, the private bar became less involved in volunteer criminal defense.

Coincident to the changes taking place in legal practice, criminal law was becoming harsher and the legal process more complicated, particularly in the largest urban centers.[39] Criminal defense became more time-consuming, difficult, and costly. A leading historian of the bar found, "In the twentieth century, the defense of accused persons became more and more the specialty of a small part of the bar, even as the reach of criminal law expanded. Only in cases that involved the new types of economic crime, turning on the conduct of business, did the average or leading practitioner continue to play a role."[40] He adds, "There is no clearer example of belated, narrow, and shallow treatment of the bar's ethical problems than in the matter of making legal services available to people of small means. Toward an issue which challenged the professed ideals of the profession and of American society the organized bar was inert, insensitive, and unimaginative."[41]

Between 1870 and 1914, more than 25 million immigrants entered the United States, changing the social composition of the country.[42] American cities were teeming with poor who had virtually no access to legal representation. The social and cultural changes alarmed Anglo-Saxon Americans. By the early twentieth century, an angry "nativist" reaction to foreign immigration and black competition raged in America. To its disrepute, the legal pro-

---

38. LAWRENCE M. FRIEDMAN, A HISTORY OF AMERICAN LAW (Simon & Schuster 1973), 549: "The slow estrangement of the lawyer from his old and natural haunt, the court, was an outstanding fact of the practice in the second half of the (nineteenth) century. Most lawyers still went to court; but the Wall Street lawyer, who perhaps never spoke to a judge except socially, made more money and had more prestige than any other lawyer."

39. Hurst, *supra* note 26 at 152, court appointed legal aid: "in the great cities it was often the means by which police-court hangers-on victimized the families or relatives of the accused."

40. *Id.* at 363.

41. *Id.* at 365.

42. *Id.* at 255. The ABA and the organized bar on the state and local level did nothing to open the profession to women, blacks and other minorities. "By administrative practice, the American Bar Association effected their (blacks') exclusion from the chief body of the organization."

fession, which by and large shared white middle-class values, did little to challenge the gross infringements of American civil rights and civil liberties that mark this period.[43]

The re-professionalization of the bar imposed on American lawyering increasingly rigid and expensive standards for admission to practice. The requirements tended to limit access by the poor and immigrant classes to its ranks. By the first half of the twentieth century, lawyering had become a relatively small, select occupation very unlike the nineteenth-century institution from which it evolved.[44] At the same time, by failing to make any provision to include free or low-cost legal services for the poor as part of the accepted requirements for practice, the legal profession tacitly approved the practice of allowing market forces to determine access to legal assistance in America.

The Development of a Legal Aid Movement

By the end of the nineteenth century, the failure of the American system of justice was manifest. A movement to reform the administration of justice surfaced first in private societies and spread later to the ABA, whose involvement gave it a semi-public direction and purpose. For nearly 90 years, from 1876 to 1954—which marks the decision of the United States Supreme Court in *Brown v. Board of Education*—the bar and the community initiated a patchwork of public and private activities to address the insufficiency of legal advocates for the poor and non-elites, an essential lack in the administration of American justice in the United States. *Brown v. Board* magnified the lack of legal aid in the judicial system, particularly for poor southern blacks, who

---

43. ALFRED H. KELLY, WINFRED A. HARBISON, & HERMAN I. BELZ, THE AMERICAN CONSTITUTION: ITS ORIGIN AND DEVELOPMENT, SIXTH ED. (1983), 523, Civil rights are usually thought of in terms of the social and economic pursuits of everyday life in the United States. Civil liberty protections, mostly under the First Amendment to the Constitution, protect individuals against government interference with religious belief, speech, press, and association. Modern civil rights guarantees are legal protections that individuals enjoy against injury, discrimination, and denial of rights by private persons and by government.

44. CENSUS OF THE POPULATION: 1950, PART 1: UNITED STATES SUMMARY, prepared under Howard G. Brunsman, Chief of Population and Housing Division, U.S. Dept. of Commerce (U.S. Government Printing Office 1953) at 8: In 1950 there were 154,230,000 Americans; Table 124: There were 174,205 employed lawyers and judges, comprising 0.31% of the population. In 1950 there were 6,333 women practicing law in the United States. Table 133: For all lawyers and judges the median income for men was $6,257 and for women, $3,616. The median income for the Northeast in 1950 was between $3,000, and $3,499.

became frustrated by their inability to claim their rights through the courts and turned increasingly to political action. After the 1955 decision of the Supreme Court, the white bar in the South refused to defend minority rights and what legal aid had been available to blacks disappeared. The following will offer a review of the evolution of an organized program of legal aid in the United States and its influence on the administration of justice for the poor and underrepresented.

Immigrant Societies

It is not surprising, given the direction of the bar in the second half of the nineteenth century, that the first efforts to reform the administration of justice came from outside the bar. On March 8, 1876, the New York City German Society established the first private legal aid organization, Der Deutsche Rechts-Schutz Verein. Its function was to discourage exploitation of newly arrived German immigrants. In Chicago in 1886, the second legal aid society was formed by the Protective Agency for Women and Children, because of the "great number of debaucheries of young girls under the guise of proffered employment." The Chicago Ethical Cultural Society began the first legal aid society opened to people of any nationality or gender, the Bureau of Justice, in Chicago in 1888. What marked the first attempts to provide the poor with legal aid was that they were private, charitable organizations.[45]

The first public defender's office in the country began in California in 1913.[46] By 1917, there were 37 cities with 41 organizations carrying on some sort of civil and criminal legal aid.[47] In all, there were six types of legal aid organizations:

- legal aid societies,
- departments of social agencies,
- public bureaus,
- bar association offices,

---

45. REGINALD HEBER SMITH, JUSTICE AND THE POOR (Carnegie Foundation 1919), ch. XVII, reviews the early history of the New York Legal Aid Movement and describes the development of the Legal Aid Movement in the United States. The information in this paper on the early legal aid movement is taken from *Justice and the Poor.*

46. ESTER LUCILE BROWN, LAWYERS AND THE PROMOTION OF JUSTICE (Russell Sage Foundation 1938) 255: "Although the concept of public defender was discussed in America as early as the eighteenth century, it was not until 1913 that provision was made for such an office. In that year Los Angeles County provided for the first defendant in criminal cases. Shortly afterwards defenders were brought into the municipal courts in Portland, Oregon, and in Columbus, Ohio. . . ."

- law school clinics,
- and public and voluntary organizations.[48]

These organizations supplied services in four basic areas: economic, family, property, and crimes and security rights.[49]

The two most common types of aid organizations were independent legal aid societies and departments of social agencies. However, the four public bureaus served more clients than either of these dominant groups. Bar association legal aid programs were few in number and weak. Law school clinics were feeble experiments, considering the magnitude of the need. Public legal aid services in criminal cases were just emerging, the lead being taken by the public defender's office in Los Angeles County.[50] Together, these groups had 62 full-time and 113 part-time lawyers, who spent as much as half of the working day on legal aid. In 1917, the 41 organizations handled 117,201 cases.[51]

The ABA

Until the 1920s, the legal aid movement in America remained a loose, unorganized collection of groups. In 1920, the American Bar Association was persuaded to become involved. The catalyst for legal aid reform within the ABA was the publication of the first comprehensive analysis of justice and the poor in the United States in 1919. The study was done by Reginald Heber Smith, a young Harvard Law graduate whose first job in 1916 was as director of the newly formed Boston Legal Aid Society. The 25-year-old Smith was so appalled by the dichotomy between American legal theory and the situation of the poor in Boston that he applied to the Carnegie Foundation for a grant to research legal aid in America. His book, *Justice and the Poor*, made sorry reading for the bar, which held to the belief that the public interest was sufficiently protected by current legal practices. Smith's findings showed that view to be absurd.

---

47. EMERY A. BROWNELL, LEGAL AID IN THE UNITED STATES: A STUDY OF THE AVAILABILITY OF LAWYERS' SERVICES FOR PERSONS UNABLE TO PAY FEES (Lawyers' Co-Operative Publishing Co. 1951) 20.

48. John S. Bradway & Reginald Heber Smith, *Growth of Legal Aid Work in the United States,* U.S. DEPT. OF LABOR BULLETIN No. 607, chs. XIX, XV. *Also see id.* at 10, defining "public bureaus" as "any legal aid office which is tax supported and which is operated as a function of government. Established by local ordinance of state law."

49. BROWNELL, *supra*, note 47 at 43.

50. *Id.* at at 20.

51. SMITH, *supra* note 45 at 142-47.

Justice and the Poor listed the problems with the existing legal aid system.[52] Smith concluded that conventional lawyering was failing the poor and its public purpose.[53] He wrote, "One fact which very forcibly strikes the observer of the work in different cities is that legal aid success or failure goes hand in hand with good or bad support from the bar. Given the amount of interest and cooperation accorded by the local bar, the strength of the legal aid work can be accurately estimated and foretold."[54]

Smith was ridiculed and his findings were hotly disputed. The ABA went so far as to refuse to turn over membership lists for use in distribution of the book.[55] Luckily, Smith found a champion within the organization. At the annual convention of the ABA in 1920, Charles Evans Hughes, a former presidential candidate and future Supreme Court Justice, called for a special session to discuss legal aid for the poor in light of Smith's findings. From that meeting came the creation of the ABA's Special Committee on Legal Aid. Charles Evans Hughes served as its first chairman.[56]

Smith deserves great credit for prodding the ABA to do more than just give lip service to the bar's public role. Believing that it was the obligation of each American lawyer to volunteer legal service for the public good, he wanted the ABA committee to provide "leadership, supervision and financial support" of a professional program.[57] His objective was to create a mechanism within the private bar and the community that would match volunteers with the legal needs of persons unable to pay for legal services. Smith's recom-

---

52. *Id.* at 193-99: He listed six principal weaknesses of legal aid in the United States: 1, its greatest weakness, lack of funding; 2, constant change of personnel; 3, no centralized responsibility or authority; 4, the movement was in desperate need of intelligent propaganda and missionary work; 5, no coordination of legal aid work in the fields of civil and criminal law; and 6, a means should be provided by which the accumulated experience of legal aid organizations could be made use of in various instruments for the administration of justice.

53. *Id.* at 19, 87: "The charitable societies in all their work, they are relieving the bar of a heavy burden by performing for the bar its legal and ethical obligation to see that no one shall suffer injustice through inability, because of poverty, to obtain needed legal advice and assistance . . . . it is doing the work of the bar for the bar."

54. *Id.* at 37.

55. JOHNSON, EARL, JR. JUSTICE AND REFORM: THE FORMATIVE YEARS OF THE OEO LEGAL SERVICES PROGRAM. (The Russell Sage Foundation 1974), 7.

56. SMITH, *supra* note 45. In 1921, Smith became the chairman of the committee and the Legal Aid Committee was substantially upgraded to a standing committee of the ABA, which meant that it was a permanent concern of the organization. In 1923, at Smith's urging, the National Association of Legal Aid Organizations was formed in Cleveland. This organization later became the National Legal Aid and Defender Association.

57. *Id. See Legal Aid and the Bar*, ch. XXIV.

mendation for the establishment of a national organization of agencies and persons interested in legal aid became a reality when the National Association of Legal Aid Organizations, which later became the National Legal Aid and Defender Association, was formed in 1923. It was a great step forward,

Unfortunately, it faltered in its promise. The momentum of the ABA's legal aid program ended with the onset of the economic depression in 1929.[58] Despite the needs created by the Depression and the war, the practices of the profession remained constant. In 1962, there were only five municipal legal aid bureaus still in existence—four fewer than in 1919, seven fewer than in 1932. Where municipal legal aid offices made up 28 percent of the total legal aid organizations in 1919, only 4 percent were government funded in 1962.[59] When a follow-up study to *Justice and the Poor* posed the question "to what extent are the Legal Aid services meeting the existing needs," it found "the unhappy truth is that we had made almost no substantial progress up to the close of 1947."[60] The principal problem, according to a professional study, was the "failure of the bar to recognize the problem and to deal with it realistically. Whether due to unfounded fear of competition, inherent lethargy, or mere lack of interest, the failure of local bar associations to give leadership, and in many cases the hostility of lawyers to the idea, have been formidable stumbling blocks in the efforts to establish needed facilities."[61]

The National Lawyers' Guild

There were exceptions in the conduct of the private bar, of course, particularly in the major urban centers of the East. In 1936, the National Lawyers' Guild (NLG) was created by men and women who were dissatisfied with the profession's insensitivity to the troubled justice system. The NLG repudiated the professional standards and legal ethics practiced by the American Bar Asso-

---

58. BROWNELL, *supra* note 47, at 168. The Depression of 1929 brought trouble to both the legal aid movement and the bar. "Corporations were going bankrupt, people were broke, and those clients that were not either bankrupt or broke were out to trim expenses. Lawyers were hurting economically and the legal aid offices had more cases than they could handle. The case load went from almost 172,000 cases in 1929 to just about 332,000 cases in 1933 and financial support dropped." *Also see* Isador Lazarus, *The Economic Crisis in the Legal Profession,* 1:1 THE NATIONAL LAWYERS GUILD QUARTERLY (December 1937): In the depression, "almost half of the attorneys in the United States earned less than $2,000 annually when $2,000 was considered the poverty line for a family of four."

59. JOHNSON, *supra* note 55, at 17.

60. *Id.* at 33.

61. BROWNELL, *supra* note 47 at 29.

ciation,[62] which in turn viewed the NLG as an association of radicals. The Lawyers' Guild drew its membership primarily from the East Coast. NLG members represented the ethnic, religious, and cultural diversity of the largest East Coast cities. Its charter proclaimed its goal was to "protect and foster our democratic institutions and the civil rights and liberties of all people . . . to aid in the establishment of governmental and professional agencies . . . to supply adequate legal services to all who are in need or cannot obtain it." It maintained that the American bar should "function as a social force in the service of the people to the end that human rights shall be regarded as more sacred than property rights."[63]

National Lawyers' Guild members, like their counterparts in the ABA, were private practitioners. They provided untold hours of volunteer legal assistance to organizations such as the American Civil Liberties Union (ACLU), the National Association for the Advancement of Colored People (NAACP), and its Legal Defense and Education Fund (LDEF). The association of NLG lawyers with the high-profile and controversial civil liberties and civil rights cases of the day marked it as an ultra-liberal organization within the mainstream professional bar.

Despite the NLG's call for federal support of legal aid, the organization did not offer its own legal aid proposal until 1950, and then it was a rather "conservative recommendation."[64]

Legal Clinics

Lawyers' incomes had suffered during the 1930s, and the profession was searching for clients. Lawyers were strictly prohibited from soliciting clients or advertising their services. In the late 1930s, a movement began within the ABA to find ways to loosen professional standards and reach out to a greater

---

62. THE NATIONAL LAWYERS' GUILD: FROM ROOSEVELT THROUGH REAGAN, Ann Fagan Ginger & Eugene M. Tobin, eds. (Temple Univ. Press 1988), xviii: "Are members of the National Lawyers' Guild a distinct subgroup within the bar? Certainly the founders of the guild thought so . . . . Guild lawyers reflected the tradition of poor kids becoming the first lawyers in the family, joining a handful of lawyers from prosperous families who got the pro bono spirit in the second or third generation after immigration . . . . the Guild was led by an inspired group of East Coast lawyers most deeply concerned with national and international issues, which they sought to move forward by resolutions, analytical reports to Congress, creative amicus briefs, and coalition work with labor unions and left-progressive-liberal groups of all sorts. Their ideology was a mixture of humanism, Marxism, populism, and the democratic tradition."

63. *Id.* at art. 1, § 2 of the Constitution of the National Lawyers' Guild, also the Preamble.

64. JOHNSON, *supra* note 55, at 18.

portion of the population. Not because of but coinciding with this effort, the Standing Committee on Legal Aid of the ABA resolved in 1937 that "every man accused of a serious crime is absolutely entitled to counsel and that, if he is too poor to employ one, society must furnish him one."[65] This opened the way for private lawyers to begin limited experiments, in small cases, with legal aid clinics for people of small means. In effect, the clinics were law firms for people who could not qualify for legal aid but who also could not pay what the conventional system charged. These clinics were a significant step forward in opening up the justice system. In the largest urban centers in the country, they resulted in the enhancement of legal assistance.[66]

Legal Aid in the Military

With the outbreak of war in 1941, for the first time in American history, the provision of skilled legal assistance was recognized as essential for the morale of the men and women in the armed services. "The capacity of democratic forms of government to satisfy the minimum wants of citizens was being persuasively challenged by a menacing alliance of totalitarians," according to leaders of the ABA. "Legal aid services more and more appeared to thoughtful citizens less like a lawyer's charity and more like a bulwark of freedom." The ABA established a Committee on the National Defense that became the ABA Committee on War Work. The chairman of the ABA War Work Committee was Harrison Tweed, a leading New York corporate lawyer.[67] The ABA Committee on War Work closely assisted the Army and Navy in the organization of a system of legal assistance offices. Existing legal aid organizations and civilian bar committees formed a key part of the ABA plan. The legal services provided for servicemen and their dependents were investigations, negotiations, and court work required in the states. At the war's conclusion, the United States Army decided to continue legal assistance.

---

65. BROWNELL, *supra* note 47, at 65. Also, in 1940 the ABA amplified its 1937 resolution: "In connection with legal aid in the criminal courts. . . . the position of the American Bar Association is that the method and instrumentality of securing adequate representation of poor defendants in the criminal courts is a local question for determination in the light of local conditions, needs and wishes. The concern of the Association is to secure proper representation of poor defendants in the criminal courts as broadly and as promptly as possible without preference of partiality as to method or instrumentality."

66. Ginger & Tobin, *supra* note 62, at 3.

67. BROWNELL, *supra* note 47, at 153-154.

Lawyer Referral Services

The electorate in the United States was changed by the experiences of World War II. As mid-century approached, improved access to the law, which required legal aid reform, became an issue of political importance. Black soldiers returning to the South were unwilling to settle for second-class citizenship, and women refused to yield in peacetime the social and economic advances they had won in wartime. The war had created increased economic, social, and legal expectations among people from all classes. Other factors that were providing an impetus for changes included technological advances, an accelerated expansion of mass production in industry, and an ever-rising standard of living. The changes intensified the complexity of everyday life, which resulted in an increase in legal regulations. More people needed lawyers and lawyers needed the work. International politics also played a role in the development of new legal assistance services.

The legal establishment's sense of professional security and independence was shaken by the depth of post-war social reform in England. On July 5, 1945, a Labour Party victory in England led to socialization of railroads, coal mines, and other industries. The Labour Party's legal aid reform bill, the Legal Aid and Advice Law, which was introduced in 1946 and passed in 1949, was in the view of many American lawyers "another step . . . toward complete socialism."[68] Reginald Heber Smith, who was among those working for an expansion in the availability of legal assistance in the United States, wrote an article for the *ABA Journal* that painted a picture of the professional fear of legal aid reform.

> I believe the picture which "socialization of the profession" brings into the minds of American lawyers is substantially as follows: The government opens a bureau or a chain of bureaus. The staffs of the bureaus consist of lawyers on salary. The lawyers are political appointees. Persons needing legal aid go to the offices of the bureaus. Gradually the rules as to eligibility for free assistance are expanded, for political reasons, until finally the private practitioner is crowded to the wall.[69]

One response to the changing circumstances was the proposal of the creation of lawyer referral services by leaders of the ABA. A Standing Committee on Lawyer Referral Services was created in 1948. The idea of an ABA referral service came from the data that was being collected for a new profes-

---

68. Reginald Heber Smith, *The English Legal Assistance Plan: Its Significance for American Legal Institutions,* 35 A.B,A. J. 454 (1949).

69. *Id.* at 455.

sional study on the state of legal aid in the United States. The information collected made it clear that existing legal aid facilities were already referring a percentage of their cases to private lawyers.[70] The referral services would be administered by local and state bar associations. The legal assistance provided would not be free but would benefit the community by increasing access to the judicial process.

The chairman of the ABA Committee on Public Relations saw the new service as "a highly important contribution to the attainment by the public of a better understanding of the function and usefulness of lawyers." Unfortunately, he also found that most lawyers did not make use of the referral service, noting, "One of the curious mysteries of the legal profession is its seeming reluctance to make its existence better known. One reason may be its traditional, and understandable, aversion to anything that smacks of solicitation. But whatever the reason, that fact remains that it is easier for Mr. John Q. Citizen to turn up the name of a good plumber or electrician than it is that of a trustworthy lawyer."[71]

The National Legal Aid Association

The experience with the legal aid system during the war convinced Harrison Tweed, chairman of the ABA Committee on War Work, that the profession needed to do more. He believed that if the bar was going to prevent its own "socialization," the ABA would have to play a larger role in the overall management of legal aid services. The underfunded and understaffed National Association of Legal Aid Organizations, which coordinated the efforts of the bar and existing private legal aid organizations, was not up to the demands of the post-war era.

In 1946, Tweed secured from the ABA an appropriation to pursue this goal through state and local bar organizations. In 1949, a new national legal aid organization, the National Legal Aid Association (NLAA), was created. Tweed became its first president while continuing his full-time practice of law with the Wall Street firm of Milbank & Tweed. The NLAA's board of directors reflected the importance the profession placed on the new organization. The 38-member board was made up of representatives from the top echelons of the bench and the bar, as well as industry and banking.[72]

The first major undertaking of the NLAA was the study referred to above

---

70. BROWNELL, *supra* note 47, at 86, Table XXV, "Referrals of Cases to Lawyers by Typical Legal Aid Organizations in 1947." Out of a total of 80,550 cases, 8.9% or 7,156 were referred.

71. Thomas L. Sidlo, *Lawyer Referral Service: A Code of Basic Principles*, 36 A.B.A. J. 197 (1950).

72. *Id.* at 155.

on the condition of legal aid in the United States. Reginald Heber Smith, the author of *Justice and the Poor*, directed the new study, "Legal Aid in the United States," which was published in 1951. In the foreword, Harrison Tweed wrote that the NLAA "was organized, is working, and seeks funds in order that the deficiencies of the present situation may be remedied as promptly as possible. If they are not promptly met, government will take over both the financing and the administration of the work, with grave risk to the rights and liberties of lawyers and laymen alike."[73]

The study defined the scope of legal aid as "the organized effort of the bar and the community[74] to provide the services of lawyers free, or for a token charge, to persons who cannot afford to pay an attorney's fee and whose cases are unremunerative on a contingent fee basis. Such services may involve no more than a professional consultation or they may include assistance in negotiation, the preparation of documents or representation in court. The term 'Legal Aid' applies if they are supplied through a facility organized for this special purpose and if they represent something more than the free service which individual attorneys render in the course of private practice."[75]

Emery A. Brownell, who compiled the report, saw money to be the most serious obstacle confronting the program:

> Equally troubling is the question of where the funds should come from—whether the work should be sustained as a sole obligation of the organized bar, as a private charity of the general public, as a responsibility of government, or a combination of these. . . . For good or ill, the issues have since been caught up in the emotional fire of heightened concern over the increasing scope and power of the government. . . . This is the dilemma . . . the fact remains that the extent and adequacy of the service has barely kept pace with the increasing need and has made no substantial progress in bettering the coverage of 30 years ago.[76]

Harrison Tweed put it more succinctly:

---

73. Harrison Tweed, *Legal Aid in the United States*, Foreword (ABA 1951).
74. *Id.* at 230. In 1950 60% of the financial support of legal aid work was provided by the Community Chests with an additional 24½% from individual contributions, including lawyers and bar associations, and from capital income. Clients carry 6% of the cost. Tax funds accounted for 9½% of the total income, and this figure takes into account the value of rent-free quarters in public buildings.
75. *Id.* at 3.
76. BROWNELL, *supra* note 47, at 243.

If the government becomes the lawyers' paymaster, it may soon become his master . . . government is steadily looming larger and larger in the role of being a party to the litigation . . . they all enforce their rules and regulations and decisions by going into court as the complainant party. . . . its lawyer is paid out of the public treasury . . . . If lawyers for the poor are to be paid out of the public treasury, will the next step be that all persons of moderate means shall be supplied with lawyers paid, in part at least, out of the public treasury? And if we got that far, could an independent bar survive?[77]

Legal Aid Services

The services administered under the NLAA were divided into two categories, criminal and civil. Indigents in criminal cases were represented in one of three ways:

- by assigned unpaid counsel, serving in response to public and professional duty;
- by assigned paid counsel, with compensation fixed by general statute or by the court; and
- by criminal defense lawyers, either public defenders or private defenders.

Criminal Cases

Counsel in the majority of criminal cases was by assigned lawyer,[78] and in eight states (Alabama, Florida, Maine, Massachusetts, Mississippi, Pennsylvania, South Carolina, and Texas) counsel was assigned only in capital offenses. In these states there were 33 cities with a population of at least 100,000, and in only three of those were there any organized criminal legal aid services. In the other 40 states, assigned counsel was mandatory in only 18 and discretionary with the court or only at the request of the defendant in the remainder. In a number of jurisdictions, if the accused did not demand his right to have counsel at trial, he was presumed to have waived it.

---

77. *Id.* at xviii.
78. Lee Silverstein. *Defense of the Poor in Criminal Cases in American State Courts: A Field Study and Report*, vol. 1, NATIONAL REPORT 15 (AM. BAR FOUND. 1965). In 1964, approximately 70% of the felony defendants in the United States were in counties using an assigned counsel system. This system was the only one used in about 2,900 of the 3,100 counties in the United States.

"The facts show clearly that the existing means for providing the services of lawyers in criminal cases fall woefully short of meeting the need. In many cities there is still a shocking denial of fundamental justice."[80]

"The importance of developing additional legal aid for the poor in criminal courts cannot be exaggerated . . . ," according to the ABA. "Undoubtedly, there are many places where the poor are adequately represented under the system whereby the court appoints a practicing lawyer to represent a particular defendant. But frequently this system has led to the abuse and halfhearted representation or cold-blooded extortion of compensation from the family and friends of the defendant."[81]

In light of the deficiencies of the assigned counsel system, organized facilities for the defense of criminals were established. There were two kinds, public defenders and voluntary defenders. The essential difference between the two is that the former were tax supported, and the latter largely financed by private contributions and Community Chest funds. There were 28 public defender offices in 1948.[82]

---

79. Brownell, *supra* note 47, at 124-25. Compensation for assigned counsel is provided in 21 states; California, Colorado, Indiana, Maine, and Michigan left the fee to the discretion of the court. In six others, the court has discretion within limits (Arizona, $5 to $100; Idaho, $10 to $25; Iowa, $10 except in cases where the punishment is life imprisonment, then $20 per diem for court time; Montana, $25 to $50; New Mexico, $25 to $100; and Wyoming, $15 to $25). In six states there was a fixed maximum (Iowa, $20; Maryland and Nebraska, $100; Nevada, $50, except in manslaughter, in which the maximum is $350; and Virginia, $15). In four states a per diem maximum was established (Kansas, $10; Minnesota $25; Oregon, $15, with a limit of two days, and Washington, $25). Connecticut and Rhode Island were completely covered by public defender services. Included among the states that pay nothing to assigned counsel are some of the most populated, with the highest rates of prosecutions—Arkansas, Delaware, Georgia, Illinois, Kentucky, Louisiana, South Dakota, Tennessee, Utah, Vermont, and West Virginia.

80. *Id.* at 40.

81. ABA Report 62 (1937), 714.

82. Brownell, *supra* note 47, at 126. The first in Los Angeles County, 1913; by 1921, Columbus, Ohio; all counties of Connecticut; Memphis, Tennessee; Omaha, Nebraska; Portland, Oregon; and San Francisco, California; the city of Los Angeles also established an office; Oakland, California, 1926; Chicago, 1930; Tulsa, Oklahoma, 1937; St Louis, Missouri, 1938; Oklahoma City, 1939; Rhode Island, 1941; Indianapolis, Indiana, 1945; Long Beach, California, 1945; and Minneapolis, Minnesota, 1947. In 1948, five counties in California—Orange, Riverside, Sacramento, San Joaquin, and Tulare—established offices.

There were two types of private defender organizations, criminal law divisions of existing legal aid societies and independent voluntary defender organizations. In 1948, the first type were four in number and located in Cincinnati, New Orleans, New York City, and Pittsburgh There were two of the second type of organization, in Boston and Philadelphia.

Civil Cases

In the United States, legal aid for civil cases was handled by a patchwork of private and public facilities. They were legal aid societies, social agencies, public bureaus, bar association offices, law school clinics, and community volunteers.[83] "At the close of 1949, there were a total of 90 legal aid offices operating in the United States. Of these, 66 had one or more paid lawyers on the staff and 24 were dependent upon volunteer lawyers for the legal services rendered to clients."[84]

Legal Aid Facilities in the South

As for the legal aid system in the South, the text of *Legal Aid in the United States* makes only one direct reference to it. It reports, "It is true . . . that the larger unserved cities—those in which the need seems to be relatively more acute—are in the Southeast. One reason for this is that the communities are economically poor. A special reason may be the rural tradition of the South and the fact that only recently has it faced major problems of industrialization. But this cannot be said of cities like Birmingham, Memphis, and Tampa. The relatively small number of foreign-born residents and a somewhat patriarchal system of dealing with problems both legal and social have no doubt contributed to the lag."[85]

---

83. *Id.* at 87-109. Of the 37 societies, 32 have salaried lawyers. All cities having a population in excess of 1 million—except Chicago—are served by this form of organization, with Los Angeles providing additional service in civil cases through the city and county public defender offices. In 1949 there were 13 legal aid offices being conducted by private social service agencies. Public bureaus are operated by social welfare agencies supported entirely by public funds. For all practical purposes the services are restricted to residents of the city. There were about 60 operating. Public Bureaus also include public defender offices, which offer civil as well as criminal services. There were five such offices. In 1916 there were three bar association offices, which had grown to 20 at the close of 1949. Much of the growth occurred from 1946 to 1949. Finally, law school clinics were of two types, those giving direct services and those operated as a cooperative activity.

84. *Id.* at 87.

85. *Id.* at 29.

The patchwork of facilities that made up the legal aid movement were primarily located in the largest urban centers of the country.[86] The few that existed in the South were locally run agencies, or in the case of public defenders, supported by local electorates that reflected the predispositions of the white community.

In 1950, black lawyers made up less than 1 percent of the American bar. Few of them were admitted in the South. Blacks relied on the largesse of the white bar for legal assistance in civil and criminal matters in the South.[87] As a class, however, blacks were represented by private advocacy groups. These groups did provide some conventional legal aid, but they were not legal aid groups. They acted through litigation and lobbying campaigns aimed at securing social reform.

The Movement at Mid-century

The major finding of legal aid in the United States was that little real change had taken place in 30 years. In 1950, in its most serious look at the question in decades, the legal establishment chose to focus on process over policy, the process of administering legal aid over the failure of American lawyers to provide adequate access to procedural justice, begging the question of reform of professional standards. In a country of 154 million people, which was growing at historic rates, the legal aid system that was described in the NLAA study was insufficient.[88] Relatively speaking, there was still no law for the poor in America.

In 1961, the dean of the Yale Law School, Eugene Rostow, when addressing problems facing the legal profession, said:

---

86. BROWNELL, *supra* note 47, Appendix D: Legal Aid Offices, 307-16.

87. Census, 1950, Tables 124 and 128. There were approximately 180,000 lawyers in the United States; 3.5% were female, 6,333. All black legal professionals were only 1.3% of the legal force. Also, Census of the United States, 1960, vol. 1, United States Summary, Eighteenth Decennial (United States Printing Office, 1964). Table 256, "Occupation by Race." In the Northeast there were 66,593 lawyers, including 475 black legal professionals; in the North Central there were 51,604 lawyers, including 731 black legal professionals; in the South there were 55,454 lawyers, including 593 black legal professionals; and in the West there were 28,756 lawyers, including 205 black legal professionals and 433 legal professionals of other races.

88. Census, 1950 at 8. The population of the United States increased 14.5% over the 1940 figures. It was the largest increase in actual numbers since the census figures began to be compiled.

In many instances we have become so identified with our clients, so much a part of their daily lives, that we have lost a large
part of our professional freedom and our professional standing,
both in our own minds and in public opinion. Too many lawyers
find themselves in situations of conflict between their professional convictions and their continuing connections with their
clients. We all know counterparts in business, in labor, and in
government to the moment when President Franklin Roosevelt
turned on a distinguished lawyer, who held a high post . . . and
had just given him some unpalatable advice. In a state of considerable irritation, the President said, "When I want to do something, I expect my lawyers to tell me how it can be done, and
not why it can't be done." And beyond the implications of this
anecdote, somber as they are, it is apparent that lawyers exclusively involved in the affairs of one client, or one limited class
of clients, have lost a large part of their freedom to represent the
Tom Paines of this world. . . . I put so much emphasis on the
fundamental importance of an ethical code and a sense of professional discipline, which could confirm in fact our belief that
lawyers should be a free guild within society, serving their clients best by serving the law first. . . . And such a Bar, visibly
independent, should be able to do much more than we have been
able to do thus far in those situations that most urgently challenge the legal process—the provision of counsel for the poor
and for unpopular litigants. The provision of legal services to
the poor, in both civil and criminal matters, is in most communities of the nation scandalously inadequate. And for that failure
we of the Bar are primarily responsible. There are outstanding
legal aid bureaus here and there, and some effective public defender programs. But their strength only highlights our general
failure to meet a real social need.[89]

The Emergence of Private Advocacy Groups

It has been noted above that in the early twentieth century there was a
nativist movement in the United States that was anti-immigrant, anti-Catholic,
and anti-black. The reactionary mood in the country at that time produced

---

89. Eugene Rostow, *The Lawyer and His Client*, 48 A.B.A. J. 146-48 (1962).

blatant violations of civil liberties and civil rights that went, by and large, unchallenged by the mainstream legal profession. It was during this period that a number of small private groups organized to advocate for the rights of the aggrieved. These were not legal groups per se, but their experience has had a profound effect on the American system of justice and, as a result, on the conduct of lawyering in America. The most notable of the private groups are the NAACP and its Legal Defense and Education Fund (LDEF), and the ACLU.[90] They were formed by concerned private citizens to protect special interests in American society. Through public education, social networking, political mobilization, lobbying, and courtroom litigation, they aimed at legal reform of social and civil wrongs. These organizations were the advance contingent in the modern movement of law for social change. Their advocacy for the rights of the poor and underrepresented is a model for the public interest law movement, which blossomed in the United States after 1963. Nonetheless, when they appeared, they were not public interest law groups as we know them today, as none of them, including the LDEF, as its name will attest, were originated solely as litigation groups. Litigation as a tool for law reform becomes more relevant after 1965 and the passage of federal civil rights and voting legislation.[91]

In 1963 the Lawyers' Committee for Civil Rights Under Law was formed to marshal the resources of the private bar to help mediate the civil rights crisis in the South. In many ways, as the committee evolved, its organization, legal strategy, and public policy advocacy began to resemble the private advocacy groups that will be discussed in this section. The question is frequently asked as to how the groups differ. The Lawyers' Committee is nonpartisan, made up solely of members of the bar. Despite the use of "civil rights" in its title, the committee was formed not as a private civil rights advocacy group but as a professional organization whose objective was to work with the bar to reform the administration of justice and thereby help to ameliorate racial conflict. Its most important contribution is that it helped

---

90. The discussion of the ACLU, the NAACP, and the LDEF is taken primarily from CHARLES FLINT KELLOGG, A HISTORY OF THE NATIONAL ASSOCIATION FOR THE ADVANCEMENT OF COLORED PEOPLE (Johns Hopkins Univ. Press 1967), vols. 1 & 2; ROBERT L. JACK, HISTORY OF THE NATIONAL ASSOCIATION FOR THE ADVANCEMENT OF COLORED PEOPLE (Meador Publishing 1943); PEGGY LAMSON, ROBERT BALDWIN: FOUNDER OF THE AMERICAN CIVIL LIBERTIES UNION: A PORTRAIT (Houghton Mifflin 1976); Robert L. Rabin, *Lawyers for Social Change: Perspectives on Public Interest Law*, 28 STAN. L. REV. (1976) 207-61.

91. In the early 1960s, when the LDEF devotes itself almost totally to litigation, it is more commonly referred to as the LDF, or Legal Defense Fund. It also is known as the INC. Fund.

change the legal practices of lawyers and law firms—a change that improved access to the legal process. In its early years, the committee helped form a bridge between the resources of the moderate elements in the traditional bar and social reform activists.

The American Civil Liberties Union

The ACLU was created during WWI in response to American xenophobia. In 1916, a group of white pacifists and social reformers formed the American Union Against Militarism (AUAM).[92] In March of 1917, Roger Baldwin went to work for the AUAM in Washington "to develop a negotiated peace in Europe that would ultimately lead to world federation." On April 6, 1917, America declared war on Germany. Baldwin said later, "I couldn't believe . . . such savage attitudes. People mobbed and persecuted—even their mail was stopped. A sudden sort of hysteria happened very quickly." Still part of the AUAM, Baldwin organized a Bureau for Conscientious Objectors. The name of the new organization was felt to be too inflammatory, so Baldwin "came up with Civil Liberties Bureau, which sounded more universal. I don't think anyone had ever called anything civil liberties in the United States before we did," he noted. "But the British had used it. In fact it's an old phrase that goes back for several centuries in British history, but it wasn't used as the name of an organization until the British used it in the World War. And then we took it over because it seemed to fit."

In October of 1917, Roger Baldwin became director of the independent National Civil Liberties Bureau (NCLB), which was based in New York.[93] Baldwin devoted his time to lobbying the War Department for fair treatment and regulations for conscientious objectors. Soon the organization's activities broadened to include publicity and lobbying against the Espionage and Sedition Acts. Roger Baldwin, the social worker from St. Louis, remained the chief influence in the ACLU for another 30 years.

During its early years, the NCLB made effective use of its members, many of whom were well connected and quite famous. The NCLB did not want to do litigation or grassroots organizing. It did have a good deal of contact with the International Workers of the World (IWW). Strikes during the war led to prosecutions of labor agitators under the espionage acts. Also, the U.S. Postal Service had the power to censure and search. During this period, the NCLB relied on persuasion and publicity, not litigation. In 1920, the NCLB was renamed the American Civil Liberties Union in an effort to broaden its identification. Despite its modern reputation, the ACLU did not organize as a legal organiza-

---

92. LAMSON, *supra* note 90, at 67-68.
93. *Id.* at 71-73.

tion. One writer calls the early ACLU "a socially conscious activist version of a small, select gentleman's club . . . that was based on personal influence, and the corresponding organizational structure," which was informal and highly personalized.[94] Inevitably the activities the ACLU was involved with—prosecutions, censorship, and deportations—led the organization into court. The ACLU never abandoned its lobbying and publicity campaigns nor its protest activities. Courtroom activity was "only a single element in a well-orchestrated campaign of resistance. And when the organization turned to litigation, its norms remained consistent: if like-minded citizens could be entreated to protest and publicize, why not to volunteer representational skills?"[95]

A number of the founders and supporters of the ACLU were famous New York lawyers who offered their professional services, guidance, and commitment to the causes the ACLU represented. The Cold War era and McCarthyism brought fundamental changes in the character of the organization. By 1950, the ACLU had established a national reputation through participation in conflicts over governmental encroachment on the Bill of Rights. Beginning in 1950, ACLU membership doubled every five years as local chapters sprung up around the country. In 1960, the ACLU's permanent staff consisted of only two lawyers in New York and one each in Los Angeles, San Francisco, and Chicago. Occasionally, ACLU lawyers volunteered legal representation in civil rights cases in the South.

As the ACLU grew, it needed to decentralize. Local groups, or chapters, developed. The local groups assumed more and more responsibility for defining priorities. It may be that the ACLU's commitment to a singular goal, the protection of civil liberties, was responsible for its success and survival. A small professional staff on the national level kept the work of the group in focus. The national staff was responsible for the organizational image and for coordination of goals.

The National Association for the Advancement of Colored People

In 1906, an all-black group, headed by the historian W.E.B. DuBois, met at Niagara Falls, New York. This group "formulated the left wing of the American Negro, and was determined to secure full manhood suffrage for the race." DuBois's activist philosophy was at odds with the accommodationist approach of Booker T. Washington, the best-known black leader of the day. At that meeting, the Niagara Movement, as the group became known, resolved:

We shall not be satisfied with less than our full manhood rights. We

---

94. Rabin, *supra* note 90, at 212.
95. *Id.*

claim for ourselves every right that belongs to a free-born American, civil and social, and until we get these rights we shall never cease to protest and assail the ears of America with the stories of its shameful deeds towards us. We want our manhood suffrage and we want it now. Second, we want discrimination in public accommodations to cease. Third, we claim the right to associate with such people as wish to associate with us. Fourth, we want the laws enforced against rich as well as poor, against capitalists as well as laborers, against whites as well as blacks. We are not more lawless than the white race, we are more often arrested, convicted, and mobbed. Fifth, we want our children educated.

From the beginning, money was a problem for the group, and bankruptcy persuaded DuBois to ally the Niagara group with a liberal white group that originated in Illinois after a race riot in Springfield in 1908. William Walling, a journalist, wrote a newspaper article titled "Race War in the North"[96] about the deterioration of race relations. He called for a "large and powerful body of citizens . . . to come to [the Negro's] aid." Walling's article became a rallying point for progressive, well-to-do whites, many of whom were rooted in the abolitionist tradition. In 1910, DuBois's Niagara Movement joined with this group to become a new organization known as the National Association for the Advancement of Colored People, or the NAACP.

The only founding member of the NAACP who was a lawyer was Moorfield Storey, who, until his death in 1930, was president of the organization. Of the six officers in the new organization, only DuBois, who was made director of publicity and research, was black.[97] The NAACP was the generally acknowledged leader of the black civil rights movement from the death of Booker T. Washington in 1915 until the emergence of more activist black organizations between 1957 and 1961.[98]

Like the ACLU, the NAACP did not begin as a litigating group.[99] From 1910 to 1930, the NAACP brought no landmark cases. Although it viewed

---

96. William English Walling, *Race War in the North*, Illinois Independent (Sept. 3, 1908).

97. Jack, *supra* note 90, at 7.

98. Allan H. Spear, *NAACP*, in International Encyclopedia of the Social Sciences vol. 9, David L. Sills, ed. (Macmillan & The Free Press 1968), 400.

99. Arnold H. Taylor, Contributions in Afro-American and African Studies, Travail and Triumph: Black Life and Culture in the South Since the Civil War (Greenwood Press 1976) 244.

litigation as an important tool right from the beginning, it used it on an ad hoc basis. Lawyers were costly and usually not the tool of choice in the South, where racial discrimination was protected by law. In the early years, the NAACP did undertake litigation against the effects of racial discrimination. A fundamental reason that the NAACP came into existence was the lynchings in the South and the desire to pursue justice for the black men who were murdered. More commonly, however, the NAACP attacked problems in a number of other ways. Much of the early work of the organization was education and lobbying. DuBois, as editor of the NAACP's newsletter, *The Crisis*, wrote extensively about the effects of racial discrimination. During World War I, the NAACP worked to combat discrimination against black servicemen. Then, in 1930, the NAACP was given a grant of $100,000, a huge amount of money for the day. The grant was a turning point for the organization as it continued its commitment to lobbying and other political action for social justice.

The Legal Defense and Education Fund

NAACP leadership decided to use the grant money to fund a litigation campaign. Nathan Margold, a lawyer and a NAACP member, designed the strategy for a legal attack on Jim Crow, the official system of segregation. In his report to the NAACP, he detailed a long-range plan for a litigation campaign that was estimated to last for at least 25 years. A subcommittee of the NAACP, the Legal Defense and Education Fund (LDEF), was created to pursue the litigation campaign and to instruct the membership about the law.

The NAACP's commitment to the work of the LDEF led to the hiring of Charles Houston and later Thurgood Marshall as special counsel to the NAACP. The two organizations remained close. They shared office space and leadership. In 1954, the LDEF won a historic victory in the civil rights struggle in the United States Supreme Court ruling in *Brown v. Board of Education of Topeka*. Subsequently, the LDEF became the Legal Defense and Education Fund, Inc., commonly referred to as the Inc. Fund. Up to 1960, the legal staff of the Inc. Fund consisted of four and sometimes five lawyers. Beginning in 1960, the staff began to expand rapidly. Outside the planned attack on segregation, criminal defense cases and school desegregation cases filled the docket of the Inc. Fund.

The *Brown* decision marks a plateau in the civil rights struggle. *Brown v. Board of Education* overturned the practice of "separate but equal" in public education in America. For black Americans, the Court's ruling made real the theoretical right of equal education and for the first time made that right susceptible to vindication in southern courts.

For the NAACP, the immediate result of the *Brown* decision was its retrenchment. The organization faced many obstacles. In a number of southern states, the NAACP was under full-scale legislative attack, some even going so far as to outlaw it entirely.[100]

Brown v. Board had another unanticipated consequence for the organization. It encouraged a more militant black political philosophy, which resulted in the eclipse of the NAACP's premier position in the black community. In 1955, black perceptions of improved social and political prospects launched the civil rights movement onto a new stage—direct political action. The ascendancy of the Southern Christian Leadership Conference (SCLC), an organization founded by Martin Luther King, Jr., challenged the hegemony of the NAACP in the black community. After *Brown v. Board,* the civil rights movement progressed very rapidly through distinct and ever more activist stages. The biracial NAACP was quickly surpassed in influence by the SCLC, which was a predominantly black middle-class organization. However, the SCLC's dominance was short-lived, as in the early 1960s it yielded to the younger, less established leadership of the Student Nonviolent Coordinating Committee (SNCC), which spawned a Black Power movement that embraced a strong anti-white sentiment

The Response to Brown v. Board of Education

The White Response in the South

To whites in the South, the *Brown* ruling was anathema. The titular head of the national Democratic Party, Adlai Stevenson, asked that the white South be "given time and patience" to desegregate and rejected the idea of using federal troops to enforce court orders.[101] For the white bar, the chief consequence was to further antagonize lawyers, who began to openly question the power of the federal authority to enforce desegregation. Lawyers in the South mirrored southern racial attitudes. The journalist Hodding Carter III, arguably one of the most moderate southerners of the era, observed about white society that "everybody more or less agrees on everything anyway." What united them was "a common anti-black attitude."[102]

Segregationists throughout the South reacted swiftly to the decision. Mississippi, the southern state with the highest percentage of black citizens, set a

---

100. *Id.* at 6.
101. Harvard Sitkoff, *The Struggle for Black Equality: 1954-1980,* THE AMERICAN CENTURY SERIES 25 (Hill and Wang 1981).
102. Hodding Carter III, *as quoted in* JOHN DITTMER, LOCAL PEOPLE: THE STRUGGLE FOR CIVIL RIGHTS IN MISSISSIPPI (Pantheon Books 1965) 128.

standard for obstruction of the federal order by creating the infamous White Citizens Council. This quasi-official institution pursued "the agenda of the Klan with the demeanor of the Rotary" and was made up of the white establishment, the "professionals, businessmen, and planters." The council officially eschewed violence and other extralegal tactics. Instead it used economic reprisal against anyone, "black or white," seen as a "threat to the status quo." Regional presidents were often local bank presidents and, despite official disclaimers, violence frequently followed in the wake of the council's economic intimidation campaigns. "The organization was so deeply entrenched in state affairs as to have a quasi-official status; it even received funding from state revenue."[103]

The Southern Delegation in Congress

In the mid-1950s, a conservative coalition of midwestern Republicans and southern Democrats controlled both the House of Representatives and the Senate. In 1956, 101 members of Congress from the South signed a "Declaration of Constitutional Principles," asking their states to refuse to obey *Brown v. Board*. They labeled the decision unwarranted and contrary to the Constitution and declared that the Supreme Court had no power to demand an end to segregation. This "Southern Manifesto" declared that only a state, not the federal government, could decide whether or not a school should be segregated, and that the states would be in the right in opposing the Supreme Court's order.

Southern States

"Defiance of the Court and the Constitution became the touchstone of Southern loyalty, the necessary proof of one's concern for the security of the white race. With the overwhelming support of the South's white press and pulpit, segregationist politicians resurrected John C. Calhoun's notions of 'interposition' and 'nullification' to rationalize their effort to thwart federal authority."[104] The most successful white tactics used to obstruct school desegregation were the pupil placement laws enacted throughout the South. Theoretically, they guaranteed each child freedom of choice in school placement. Local authorities could not consider race in placement but they could use such criteria as psychological qualifications, or the morals, conduct, health, and personal standards of the pupil. With these standards, school boards through-

---

103. CHARLES M. PAYNE, I'VE GOT THE LIGHT OF FREEDOM: THE ORGANIZING TRADITION AND THE MISSISSIPPI FREEDOM STRUGGLE (Univ. of California Press 1995) 34-35.

104. *Id.*

out the South continued segregated education. In 1958, the United States Supreme Court upheld the constitutionality of pupil placement laws.

The Federal Government

The President of the United States, Dwight D. Eisenhower, a Republican, preferred education to coercion, and initially refused to use his authority to back school desegregation. Eisenhower was quoted as saying that the appointment of Earl Warren to the Supreme Court was the "biggest damfool mistake I ever made." Ironically, Eisenhower became the first president since Reconstruction to use federal troops in the South to enforce black rights. In September 1957, Arkansas Governor Orval Faubus claimed he was unable to obey a court order to desegregate the Little Rock Central High School. "In defense of the union,"[105] Eisenhower sent 1,000 men from the U.S. Army 101st Airborne Division into Little Rock to secure order in Arkansas.

In 1954, the Eisenhower Administration declined to give the United States Justice Department authority to initiate lawsuits on behalf of the victims of discrimination. In a subsequent Supreme Court decision, the high court ruled that jurisdiction for *Brown* was to rest in the district courts. This effectively left enforcement authority for school desegregation in the hands of southern judges, who were supported by a racially biased bar. As a result, very little desegregation occurred in the South in the following six years.[106] According to one historian, the *Brown* decision was "essentially a statement of principle rather than a mandate for desegregation." Further, "civil rights lawyers, mainly from the Legal Defense Fund of the NAACP, fought alone to make the Supreme Court's decree a reality in the 1950s."[107]

In 1960, the Republicans lost the White House to John F. Kennedy. President Kennedy owed his election in large part to his support of civil rights reform, and his election generated renewed hope in the black community.[108] Kennedy named his brother Robert as Attorney General. The younger Kennedy was not eager to involve the Administration in the South. The Kennedy Justice Department took some time to become fully engaged with desegregation enforcement. In 1962, in an interview with Anthony Lewis of *The New York Times*, Kennedy said that "everyone in the Justice Department agreed that 'our authority was limited . . . it's better not to

---

105. *Id.* at 32.
106. CARL M. BRAUER, JOHN F. KENNEDY AND THE SECOND RECONSTRUCTION (COLUMBIA UNIV. PRESS 1977) 1, 5.
107. *Id.* at 6.
108. *Id.* at 33-36.

impose things from above because people resent it."' Later, Burke Marshall, former assistant attorney general for civil rights, observed, "We didn't have the power" and, he added candidly, "We didn't want it." Leslie Dunbar, the head of the Southern Regional Council, an organization formed in the 1940s to promote racial understanding, said about the federal government, "There was a great reluctance . . . to accept the fact that you had to be on somebody's side in the South."[109]

The Kennedy Justice Department, unlike the Eisenhower Administration, did take its responsibility to investigate and litigate matters seriously. Nonetheless, one study concludes that civil rights activists:

> . . . encouraged by the government put on the armor of federal law and assailed the ramparts of lily-white democracy. . . . The Justice Department, to be sure, had not remained neutral; but neither had it provided the active support they believed it had promised. While it had supplied doughty lip service and brandished unfailingly its policy of litigation, it had done little either to prevent or punish even the most flagrant acts of violence and coercion.[110]

The failure of the federal government to enforce school desegregation in the South proved to be a turning point for black leadership of the civil rights movement. Black frustration with the failure of the justice system after 1955 changed the nature of the movement for racial equity. A younger leadership abandoned the NAACP's strategy of incremental change through litigation. A strategy of peaceful but determined political resistance was adopted. The white community, which opposed the goals of the civil rights movement, countered the new strategy with further repressive actions.

The mass arrests and imprisonments of the late 1950s and early 1960s necessitated the aid of lawyers in a way that had not been seen before in the southern struggle. The meager resources, both financial and human, of the public interest advocacy groups were overwhelmed. The bar, both in the South and throughout the nation, failed to come to the aid of the courts. From 1955 to 1963, the fundamental failure of the southern bar was not its paucity of legal aid but its callousness to the judicial process. Because of racial prejudice, the bar allowed itself to be blinded to the crippling effects that the lack of procedural justice was having on southern society. Without

---

109. Dittmer, *supra* note 102 at 93-94.
110. Neil R. McMillen, *Black Enfranchisement in Mississippi: Federal Enforcement and Black Protest in the 1960s,* 3 JOURNAL OF SOUTHERN HISTORY XLIII (1977) 363-65.

lawyers, the constitutional system for peaceful settlement of social conflict was inoperable in the South in the 1950s and early 1960s.[111]

The Black Response

To blacks in the South, the Supreme Court's decision in *Brown* was reason for rejoicing. It confirmed their faith in the principles professed in the Constitution and their hope for legally mandated reform. All over the South, black citizens began to demand not only educational rights but social change. The deluge began quite unexpectedly in early December 1955, when Rosa Parks was arrested for refusing to relinquish her seat to a white man on a public bus in Montgomery, Alabama. Four days after her arrest on December 5, a new presence in the civil rights movement appeared, the Reverend Martin Luther King, Jr. The young preacher captured the imagination of southern blacks. King said, "There comes a time when people get tired. We are here this evening to say to those who have mistreated us for so long that we are tired—tired of being segregated and humiliated, tired of being kicked about by the brutal feet of oppression. We have no alternative but to protest."[112]

So began a successful year-long boycott of the Montgomery bus system. "The great crusade in Montgomery inspired black leaders throughout the South. To young black people in the South, the Montgomery boycott was the only important social action ever brought off by blacks in the nation's history. To them, King became an instant hero—something of a black superman."[113]

The Southern Christian Leadership Conference

Martin Luther King's strategy of nonviolent resistance to southern segregation laws revolutionized the black struggle. It recruited for the first time the active participation of the southern black middle class. In 1957, Dr. King and "his ministerial lieutenants" formed the Southern Christian Leadership Conference (SCLC).[114] The SCLC was based in Atlanta, Georgia, and "repre-

---

111. Census, *supra* note 87.
112. MARTIN LUTHER KING, JR., STRIDE TOWARD FREEDOM: THE MONTGOMERY STORY (Harper & Row 1958) 46.
113. ROBERT BRISBANE, BLACK ACTIVISM (Judson Press, 1974) 43.
114. A Guide to Subversive Organizations and Publications (Committee on Un-American Activities, U.S. House of Representatives, 1944, rev. 1961), Report 1311, 149. The Program, *Freedom Now,* Seventh SCLC Annual Convention, Sept. 24-27, 1963. The Foreword to the program states, "The Southern Christian Leadership Conference is a service agency committed to non-violence and voter registration. It hopes to facilitate coordinate action of local protest groups and to assist in their sharing of resources and experiences."

sented the black church militant; and until the beginning of the student sit-ins in 1960, black Baptist ministers, mostly graduates of black colleges, provided the leadership of the protest movement."[115]

From the beginning, the relationship between the leadership of the national NAACP and the SCLC was tense. Focusing on their conflict in Mississippi, a recent work found:

> The Southern Christian Leadership Conference never did establish a base in Mississippi, in part because of NAACP opposition . . . the national NAACP officials had no program to deal with the range of problems facing Mississippi blacks. . . . Although its major resources were directed elsewhere, the New York office nonetheless wanted Mississippi to remain exclusive NAACP territory. NAACP activists in Mississippi, on the other hand, were more open to cooperation with other groups . . . . (Medgar) Evers complained, "Our goals are identical. Why can't we join hands to get there?"[116]

The NAACP consistently struggled for southern membership. Joining the organization, particularly in places like Mississippi, was dangerous.[117] In that state there were only 129 members of the NAACP in 1944.[118] The organizations did not even begin to establish a political network there until the late 1940s, when black veterans began to return from the service. Not until 1954 and *Brown v. Board* did the NAACP consider hiring a full-time state secretary. At that time, organization leaders brought on Medgar Evers to pursue school desegregation cases. "Given the powerful segregationist opposition, the federal government's inaction, and the lack of a deep base of support in the black community, the school petitioners in Mississippi were sitting ducks, to be picked off one by one by the sharpshooters of the Citi-

---

115. *Id.* at 239.

116. DITTMER, *supra* note 102 at 76-78.

117. AFRICAN AMERICANS AND THE LIVING CONSTITUTION, John Hope Franklin & Gena Rae McNeil eds. (Smithson Institution Press 1995) 97. Percentage of blacks in Mississippi in 1960 was 42%. Recorded lynches in Mississippi were 534 from 1882 to 1952. Also, DITTMER, *supra* note 102 at 6, Mississippi's two-year residency requirement and two-dollar poll tax were the most exacting in the South. Beyond that, the registrars administered the law selectively. The Mississippi voting statute was the product of the 1890 constitutional convention, which was called for the express purpose of eliminating the Negro vote. The heart of the electoral provision was the "understanding clause."

118. DITTMER, *supra* note 102 at 29. In 1944 there were only 129 members in the NAACP's six branches in the State.

zens' Council. The national NAACP office responded to this defeat by drop-ping Mississippi like a hot potato. Eight years passed before the NAACP filed its first desegregation suit against the Mississippi public schools, and it did so only after repeated, increasingly insistent, requests by state field secretary Medgar Evers."[119]

Student Nonviolent Coordinating Committee

Into the impasse created by the "turf battles" between the two main civil rights organizations came a new group of black activists, southern black col-lege students. The students formed the Student Nonviolent Coordinating Com-mittee (SNCC) in 1960.[120] Historian Howard Zinn calls them "the new abolitionists." He credits the students with starting "the explosion of sit-ins throughout the South in early 1960 that led to the formation of the Student Nonviolent Coordinating Committee," which launched a new wave of mili-tant political resistance.

The sit-ins began on February 1, 1960, when four freshmen at A&T College in Greensboro, North Carolina, sat down at the lunch counter of Woolworth's and waited for service. "In a matter of days, the idea leaped to other cities in North Carolina. During the next two weeks, sit-ins spread to fifteen cities in five southern states. Within the following year, over 50,000 people—most were Negroes, some were white—had participated in one kind of demonstration or another in a hundred cities and over 3,600 demonstrators spent time in jail. It is hard to overestimate the electrical effect of that first sit-in in Greensboro."[121]

The political power and moral determination of southern blacks to se-cure their legal rights was greater than it had ever been in American history. The Negro "was rebelling now," according to Howard Zinn, "not with the blind, terrible understandable hatred of the slave revolts, but with skill in organization, sophistication in tactics, and an unassailable moral position. With these went a ferocious refusal to retreat. What had been an orderly, inch-by-inch advance via legal processes now became a revolution in which unarmed regiments marched from one objective to another with bewildering

---

119. *Id.* at 52. Also see Sitkoff, *supra* note 101 at 27. Black parents and NAACP lawyers initiated desegregation suits in more than 2,000 southern school districts.

120. Marion Barry was elected as the first chairman of the Student Nonviolent Coordinat-ing Committee. Barry, who later became a well-known elected official in Washington, D.C., was doing graduate work at Fisk University in Atlanta. It was decided to set up an office in Atlanta and to hire staff, raise money, and coordinate the various student activities throughout the South.

121. HOWARD ZINN, SNCC: THE NEW ABOLITIONISTS (Beacon Press 1964) 16,

speed."[122] Zinn later noted that, "Naked physical confrontation of the Jim Crow establishment became the order of the day. Blacks demanded rather than pleaded, bargained rather than cajoled. Thus within the Southern environment the movement was radical, even revolutionary, in its tactics."[123] Yet, state-sponsored segregation remained the rule. Blacks continued to be denied the vote and economic and physical violence increased.

Congress for Racial Equality

In Washington in 1961, the recently inaugurated Kennedy Administration hoped to avoid taking on a congressional fight for civil rights legislation, one they felt they were sure to lose. But another civil rights advocacy group, the Congress for Racial Equality (CORE), led by James Farmer, had a different plan. CORE initiated a campaign to test a recent Supreme Court ruling that declared segregated interstate bus terminals unconstitutional. CORE organized "freedom rides," the first in May 1961, to force the Kennedy Administration to execute the law in the South. The brutal treatment of the multiracial freedom riders stunned the nation and turned the freedom rider issue into a national dilemma. Still the Kennedy Administration withheld federal intervention. CORE did succeed in gaining the attention of the attorney general and the Civil Rights Division of the Justice Department about the seriousness of the growing conflict. In September 1962, the federal government intervened in the South.

Federal troops were sent to Mississippi to quell rioting that broke out in Oxford over the court-ordered desegregation of the University of Mississippi. In the struggle to enroll James Meredith in the university, two people died, 375 were injured, and more than 300 were arrested. The absence of the Mississippi bar in the conflict so outraged Attorney General Robert F. Kennedy that he denounced the organization publicly. While making a speech in California for Law Day, in an extraordinary show of anger, Kennedy condemned the southern legal profession for its failure to uphold the principles of justice and freedom. He wrote, "I wouldn't have believed it could happen in this country, but maybe now we can understand how Hitler took over Germany."[124]

Mississippi

Without the intermediation of law, the South appeared to be headed toward

---

122. *Id.* at 26.
123. TAYLOR, *supra* note 99, at 243.
124. Robert F. Kennedy, *On the Duty of Lawyers*, Sept. 29, 1962, *reprinted in* Edwin O. Guthman & C. Richard Allen, RFK: COLLECTED SPEECHES (Viking, 1993) 89-90.

anarchy. Mississippi in the early 1960s was a microcosm of the southern struggle. The state led the country in recorded lynchings, the ultimate form of social control. Its legal system protected the most oppressive political, social, and economic policies of segregation in the South.[125] The NAACP's strategy of incremental legal progress was passed over in favor of the tactics of confrontation by the activists who controlled the movement in the state. The activists, young and poor, encountered violence, mass arrests, unjust imprisonment, and, despite it all, the movement grew in size, strength, and determination.

The movement in Mississippi was not driven by a master plan but rather two extraordinary young men. They were Robert Moses, who represented SNCC and the SCLC, and Medgar Evers of the NAACP. Moses, a schoolteacher from New York, became convinced that the key to black advancement was the franchise. From 1940 to 1954, the percentage of voting age blacks registered in the South had risen from 5 to 20 percent. In 1956, the figure was 25 percent. The Civil Rights Act was passed in 1957, but the percentage remained unchanged in 1958, even though the NAACP had, after the passage of the act, unveiled the Crusade for Citizenship, which aimed to register three million Negroes by 1960. A national voter registration drive sponsored by the national Democratic Party in 1960 managed to increase the figure to only 28 percent in that year. "Mississippi, however, lagged far behind even the most dilatory of its southern sisters. . . . [it] permitted fewer blacks to vote for Lyndon Baines Johnson in 1964 than had been eligible to vote for William McKinley in 1896."[126] In 1961, the United States Civil Rights Commission reported that in 69 (out of 82) Mississippi counties where the commission was able to acquire data, blacks constituted 37.7 percent of the voting-age population, but only 6.2 percent of them were able to vote.[127] A professor of history at the University of Southern Mississippi, Neil McMillen, found:

> . . . that even with more favorable demographic characteristics blacks could not have registered to vote in significantly greater numbers; for Mississippi, the pioneer state in the southern disenfranchisement movement, had no peer in the denial of black rights. Whether by force or fraud or by such legal sophistries as the all-white primary and stringent literacy, poll-tax, and residency requirements, Mississippi for three quarters of a century provided

---

125. FRANKLIN & MCNEIL, *supra* note 117.
126. MCMILLEN, *supra* note 110 at 352.
127. CARL M. BRAUER, JOHN F. KENNEDY AND THE SECOND RECONSTRUCTION (Columbia Univ. Press 1977) 113.

the standard by which all southern states could measure their devotion to white supremacy. In 1965, on the eve of the enactment
of the Voting Rights Act, even as in 1890 when white rule was
formalized, the state's black citizens found the obstacles to suffrage insurmountable.[128]

Robert Moses moved to Mississippi to launch a series of voter registration campaigns that would change the history of the South. His work in
Mississippi was supported primarily by the young activists from SNCC.[129]

At the same time that Moses was organizing the rural blacks to register,
Medgar Evers was the key force behind the organization of a series of increasingly effective economic boycotts and sit-in demonstrations in Jackson, the
state capital. Evers was an American combat veteran who, despite repeated
efforts, was never allowed to register to vote in his home state of Mississippi.[130]

---

128. McMillen, *supra*, note 126.
129. JAMES MACGREGOR BURNS & STEWART BURNS, THE PEOPLE'S CHARTER: THE PURSUIT OF
    RIGHTS IN AMERICA (Alfred A. Knopf 1991), 311-12. In February of 1960 the executive
    secretary of the SCLC in Atlanta, Ella Barker, called for a meeting of the young leaders
    of SNCC. She knew that the organization needed structure to endure and proposed that
    SNCC incorporate with the more moderate SCLC. However, "the urge for freedom
    from adult fetters and formal ties had marked the student movement from the begin-
    ning," and it was decided that the new group would remain independent. Ella Barker,
    who had become critical of the SCLC, resigned because of the "SCLC's rigid, preacher
    dominated hierarchy." Barker's experience in the southern movement is illustrative of
    the rapid pace of change in the 1950s. She had been a civil rights activist for over 30
    years. She was the descendant of a slave who became valedictorian of her college class
    in the 1920s. As a young woman she set up black consumer cooperatives during the
    Depression. She joined the NAACP and recruited for the organization throughout the
    South, serving as the director of a number of NAACP branches including its New
    York office, which she left to become a founding member of the SCLC. Barker, along
    with Bayard Rustin and a white New York lawyer, Stanley Levinson, were the ones
    who urged Martin Luther King, Jr. to use his fame from the Montgomery boycott to
    fuse a "South-wide federation of the church-based movements that had arisen in
    several cities." Ella Barker's commitment to a faster advancement of civil rights
    caused her, at 56, to oppose "the centrality of charismatic leaders who were best at
    organizing the media," and to back SNCC activists who "lived out the idea that real
    change came through the empowerment of the people at the grass roots." The SCLC
    did try unsuccessfully to launch a grassroots Crusade for Citizenship that had two
    important results. It proposed a strategy for a voter registration campaign in the South
    and it attracted a group of activists dedicated to winning the vote for blacks.
130. Medgar Evers, *Why I Live in Mississippi*, EBONY (September 1963) 142-44, *as quoted*
    in DITTMER, *supra* note 102 at 2: "I was born in Decatur, was raised there, but I never
    in my life was permitted to vote there."

In the beginning, both initiatives were small.[131] Their value lay in ener-
gizing of the mass of the black community, which transformed race relations
in Mississippi into power relations.[132]

From 1961 to 1963, blacks fought against tremendous odds to advance
their social goals in Mississippi. "There were only three black lawyers practicing in the state, Carsie Hall . . . Jack Young . . . (and) Jess Brown," all three
of whom practiced in Jackson.[133] As one black Mississippian observed, "We
have next to no lawyers to defend our rights. . . . There are no white lawyers
and only three Negro lawyers that will handle civil rights cases. These Negro
lawyers are just about totally overburdened. Out-of-state lawyers are generally barred from practicing, including in the federal district courts. The present
legal set-up is inadequate."[134]

Throughout it all, the bar and its leadership watched silently as the racial
divide widened.

---

131. Doug McAdam, Freedom Summer (Oxford Univ. Press, 1988), 6-7. The injustice in
    Mississippi struck a chord in the college-age generation in the United States that was
    to reverberate through the American experience. Non-southerners, black and white,
    began to volunteer time and money to the black cause. "I was struck by the number of
    references to whites trained in civil rights organizing who went on to prominent roles
    in the other major movements of the Sixties. I had been aware of the debt those later
    movements owed the black struggle . . . . I had experienced the debt as primarily one
    of tactics and ideology rather than of personnel . . . . the importance of these early
    white civil rights activists lay in the political and cultural bridge. . . ."
132. Joseph S. Himes, *A Theory of Racial Conflict,* 50 Social Forces (1971) 53-60. Also,
    Joseph S. Himes, *Functions of Racial Conflict,* 45 Social Forces (1966) 3-5.
133. Dittmer *supra,* note 102, at 81.
134. Robert Hunter Morley, Dictated Notes, March 3, 1964, from the personal file of J.J.
    Shestack.

CHAPTER 2

"There Isn't Any Middle of the Road"— Alabama, 1963

On May 17, 1954, the Supreme Court of the United States issued a unanimous ruling on school segregation that struck at the heart of white supremacy in the South.[1] To the dismay of segregationists, the Court, led by a new Chief Justice, Earl Warren, chose to override the legal precedent on which segregated public education in the South rested—"separate but equal." Established in 1896,[2] the system had been repeatedly upheld by previous Courts.[3] Chief Justice Warren wrote for the Court, "We must consider public education in the light of its full development and its present place in American life throughout the Nation. Only in this way can it be determined if segregation in public schools deprives these plaintiffs of the equal protection of the laws."[4] The Court ruled that "in the field of public education the doctrine of 'separate but equal' has no place."[5] The furor aroused by the Supreme Court's ruling in *Brown v. Board of Education* was "without parallel even in the turbulent history of the Court."[6] A number of states refused to

---

1. Brown v. Board of Educ., 347 U.S. 483 (1954); Bolling v. Sharpe, 347 U.S. 497 (1954).
2. Plessy v. Ferguson, 163 U.S. 537 (1896).
3. Cumming v. Board of Educ., 175 U.S. 528 (1899); Berea College v. Kentucky, 211 U.S. 45 (1908); Gong Lum v. Rice, 27 5 U.S. 78 (1927).
4. *Brown*, 492-93.
5. *Id.* at 495.
6. Robert B. McKay, *With All Deliberate Speed: A Study of School Desegregation*, 31 N.Y.U. L. Rev. 991, 998 (1956).

comply with the order,[7] asserting that they had a right of interposition. This contention was in direct opposition to a bedrock principle of American justice, the doctrine of judicial supremacy.[8]

In the South, a seriously flawed judicial process was further discredited in the eyes of blacks by the white bar's refusal to defend minority rights. The American bar, a key legal institution with responsibility to the Constitution and the courts, was ambivalent in its response to the attack on the authority of the Supreme Court. On the one hand, lawyers had an obligation to support the supremacy of the judicial system but, on the other, the predominantly white bar shared the racial prejudices of American society. During a crucial period of social adjustment to the new law of the land, 1954 to 1963, the organized bar, the recognized spokesman for the profession in the United States, was equivocal about the desegregation decision and silent on the duties of the lawyer to uphold the law.

By 1963 the integrity of the American system of justice was in jeopardy in the South. In June of that year, the crisis surrounding desegregation and federal authority came to a critical juncture in Alabama when the governor, an avowed segregationist, prepared to resist, with force if necessary, federal efforts to integrate his state's public system of higher education. All during the winter and spring of 1963, the bar continued to be an ineffective advocate for the American system of justice. It wasn't until the governor of Alabama moved toward open rebellion that a few prominent members of the organized bar denounced, as lawyers, his position as illegal and untenable. This pivotal incident marks the beginning of a movement that, within a decade, would transform the legal profession in America from its almost total devotion to the interests of the well established into an institution beginning to come to terms with its responsibility for maintaining equity between the public and private needs of society.

Southern Resistance to Brown v. Board

In the minds of many in the South, *Brown v. Board* meant the end to a revered way of life, and resistance to its implementation became paramount. White supremacists in the South believed that *Brown* was merely part of an orches-

---

7. The states that refused to desegregate their schools were Alabama, Florida, Louisiana, Mississippi, North Carolina, South Carolina, and Virginia. Also, Leflar & Davis, *Segregation in the Public Schools 1953*, 67 Harv. L. Rev. 377, 378-79 n.3 (1954). Segregation was required by statute in 17 states and the District of Columbia and was permitted in four additional states.
8. McKay, *supra* note 6, at 1020-38.

trated attack on the southern way of life by blacks and "leftists."[9] "Anyone who looks beneath appearances to reality must see that the attack upon the southern school system is but one front of a general attack upon the principle of an independent, self-directing social order with a set of values proper to itself."[10] White southerners actively supported semi-official groups, such as the White Citizens Council, whose goal was to maintain a segregated South. The eminent historian and southerner Charles Callan Tansill described the importance of segregation to the southern social system. In the South, he wrote: "From Tidewater, Virginia, to the western boundary of Texas there is a common factor of blood, beliefs, and behavior that sets the inhabitants of that region apart from other sections of the nation. In order to prevent aspiring Negroes from changing the culture pattern of the South, certain barriers have been erected to prevent such action. The first barrier is blood intermarriage is strictly forbidden . . . . closely related to the barrier of blood is the barrier of segregation . . . . The third barrier raised against aspiring Negroes has been that of suffrage."[11]

Some 96 of the South's Congressional delegation from 11 southern states signed a Declaration of Constitutional Principles,[12] which was read in both Houses. It declared their region's opposition to the imposition of federal authority by "judicial activist's" in a sphere that they believed was reserved for the states.[13] The southern bloc declared *Brown v. Board* "judicial legislation." In what has become known as the Southern Manifesto, they pledged "to use all lawful means to bring about a reversal of this decision which is contrary to the Constitution and to prevent the use of force in its implementation."[14] Political and other leaders in the South contended that, rather than a federal court order, a constitutional amendment was required to force such a change

---

9. Charles C. Tansill, *How Long Will Southern Legislatures Continue to Acquiesce in the Alleged Decision of the Supreme Court on May 17, 1954?*, ALA. LAW. 24:1 (1963) at 371.

10. Richard M. Weaver, *The Regime of the South*, NAT'L REV., Mar. 14, 1959, at 588-89.

11. Tansill, *supra* note 9, at 364, 372-74.

12. CONGRESSIONAL RECORD 102, Mar. 12, 1956, at 3948, 4004.

13. Southerners didn't have the votes in Congress to pass legislation that would ensure the continuance of segregation. However, what they could do was filibuster—that is, use obstructive tactics in Congress to block the Kennedy Administration's legislative agenda. In order to break any filibuster, 67 out of the 100 votes in the Senate are needed. In 1963, "the Administration will have to round up something like 25 Republican votes. It is touch and go whether this can be done," Robert J. Donovan, *Racial Crisis—The Official View,* N.Y. HERALD TRIB., June 6, 1963, at 1.

14. *The Southern Manifesto*, N.Y. TIMES, Mar. 12, 1956, at 1.

in the South. As one constitutional law professor wrote of the southerners, "The protestants, however sincere, are doing enormous public harm."[15]

The states of Alabama, Georgia, and Mississippi went even further in their opposition to the ruling. They passed interposition laws for the purpose of nullifying the segregation decisions[16] of the Supreme Court.[17] The Alabama Act, passed on February 2, 1956 states:

> Whereas the Constitution of the United States was formed by the sanction of the several states, given each in its sovereign capacity; and whereas the states, being the parties to the constitutional compact, it follows of necessity that there can be no tribunal above their authority to decide, in the last resort, whether the compact made by them be violated; and, consequently, they must decide themselves, in the last resort, such questions as may be of sufficient magnitude to require their interposition. . . . be it resolved . . . that until the issue between the State of Alabama and the General Government is decided by the submission to the states, pursuant to Article V of the Constitution, of a suitable constitutional amendment that would declare, in plain and unequivocal language, that the states do surrender their power to maintain public schools and other public facilities on the basis of separation as to race, the Legislature of Alabama declares the decision and orders of the Supreme Court of the United States relating to separation of races in the public schools are, as a matter of right, null, void, and of no effect; and the Legislature of Alabama declares to all men that as a matter of right, this State is not bound to abide thereby; we declare, further, our firm intention to take all appropriate measures honorably and constitutionally available to us, to avoid this illegal encroachment upon our rights. . . .[18]

From 1954 to 1962, the rancor incited by the segregation decision remained relatively calm. For blacks in the deep South, the Supreme Court's order remained largely theoretical due to the failure of the legal profession to

---

15. Charles Fairman, *The Supreme Court 1955 Term: Foreword: The Attack on the Segregation Cases*, 70:83 HARV. L. REV. (1956).

16. The Supreme Court extended *Brown* to include the District of Columbia in *Bolling v. Sharpe*, 347 U.S. 497 (1954).

17. Alabama Acts 1st Special Session 1956, No. 42; Georgia Laws 1956, Res. Act No. 130, at 642; Mississippi Laws 1956, S. Con. Res. 125.

18. Alabama Act No. 43.

support its implementation through the courts, and because of the reluctance of the federal government to confront southern defiance.[19] In their efforts to force execution of the law, southern blacks were stymied by a labyrinth of obstacles enacted by state officials.

However in 1962, after a long series of court battles that went all the way to the Supreme Court, the situation took a radical new direction. For the first time, the federal courts ordered the end to official resistance. Mississippi was directed to admit James Meredith, a native of the state and a young black war veteran, to a branch of the state university at Oxford. Under the constitutional system, there was no further legal question of review or vacillation. The stage was set for confrontation at the highest levels of state and federal authority. "When open and avowed defiance continued in a manner unprecedented for a century, the United States Court of Appeals for the Fifth Circuit consisting of eight Southern jurists found Mississippi's Governor Ross Barnett and Lieutenant Governor Paul Johnson guilty of contempt for blocking Meredith's admission. The judges . . . then directed the Federal Government to enforce the court's order and to put down what bordered on rebellion."[20]

United States marshals were sent to Mississippi to enforce compliance. By Sunday, September 30, 1962, when Meredith was to register, the marshals numbered 550. That night at 10 P.M., President John F. Kennedy went on television. He said, "Our nation is founded on the principle that observance of the law is the eternal safeguard of liberty . . . . Americans are free to disagree with the law, but not to disobey it."[21] Even as the President was speaking, a crowd of more than 2,500 began attacking the federal marshals. Thirty-five marshals were shot and more than 150 others required medical attention. The attack forced the President to order the use of federal troops, which eventually numbered 20,000 men. In defense of his actions, President Kennedy explained, "This country cannot survive . . . and this government would unravel very fast, if . . . the Executive Branch does not carry out the decisions of the Court."[22]

---

19. CARL M. BRAUER, JOHN F. KENNEDY AND THE SECOND RECONSTRUCTION 142 (Columbia Univ. Press 1977) 3-5. The Eisenhower Administration did little to discourage resistance to desegregation in the South, and Eisenhower himself believed segregation to be a local problem. In 1957, he did send paratroopers and the National Guard into Little Rock, Arkansas, after desegregation of Little Rock High School led to rioting. "The Little Rock crisis did not initiate a change of policy. On the contrary, the Administration still sought to avoid involvement. . . . Although Congress in 1957 and in 1960 had given the Justice Department new authority to investigate voting rights infractions, the Department responded lethargically and brought few cases."

20. THEODORE C. SORENSEN, KENNEDY 483 (Harper & Row 1965).

21. *Id.* at 485.

22. *Id.* at 488.

The Kennedy Administration found itself isolated and without official or traditional allies in the desegregation battle in Mississippi. One of the harshest disappointments for the Attorney General was the failure of the legal profession to stand by the judicial process. In an extraordinary show of anger over the profession's attitude in Mississippi, Robert Kennedy publicly rebuked southern lawyers, comparing them to Germans in the 1930s. "I wouldn't have believed it could happen in this country," he said, " but maybe now we can understand how Hitler took over Germany."[23] Some of the Attorney General's closest colleagues at the Department of Justice recall that during the Oxford crisis a constant refrain of his was, "Where are all the lawyers?"[24] The exceptional rebuke did nothing to change the southern bar's belief that racial policy was not a federal but a state decision and segregation of schools was within the states' purview. Nor did the Attorney General's reproof sway the leaders of the American Bar Association, who were also singled out for criticism by him. Up until this period, the ABA had remained aloof from the civil rights struggle in the South, skirting any debate within the organization about the profession's obligations to the judicial process. Nor did it offer any guidance to state or local bar organizations concerning the profession's responsibilities to the law and judiciary. Kennedy was angry at the organization for withholding what could have been formidable aid in the South.

The American Bar Association was the foremost national spokesman for the legal profession in the United States. The ABA was larger—more than 120,000 members—and better organized than any other professional association, and its membership represented the cream of the mainstream profession. Through its official organ, the *ABA Journal*, published monthly, it had the ability to reach the country's legal world and to influence associated organizations at the local and state levels. Its objectives, which are printed on the first page of each issue, are "to uphold and defend the Constitution of the United States and maintain representative government; to advance the science of jurisprudence; to promote the administration of justice and the uniformity of legislation and of judicial decisions throughout the nation; to uphold the honor of the profession of law; to apply its knowl-

---

23. Robert F. Kennedy, *On the Duty of Lawyers, reprinted in* RFK: COLLECTED SPEECHES 89 (Edwin O. Guthman & C. Richard Allen eds., Viking 1993).

24. Interviews with Louis Oberdorfer, John Nolan, John Douglas, and Joseph Dolan, all of whom worked with Attorney General Robert Kennedy at the Department of Justice during this period. Individually, each remarked on Kennedy's frequent disbelief at the absence of the bar in the civil rights conflict in the South. Each commented on his frequent use of the expression, "Where are all the lawyers?"

edge and experience in the field of the law to the promotion of the public good; to encourage cordial intercourse among members of the American Bar; and to correlate and promote such activities of the bar organizations in the nation and in the respective states as are within these objects, in the interest of the legal profession and of the public."[25]

Each month the *Journal* publishes about 100 pages of information relevant to the profession: current judicial opinions; professional literature; social activities; bar association reports; profiles on prominent state associations, young lawyers, and prominent attorneys, as well as a half dozen usually brief articles on legal issues of national concern in areas such as labor, tax, corporate, or international law. Articles are submitted for publication by individual lawyers around the country. Since the segregation cases in the South should have been of intense interest to the profession, it must be concluded that the *Journal*'s lack of attention to the issue was an editorial decision.[26] For instance, after a flurry of criticism over the executive decision in 1957 to intervene in Little Rock, Arkansas, what comment was forthcoming from an organization that saw as its duty to support the Court's authority was ambiguous at best. Instead of supporting the federal courts, the ABA adopted an equivocal position. This was a disservice to the constitutional system.

It was not until 1962 that the publication chose to include an article that addressed the issue of the responsibility of the lawyer to the changing law. In its January issue it published an exceptionally long piece for the *Journal*, *The Lawyer and His Client*, by Eugene Rostow, the dean of Yale Law School. It was a reprint of the Alexander F. Morrison Lecture for 1961, delivered by Dean Rostow the previous September in Monterey, California. Due to its length it was published in two parts, the second appearing the following month. Rostow's main point was that the profession had become too specialized and had as a result lost a good portion of its independence. He addressed the blatant failure of the southern bar and the theory of interposition. He wrote, "The lawyer is an integral part of our legal system . . . . It is easy to fall into error about the rules of a given legal system by viewing it too abstractly, and without reference to the social context." He argued that lawyers should rethink their responsibility to society and the law. That "protecting the rights of persons involved in controversies which stir great passions" presents, for the profession, the simplest and most searching test of

25. A.B.A. J. 46 (January 1960) at 5.
26. The author's review of the A.B.A. J. from 1959 to 1963 found not one article on the legal aspects of the southern black struggle. Few and cursory articles on judicial review, federal jurisdiction, and the origins of the Fourteenth Amendment appeared.

our legal system. "In the transformations occurring in American society, we can expect conflicts over civil rights. . . ," he believed, "unless the mediating influence of the law is made more effective by the wise and vigorous action of the courts, the legislatures and the Bar."[27]

Nothing else appeared in the *Journal* concerning the role of the lawyer until the following October, when the outgoing president of the ABA, John C. Satterfield of Mississippi, used the topic for the traditional farewell address to the association. The publication of *Law and Lawyers in a Changing World: The President's Annual Address*,[28] coincided with the struggle over the desegregation of the University of Mississippi and Kennedy's censure. Satterfield begins his address by noting that the official title could as well be "The Destruction of the United States of America" because of a "process now quietly but rapidly going forward through which the indestructible Union composed of indestructible States . . . is now being transformed into a strong centralized government in which the states may soon become little more than local governmental agencies largely subject to the control of the central government and the central government may be permitted by the courts to exercise broad and sweeping control over the individual actions of citizens in almost every phase of their existence."[29] In a carefully crafted analysis, Satterfield criticized the Supreme Court for "inroads into the area of action assigned to the states under the provisions of the Constitution as originally adopted and subsequently amended. This has been accomplished through a construction of the Fourteenth Amendment, which seeks to embrace, as limitations upon state action, many of the guarantees which the first eight amendments gave to the people exclusively against their newly created national government."[30] Satterfield's counsel to the profession was that lawyers have a responsibility to use constructive criticism to alert the people to the dangers that creeping centralism pose for the American system. Not one other article was printed in 1962 or 1963 about the southern struggle between federal and state authority.

George Wallace

Lawyers knew from the public press that it was only a matter of time before the last remaining bastion of segregated higher education in the South, the

---

27. Eugene Rostow, *The Lawyer and His Client*, part 1, 48 A.B.A. J. 25 (1962); Part 2, 48 A.B.A. J. 146 (1962).

28. John C. Satterfield, *Law and Lawyers in a Changing World: The President's Annual Address,* 48 A.B.A. J. 922 (1962).

29. *Id.*

30. *Id.* at 926.

University of Alabama, would be ordered to integrate. Thus, the ongoing race for governor of Alabama was catapulted into the national spotlight. George Corley Wallace, a democrat "whose segregationist ideas would make Orval Faubus (the governor of Arkansas) seem like an admirer of the NAACP,"[31] was the front-runner. Wallace proudly defended white supremacy and states' rights. His racist rhetoric quickly made him the national spokesman for southern resistance to federal authority. Wallace recast the essentially political issue into legal terms.

He based his legal position on the states' right doctrine of interposition, a theory about the origins of federal-state power in the Constitution. Interposition was first popularized by John C. Calhoun in 1832[32] and was thought to be discredited by the outcome of the Civil War. The doctrine rests on three beliefs: first, that the U.S Constitution is a compact entered into by and between the several states acting in their sovereign capacity;[33] second, that the central government authorized by the Constitution was simply an agent of the states for the execution of certain delegated powers, but that the states retained the power to judge the scope of that delegation; and third, that in the event of an attempt to infringe on the reserved powers or to abuse the delegated powers, the states possess the right of interposition, that is, refusal to obey the wrongful command of the central government.[34] The doctrine of interposition necessarily rejects the legal principle of judicial supremacy. As a lawyer and a former state judge, Wallace understood the tenuous nature of his challenge to the federal system. When criticized by the press for his extreme position, Wallace retorted, "How can you be too strong on what you believe in? There isn't any middle of the road."

Wallace was taught, as all law students are taught, that the question of

31. *What You Believe In,* TIME, June 8, 1962, at 25. Orval Faubus was governor of the state of Arkansas when President Dwight D. Eisenhower sent troops to Little Rock to support the desegregation of public education in the city in 1957. Little Rock became a rallying point for extreme segregationists.

32. John C. Calhoun, 6 Works 144 (Cralle ed. 1863). The most complete exposition of the theory of interposition is found in a letter from John C. Calhoun to James Hamilton, governor of South Carolina, dated Aug. 28, 1832.

33. Interpositionists argue that the compact of states theory is supported by the language of art. VII of the Constitution: "The Ratification of the Conventions of nine States shall be sufficient for the Establishment of this Constitution between the States so ratifying the same." Therefore, authority comes from the states. However, ratification was by conventions representing the people. On the other side of the debate is the language of the Preamble to the Constitution, which states that the people established the Constitution.

34. McKay, *supra* note 6, at 1018.

judicial review of state legislation was settled early in the history of the American republic.[35] Most Americans of the time believed that any lingering questions of state interposition or nullification were put to rest by the North's victory in the Civil War. Lawyers accepted that "it was a firmly established constitutional doctrine that the United States Supreme Court may pass on the federal constitutionality of state legislation, and of course it follows that other forms of 'state action' are also subject to review—federal judicial review of state action is an essential part of federalism, as revealed in the records of the Constitutional Convention."[36] According to the constitutional law professor Paul Freund, "The role of the courts in maintaining a working federalism is precisely this task of mediation between large principles and particular problems, the task of interposing intermediate principles more tentative, experimental, and pragmatic. The courts are the substations which transform the high-tension charge of the philosophers into the reduced voltage of a serviceable current."[37] Wallace's claim of interposition, if successful, would send a lightning bolt right to the heart of the generator.

George Wallace campaigned on a platform of resistance to, and defiance of, federal authority. He ran against the federal judiciary and won large audiences with his inflammatory denunciations of the Kennedys and the federal government. Over and over he lambasted the federal courts as "lousy and irresponsible." Alabama Federal District Judge Frank M. Johnson was singled out by Wallace as a scapegoat for white animosity. In campaign speeches, Wallace branded Johnson as an "integrating, scalawaging, carpetbagging liar" for turning over voting records to the Civil Rights Commission.[38] Assistant U.S. Attorney General for Civil Rights Burke Marshall publicly defended Judge Johnson. Marshall, in his criticism of Wallace and his campaign, noted the lack of support for the justice system by the bar. Marshall indicated that he believed that this failure was even more worrisome than the campaign rhetoric. He said "that not one voice from the Bar of the State of Alabama— or for that matter from the bar anywhere—was raised to protest an attack on a federal judge which was based upon nothing but his acceptance of his responsibility to give effect to federal law."[39]

As in Mississippi, the Alabama Bar refused to support the efforts of the Justice Department to move civil rights grievances into the courts. The Attor-

---

35. Fletcher v. Peck, 10 U.S. (6 Cranch) 87 (1810).
36. McKay, *supra* note 6, at 997.
37. Paul A. Freund, *Umpiring the Federal System*, 54 Colum. L. Rev. 561 (1954).
38. *Id.*
39. Brauer, *supra* note 19 at 142.

ney General's disdain for the failure of the institution to uphold its professed values and the nation's legal traditions continued to be palpable. He believed that demagogues, like Wallace, are able to advance their interests in large part because of the failure of responsible people and organizations to stand up to them. That certainly was the case in Alabama in the winter and spring of 1963.

In the heated atmosphere that surrounded the implementation of the Court's desegregation order, it was hard for southern lawyers to separate themselves from the attitudes of their culture and to view the implications of Wallace's refusal to abide by the decision of the federal courts dispassionately. Judged through the official publication of the bar of Alabama, *The Alabama Lawyer*, the legal establishment in that state was in sympathy with Wallace's defiant legal views. In a survey of *The Alabama Lawyer* from 1955 to 1963 there was not one article in defense of the constitutional system of justice.[40] On the other hand, the controversy surrounding the ratification of the Fourteenth Amendment, the growth of federal power, and the constitutional theory of states' rights received regular attention.[41] Alabama state Judge Walter B. Jones actually wrote a new "Confederate Creed" that was printed in *The Alabama Journal*. "It is my duty to respect the laws and ancient ways of my people," according to Judge Jones, "and to stand up for the right of my State to determine what is good for its people in all local affairs."[42] In 1963 Professor Marvin E. Frankel of Columbia Law School examined 10 years of back issues of *The Alabama Lawyer* only to discover an absolute "monolithic" stand against the Supreme Court's civil rights decisions. A leading Birmingham newspaper published the law review article and asked lawyers

---

40. THE ALABAMA LAWYER is available in the Library of Congress, the law reading room in the James Madison Building. The author surveyed the journal from 1955 to 1963, in addition to THE VIRGINIA BAR NEWS and THE TEXAS BAR JOURNAL. The bar journal from the state of Mississippi was missing.

41. John C. Satterfield, *The Growth of Federal Power*; Joseph L. Call, *The Fourteenth Amendment and Its Skeptical Background*; Charles J. Bloch, *Rock of Ages*; Charles H. Roe, *What Happened to the Constitution?*; Walter J. Suthon, Jr., *Unconstitutional Creation of the 14th Amendment*; Frank W. Hawthorne, *Public Confidence and the Courts*; Alfred Avins & Sam S. Crutchfield, Jr., *Prima Facie Tort and Injunction: New Remedies Against Sitdowns*; *A Georgia Federal Judge Respects State Rights*; Charles J. Bloch, *The Law of the Land*; Thomas B. Hill, Jr., *The South and Some of Her Problems*; Charles J. Bloch, *A Second Tragic Era—The Role of the Lawyer In It*; Charles C. Tansill, *How Long Will Legislatures Continue to Acquiesce in the Alleged Decision of the Supreme Court on May 17, 1954?*, ALA. LAW., vols. 24-26.

42. Walter B. Jones, *The Confederate Creed*, ALA. LAW., vols. 24-26.

to comment on Frankel's findings. "Its offer was met by total silence. Not a single lawyer was willing to go on record as approving the law laid down by a unanimous Supreme Court."[43]

George Wallace's ambitions didn't rest with the governorship of Alabama. The acquiescence of the legal profession gave him succor. The Alabama Bar's sympathy with his states' rights argument not only obstructed the implementation of the law but skewered the public debate over the legitimacy of the civil rights movement. As well, the attitude of the private bar damaged public confidence in the judicial process and helped to repress responsible criticism within the political and legal establishment. The profession's silence about what it knew to be an untenable theory about judicial review undermined the American system of justice and helped steamroll the discontent in Alabama, both black and white, into a serious threat to the soul of the nation. In November 1962, Wallace scored an impressive victory of 338,961 to 267,612 over his pro-segregationist opponent Ryan de Graffenried.[44]

When the new governor took his oath of office in Montgomery, Alabama, on January 14, 1963, he made it clear that he intended to follow through on his campaign promises to defy the federal government and to take the southern challenge to federal authority to the American people.[45]

> Today I have stood, where once Jefferson Davis stood, and took an oath to my people. It is very appropriate then that from this Cradle of the Confederacy, this very Heart of the Great Anglo-Saxon Southland, that today, we sound the drum for freedom as have generations of forebears before us done, time and again down through history. Let us rise to the call of freedom-loving blood that is in us and send our answer to the tyranny that clanks its chains upon the south. In the name of the greatest people that have ever trod this earth, I draw the line in the dust and toss the gauntlet before the feet

---

43. Leon Friedman, *The Federal Courts of the South: Judge Bryan Simpson and His Reluctant Brethren*, SOUTHERN JUSTICE 188 (Leon Friedman, ed., Pantheon 1966). Also Jack Oppenheim, *The Abdication of the Southern Bar* 133 .

44. TIME, June 8, 1962.

45. One notable exception to the silence of the bar was Richmond Flowers, who was elected attorney general of Alabama with George Wallace in 1962. Immediately before Wallace's inauguration address, Flowers issued a statement warning that "to defy the same federal arm that speaks for America to Castro, Khrushchev, and Mao Tse-Tung . . . is only a chance to fight and can bring nothing but disgrace to our state, military law upon our people, and political demagoguery to the leaders responsible." As quoted in BRAUER, *supra* note 39, at 253.

of tyranny . . . and I say . . . segregation now . . . segregation tomor-
row . . . segregation forever. . . . Let us send this message back to
Washington by our representatives who are with us today . . . that
from this day we are standing up, and the heel of tyranny does not
fit the neck of an upright man . . . that we intend to take the offensive and carry our fight for freedom across this nation, wielding
the balance of power we know we possess in the Southland . . .
that we, not the insipid bloc voters of some sections . . . will determine in the next election who shall sit in the White House of the
United States . . . that from this day . . . from this hour . . . from
this minute . . . we give the word of a race of honor that we will
tolerate their boot in our face no longer . . . and let those certain
judges put that in their opium pipes of power and smoke it for
what it is worth.[46]

The administration in Washington hoped to prevent another "Ole Miss"
tragedy or worse, and launched a two-pronged effort to defuse the defiance of
the new governor. First, the administration tried to reason with Wallace. The
newly elected Alabama Attorney General, Richmond Flowers, was asked to
talk to him about his real intentions. Flowers reported that Wallace said,
"Dammit, send the Justice Department word, I ain't compromising with anybody. I'm gonna make 'em bring troops into this state."

By April the integration of the university appeared to be on track.[47] The
university's president and board of trustees were ready to comply with the
court. Nonetheless, at a meeting of the trustees on April 8, 1963, Wallace
refused to relent and demanded that he be appointed acting university president for the purpose of confronting the federal authorities on June 11, 1963,
the day that the students were to be presented for registration. Alerted to
Wallace's plans, Robert Kennedy went to Montgomery on April 25 to talk
with him. After the meeting, Kennedy called on Grover C. Hall, Jr., editor of
the *Montgomery Advertiser* and a confidant of Wallace. Hall agreed that it
would be foolish of Wallace to stand in the doorway of the university but
believed that Wallace was committed to do so. Kennedy asked Hall whether
any pressure could be brought to bear on the governor that could change his
mind. Hall said he didn't think so. Three weeks later, on May 18, President

---

46. George C. Wallace, *Inauguration Address, reprinted in* BIRMINGHAM NEWS, Jan. 14,
    1963, at 4.
47. ARTHUR M. SCHLESINGER, JR., ROBERT KENNEDY AND HIS TIMES 337 (Houghton Mifflin
    1978): "On May 21 (1963) the federal district court ruled that the university must
    admit the black applicant to its summer session."

Kennedy went to Tennessee, where Wallace joined him. Flying by helicopter to Muscle Shoals in Huntsville, Alabama, the pair had a chance to size each other up. Once again Wallace declared his intention to honor his promise to resist. Three days later, the Justice Department began to organize a massive effort to exert economic pressure on Wallace. Winton M. Blount, president of a major construction company in Montgomery, president of the state chamber of commerce, and trustee of the University of Alabama, supplied a list of the state's 375 leading executives to the Justice Department.

Nearly 80 percent of the executives reached agreed to get in touch with Wallace personally or through subordinates. Wallace broke off communications with the Kennedy Administration.[48] Attorney General Robert Kennedy had requested, "the names of every company with more than one hundred employees . . . in the whole state of Alabama. All those names were distributed at a cabinet meeting. . . . A cabinet member . . . called . . . every one of them."[49] Involved in the effort was Assistant U.S. Attorney General Louis F. Oberdorfer, a prominent native of the state.[50] According to Burke Marshall, the appeal to the business leaders in the state had a tremendous consequence for the outcome of the crisis. Wallace "was getting fifteen to twenty calls every day from business people," and he would "have to guarantee them that there wouldn't be any repeat of the Oxford incident, that there wouldn't be any violence." The Attorney General believed that "Wallace really didn't know what he was going to do . . . up until at least a couple of days before and, maybe, a few hours before . . . . If he had received great popular support in the state . . . standing in the door, continuing to stand in the door, I think that's what he would have done. But he was trying to get off the hook."[51]

Birmingham, Alabama

While the Kennedy Administration was working to avert another "Ole Miss," Martin Luther King, Jr., and the Southern Christian Leadership Conference (SCLC) launched a campaign early in April to challenge the practices of institutionalized segregation in Alabama's largest city, Birmingham. On Good Friday, April 12, 1963, Martin Luther King refused to obey an injunction of the state court to refrain from demonstrating and was arrested. King was placed in solitary confinement in a Birmingham jail. Within hours of his jailing, young blacks went on a brief but violent rampage in the city and Eugene

48. Brauer, *supra* note 39, 253-57.
49. As quoted in Schlesinger, *supra* note 47, at 337.
50. Interview with Louis F. Oberdorfer, former assistant U.S. attorney general.
51. Schlesinger, *supra* note 47, at 342.

"Bull" Connor, the chief of police, filled the jails. On May 2, King, who had been released from jail on bond, decided that the time had come to allow children to take part in the demonstrations. National and international television and press coverage caught the dogs and firehoses that the Birmingham police turned on the demonstrators. Negotiating in secret with a group of white Birmingham leaders, King reached a settlement to end the demonstrations. Immediately, Bull Connor and other prominent segregationists attacked the accommodations that had been made and proposed that the white community boycott the businesses owned by the whites who were involved in the settlement. He allowed the Ku Klux Klan to hold a rally in a local park, after which the home of Martin Luther King's brother was bombed.

President Kennedy went on television and radio. He warned that the federal government would support the settlement in Birmingham, and as tangible evidence of the government's determination, he announced three steps that he had taken. He was sending Burke Marshall to Birmingham to consult with local citizens; he alerted units of the military trained in riot control and some were dispatched to Birmingham; and he had ordered the execution of the necessary preliminary steps for calling the Alabama National Guard into federal service.[52] The Birmingham campaign had a tremendous effect on American public opinion. It made the rest of the nation take notice of the changing tide in the South. As *Time* magazine wrote, the fever was everywhere, and every act seemed to fan the flames in another place. "Spring of 1963 will long be remembered as the time when the U.S. Negro's revolution for equality exploded on all fronts. . . . Negroes faced snarling police dogs. They went to jail by the thousands. They risked beatings as they sat on lunch counter stools. They were bombed in their homes. They were clubbed down by cops. They sent out their children to battle men. In the weeks, months, and even in the years to come, there will be lulls in the revolution. But it will revive, for, after the spring of 1963, there can be no turning back."[53]

Outside of the South, Wallace's legal arguments were captivating new audiences. Martin Luther King, Jr., believed that Wallace was "perhaps the most dangerous racist in America today. . . . 1 am not sure that he believes all the poison he preaches, but he is artful enough to convince others that he does."[54] Wallace's psychological appeal to northern whites was nothing new in the battle against desegregation. As the writer Helen Fuller, "a southerner by birth and education," wrote in an acclaimed series in 1959 on "Southerners and Schools" in *The New Republic*, "A second battle of Gettysburg is

---

52. *The Resounding Cry*, Time, May 24, 1963.

53. *The Nation: Races*, Time, June 7 1963, at 7.

54. Playboy, January 1965, interview with Martin Luther King, Jr.

about to begin, this one to be fought with the techniques of psychological warfare, aimed at the public outside the South, the Congress and conservative leaders in both major political parties. Object: to win sympathy for the segregationist view behind the enemy lines, support for curbing the powers of the Supreme Court by law, and agreement to nullify the New Reconstruction of 1954 as the Compromise of 1877 nullified Reconstruction before."[55] Wallace's logic had the effect of throwing up a political smoke screen around events in the South and further clouded the essential constitutional issues underpinning the civil rights struggle. By the spring of 1963, many in the North empathized with the need for blacks to abide by the law as well.

On May 21, 1963, the Federal Appeals Court in Birmingham issued a final order ruling that the University of Alabama must admit for the summer session the Negro students Vivian J. Malone of Mobile and James A. Hood of East Gadsden to the main campus at Tuscaloosa and, David M. McGlathery to Huntsville. The following day at a White House conference, President Kennedy said that he was obligated to carry out the court's order as part of the constitutional system. Now, there was no choice in the matter, the state had exhausted all legal appeals, and its officials must obey or resist illegally.

Kennedy's warning was heeded by state administration officials in Alabama, who were promptly removed by Wallace, who had himself appointed as the chief operating officer for the university. *TIME* magazine reported that Wallace forced through the legislature a vote of confidence in his stand at the schoolhouse door. "But before it passed, State Senator James E. Horton, Jr. cried to his colleagues, 'the presence of Governor Wallace will by implication attract a mob which by comparison will make Oxford, Miss., look like a Sunday School picnic.' And Senator George Hawkins warned, 'this resolution is a call to arms to every hoodlum in the state.'" Wallace's plan, as outlined to confidants, went like this: "(1) He will ring the Tuscaloosa campus with highway patrolmen; (2) escorted by a large force of patrolmen, he will go to the campus himself; (3) U.S. marshals will presumably bring Vivian Malone to the campus, and Wallace personally will bar the way; 4) if the marshals attempt to push past, Wallace may order his state cops to remove the Negro girl bodily from the premises. After that not even George Wallace knows what will happen, but the results are not apt to be pleasant."[56]

Department of Justice lawyers were trying to legally maneuver around Wallace's proposed plan. But the governor, who was protected during the last days of the crisis by helmeted state troopers, was able to avoid process of a

---

55. Helen Fuller, *Southerners and Schools-III: The Segregationists Go North,* THE NEW
      REPUBLIC 140:6 (Feb. 9, 1959).

56. TIME, May 22, 1963, at 19.

federal subpoena. In open defiance of the federal government, Wallace flew to New York on Saturday, June 1, 1963, for an appearance on NBC's Sunday television interview show "Meet the Press."[57] Wallace explained to the viewing audience that he would bar the students, "not as an individual but as the people of Alabama." He would "stand in the door as the Governor of the state embodying the sovereignty of the state. In my opinion we can raise some constitutional questions that can be adjudicated by the courts."[58]

The following Thursday, June 5, Judge Seybourn H. Lynne, the Chief Judge of the United States District Court for the Northern District of Alabama, issued an order enjoining Wallace from "preventing, blocking or interfering with, by physically interposing his person or that of any other person under his control" the students and to obey the court's judgment, which is final.[59] Lynne, a 56-year-old Alabamian, wrote:

> Thoughtful people, if they can free themselves from tensions produced by established principles with which they violently disagree, must concede that the Governor of a sovereign state has no authority to obstruct, or prevent the execution, of the lawful orders of a court of the United States . . . . No legalistic formula is required to express the craving of honest, hard-working, God-fearing citizens for a moral order logically supported, an attitude long ago expressed when Coke informed King James that there was a law above the King . . . . In the final analysis, the concept of law and order, the very essence of a republican form of government, embraces the notion that when the judicial process of a state or federal court, acting within the sphere of its competence, has been exhausted and has resulted in a final judgment, all persons affected thereby are obliged to obey it . . . . May it be forgiven if this court makes use of the personal pronoun for the first time in a written opinion . . . . I love the people of Alabama . . . . I know that many of both races are troubled and, like Jonah of old, are angry even unto death as the result of distortions of affairs within this state practiced in the name of sensationalism . . . . My prayer is that all of our people in keeping with our finest traditions will join

---

57. *Move to Subpoena Governor Wallace Fails*, N.Y. HERALD TRIB., June 1, 1963, at 1.

58. Charles Partis & Earl G. Talbert, *A Guarded Governor: Law Vow*, N.Y. HERALD TRIB., June 3, 1963, at 1: "he would stand in the door as the Governor of the state embodying the sovereignty of the state. . . ."

59. *Law for Alabama: GOP Rights Plan: The Judge*, N.Y. HERALD TRIB., June 6, 1963, at 1.

in the resolution that law and order will be maintained both in Tuscaloosa and in Huntsville.[60]

Lynne had reason to fear for his state. The Kennedy Administration expected the situation to become increasingly difficult and "fraught with more and possibly greater violence." In Washington, it was feared that the "Negroes will lose confidence in the government and in white men generally and will attempt to take the law in their own hands, which might bring violent counteraction from whites."[61] An editorial in support of Lynne's order in the ne *New York Herald Tribune* said, "There is no question about who must and will prevail. State defiance obviously won't be tolerated. This has no standing in law or otherwise,"[62] while in the rest of the country in the first week in June, by a Justice Department count, "more than 30 Negro mass demonstrations against racial discrimination occurred."[63]

The Bar Responds to Wallace

Wallace had his supporters in and out of the South. The widely read and admired nationally syndicated columnist and southerner by birth David H. Lawrence supported Wallace's position. He argued that Wallace had every right to test the law's "validity."[64] The day after Lynne's ruling, Lawrence wrote a column, "Wallace Attitude Called 'Challenge, Not Defiance'" in defense of Wallace's "constitutional right to challenge any decision of the Supreme Court in order to try to get a different ruling from that which has prevailed." Under our Constitution, explained Lawrence, "an individual can test any law or ruling and has a right to pursue the matter from the lower courts to the highest court, arguing new points not covered in previous cases. Wallace emphasized this on the 'Meet the Press' program on TV last Sunday. The layman may call all this 'legalism' but that's the way the judicial system operates in America. It is hard not only for laymen but for lawyers

---

60. *Id., The Words.*

61. Robert J. Donovan, *The Racial Crisis—The Official View,* N.Y. HERALD TRIB., June 6, 1963, at 1.

62. *Who Speaks for Alabama?,* N.Y. HERALD TRIB., June 6, 1963.

63. Joseph Alsop, *Why Legislate?,* N.Y. HERALD TRIB., June 6, 1963. "In Chicago, 1,700 Negroes gathered to protest a cemetery's refusal to cremate the body of a Negro woman. In Los Angeles, 30,000 filled the city stadium to mark their sympathy with the Negroes of Birmingham. In North Carolina, alone, there were six major or minor demonstrations."

64. Frank A. Sieverman, letter to the editor, BIRMINGHAM NEWS, June 8, 1963.

to be sure what the decisions of the high court mean or how long they will remain in effect."[65]

The Lawrence article would have gone unchallenged if it hadn't so irritated one man, Bernard G. Segal, a corporate lawyer in Philadelphia, Pennsylvania. Segal remembers:

> I recall . . . a day which was destined to become a highly significant one in my life . . . Friday, June 7, 1963. At breakfast, I read aloud to my wife a newspaper column by David H. Lawrence attacking the Kennedys . . . for their threat to call out the National Guard if Governor Wallace should persist in his announced intention to defy the injunction. . . . I remember the biting response of my wife . . . "What is the bar of the nation doing about this? What should *you* be doing?"[66]

The question of the bar's role bothered him all day, and when he heard "several highly intelligent laymen express puzzlement over whether the governor was entitled to flout the express terms of a court decree under these circumstances on the grounds of a 'test,'" he resolved to organize a group of lawyers to refute unequivocally Wallace's erroneous legal arguments.[67]

Segal, as a former chairman of the American Bar Association's Standing Committee on the Federal Judiciary, a position that he held for five years, 1957 to 1962, was no stranger to the legal issues involved nor to the internal politics of the ABA and the Kennedy Administration.[68] As chair-

---

65. David Lawrence, *Wallace Attitude Called Challenge, Not Defiance*, N.Y. HERALD TRIB., June 6, 1963.

66. Remarks of Bernard G. Segal, 15th Anniversary dinner, Washington, D.C., June 21, 1978. The author is unable to locate the article that Mr. Segal referred to in the June 7, 1963 editions of *The Philadelphia Inquirer, The Washington Post* or *The New York Times*. Mr. Segal allowed access to his personal scrapbooks and a cross-reference to the Lawrence article appears there in the form of a letter to the editor in the *Birmingham News*.

67. *Id.*

68. VICTOR NAVASKY, KENNEDY JUSTICE 253 (Athenaeum 1971). Navasky believes that the ABA has become the "real bureaucrats of judicial selection." Judicial selection is a balance between the President and the Senate that is complicated by the role of the ABA: "the ABA, self-appointed overseer of judge picking. . . . The other participants—the President's men and the senators—act partly in response to or anticipation of the ABA's ratings."

man of the committee,[69] Segal had become an important presence at the Kennedy Justice Department after Congress passed a bill creating 71 new judgeships in May 1961.[70] By mid-October 1962, less than 16 months from assuming the office of the presidency, Kennedy nominated 128 people to the federal bench. For awhile the Justice Department was sending names to Capitol Hill at a rate of nearly 10 a month.[71] Segal's ties to the Attorney General and Deputy Attorney General Byron White, with whom he worked closely, were purely professional. He never became one of Bob Kennedy's close advisors.[72] Not only did he represent an organization, the ABA, that was in Robert Kennedy's disfavor, but he had a personality that was in dramatic contrast to the more circumspect and self-effacing men that the Attorney General worked so well with at Justice. However, during this time, Segal became an important consultant to the Kennedy Justice Department.[73] He had numerous connections both in and out of the legal profession and a pleasant personal

---

69. The American Bar Association became significantly involved in the nominating process only in the twentieth century when it set as one of its goals the upgrading and professionalization of the bar. The tendency of the ABA was to establish criteria that favored the Ivy League Anglo-Saxon establishment. President Harry S. Truman, a circuit judge in Missouri who won his appointment to the bench through political patronage, rejected the ABA's interference in Democratic politics and marginalized the ABA's influence at the Department of Justice. Under President Dwight D. Eisenhower, Ross Malone, chairman of the ABA Standing Committee on the Federal Judiciary, who preceded Bernard Segal, reestablished the ABA's influence within Justice. Eisenhower was the honored speaker at the 1960 ABA convention.

70. NAVASKY, *supra* note 68, at 254. Deputy Attorney General Byron White was in charge of the judicial nomination process. He delegated the vetting to Joseph Dolan, assistant deputy attorney general. Early in the administration Byron White suffered a duodenal ulcer. Because Dolan was the initial nominee-screener, "it meant that Dolan . . . was the working judge picker." In an interview with Mr. Dolan on March 8, 1995, he said, "The work at the Department was very compartmentalized. There was not a lot of unnecessary discussion. You did your work and explained when asked." If the Attorney General had a question, he would talk about it with his top staff at the regular Tuesday and Thursday luncheons in his office.

71. HAROLD W. CHASE, FEDERAL JUDGES: THE APPOINTING PROCESS 49 (1972).

72. Interviews with Joe Dolan, Louis Oberdorfer, Jerry Shestack.

73. Interview with Joseph Dolan, deputy to the deputy attorney general, March 8, 1995. The function of vetting the judicial nominees came at a time when the Justice Department personnel, particularly RFK's closest advisors, were under enormous strain because of the dual crises of Cuba and civil rights. Deputy Attorney General Byron White delegated the vetting to Dolan, White's deputy. Dolan found the "FBI background checks worthless. The FBI polluted the atmosphere, not on purpose. But once

style, coupled with fierce competitive instincts. Once Bernie Segal was on an issue, he would not let go until he had achieved results.[74] Segal, a Republican and partner in the prominent Philadelphia law firm of Schrader Harrison Segal & Lewis, was a former chairman of the American Judicature Society, a former chancellor of the Philadelphia Bar Association, and the treasurer and counsel to the professionally prestigious American Law Institute. He was ambitious,[75] and judging by his tireless dedication to the ABA, he hoped to add the title of president of the American Bar Association to his impressive resumé,[76] a position that had never been granted to someone of the Jewish faith. He had a good working relationship with the Attorney General, but "he wasn't Bob's type," according to Joseph Dolan who worked with Bob Kennedy for eight years "He was a non-stop talker."

In 1962, Deputy Attorney General Byron White left the Department of Justice for a seat on the Supreme Court. From that time on, Segal worked primarily with Deputy Attorney General Nicholas Katzenbach and Deputy Assistant Attorney General Joseph Dolan. According to Nicholas Katzenbach, "the American Bar Association's Standing Committee on the Federal Judiciary spoke for the legal establishment," but the Justice Department "regarded the ABA imprimatur as desirable but not essential."[77] It was Dolan who did

---

the FBI got on it, they (the person being interviewed) felt that they (the future judge) would surely get it." Dolan said that people were afraid that what was said in confidence would find its way back to a judge they were bound to meet in court. As a result, Dolan said that Justice learned to rely on the ABA's judicial selection committee for sensitive information, in particular Bernie Segal. Dolan said, "We could work with them. . . ."

74. *Id.*
75. Anthony Day, *Clark Puts Final Veto on Judgeship for Segal*, PHILADELPHIA EVENING BULLETIN (Jan. 24, 1963): "Bernard Segal's nomination for the U.S. Court of Appeals on the Third Circuit was blocked by Democratic Senator Joseph S. Clark, of Pennsylvania." Ten years earlier, Segal and Clark, when he was mayor of Philadelphia, had a falling out over the subject of the election of judges.
76. *Supra* note 73.
77. SCHLESINGER, *supra* note 47, at 373. According to Navasky, *supra* note 68, at 261, the ABA's "committees, membership, and leadership were dominated by Republicans and the elite Ivy Leaguers, and the tough-minded Democratic and liberal lawyers whom Kennedy attracted to the Justice Department were hostile to the ABA." Also, according to Joseph Dolan, who was deputy assistant attorney general at the time, "It was Segal who contacted Byron White and offered his help." "Segal was sensitive to the reservations about the ABA and he suggested a system whereby he would render 'informal' ratings. He believes that it was Mr. Segal who suggested a system of qualified, very qualified, and not qualified ratings. After the Kennedy assassination, Mr.

the preliminary screening of all judicial possibilities. Joe Dolan remembers that time as hectic and very fast paced.[78] Segal remembers, "There was not a day that I was not on the phone to Dolan or Katzenbach or White, or in rarer cases, to Bob. My time sheets show I put in forty to forty-five hours a week on it."[79] The people at Justice thought Bernie Segal's information was beneficial— "he could find out things that the FBI couldn't." "One of Segal's most useful roles," according to Dolan, "was his ability to filter uncensored information back that was extremely helpful." Lawyers who might have to appear before a future judge were reluctant to go on record with any negative information about the nominee for fear of its leaking back. As a result, Segal, even after stepping down from his ABA chairmanship, was a back channel for Katzenbach, Dolan, and the Attorney General, and it was not unusual for him to phone them both at the Justice Department and at home."[80]

When Bernie Segal got to work on Friday, June 7, 1963, he phoned *The Birmingham News* and *The Birmingham Post-Herald,* the two leading newspapers in Birmingham, Alabama, to reserve front page space—not advertising space but space for a news story—for a statement by leaders of the bar about Wallace. Segal knew if he could gather a representative group of lawyers, including some from the South, to speak out about Wallace it would be news. He then enlisted the help of his young law partner, Jerome J. Shestack, in a round-the-clock phonathon, persuading bar leaders in all parts of the country to stand with them in refuting Wallace's contention that he could legally test the court

---

Dolan searched his records for any informal discussions that he had in his personal files and destroyed all but what he felt was of historic importance. To his knowledge, no records remain from informal dealings at the Justice Department.

78. *Id.* In contrast to the vetting of court nominees by the Clinton Department of Justice, the author interviewed Peter Erichsen, assistant deputy attorney general for the Office of Policy Development, on March 10, 1995. He reported that the responsibility for judicial selection is split between the White House Counsel's Office and the Office of Policy Development at Justice. Overall, the White House is in charge and primarily involved with the Court of Appeals nominees. At Justice, a working group of approximately 15 lawyers, some working on the judiciary part-time, process the federal district court nominees. In the first 12 months, 28 nominees were appointed, and the Clinton Administration nominated 129 in all. Today the Justice Department has the complete cooperation of the FBI, unlike the situation in the early 1960s when the FBI was run by J. Edgar Hoover.

79. NAVASKY, *supra* note 68, at 261. Segal told Assistant Deputy Attorney General Dolan that he put in as much time on judicial selection as on his own law practice. Dolan also believes that Segal wanted to be president of the ABA.

80. *Supra note* 73.

order to desegregate the university.[81] The success of the Segal effort rested in large part on the reaction of the leadership of the ABA; without their cooperation it would be questionable whether other bar leaders would want to take the lead against Wallace. Sidestepping the civil rights question entirely, Segal began with calls to the officers of the ABA "to ascertain from them whether they would consider it inappropriate" for him to try to get other lawyers to sign a statement that would clarify the law.[82] Segal's first call was to the chairman of the ABA House of Delegates in Little Rock, Arkansas. Edward Wright agreed "enthusiastically," giving Segal's effort an important imprimatur. Segal focused on the bar and its responsibility to the justice system, which gave the leadership the opportunity to comment on Wallace's legal views outside of the race issue. They could speak out without aligning themselves with the civil rights movement or the Kennedy Justice Department. Obviously, from the response, there were many who were willing to go on record.

Over the weekend, Segal contacted Assistant Attorney General Louis F. Oberdorfer for advice.[83] It is not clear how Oberdorfer, a native of Birmingham, Alabama, and Segal were put in touch with one another. Oberdorfer, a part of the Attorney General's inner circle, was deeply involved in negotiations with the University of Alabama, as well as the Justice Department's effort to get

---

81. On June 17, 1963, Mr. Segal wrote a confidential letter to the members of the Standing Committee on the Federal Judiciary of the American Bar Association (Robert Meserve, Cloyd Laporte, Arthur Littleton, Robert T. Barton, Leon Jaworski, Harry G. Gault, Barnabas F. Sears, Roy E. Willy, Eugene D. Bennett, Gerald B. Klein, and Robert Ash) to explain how he chose the group to sign the lawyers' letter to Wallace. "I first called the officers of the American Bar Association to ascertain from them whether they would consider it inappropriate for me to try to secure agreement of a group of lawyers on a statement, and if not, whether they would sign it. The first person I reached was Edward Wright, chairman of the House of Delegates, who lives and practices in the former embattled city of Little Rock, Arkansas. When Ed and the others enthusiastically endorsed the idea, I proceeded to call practicing lawyers and deans of law schools throughout the country, endeavoring first to include the top officers of our leading professional organization, and second, to get geographical distribution, including, of course, the deep South. Since the calls had to be made over a weekend in mid-June, with many people away at their summer places and other vacation spots, I felt very fortunate in having been able to assemble a reasonably representative group of 46. 1 also want you to know why I did not call any member of the Standing Committee on the Federal Judiciary . . . I felt, as I always have, that the members . . . should insofar as possible remain aloof from controversial matters, and all the more when they affect an action by a Federal Judge."
82. Confidential Letter (unsigned) to the ABA Standing Committee on the Federal Judiciary, June 1963.
83. In author interviews with Jerome Shestack, Louis Oberdorfer, and Joseph Dolan, it is unclear exactly when and how Segal connected to the Justice Department.

leading hotels and businesses to voluntarily desegregate. Oberdorfer was the only southerner among the Attorney General's closest advisors. His distinct understanding of the issues in Alabama, his personal contacts, and his appreciation of southern society were important assets. "You could say I spoke the language," as Oberdorfer put it.[84]

During the spring of 1963, the Attorney General convinced the President to invite small groups of southern community leaders to the White House to persuade them to voluntarily open their facilities to blacks. "The President was engaged in what amounted to a tactic of envelopment," according to one political observer, Chalmers M. Roberts. "He met with businessmen, with mayors, with leaders in Congress. He planned more meetings with labor leaders and with clergymen, all designed to enlist the widest possible support before he went to Congress."[85] Oberdorfer knew of Segal but had never worked with him. Over the weekend they consulted by telephone about the statement.[86]

At 3 A.M. on Sunday, June 9, almost two days after Bernie Segal and Jerry Shestack began their effort to enlist lawyers to sign a statement challenging Wallace, they placed their last call.[87] Forty-six prominent members of the American legal establishment agreed to sign a statement that would explain why Wallace could not legally challenge the desegregation order.

On Monday, June 10, 1963, the Segal statement was picked up by papers throughout the country, including *The New York Times*, as well as the front pages of the leading Birmingham newspapers. To Wallace's argument that he had a right to test a valid court order, they replied:

> He would justify this interference as a proper way of 'testing' constitutional issues. But these issues have already been decided—

---

84. Interview with former Assistant Attorney General Louis F. Oberdorfer, Jan. 22, 1994. Oberdorfer recalls that Robert Kennedy would use his assistants in unorthodox areas. Oberdorfer was chosen to work on civil rights because he understood the South in a way that non-southerners could not. At the end of May 1963, Robert Kennedy convinced JFK to hold meetings "two or three a week, sixty or seventy people at a time, both white and Negro leaders to begin to build local support for civil rights legislation and for hiring Negroes." Plans for the voluntary desegregation meetings were under way at the White House and Justice when the Tuscaloosa incident changed the course of history.

85. Chalmers M. Roberts, *Kennedy Speaks Out*, WASH. POST, June 12, 1963, op-ed page.

86. *Supra* note 84.

87. Segal Remarks, 15th Anniversary of the LCCR. Segal and Shestack were rejected on a number of occasions, "I still feel the pain when lawyers who we had been confident would join us, abruptly said no, sometimes sharply."

again and again—by the tribunal having final authority under our constitutional system. Under these circumstances, it is not permissible to "test" these issues by defying an order issued by a court of competent jurisdiction . . . . If the issues that trouble the nation are to be peacefully resolved, all parties must respect the law. In a government of laws, the governor is not free to flout the court's decree so long as it remains in force, particularly when the issues have been so recently and so frequently resolved by the highest court in the land. Lawyers have a special responsibility to support the rule of law in our society and to obey the fundamental legal principles that guarantee safety and justice for all. To this end, as lawyers, we ask Governor Wallace to refrain from defiance of a solemn court order. If he is present when the students present themselves for registration, we call upon him to stand aside and to forebear from any act or gesture of interference with the carrying out of the court's order.[88]

---

88. James Free, *Stand Aside, U.S. Lawyers Plead*, THE BIRMINGHAM NEWS, June 10, 1963, at 1. Plea was signed by Walter P. Armstrong, Jr., Memphis, Tennessee (chairman, National Conference of Commissioners on Uniform State Laws; president, Board of Education, City of Memphis); Francis Biddle, Washington, D.C. (former attorney general of the United States); Henry P. Brandis, Jr., Chapel Hill, North Carolina (dean, University of North Carolina Law School); Bruce Bromley, New York (former judge, Court of Appeals of New York); Cecil E. Burney, Corpus Christi, Texas (past chairman, National Conference of Bar Presidents; past president, State Bar of Texas); Brant B. Cooper, Los Angeles, California (president, American College of Trial Lawyers); Walter E. Craig, Phoenix, Arizona (president-elect, American Bar Association); Lloyd N. Cutler, Washington, D.C. (president, Yale Law School Association); Norris Darrell, New York (president, American Law Institute); Arthur H. Dean, New York (chairman, U.S. Delegation to Geneva Conference on Nuclear Testing & Disarmament); Robert F. Drinan, S.J., Boston, Massachusetts (dean, Boston College Law School); Harry L. Dunn, Los Angeles, California (officer, Harvard Law School Association; trustee, Claremont College); Robert J. Farley, Oxford, Mississippi (dean, University of Mississippi Law School); Jefferson B. Fordham, Philadelphia, Pennsylvania (dean, University of Pennsylvania Law School); Cody Fowler, Tampa, Florida (past president of the American Bar Association); E. Smythe Gambrell, Atlanta, Georgia (past president, American Bar Association); William P. Gray, Los Angeles, California (president, California Bar Association); Edwin N. Griswold, Cambridge, Massachusetts (dean, Harvard Law School); Louis Hector, Miami, Florida (former member of the Civil Aeronautics Board; trustee, University of Miami Law School); John O. Hannold, Philadelphia, Pennsylvania (professor of Constitutional Law, University of Pennsylvania Law School); Herbert Johnson, Atlanta, Georgia (ex-president, Lawyers Club of Atlanta; delegate

The lawyers' statement was signed by the president, the president-elect, the chairman of the Board of Governors, and six past presidents of the ABA; three former attorneys general of the United States; the president of the American Law Institute; the president, the president-elect, past president, and four regents of the American College of Trial Lawyers; the president of the National Conference of Commissioners on Uniform State Laws; and the deans of 10 law schools. Included also were ranking officers, past and present, of state and local bar associations throughout the country. And even though the lawyers signed the statement in their personal capacities, not as official representatives of their

---

from Atlanta Bar Association to the American Bar Association); Paul Johnston, Birmingham, Alabama (Birmingham, Alabama, State, and American Bar Associations; member American Law Institute); C. Baxter Jones, Macon, Georgia (general counsel, Board of Education of Bibb County, Georgia; former delegate, Georgia Bar Association to American Bar Association); Harry B. Kelleher, New Orleans, Louisiana (former secretary-treasurer, Louisiana State Bar Association); Earle W. Kintner, Washington, D.C. (president, National Lawyers Club; past president, Federal Bar Association); David F. Maxwell, Philadelphia, Pennsylvania (past president, American Bar Association); Walton J. McLeod, Walterboro, South Carolina (state delegate from South Carolina to American Bar Association); John Lord O'Brian, Washington, D.C. (former regent of University of State of New York; former overseer of Harvard University); Joseph O'Meara, South Bend, Indiana (dean, University of Notre Dame Law School); John N. Randall, Cedar Rapids, Iowa (past president, American Bar Association); Charles S. Rhyne, Washington, D.C. (past president, American Bar Association); Frederick D.G. Ribble, Charlottesville, Virginia (dean, University of Virginia Law School); William P. Rogers, New York (former Attorney General of the United States); Eugene V. Rostow, New Haven, Connecticut (dean, Yale Law School); Bernard G. Segal, Philadelphia, Pennsylvania (former board chairman, American Judicature Society; treasurer and counsel, American Law Institute); Whitney North Seymour, New York (past president, American Bar Association); James L. Shepherd, Jr., Houston, Texas; (past president, State Bar of Texas; former chairman, House of Delegates of the American Bar Association); Jerome J. Shestack, Philadelphia, Pennsylvania; Sylvester C. Smith, Newark, New Jersey (president, American Bar Association); William B. Spann, Jr., Atlanta, Georgia (Board of Governors, State Delegate from Georgia, American Bar Association); Charles P. Taft, Cincinnati, Ohio (past president, Federal Council of the Churches of Christ in America; former mayor of Cincinnati); John W. Wade, Nashville, Tennessee (dean, Vanderbilt Law School); William C. Warren, New York (dean, Columbia Law School); Francis E. Winslow, Rocky Mount, North Carolina (past president, North Carolina Bar Association); Edward L. Wright, Little Rock, Arkansas (chairman, House of Delegates, American Bar Association; regent, American College of Trial Lawyers), Wilson Wyatt, Louisville, Kentucky (former mayor, Louisville). **Note**: The signers' titles have been supplied by the author for this paper; they were not connected to the statement.

institutions,[89] they did lend legal authority to the position of the federal government, weakening Wallace and the passive attitude of southern lawyers. The publication of the lawyers' statement provided some long-delayed professional support to the beleaguered judiciary as well as giving needed encouragement to civil rights activists who had to rely on the courts for vindication. However modest a gesture, the statement marks the first organized effort by the conventional private bar to assume a public role in the civil rights struggle. Commenting on Tuscaloosa years later, Attorney General Robert Kennedy reflected that Wallace lost essentially "because of the appeal to respectable opinion in the state."[90] In this regard, the bar could point with pride to the lawyers' statement of June 10, 1963.

The Desegregation of the University of Alabama at Tuscaloosa

The next day, June 11, proved to be a turning point in American history. Wallace's planned resistance proved to be a charade. The Kennedy Administration, determined not to find itself in another "Oxford debacle" in Alabama, put over 5,000 troops on full alert for quick deployment,

> Shortly before 11 a.m., Katzenbach arrived and began the long walk under the broiling Alabama sun to the registration building. Inside the building a highly nervous Wallace repeatedly asked a state detective, "Ben, do you think they'll actually arrest me?" He sent word to Katzenbach through the National Guard commander that there would be no problem; he just wanted a chance to say something. Now, standing incongruously behind a lectern, a microphone draped around his neck, he awaited Katzenbach. White semicircles painted in the doorway indicated where Wallace should stand in order to look his best on television; this irritated Katzenbach, who felt the situation was sufficiently theatrical already. Katzenbach began by saying he had a presidential proclamation commanding Wallace to cease and desist from unlawful obstructions. Wallace, holding up his hand like a traffic cop, stopped Katzenbach and read a proclamation of his own denouncing the "Central Government." They stood together, the rangy Katzenbach towering over the bantam governor, "exchanging vaguely irritable and exasperated phrases . . . like a short, idle, haphazard argument on some street corner,

---

89. The Lawyers' Statement indicated the city and state of the signers.
90. Schlesinger, *supra* note 47, at 342.

Katzenbach with arms folded tightly and a faint expression of pained sufferance, beginning to glisten a little with sweat." Katzenbach again asked Wallace to step aside: 'If you do not, I'm going to assure you that the orders . . . will be enforced. From the outset, Governor, all of us have known that the final chapter of this history will be the admission of these students." "I stand according to my statement," said Wallace. Katzenbach went back to the car. Wallace retired inside the auditorium. The President federalized the National Guard. Katzenbach took the students to their dormitories. No one stood in the doorway there. When the students appeared again for registration in the after-noon, Wallace stepped aside.[91]

After the confrontation with Wallace was over, Katzenbach used a public phone to call the Justice Department to inform the Attorney General that the integration of the University of Alabama was a fact.[92]

The Decision to Introduce Federal Civil Rights Legislation

That very afternoon, after sitting alone and viewing the tapes from Tuscaloosa in the White House, John Kennedy made a decision that changed the course of the civil rights struggle in the South and cast its future in legal terms. He decided to introduce revolutionary civil rights reform legislation.[93] As the

---

91. *Id.*, at 341-42
92. The telephone call from Katzenbach is recorded on a videotape made in the Department of Justice on June 11, 1963. Louis Oberdorfer owns a copy of the videotape. The author watched the tape with Mr. Oberdorfer.
93. SCHLESINGER, *supra* note 47, at 343, reproduction from JFK Oral History Program. "He just decided that day . . . He called me up on the phone and said that he was going to go on that night." Also "Kennedy Versus Wallace" videotape, Direct Cinema Limited. In an interview on the tape, he recalls that after John Kennedy finished reviewing a tape of the Tuscaloosa encounter that had been sent to the White House, he picked up the phone and called his brother to tell him that he was gong on television that night. There was no live television coverage of the Tuscaloosa confrontation. The Attorney General and his staff followed the events by shortwave radios and telephone. President Kennedy had to wait until a government videotape reached the White House to actually see the meeting between Katzenbach and Wallace. RICHARD REEVES, PRESIDENT KENNEDY, PROFILE IN POWER 516 (Simon & Schuster 1993). Kennedy was told about the immolation of a 73-year-old monk named Thich Quang Duc in Saigon the night before. The Associated Press blanketed the American press with the gruesome pictures June 11. RFK in recorded interview by Anthony Lewis, Dec. 4, 1964.

historian Calvin Woodward points out, "The terms in which a problem is cast are decisive in determining the relative significance of social institutions."[94] Kennedy's decision to introduce civil rights legislation at that moment, rather than at a later time when the congressional politics for passage were clearer, appears to have been strongly influenced by the events at Tuscaloosa.[95]

At the end of May, the Administration had made the theoretical decision that the time had come to make equal access to places of public accommodation a matter of law. Legislation was in the works, but because of the strength of southern opposition in Congress, fear for the failure of other important administration legislative priorities in retaliation, and reelection considerations, no timetable for introduction of the legislation had been agreed upon. In fact, when President Kennedy announced his intention to go ahead with wide-ranging reforms on June 11, only his brother Robert supported the decision. In a televised speech to the American public that evening, John Kennedy said, "I shall ask Congress . . . to make a commitment it has not fully made in this century to the proposition that race has no place in American life or law."[96] According to Robert Kennedy, the events in Alabama had not only created the "mood but demonstrated the need" for legislation. "People were enough concerned about it, and there was enough demand about it that we could get to the heart of the problem and have some chance of success."[97]

The "Kennedy Manifesto," as his biographer, Theodore C. Sorensen, named the speech, not only marks the end of overt resistance to college desegregation, but also marks the beginning of the federal government's full-scale commitment to the fight against all discrimination.[98] Sorensen, White House Counsel on June 11, had made tentative plans for the Presi-

---

94. CALVIN WOODWARD, REALITY AND SOCIAL REFORM: THE TRANSITION FROM LAISSEZ-FAIRE TO THE WELFARE STATE 72 (1962), 286-328. "Every society has standards (tradition and reality) which render certain conduct and conditions intolerable. And each society endeavors, by pressure exerted through its various institutions, to abolish such conduct and conditions. One such institution is the state which acts through the law."

95. SCHLESINGER, *supra* note 47, at 494. "For several weeks the White House and Justice Department had been preparing a new package. The President's decision to go ahead definitely on a sweeping bill had been made on May 31, over the opposition of some of his political advisers who saw both congressional and electoral defeat. Democratic leaders were being consulted. Republican support was being rounded up. The details of the program had not yet been concluded."

96. JOHN F. KENNEDY, PUBLIC PAPERS OF THE PRESIDENT 1963 469 (1964).

97. SCHLESINGER, *supra* note 47, at 347.

98. SORENSEN, *supra* note 20, at 493.

dent to go on television in the event of violence in Alabama.[99] But events went smoothly and as Sorensen remembers, "no address to the nation had been written. Having assumed that the tranquil resolution at Tuscaloosa that afternoon would make a speech unnecessary, I did not start a first draft until late in the afternoon or complete it until minutes before he [JFK] went on the air. . . . He did, in fact, wholly extemporize a heartfelt conclusion."[100] What actually persuaded John Kennedy "to unequivocally place his office, his country, and himself behind the proposition that 'race has no place in American life or law,' that particular day will never be known.[101] But it is clear from the record that at some point Kennedy instinctively understood that this was the right time to act."[102] Once he had made up his mind, preparations for the TV address progressed. In what is indisputably one of the most memorable moments of his presidency, John Kennedy simply and clearly explained his decision. He said:

> This was not a sectional issue, nor a partisan issue, nor even a legal or legislative issue alone. It is better to settle these matters in the courts than on the streets, and new laws are needed at every level. But law alone cannot make men see right. We are confronted primarily with a moral issue. It is as old as the Scriptures and is as

---

99. SCHLESINGER, *supra* note 47, at 341. "Secretly, Wallace had sent word to Katzenbach that there would be no trouble, all he wanted to do was to have his say."

100. *Id.* In June of 1963, it was the policy of the Special Counsel's office to keep only one secretary, out of the three assigned to Sorensen, on call for evening work. On June 11, a single secretary, Mary White, was working in the office with Sorensen. She typed the President's speech, with a carbon copy. Kennedy was concerned about meeting air time and kept peering over shoulder to review the copy. Mary White recalls being flustered and slowed by his constant presence. A few minutes before he was to go on national television to announce sweeping changes in American society, Sorensen's secretary turned to JFK and, as sweetly as she could, suggested "Why don't you go get your makeup done? He laughed good-naturedly," turned and left the   room. Interview with Mary White, secretary to Theodore Sorensen, Jan. 13, 1994. Interview with Gloria Sitrin, secretary to Theodore Sorensen, Jan. 20, 1994. Interview with Lee C. White, White House counsel, Jan. 24, 1994.

101. See note 93, *supra.* Also "Kennedy Versus Wallace" videotape, Direct Cinema Limited.

102. BRAUER, *supra* note 39, at 318. "Kennedy needed to feel that he was leading rather than being swept along by events. As President, he was uncomfortable playing a passive role. Therefore, when in the spring of 1963 he perceived that he was losing the reins of leadership, he boldly reached out to grasp them once again."

clear as the American Constitution. . . . Now the time has come for this nation to fulfill its promise . . . . It cannot be met by repressive police action. It cannot be left to increased demonstrations in the streets. It cannot be quieted by token moves or talk. It is time to act . . . . Those who do nothing are inviting shame as well as violence. Those who act boldly are recognizing right as well as reality.[103]

The President promised to send the bill to the Hill within the week.[104] Ironically, just four days before, the national media reported that the best Negroes could expect from the administration "was a bill, to be sent to Congress, proposing to use the interstate commerce clause of the Constitution as a weapon to bring federal suits against private segregated firms and stores."[105] The Omnibus Civil Rights Bill, as Kennedy's proposed civil rights legislation was known, also revived the voting rights proposals that the Kennedy administration fruitlessly submitted to the Congress the preceding February,[106] as well as authorizing the Attorney General of the United States to sue for school desegregation.

Not included in the legislation was a section on fair employment practices, which the President endorsed but believed would sink any chance for passage. As it was, Vice President Lyndon B. Johnson told Kennedy that he believed civil rights legislation could not be passed, in part because "so little had been done to prepare the country for it."[107]

---

103. JOHN F. KENNEDY, PUBLIC PAPERS OF PRESIDENT JOHN F. KENNEDY 1963 469 (1964).

104. The two principal features of the bill were a ban on discrimination in places of public accommodation—including hotels, restaurants, places of amusement, and retail stores, with a substantial effect on interstate commerce—and authority was given to the attorney general to seek desegregation of public education on his own initiative when a lack of means or fear of reprisal prevented the aggrieved students or their parent from doing so. SORENSEN, *supra* note 20, at 497.

105. *The Nation*, TIME, June 7, 1963, at 8.

106. SORENSEN, *supra* note 20, at 494. Kennedy's first civil rights message in February, 1963, called for a variety of improvements in the voting rights laws: abolishing literacy tests for those with a sixth-grade education, prohibiting the application of different standards to different races, and speeding up the registration of voters in contested areas. Also SCHLESINGER, *supra* note 47, at 328. On the voting rights features of the February bill, RFK said, "The bill fell into a vacuum of apathy. There wasn't any interest in it. There was no public demand for it. There was no demand by the newspapers or radio or television. There was no interest by people coming to watch the hearings. . . . Nobody came. Nobody paid any attention."

107. Norbert Schlei, *Comments of the Vice-President on the Civil Rights Legislative Proposals*, June 4, 1963, 47-49. Robert F. Kennedy Papers, AG File 1963, John F. Kennedy Memorial Library.

The bill was submitted to Congress on June 19, 1963.[108] The need for the constructive participation of the bar in the South would be more necessary than ever. Despite the prospect of new federal legislation, it was by no means clear that the white southern bar would respond any differently than it had since the Supreme Court handed down the *Brown* decision in 1954. Except for the lawyers' statement in Alabama, there was no indication that the profession would act responsibly. The editors of *The Birmingham News* posed a relevant question on the morning of June 10. Commenting on the appearance of the Segal statement, they asked, "To what extent does his action (Wallace) carry endorsement of his fellow members of the Alabama Bar or the nation?"

A White House Conference for Lawyers

Immediately after the television address, Robert Kennedy was put in charge of strategy for the bill's passage. Building on a plan from the spring, entertaining small groups in the White House, Bob Kennedy suggested that the President now host much larger gatherings of the nation's opinion makers to garner support for the legislation. A social invitation to the fabled Kennedy White House was a prestigious enticement for many who might not otherwise want to involve themselves. According to Burke Marshall, it was Bob Kennedy's Show.[109] "Robert planned the effort, saw that the meetings took place, did the groundwork for them, did the follow-up on them,"[110] Assistant Attorney General Oberdorfer, who had been involved all spring with the Attorney General's voluntary desegregation project, worked with Lee White, the White House Counsel, on the details of inviting chain-store executives, hotel managers,[111] educators, clergymen, businessmen, labor leaders, and others to the proposed civil rights conferences. President Kennedy was scheduled to leave the country for a European conference on Saturday, June 22, and both the White House and Department of Justice scrambled to

---

108. *JFK Prods Congress on Rights,* WASH. POST, June 20, 1963, at A-1. The article states that the President "calls for Congress to stay in session until it has enacted— preferably as a single omnibus bill"—the civil rights package that was submitted the day before.

109. Interview with former Assistant Attorney General for Civil Rights Burke Marshall, Mar. 27, 1994, Yale University Law School.

110. SCHLESINGER, *supra* note 47, at 349.

111. In May 1963, Robert Kennedy had persuaded the President to meet with southern executives and business leaders to help convince them to support the Administration's voluntary desegregation plan. This effort was under way when the Tuscaloosa crisis intervened. Assistant Attorney General for Tax Louis Oberdorfer, was working with the Attorney General in this effort.

put together invitation lists and agendas for the White House sessions.[112] "The whole point was to display the 'active involvement of the President,'" according to the Attorney General, as well as to show local leaders "why it was in their interest to do something rather than to wait until violence occurred."[113]

Robert Kennedy understood that the President's time was at a premium, and he targeted his guest list for the greatest possible public relations effect. He did not include the bar on the original guest list. At that time the Attorney General had no reason to believe that the legal establishment would be any more responsive to the President's legislative proposal than it had been to the Court.[114] It was quite by chance that the Attorney General telephoned Bernard Segal on an unrelated matter sometime that week.[115] Segal "challenged him" that having convened White House Conferences for various other key groups, the President should now schedule one for lawyers, "at least their advice should be sought."[116] It is not certain that Robert Kennedy was even aware of the publication of the lawyers' statment on June 10 in Alabama, when he phoned Segal.[117] It cannot be doubted that Segal relayed his experi-

---

112. More than 1,600 people were invited to the conferences.

113. Robert F. Kennedy to Anthony Lewis, interview Dec. 6, 1964, John F. Kennedy Oral History Project I, 52-53, Civil Rights, John F. Kennedy Memorial Library, Cambridge, Massachusetts.

114. In the research for this paper, the author has not been able to uncover any specific reason RFK omitted the bar. Conjecture has been made that the omission reflected the Attorney General's pique at the southern bar and the ABA for its failure to respond to the civil rights crisis. Repeatedly, in the course of the oral interviews with those close to Kennedy at Justice, the phrase "Where are all the lawyers?" comes up as one that was so oft repeated by the Attorney General that it became a mantra around the department.

115. Bernard G. Segal, confidential letter, June 17, 1963, to Robert Meserve, Cloyd Laporte, Arthur Littleton, Robert T. Barton, Leon Jaworski, Harry G. Gault, Barnabas F. Sears, Roy L. Willy, Eugene D. Bennett, Gerald B. Klein, and, Robert Ash. The exact date of RFK's contact with Bernard Segal is unknown, but a telegram inviting Segal was sent from the White House dated June 15, 1963.

116. Bernard G. Segal, *Remarks*, 15th Anniversary Dinner for the LCCR.

117. Interview with former Assistant Attorney General Louis Oberdorfer. Oberdorfer does not remember when the Attorney General became aware of the Lawyers' Letter and Segal's contribution in Alabama. Also, interview with former Deputy Attorney General Nicholas Katzenbach, April 4, 1994. Katzenbach does not recall if he was aware of the publication of the Lawyers' Letter on the morning of June 10, 1963. Interview with Assistant Attorney General for Civil Rights Burke Marshall. Marshall does not recall discussing the Segal letter with the Attorney General on June 10.

ence and the cooperation from the leaders of the profession to the Attorney General. It is also probable that Segal predicted a similar response from the establishment bar if they were included in the White House events. The Attorney General was persuaded by Segal. He did not commit to anything during that phone call, but less than half an hour later the White House Counsel, Lee White, called Segal to arrange for a lawyers' conference.[118]

The President's scheduled departure for European talks on a proposed Test Ban Treaty meant that preparations for the lawyers' conference had to be handled swiftly. On Saturday morning, June 22, the day of departure for Europe, the President was to meet with the national leaders of the civil rights movement with hope of engendering some bipartisan support for the President's proposal. As Segal remembers it, Lee White told him "to prepare a list of at least 250 lawyers, at least one from every state, Puerto Rico, and the Virgin Islands, including the 46 lawyers who had joined in the Statement to Governor Wallace and at least 50 members of minority groups, to be invited to attend on June 21 a White House conference for lawyers on the subject of civil rights."[119]

Oberdorfer and White were happy to have Segal's help.[120] White's office was also involved in preparations for the President's trip to Europe, which coincidentally had been announced on June 11.[121] It was "hectic," according to White, "and remember," he said, "that in those days we didn't even have Xerox machines"—every list and memorandum had to be manually typed, and usually there was only one carbon copy.[122] The historian Arthur Schlesinger, Jr., a Kennedy biographer and friend, writes of the Kennedys, "They were not systematic calculators but brilliant improvisors. . . . Robert Kennedy's genius as a manager lay in his capacity to address a specific situation, to assemble an able staff, to inspire."[123] Assistant Attorney General Oberdorfer said Kennedy expected his people to keep him informed about anything that had public implications, but he "did not interfere unless they

---

118. Interview with former White House Counsel Lee C. White, Jan. 24, 1994, Washington, D.C. Mr. White remembers that it was difficult to find a time for the lawyers' meeting because the President was busy and he was to leave for Europe on June 22.

119. Segal, *supra* note 116 at 3.

120. *Supra* note 84.

121. *Big 3—Set Moscow Test Ban Treaty*, WASH. POST, June 11, 1963, at A-1.

122. Interview with Lee White. Mr. White remembers that frequently the vice president did not have copies of the materials that were handed to the President when he came into one of these meetings, and as a result, Johnson believed that Kennedy's staff was trying to snub him.

123. SCHLESINGER, *supra* note 47, at 193.

requested his counsel or support." Kennedy "had that quality of leadership that made all of us play above our heads."[124]

Oberdorfer and Segal realized that they had a completely unique opportunity to address the representatives of the organized bar—state, local, and national—about the crisis in the South. They jumped at the chance. They knew that they would have to be very careful not to offend the leadership of the ABA, who guarded their position within the profession jealously.[125]

Just four days after the President's television announcement, Saturday, June 15, 1963, the White House began telegraphing 250 invitations to the selected lawyers. They read:

> At 4 o'clock on Friday, June 21, I am meeting with a group of leaders of the Bar to discuss certain aspects of the Nation's civil rights problem. This matter merits serious and immediate attention and I would be pleased to have you attend the meeting to be held in the East Room of the White House. Please advise whether you will be able to attend.
>
> John F. Kennedy[126]

The following Friday, 244 lawyers[127] gathered with the President, Vice President Lyndon B. Johnson, and the Attorney General in the East Room of the White House.[128] Included in the group were several members of the Board

---

124. SCHLESINGER, *supra* note 47, at 240, quoting Louis Oberdorfer.
125. *Supra* note 84.
126. Western Union Telegram, John F. Kennedy to Bernard G. Segal, from the files of the LCCR, Washington, D.C.
127. Marjorie Hunter, *Lawyers Promise Kennedy Aid in Easing Race Unrest*, N.Y. TIMES, June 22, 1963, at 1.
128. From the records of the LCCR, June 21, 1963 Meeting File, Lawyers Who Attended President's Meeting, June 21, 1963: Morris Abram, New York; Walter E. Alessandroni, Philadelphia, Pa.; Mrs. Sadie T.M. Alexander Philadelphia, Pa.; Oscar J. Andre, Clarksburg, W.Va.; J. Garner Anthony, Honolulu, Haw.; Douglas Arant, Birmingham, Ala.; Walter P. Armstrong, Jr., Memphis, Tenn.; Robert Ash, Washington, D.C.; George Barrett, Nashville, Tenn.; John C. Bartlett, Reno, Nev.; Lowell Beck, Washington, D.C.; Berl Bernhard, Washington, D.C.; Theodore Berry, Cincinnati, Ohio; Francis Biddle, Washington, D.C.; Thomas W. Blackwell, Jr., Winston-Salem, N.C.; Luis Torres Bonet, San Juan, P.R.; Henry P. Brandis, Jr., Chapel Hill, N.C.; Wiley A. Branton, Atlanta, Ga.; Charles D. Breitel, New York, N.Y.; Hon. Edward W. Brooke, Boston, Mass.; John G. Buchanan, Pittsburgh, Pa.; Herbert Brownell, New York, N.Y.; Mason Bull, Morrison, Ill.; Charles Bunn, Charlottesville, Va.; Cecil E. Burney, Corpus Christi, Tex.; Howard F. Burns, Cleveland, Ohio; Kenneth J. Burns, Jr., Chicago, Ill.; Lawrence Burns, Jr., Coshocton, Ohio; Joseph D.

Calhoun, Media, Pa.; Charles V. Carr, Cleveland, Ohio; James J. Carter, Montgomery, Ala.; Robert L. Carter, New York, N.Y.; Donald Channell, Washington, D.C.; Walter G. Chuck, Honolulu, Haw.; Clark M. Clifford, Washington, D.C.; John F. Cogan, Jr., Boston, Mass.; David Cole, Paterson, N.J.; William T. Coleman, Jr., Philadelphia, Pa.; Nathaniel Colley, Sacramento, Calif.; John Conyers, Jr., Detroit, Mich.; Grant B. Cooper, Los Angeles, Calif.; Jerome A. Cooper, Birmingham, Ala.; Glenn A. Coughlan, Boise, Idaho; Glenn M. Coulter, Detroit, Mich.; Walter E. Craig, Phoenix, Ariz.; George W. Crawford, New Haven, Conn.; George W. Crockett, Jr., Detroit, Mich.; Marshall Crowley, Newark, N.J.; Lloyd N. Cutler, Washington, D.C.; Norris Darrell, New York, N.Y.; Jay A. Darwin, San Francisco, Calif.; Arthur H. Dean, New York, N.Y.; James C. Dezendorf, Portland, Ore.; Arthur Dixon, Chicago, Ill.; Hugh M. Dorsey, Jr., Atlanta, Ga.; Robert F. Drinan, S.J., Boston, Mass.; Robert E. Driscoll, Jr., Lead, S.D.; Edward R. Dudley, New York, N.Y.; Harry L. Dunn, Los Angeles, Calif.; W.J. Durham, Dallas, Tex.; Bert Early, Chicago, Ill.; Allen B. Endicott III, Atlantic City, N.J.; Vernon H. Eney, Baltimore, Md.; James E. Faust, Salt Lake City, Utah; James D. Fellers, Oklahoma City, Okla.; Clyde Ferguson, Washington, D.C.; William F. Fitzpatrick, Syracuse, N.Y.; Cody Fowler, Tampa, Fla.; Ralph F. Fuchs, Bloomington, Ind.; Leo V. Gaffney, New Britain, Conn.; Harold J. Gallagher, New York, N.Y.; Lloyd K. Garrison, New York, N.Y., Frank B. Gary, Columbia, S.C.; Benton E. Gates, Columbia City, Ind.; William W. Gaunt, Brighton, Colo.; Harry Gershenson, Saint Louis, Mo.; Delbridge L. Gibbs, Jacksonville, Fla.; Nathan B. Goodnow, Detroit, Mich.; Earl Q. Gray, Ardmore, Okla.; Fred D. Gray, Montgomery, Ala.; William P. Gray, Los Angeles, Calif.; Jack Greenberg, New York, N.Y.; H. Eastman Hackney, Pittsburgh, Pa.; William N. Haddad, Chicago, Ill.; Amos T. Hall, Tulsa, Okla.; Albert J. Harno, Springfield, Illinois; C. Howard Hardesty, Jr., Fairmont, W. Va., Alphonso R. Harper, Detroit, Mich.; Harold C. Havighurst, Chicago, Ill.; George E.C. Hayes, Washington, D.C.; George A. Healey, Lincoln, Neb.; Robert O. Hetlage, St. Louis, Mo.; William Higgs, Cambridge, Mass.; Francis W. Hill, Washington, D.C.; Leslie Hodson, Chicago, Ill.; Louis Hoffman, St. Thomas, V.I., Donald L. Hollowell, Atlanta, Ga.; Leon Jaworski, Houston, Tex.; Joseph S. Jenckes, Jr., Phoenix, Ariz.; Albert E. Jenner, Jr., Chicago, Ill.; Herbert Johnson, Atlanta, Ga.; Honorable Leroy Johnson, Atlanta, Ga.; Joseph F. Johnston, Birmingham, Ala.; Gerald J. Kahn, Milwaukee, Wis.; Edward E. Kallgren, San Francisco, Calif.; Lloyd Karr, Webster City, Iowa; Damon Keith, Detroit, Mich.; Harry B. Kelleher, New Orleans, La.; Earle W. Kintner, Washington, D.C.; Robert H. Knight, New York, N.Y.; Edward W. Kuhn, Memphis, Tenn.; Cloyd Laporte, New York, N.Y.; Belford Lawson, Washington, D.C.; Arthur W. Leibild, Jr., Philadelphia, Pa.; Robert E. Lillard, Nashville, Tenn.; William B. Lockhart, Minneapolis, Minn.; Laurence H. Lougee, Worcester, Mass.; Colin MacR. Makepeace, Providence, R.I.; Walter D. Malcolm, Boston, Mass.; Ross L. Malone, Roswell, New Mexico; William L. Marbury, Baltimore, Md.; Orison S. Marden, New York, N.Y.; Eugene E. Marsh, McMinnville, Ore.; Scott M. Matheson, Jr., Salt Lake City, Utah; David F. Maxwell, Philadelphia, Pa.; Paul N. McCloskey, Jr., Palo Alto, Calif.; William A. McKenzie, Cincinnati, Ohio; Walton J. McLeod, Walterboro, S.C.; Desmond J. McTighe, Norristown, Pa.; Maurice H. Merrill, Norman,

Okla.; Robert W. Meserve, Boston, Mass.; Waldo G. Miles, Bristol, Va.; Loren Miller, Los Angeles, Calif.; Robert N. Miller, Washington, D.C.; Joseph A. Millimet, Manchester, N.H.; William R. Ming, Chicago, Ill.; Ernest N. Morial, New Orleans, La.; Earl F. Morris, Columbia, Ohio; Mrs. Constance Baker Motley, New York, N.Y.; Robert S. Mucklestone, Seattle, Wash.; Edward E. Murane, Casper, Wyo.; James M. Nabritt, Washington, D.C.; Philip Neville, Minneapolis, Minn.; David A. Nichols, Camden, Me.; Honorable Austin Norris, Philadelphia, Pa.; James E. O'Brien, San Francisco, Calif.; Joseph O'Meara, South Bend, Indiana, Telford B. Orbison, New Albany, Ind.; John Lord O'Brian, Washington, D.C., Francis J. O'Brien, Providence, R.I.; Addison M. Parker, Des Moines, Iowa; Wilbur F. Pell, Jr., Shelbyville, Ky.; Jack Petree, Memphis, Tenn.; Samuel R. Pierce, Jr., New York, N.Y.; William J. Pierce, Ann Arbor, Mich.; William Poole, Wilmington, Del.; Webster Posey, Cincinnati, Ohio; Lewis Powell, Richmond, Va.; George V. Powell, Seattle, Wash.; George B. Powers, Wichita, Kan.; John R. Quarles, Boston, Mass.; Carl Rachlin, New York, N.Y.; William L. Randall, Milwaukee Wis.; Talbot Rain, Dallas, Tex.; Louis Ramsay, Pine Bluff, Ark.; Frank D. Reeves, Washington, D.C.; Charles S. Rhyne, Washington, D.C.; Frederick D.G. Ribble, Charlottesville, Va.; Hohn Riehn, Dallas, Tex.; William K. Ris, Denver, Colo.; John Ritchie III, Chicago, Ill.; Spotswood Robinson, Washington, D.C.; Edwin S. Rockefeller, Washington, D.C.; Eugene F. Rogers, Columbia, S.C.; William P. Rogers, New York, N.Y.; Eugene V. Rostow, New Haven, Conn.; John C. Satterfield, Yazoo City, Miss.; Louis B. Schwartz, Philadelphia, Pa.; Barnabas F. Sears, Chicago, Ill.; Bernard G. Segal, Philadelphia, Pa.; James L. Shepherd, Jr., Houston, Tex.; Charles F. Sheridan, Jr., Concord, N.H.; Jerome J. Shestack, Philadelphia, Pa.; Arthur D. Shores, Birmingham, Ala.; Jay S. Siegel, Hartford, Conn.; C.H. Erskine Smith, Birmingham, Ala.; Sylvester C. Smith, Jr., Newark, N.J.; Gerald C. Snyder, Waukegan, Ill.; William B. Spann, Jr., Atlanta, Ga.; Joseph Stecker, Chicago, Ill.; Jerome Steen, Jackson, Miss.; Oliver P. Stockwell, Lake Charles, La.; James R. Stoner, Washington, D.C.; Eugene B. Strassburger, Pittsburgh, Pa.; Russell B. Sugarman, Jr., Memphis, Tenn.; Roy P. Swanson, Kansas City, Mo.; Harry Swegle, Chicago, Ill.; Charles P. Taft, Cincinnati, Ohio; Bascom Talley, Bogalusa, La.; Jack Tanner, Tacoma, Wash.; Alfred W. Taylor, Johnson City, Tenn.; Hobart Taylor, Washington, D.C.; William L. Taylor, Washington, D.C.; Henry J. TePaske, Orange City, Iowa; N. Maxson Terry, Dover, Del.; John J. Thomason, Memphis, Tenn.; David Thorsness, Anchorage, Alaska; Wilbur P. Trammell, Buffalo, N.Y.; Roger J. Traynor, Berkeley, Calif.; Harrison Tweed, New York, N.Y.; Andrew R. Tyler, New York, N.Y.; David J. Vann, Birmingham, Ala.; John W. Wade, Nashville, Tenn.; A.T. Walden, Atlanta, Ga.; Lawrence E. Walsh, New York, N.Y.; William C. Warren, New York, N.Y.; Herbert Wechsler, New York, N.Y.; John G. Weinmann, New Orleans, La.; Francis Wilcox, Washington, D.C.; Samuel A. Wilkinson, Boston, Mass.; Charles Willard, New York, N.Y.; Laurens Williams, Washington, D.C.; Archie N. Willis, Jr., Memphis, Tenn.; Roy E. Willy, Sioux Falls, S.D.; J. Boone Wilson, Burlington, N.C.; William L. Wilson, Owensboro, Ky.; Francis E. Winslow, Rocky Mount, N.C.; Glenn R. Winters, Chicago, Ill.; Sherwood W. Wise, Jackson, Miss.; Paul A. Wolkin, Philadelphia, Pa.; Mrs. Ruth L. Wood, Danville, Va.; Henry L. Woolfenden, Detroit, Mich.; Ed-of Directors of the NAACP, the president of Howard University, the attorney general of Massachusetts, the president of the American Bar Association, and other leading members of the minority legal community.

The entire Board of Governors and many of the delegates to the ABA were also invited to attend. When the association's president, Sylvester C. Smith, Jr., of Newark, New Jersey, received his invitation, he was wary of Kennedy's intentions. He called an emergency meeting of the board to discuss the possibility that the organization would be asked to endorse the President's proposed civil rights legislation. Gathering in Washington before the White House meeting, the board authorized Smith to propose an ad hoc committee to look into the civil rights issue and the racial violence in the South, but there was "to be no publicity to its considerations."[129] The roster of members chosen for the Committee on Civil Rights and Civil Unrest of the ABA reflects the attitudes of the organization's leadership to the idea of intervention in the civil rights struggle. The chairman of the new ABA committee didn't believe the President had the authority to enforce judicial decrees.[130] His appointment as well as a number of others was a clear signal of the national organization's resistance to the civil rights legislation.[131] A number of its members were overt racists. Rush H. Limbaugh of Cape Girardeau, Missouri, believed that it was a positive comment on his community that it "prided itself on the fact that it never allowed a Negro to live in it and no Negro had

---

ward L. Wright, Little Rock, Ark.; Jack Young, Jackson, Miss. This list contains the names of 225 of the 244 lawyers who attended the meeting. Among the missing names are some obvious omissions, such as Burke Marshall and Louis Oberdorfer.

129. Jerry Shestack, Memorandum to Bernard Segal, July 17, 1963. Meeting with the ABA Committee on Civil Rights and Racial Unrest, July 12 & 13, Washington, D.C. On p. 2 of the memo Shestack quotes a conversation that speculates on why the President did not ask for the ABA's endorsement, "perhaps because he had been warned in advance (about the ABA's objections), the President did not so ask."

130. *Id.* at 23. Chairman of the ABA Committee on Civil Rights and Racial Unrest was Walter Schweppe, who was not invited to the White House. Mr. Schweppe held the opinion that there was not a problem with people involved in unpopular causes receiving counsel. Mr. Schweppe had written in the A.B.A. J., vol. 44, 1958, that the executive branch of government has no authority to enforce judicial decrees.

131. Alfred J. Schweppe, *Enforcement of Federal Court Decrees: A "Recurrence to Fundamental Principles,"* vol. 44 A.B.A. J. vol. 54, at 112. Mr. Schweppe from Seattle, Wash., was named chairman of the committee. He wrote about President Eisenhower's use of federal troops in Little Rock, Ark., "The statutory sections on which the President relied in his Proclamation of September 23, 1957, entitled 'Obstruction of Justice in the State of Arkansas' . . . cannot by any fair construction be made to give him, under the guise of enforcing the 'laws of the United States,' the power to enforce federal court decrees in civil rights cases." Col. Harold J. Sullivan,

ever lived there permanently." Sherwood Wise from Jackson, Mississippi, was "afraid" of the implications of the racial struggle, "If you let a camel put his nose in the tent, he would soon get the whole tent," and that recent events "gave credence to these fears." His co-member, Thomas G. Greaves of Mobile, Alabama, believed that it was the federal government that was "pushing" the "colored people on" to violate the law and to fight the police. Greaves thought that "Birmingham was not as bad as people thought." Assistant Attorney General Oberdorfer, who attended the first meeting of the group in Washington in July, believed that the committee was meant to be "a burial ground."[132] It is extremely doubtful that the ABA would have done anything without the pressure of the impending meeting in the White House.

Both the White House and the Justice Department prepared memoranda for the President for the meeting. The Justice Department outlined three issues: the groups represented at the meeting; the problem; and suggestions for the lawyers. In the section entitled "Things for Lawyers To Do," the mission for lawyers was to "(A)—Be leaders and (B)—Be Lawyers." Lawyers as leaders could form and participate in biracial committees; establish contact with city government and urge voluntary desegregation in public facilities; propose city ordinances to provide protection and support for businesses, which would change if they were assured of city government support; do the same with local newspaper publishers and staffs and church and civil groups; speak up socially (e.g., at the country club) and encourage and stand up for others who do; critically examine state and local budgets for school personnel and construction and advocate large appropriations for "Manhattan projects" to cushion integration and to provide the long-range educational opportunity so badly needed by Negroes and whites; examine and advocate the improvement of local provisions for vocational training, and for recreational opportunities for all, including Negroes; and campaign against school dropouts. Lawyers as lawyers could offer to represent Negroes in distress, "and even where you think they have violated the law"; urge repeal of city ordinances believed to violate the Constitution; and discourage lawyers from raising issues that have no apparent merit (e.g., Governor Wallace had appealed Judge Lynne's order). Specifically, lawyers could publicly answer outrageous interpretations of the law by columnists and letter writers; offer professional assistance to other groups, such as those being organized by the clergy; urge upon clients the morality and business wisdom of

---

Okla.; Rush Limbaugh, Mo.; Walton J. McLeod, Jr., S.C.; James D. Fellers, Okla.; William B. Spann, Jr., Ga.; Charles P. Light, Jr., Va.; Thomas G. Greaves, Jr., Ala.; Sherwood W. Wise, Miss.; Karl C. Williams, Ill.

132. Jerome Shestack to Bernard Segal, Memorandum, July 17, 1963, Meeting with the ABA Committee on Civil Rights and Racial Unrest on Jul 12 & 13. Shestack File, Records of the LCCR, Washington, D.C.

desegregation of public facilities, employment for Negroes, and elimination of job discrimination on the basis of race.[133]

Lee White prepared the memorandum that was used by the President. Immediately before the meeting, White handed Kennedy a briefing packet. It contained the memorandum prepared by the Justice Department indicating who was present, some suggested points to mention by way of describing the problem throughout the nation, and a section on what lawyers might do.[134] He also gave the President a summary of progress made in desegregation since May 22, a copy of the Segal letter to Wallace, and an Atlanta Bar statement from May 18 urging all citizens to have respect for the law. White also gave the President 10 specific "requests" that might be made: "(1) help form and participate in biracial committees; (2) work with state and municipal public officials in the consideration of statutes and ordinances dealing with discriminatory practices; (3) as influential molders of public opinion in their own communities, they can issue statements and publicly urge respect for judicial and legal processes (this is a special burden on Negro lawyers); (4) as educated citizens they can stress the importance to our society and individuals of adequate education and particularly participate in efforts to eliminate school drop-outs; (5) insure that legal aid groups and other voluntary associations provide legal counsel for all on a nondiscriminatory basis; (6) speak out when fallacious interpretations of court decisions or proposed legislation are made by newspaper columnists and others; (7) see to it that in their own Bar groups and legal associations all are admitted without regard to race; (8) volunteer legal and other services to religious, labor and other organizations set up to meet these problems at the local level; (9) set up an informal committee to provide a point of contact with the Federal Government similar to those proposed for clergymen, educators, etc,; (10) review carefully the legislation proposed by the Administration. Any substantive or drafting suggestions will be welcomed by the Administration and certainly the support of lawyers throughout the country for the entire package will be welcome."[135]

There is no official record of the White House conference. but many who were there remember that both the Attorney General and the Vice President spoke passionately about the situation in the South. The President preceded

---

133. Memorandum for Possible Use in June 21, 1963 Meeting With Leaders of the Bar, Records of the LCCR, Personal Records of Jerome J. Shestack, marked "JJS Personal copy."

134. Interview with Lee White.

135. Lee C. White, Memorandum for the President: Subject Notes for Meeting with Lawyers at 4:00 p.m., June 21, 1963, signed Lee C. White, Box 22, Records of the LCCR, Washington, D.C.

them. "He spoke briefly, but compellingly, of the need to muster the nation's religious, business and professional leaders in the cause of civil rights."[136] The Vice President, by all accounts, surprised the audience with his heartfelt and poignant remarks, relating personal experiences with the southern system of racial segregation, and suggested that each dwell on what it would be like to be black in the South. In *The New York Times'* report that followed the meeting, it was Johnson's remarks that received notice.[137] Robert Kennedy spoke the longest, not limiting his comments to the South but suggesting a more national mission for the bar. The Attorney General told the audience that "the surface eruptions of an internal disease cannot be cured with bandages. The only way to cure a disease is to attack its source; and the sources of this disease, this malignancy that has been allowed to grow within the tissues of our national life, are as minute and various as the various cells of any living body."

> While the dramatic incidents of racial tension have been in the South, he said, the North is far from blameless. "While there is de jure discrimination in the south, there is de facto discrimination in the north," schools, housing, employment and other areas. And he challenged the lawyers at the White House to address problems in their own communities, to marshal forces to cure the de facto discrimination and to set up "lawyers' committees for civil rights throughout the North, Midwest and West as well as the South.[138]

According to Jerry Shestack, "It was the first time a group of the nation's leading lawyers had come together to focus on civil rights."[139] Years later the meeting was recalled:

> The President, Vice President Lyndon B. Johnson, and Attorney General Robert F. Kennedy pointed to the recent events in the South as symptoms of a deepening crisis. Our constitutional system and the rule of law depended, they said, upon peaceful obedience to court orders. Official resistance necessitating enforcement by the use or display of armed force could cause the system to

---

136. Interview with Jerome J. Shestack.
137. N.Y. TIMES, June 22, 1963, at 8.
138. JEROME J. SHESTACK, A MASS IN MEMORY OF ROBERT F. KENNEDY: A PERSONAL MEMOIR 14 (Jerome J. Shestack 1993).
139. *Id.*

begin to unravel. Beyond that, pent-up and fully justified demands by blacks for access to public facilities, job opportunities, voting rights and other simple perquisites of citizenship could no longer be denied. They pointed out that the struggle of blacks for justice had been waged primarily in the courts and in the legislatures where, under our system, all citizens are supposed to seek justice and to gain it. Frustration in the courts and in the legislatures could only lead to more demonstrations and more violence. Simple justice and simple common sense, they said, demanded that the nation heed these signals without delay. To this end, President Kennedy called upon the gathering of lawyers . . . to join with him to lead the nation to fuller and more sympathetic understanding of the demands of minorities, to encourage local officials to obey court orders gracefully, to help resolve local civil rights controversies, to support voluntary integration of public facilities, to help improve minority job opportunities, and to work toward an environment in which the injustices long suffered by blacks would be ended in legislatures and in courts without resort to the streets. . . . They spoke of the unique role of lawyers in the creation and continued effective operation of our constitutional system and the rule of law. They emphasized the special skills of lawyers as negotiators and conciliators. They specifically appealed to the lawyers to mobilize the voice and work of the legal profession in support of the struggle in which blacks had been engaged, more or less singlehandedly, for so long.[140]

The press accounts that followed the "closed meeting" add more insight:

The nearly two-hour meeting was marked by one spirited but limited debate. This was touched off when a Southern lawyer, who was not identified, indicated that he believed the Administration was fostering racial street demonstrations that were leading to violence. A few Southern lawyers also said they could not support the Administration's civil rights program sent to Congress this

---

140. TEN YEAR REPORT: LAWYERS' COMMITTEE FOR CIVIL RIGHTS UNDER LAW 8 (LCCR, November 1973). Serving on the board of the LCCR at the time this was written were Bernard Segal, Jerome Shestack, Louis Oberdorfer, Harrison Tweed, Burke Marshall, Whitney North Seymour, Lloyd Cutler, Nicholas Katzenbach, and many more who attended the June 21, 1963 meeting and who took part in the planning for the event.

week, but the legislation question was not debated. The major emphasis was on peaceful solutions by cooperation.[141]

After pleading the case for professional mediation, the President of the United States issued an invitation to the leaders of the bar to work together for the public welfare, President Smith of the ABA announced the formation of the Committee on Civil Rights and Racial Unrest. "I assure you, Mr. President," said Smith, "that the American Bar Association is deeply concerned with finding solutions consistent with the rights of all individuals within the framework of the rule of law."[142] Despite the reservations of some of the lawyers before the conference, the arguments put forward by the Administration for help, for lawyers to get involved in the judicial process in the South, were compelling. Liberal or conservative, Democrat or Republican, lawyers had an obligation to the constitutional system of justice. Unbeknownst to Sylvester Smith, there was an alternative to leaving the issue in the hands of the ABA. An independent committee was about to be proposed.[143]

In the short time before the White House meeting, Bernard Segal approached Harrison Tweed about serving with him as co-chair of a lawyers' committee for civil rights.[144] Tweed was one of the corporate legal establishment's most aristocratic members and, unlike Lou Oberdorfer, independent from the Kennedy Administration. He had long been a leader in the bar's legal aid work, serving as president of the National Legal Aid Association. He was the senior partner in the highly regarded Wall Street law firm of Milbank & Tweed and chairman of the board of the American Law Institute, an internationally acclaimed group of independent legal scholars whose opinions were "legal pronouncements" both within and out of the profession. Tweed, a courtly New Yorker and a force in the ABA, agreed to join Segal.

Segal and Tweed rose and offered their services to the President. Kennedy responded enthusiastically and asked them to serve as co-chairmen of a lawyers' committee to "help open the lines of communication between the races."[145]

---

141. *Supra* note 137.
142. *The ABA House Action on Civil Rights Report,* AMER. BAR NEWS, July 19, 1963, at 4. The story reports that "the new (ABA) committee was authorized by the Board of Governors at a special meeting June 21 in Washington, D.C. shortly before the ABA officials joined more than 200 other bar leaders at a White House conference on civil rights."
143. *Id.* "The ABA Special Committee on Civil Rights functions independently of the new Lawyers Committee for Civil Rights Under Law."
144. *Id.* at 12. "Soon after the Wallace condemnation, Bobby Kennedy and Bernie Segal had a series of discussions on how to mobilize the nation's lawyers."
145. N.Y. TIMES, June 22, 1963, at 1.

Kennedy appealed to the whole group to join in the new effort. In turn, the new co-chairmen invited anyone who was interested in the President's Committee to talk to them after the meeting.

The character of the times, shifting perceptions about the function of the bar, and the deep commitment of a handful of men produced an unprecedented opening for change within the organized bar. Presidential leadership redefined the southern crisis in legal terms and elevated the struggle to the national stage. From their varied professional experiences—Bernard Segal with the judiciary, Louis Oberdorfer with the Justice Department in the South, and Harrison Tweed with legal aid—all believed that lawyers needed to do more to uphold the principles of the profession, and they were willing to work toward that end. Out of the White House Conference came a vision and direction for professional change.[146] Whether a new bar organization would be brought forth and survive in the days that followed the White House Conference was in large part a function of whether or not the profession understood, as Governor Wallace did, that there was no longer any middle of the road in civil rights revolution sweeping over America in 1963.

---

146. Interview with Lee C. White, former White House Counsel, January 24, 1994. The LCCR was the only organization to be created as a result of the 1963 White House Conferences.

CHAPTER 3

From the White House to Mississippi: Forging a New Path

In the preceding chapter, we examined the call for emergency intervention by the bar in a racial conflict that tested the efficacy of the judicial system. This chapter will examine the legal establishment's response to that call: the immediate reaction of the 244 lawyers who were at the White House on June 21, 1963; the formation of a Lawyers' Committee for Civil Rights Under Law (LCCR); its membership, purposes and policies; the group's initial legal activities; and the board's fateful decision to become active in Mississippi. This decision—a far cry from the original intent of the committee—would have a central influence on the character and direction of the organization.

The bar in America is reactive. As we have seen, American legal practice reflects social and economic trends. It does not anticipate them or precipitate them. Throughout its history it has adjusted to the political and economic priorities of the culture. The innovative, undisciplined, and democratic colonial bar was shaped by the demands of the frontier. British imperialism in the eighteenth century brought a return to the discipline and organization of the common law bar because of the demands of the American commercial classes for protection of their interests. In the early nineteenth century the bar changed again because of the republic's democratic values, which required an opened bar to advocate for the rights of the people. After the Civil War, the needs of industrialization compelled distinct legal skills, and a re-professionalized bar or organized bar emerged that was linked to the interests of American commerce and the commercial classes. Foreign immigration, urbanization, the Great Depression, the political triumph of FDR, World War II, the rise of the middle class; and, finally, the black awakening of the South transformed conventional concepts of social justice by the middle of the twentieth century.[1]

The legal historian Lawrence Friedman observes that "Twentieth-century man seems less inclined to accept the social order as given and his place within it as fixed. He demands for himself, his interests, and his aspirations, recognition and legitimacy, as well as practical achievement. There is consequently a massive demand to close the gap."[2] Lawyering returned to the courtroom, its natural habitat, to advocate for fundamental social change in the United States. A public interest bar emerged. The legal skills employed by the professional bar, masters of facts as the counselors of big business and big finance, had to adapt to the transformed social needs. Like the appearance of bar associations in the 1870s, the call for the creation of a Lawyers' Committee in 1963 reflects a reaction by the legal establishment to the changes taking place in American culture. Within the decade, the LCCR would be on the leading edge of the public interest law movement in America. However, on June 21, 1963, the thin veneer of the bar who launched the LCCR believed they were involved in a transitory effort undertaken to help relieve the southern crisis. According to Louis Oberdorfer, one of the LCCR's founders, the group did not see themselves as civil rights lawyers in the beginning.[3] The LCCR was formed specifically to help move the civil rights crisis out of the streets and into the courts, where blacks could seek justice. Its membership was united not by political ideology but by an appreciation of the professional responsibility of the bar to ensure the availability of lawyers to those seeking to address their grievances, however controversial the circumstances of the dispute.

The Bar's Reaction to the White House Conference

The immediate reaction of the 244 lawyers to President John F. Kennedy's suggestions was amazing. The 10 suggestions[4] for the bar put forward by Kennedy were embraced willingly by the lawyers. As the event ended on June 21, a number of men and women volunteered to serve on the President's

---

1. For a discussion on the effect of "demands" as the "causes of law," see Lawrence M. Friedman, *Notes Toward a History of American Justice*, in AMERICAN LAW AND THE CONSTITUTIONAL ORDER: HISTORICAL PERSPECTIVES, Lawrence M. Friedman & Harry N. Scheiber eds. (Harvard Univ. Press 1988), at 13-26.
2. *Id.* at 24.
3. In the interviews that I have had with the founding members of the LCCR [hereinafter LCCR], I have asked each one, "Did you think of yourself as a civil rights lawyer?" The universal response was no.
4. See chapter 2, at 89-90.

Committee (as the LCCR was first known) under the new co-chairmen, Bernard Segal and Harrison Tweed. Also noteworthy is the fact that no one specifically refused. There was no public disassociation from the call for a LCCR.[5] Even the leadership of the American Bar Association, who it was feared would resist the call to change, responded affirmatively. The ABA created a new committee to investigate the southern civil rights problems. The initiatives that came from the White House Lawyers' Conference were welcomed. The bar had been quiescent too long.

The state bars responded quickly. When the lawyers returned to their respective communities, they went right to work implementing the President's recommendations. Among the East Room attendees were some 25 presidents of local and state bar associations.[6] They were particularly effective in implementing the requests for professional education and the creation of biracial committees.[7] Lawyers as far away as Puerto Rico and Hawaii began reporting about these activities.[8] What follows is taken from reports sent to the co-chairmen about the efforts of the state and local bars.[9]

One of particular interest to the co-chairmen was the response of the local Alabama bar. In July 1963 the Alabama Bar Association met, less than a month after the standoff between Governor George Wallace and the federal government. For the first time in many years, it did not introduce resolutions condemnatory of the courts on civil rights. To a large extent, this was due to work done by committee members in advance of the meeting. Committee members privately let it be known that any such resolution condemning the courts would be vigorously opposed on the floor. Also, on September 29, 1963, 53 Alabama lawyers, including several members of the LCCR, issued a

---

5. Interview with Louis F. Oberdorfer. Oberdorfer and Segal did not know how the leadership of the ABA would react. "If they opposed us," according to Oberdorfer, "we couldn't have done anything. We were very careful not to offend them."
6. *Work with Bar Associations*, Minutes of the Meeting of the Board of Directors of the LCCR, Washington, D.C., Nov. 14, 1963.
7. Shestack, Memo to Tweed and Segal, July 19, 1963, at 12-21.
8. Harrison Tweed & Bernard G. Segal, co-chairmen, *Report to the Members of the LCCR,* Jan. 31, 1964: "Some 25 state Bar Associations who have joined the Committee . . . include Presidents or past Presidents of the state Bar Associations of California, Connecticut, Delaware, Georgia, Hawaii, Idaho, Illinois, Indiana, Kansas, Louisiana, Maryland, Nebraska, Nevada, New Hampshire, New Jersey, New York, North Carolina, Oregon, Pennsylvania, South Dakota, Utah, Vermont, Virginia, West Virginia, Wisconsin, and the District of Columbia."
9. LCCR, *Report to the Board of Directors on Activities by Local and State Bar Associations*, Nov. 12, 1963.

statement urging compliance with court orders. Officers and members of the LCCR had encouraged members of the Birmingham Bar to issue such a statement. After it was issued, some members of the committee, Jefferson B. Fordham, Cody Fowler, Joseph O'Meara, Eugene Rostow, and John W. Wade, wrote to Birmingham newspapers commending the lawyers who had signed the statement. *The Birmingham News* published the letters. Committee members were also instrumental in getting a public statement by some members of the Birmingham Bar opposing resolutions approving three amendments to the Constitution of the United States, which were under consideration in the Alabama legislature. Committee members also tried to open confidential discussions in the Birmingham Bar Association with the purpose of doing away with restrictions against Negro members. The work of committee members brought about a motion of the Executive Council of the Junior Bar Section of the Alabama Bar Association that, in October 1963, called upon lawyers to maintain respect for the court and its law officers.

Through the leadership of the new LCCR, state and local bar associations responded in a number of ways. In California, Michigan, and Minnesota, resolutions were passed to reaffirm their open racial policies.[10] One bar

---

10. *Id.* In California, LCCR member William P. Gray, president of the State Bar of California, called a series of three regional meetings covering the 101 voluntary bar associations in the state. At these meetings Gray proposed that lawyers form legal aid groups for Negroes and that bar associations reaffirm the existing open racial policy.

In Michigan, two members of the LCCR drafted a resolution that was adopted by the Board of Commissioners of the State Bar of Michigan, establishing a Committee of the State Bar to carry out the following nine functions: to assist the establishment of local governmental human relations committees; to establish or provide for volunteer professional services to civil organizations dealing with legitimate grievances; to assist and cooperate with national, state, or local officials and agencies in programs or specific actions designed to protect civil rights and to maintain law and order, to urge respect for the judiciary and the legal process, and to refute irresponsible and erroneous legal commentary; to encourage the 75 bar associations throughout the state of Michigan in the formation of civil rights committees to implement these resolutions; to cooperate with and assist the LCCR ; to encourage and develop programs that will ensure that adequate legal representation is available in cases affecting civil rights; to participate in or to assist in establishing fact-finding, conciliation, and arbitration services in connection with situations involving civil rights problems; and to compose, recommend, and, after approval by this Board, implement a plan by which Michigan lawyers will be inspired to furnish their professional services in the defense of clients wherever, by reason of intimidation, harassment, or threat of disbarment of our brother lawyers, adequate local legal representation is unavailable.

association, North Carolina, opened its membership to blacks for the first time.[11] In Kentucky, a statement against racial discrimination and preferential treatment in the association was included in the minutes of the board of governors of the bar and distributed to all lawyers in the state.[12] Among a number of other civil rights resolutions, California passed a resolution encouraging members who represented business clients to encourage them to "reexamine their employment practices and to remove any discrimination against the Negro people."[13] Connecticut, Idaho, and Hawaii offered their services to the LCCR,

---

In Minnesota, the Bar Association activated a Committee on Civil Rights that conducted a review of the status of civil rights in Minnesota. They issued a report supporting and encouraging the full enforcement of the antidiscrimination laws of Minnesota and made arrangements for a distribution of the Minnesota antidiscrimination laws to all state bar association members.

11. *Id.* In North Carolina, a member of the LCCR was instrumental in amending the Constitution of the Winston-Salem-Forsythe County Bar Association to allow, for the first time, full business and social membership for Negroes. In addition, a committee member was instrumental in having a biracial committee appointed in Winston-Salem. Another member has participated in public discussions explaining civil rights legislation, has worked in an advisory capacity with local officials on civil rights problems, and has urged the North Carolina Bar to hold an institute on civil rights.

12. *Id.* "In Kentucky, the Board of Governors of the State Bar approved the inclusion in the minutes of the July 26, 1963 meeting statements against discrimination and preferential treatment in the association and recommendations for Kentucky lawyers, in their respective communities, to aid and assist to the fullest extent of their influence and ability, to insure that discrimination be eliminated, violence be prevented; that the laws of our land and the decisions of our Courts may be observed and executed with promptness, fairness and impartiality."

13. *Id.* In California, LCCR member William P. Gray, president of the State Bar of California, called a series of three regional meetings covering the 101 voluntary bar associations in the state. At these meetings Gray proposed that: lawyers form legal aid groups for Negroes; bar associations reaffirm the existing open racial policy; good mediators volunteer to form biracial groups of community leaders to air racial grievances; those who represent business seek to persuade clients to reexamine their employment practices; as leaders of the community remind everybody of the need for patience and understanding; remind all that in any civilized community disputes must be resolved by discussion, or by court action if discussion falls; and courts are available to everyone, and, in any period of social unrest the decisions of the courts must be respected. A number of California city and county bar associations appointed biracial committees following Gray's advice. For example, the Los Angeles County Bar Association directed its Committee on Constitutional Rights to explore what further assistance that association can give in connection with civil rights problems. In Sacramento, at the prompting of the local bar, a biracial Human Relations Com-

while the state bar of Oregon asked the committee to help them establish a civil rights program.[14] Kansas authorized its officials to serve on the LCCR.[15] Members from Indiana and Louisiana wrote articles that were published in the state bar journals reminding their colleagues of the duty of the profession to uphold the courts.[16] Members in Chicago and New York City formed special committees to respond to racial problems and to work with city officials.[17] In general, however, the most significant and common response to the

---

mittee was formed. In California, leaders of the bar began to express opinions in public on civil rights matters. Gray appeared on television and radio news broadcasts. Pieces about the LCCR began to appear in the news and bar association periodicals. A State Bar Committee on Lawyers and Civil Rights was established and the first meeting was to be held on Nov. 22, 1963.

14. *Id.* "In Connecticut, Idaho and Hawaii, the State Bar Associations officially offered their services to the LCCR." Also, "The Board of Governors of the Oregon State Bar officially offered to cooperate with the LCCR and asked the Lawyers' Committee for a suggested program for local bar associations in the State."

15. *Id.* "In Kansas the Executive Council of the State Bar Association authorized its President and State Attorney General, William M. Ferguson, to serve on the Lawyers' Committee."

16. *Id.* A member of the LCCR, the president of the Indiana State Bar Association, Wilbur F. Pell, Jr., published an article in the bar magazine calling upon lawyers to carry out the Attorney General's objectives. Another member, Professor Ralph Fuchs, met with the biracial Human Relations Committee in Bloomington, Indiana, to consider methods of implementing local action on desegregation. Also, in Louisiana a member of the LCCR and president of the Louisiana State Bar, Bascom D. Talley, Jr., wrote in the *State Bar Journal* about the formation of the LCCR and the White House Conference. He ended his piece with the admonition that "no matter how much we may dislike a final judgment, we, as lawyers, are obligated to uphold it publicly and privately, if our system is to endure." In New Orleans another LCCR member suggested confidentially the formation of a biracial committee, while another member informed the committee that he took cases defending "those who have been attacked for handling civil rights matters."

17. *Id.* In New York City, Herbert Brownell, a former U.S. Attorney General, formed a special committee of the Bar Association of New York to work out precise ways for that association to help solve discrimination problems in the New York City area. Judge Francis E. Rivers of the Civil Court of the City of New York was named chairman. The president of the New York State Bar Association, William FitzPatrick; the president of the New York Women's Bar Association, Freda Silbowitz; and the president of the National Association of Claimants' Counsel of America, Jacob Fuchsberg, have all volunteered their services to the LCCR in New York and Chicago. Also, in Illinois, the Civil Rights Committee of the Chicago Bar Association and the Cook County Bar Association combined, for the first time, to host a luncheon for the NAACP Lawyers' Conference at the NAACP convention in Chicago on July 1.

LCCR was the outreach by state and local bar associations to black leaders and to the black community.[18]

"Committee members have been instrumental in solving various civil rights problems in Chicago," and a member of the LCCR, William Ming, was appointed by Chicago's Mayor Daley to serve on Chicago's Human Relations Committee. Other members of the LCCR undertook to organize bar association committees in downstate Illinois to help work on civil rights problems.

18. *Id.* In Maryland, the LCCR member H. Vernon Eney, president of the state bar, appointed a statewide committee to deal with civil rights problems. Messrs. Segal and Tweed suggested to the Maryland State Bar that they try to provide a role in "trying to bring about a settlement of the racial problems in Cambridge, Maryland." In Missouri, an LCCR member established a local lawyers' committee in St. Louis with the purpose of recruiting other professionals to join the committee. President of the Nevada State Bar and member of the LCCR John C. Bartlett set up a biracial committee in the Nevada State Bar Association.

At the insistence of president of the state bar association and LCCR member Joseph A. Millimet, the New Hampshire State Bar adopted a resolution recommending that all of its members volunteer their services wherever they are requested to do so in cases involving a great violation of civil rights where it appears that local counsel is not available.

LCCR member Walter Leichter, president of the New Jersey State Bar Association, called a meeting of representatives of the 21 county bar associations in New Jersey. He supplied copies of a statement about the White House Conference to all the associations. Following the meeting, a committee was established on a statewide bar level to deal with civil rights problems consisting of the presidents or vice-presidents and an alternate from each county bar association. A number of the counties in New Jersey also formed biracial committees, and Mr. Leichter encouraged other associations to do the same. Allen B. Endicott, another LCCR member, was appointed chairman of the New Jersey State Bar Civil Rights Committee. The committee adopted four resolutions, which were adopted by the state bar association on October 4, 1963. Among the resolutions was one that directed the association to "act as liaison between the County Bar Association and the LCCR, and the Federal and State Governments."

The LCCR sent the Ohio State Bar Association materials to help them formulate biracial civil rights committees. Members in Oklahoma City, Oklahoma, contacted fellow lawyers with a view toward organizing a local lawyers' biracial committee.

In Pennsylvania, Donald J. McTighe, president of the Pennsylvania Bar Association and LCCR member, proposed a resolution that was adopted by the Board of Governors of the association calling upon the 67 counties of Pennsylvania to establish biracial committees where appropriate. Many local bar associations followed up on that resolution. In Philadelphia, the Bar Association Committee on Civil Rights has been reactivated and has received suggestions from the LCCR. A member of the LCCR, Thomas McBride, was appointed co-chairman of a new Citizens Advisory Committee on Civil Rights appointed by the mayor of Philadelphia.

For the first time in the civil rights struggle, bar associations took a leadership role. Some of the changes in the restrictive tenets of the professional organizations, such as in North Carolina, reflected substantive progress. By today's standards, the majority of the resolutions and statements seem ambiguous. They were significant in the racial climate of the time. What the reports to the co-chairmen reveal is an effort by professional organizations that heretofore were silent to respond to the demands of the changing culture. They were distinct steps in the process of broadening the bar's perceptions of its professional responsibility.

This transformation would not have occurred without the vision and persistence of Bernard Segal and Louis Oberdorfer, and the help and support of Robert Kennedy, who responded to a perceived opportunity for change. Without them, the White House conference for lawyers would not have taken place. In the tumult of 1963, these men stand out in the emerging pro bono public interest law movement and in the history of the American bar. They stand out not as men who changed the direction of the bar, for no small group could effect so historic a transformation of this institution, but rather, as the examples show, because they were able to clarify a reason and direction for change to a significant segment of the profession, at a pivotal moment in the civil rights struggle.

These men—Segal, Oberdorfer, and Tweed—deserve notice for their commitment to the professed values of the country and of the profession. Each, in

---

The Executive Committee of the Rhode Island Bar Association offered its services to local and state groups in Rhode Island concerned with problems of civil rights. And in South Dakota the president of the State Bar of South Dakota, R.C. Driscoll, Jr., a member of the LCCR, appointed a Civil Rights Committee whose responsibilities were to carry out the points from the Attorney General's letter. The chairman of the committee was Ramon Roubideaux, who is one of South Dakota's leading trial lawyers and a Sioux Indian.

Working privately, the members of the LCCR in Texas were working to eliminate discrimination against Negroes in the Dallas Bar Association. A member of the LCCR, J.W. Riehm, while serving as dean of Southern Methodist University, received 100 percent participation of the faculty members of his school in a civil rights statement made by the southern law school deans and faculty members.

The president of the Virgin Islands' Bar and the president-elect of the West Virginia State Bar offered the assistance of their associations to the LCCR. The West Virginia Bar Association scheduled its annual membership meeting in October for Bluefield, West Virginia. The association was advised that some of the housing facilities would not be available to Negroes. The Association's Executive Committee met and decided unanimously that if that situation existed, it would not hold its meeting there. The result was that the situation was corrected and the facilities were made open to all.

his own way and for his own reasons, responded to a perceived duty. They gave selflessly of their time, resources, and talents to convince their colleagues that the bar had to act. They didn't know where their efforts would lead them. There is no record that they expected any professional reward or personal recognition or that they sought any. On the contrary, the record shows them acting simply in furtherance of the public welfare. In the next 20 years, private lawyers responding to an emerging perception of personal and professional responsibility would transform the character of legal service in the United States. The LCCR was on the leading edge of this movement.

The Formation of the LCCR

When the White House meeting ended on the afternoon of June 21, there was no LCCR, only a promise of something to come. The reality was that the President's Committee rested on the ability of a handful of men to pull it together. President Kennedy and the Attorney General turned their attention to Europe and the passage of the civil rights legislation. The establishment of the LCCR was left to the imagination and resources of the co-chairmen. The ABA's new Committee on Civil Rights and Civil Unrest was dominated by southerners who were skeptical about any "interference" in southern problems. The co-chairmen did not expect its help or that of the wary hierarchy of the ABA.

Essentially, the lawyers who were invited to the White House were the proposed LCCR. The 244 attendees, though receptive to the President, were scattered throughout the country, shared little in common except their positions of professional leadership, and had no clear understanding of what the committee intended to do. They were not invited to the Conference on the basis of demonstrated civil rights activity but by virtue of their representative position in the bar. Once the initial flurry of activity passed, the LCCR would have to demonstrate an acceptable reason for their continued interest and support.

Harrison Tweed and Bernard Segal began the process of establishing a LCCR as the White House meeting ended on Friday afternoon June 21. The new co-chairmen decided they should go somewhere to discuss the immediate future. Where to hold the meeting was the question. The men could have used Oberdorfer's office at Justice. But the assistant attorney general wanted to avoid any question about the committee's independence from the Kennedy Administration to protect its professional, nonpartisan character. It was decided to adjourn to the law offices of Lloyd Cutler, a former law partner of Oberdorfer and one of the first lawyers to volunteer for the committee. Cutler attended the White House Conference as president of the Yale Club in Washington, D.C. Oberdorfer joined Cutler, Segal, Shestack, and Tweed for the discussion.[19]

That evening, the structure of the LCCR began to take shape. Harrison Tweed felt strongly that the phrase "under law" should be added to the committee's name. He believed the LCCR was licensed to work within the legal process and it could not condone violence, either black or white.[20] They also discussed the location of a headquarters, fund-raising, and a tax exemption.

The decision about the location of a headquarters was postponed. Oberdorfer, the Assistant Attorney General for Tax, was asked to look into the question of tax exemption. Tweed and Segal resolved to meet in New York on Monday, June 24, to plan a fund-raising effort. One of the functions of the LCCR proposed at the White House was that it would act as a liaison between the government and the bar. Despite President Kennedy's association with the call for a Lawyers' Committee on Civil Rights, its real patron was Robert Kennedy, in the sense that he initiated the White House Conference of Lawyers and his department was at the center of civil rights policy for the Administration. As a result, Oberdorfer's office at Justice was designated as the committee's point of contact within the Administration. Shestack agreed to handle the day-to-day business of the committee.

Shestack was to act as liaison between Tweed and Oberdorfer for the month of July while Bernard Segal was attending a European Conference. Shestack assumed the responsibility for such essential details as establishing bank accounts and seeing to the purchase of committee stationery, as well as the more important details of getting out press releases, fund-raising letters, correspondence with prospective members, meeting arrangements, and the like. He juggled all this while arguing a large communications case for his firm in the summer of 1963. He wrote to Segal, "Various calls have been coming in asking for information about the Committee and in some cases, making suggestions. . . . Setting up the file, getting the paper work in order, etc., etc. has taken a tremendous amount of time."[21] Communication with the White House guests was very im-

---

19. There is no written record of the initial organization of the Lawyers' Committee. This account is taken from oral interviews with the former U.S. Assistant Attorney General for Tax, Louis Oberdorfer; Gerald Shestack; and Lloyd Cutler. At the time of this writing, Harrison Tweed was long deceased and Bernard Segal, although still alive, was too frail to be interviewed. Segal died in June 1997. The one point of discrepancy in the story is between Oberdorfer, who remembers going to Cutler's house for the meeting, and Cutler and Shestack, who remember meeting at Cutler's law offices.

20. Interview with Louis Oberdorfer.

21. Letter from Jerome J. Shestack to Bernard G. Segal, July 8, 1963. Shestack File,

portant. As one of the lawyers at the Conference on June 21 warned, "If the 244 lawyers don't hear anything for two to three weeks, many of them will have 'lost steam.' Indeed . . . I overheard a conversation between two prominent people to the effect that the entire conference wasn't really going to amount to anything at all."[22] In effect, Shestack was the administrative part of the LCCR. Without his dedication, it is doubtful whether the formation of the committee would have proceeded as quickly or efficiently. An executive director, David Stahl, a lawyer, was hired in January 1964 to run the LCCR's headquarters in Washington, D.C.

Harrison Tweed and Bernard Segal decided to adopt an organization system similar to the American Bar Association. A board of directors would comprise the governing authority. The board would appoint an Executive Committee to oversee specific projects. The principal activities of the committee were to be handled by standing committees whose chairmen were selected from the Executive Committee.[23] The membership was selective, not opened to all lawyers. It was carefully picked from the profession's elite corps.[24]

The by-laws of the LCCR say the Executive Committee "shall consist of between three and fifteen members, as determined by the Board."[25] "Members shall be elected by the Board of Directors." The directors of the committee are "to number not less than three nor more than fifty."[26]

Executive Committee members were board members as well. As for the qualifications for membership, "the only persons who shall be eligible for

---

LCCR. Shestack makes mention that Lou Oberdorfer called that day and "would like to get a member of the committee to work with the National Council of Churches. He suggested Bob Knight."

22. J. Boone Wilson, Letter to Bernard Segal, June 24, 1963 Records of the LCCR, Committee Formation File, Washington, D.C.

23. Report to the Members of the LCCR, March 1964, Harrison Tweed & Bernard G. Segal, co-chairmen, 5-7. Six standing committees were established. They were responsible to the officers and the board of directors.

24. Records of the LCCR, Board of Directors File, Letters. This file reveals that names of appropriate candidates for the committee were asked for by the co-chairmen. From names submitted, and from personal acquaintances, the co-chairmen and a small group of committee members recruited leading members of the bar from as many of the major centers as possible. *Also see* Interview with Jerome Shestack: the "stature of the Board was a fundamental part of the Lawyers' Committee."

25. Records of the LCCR, By-Laws, Washington, D.C., Attached to Memorandum, Aug. 1, 1963, from Jerome J. Shestack to Bernard G. Segal, By-Laws of LCCR, Article 5, § 5.0 1 Committees; Article 4, § 4.0 1, Members Elections, and § 4.02, Qualifications for Membership.

26. *Id.*, Article 3, § 3.02.

membership in the corporation shall be those who subscribe to the purposes and policies of the corporation and whose election to membership, in the judgment of the Board of Directors, will advance those purposes and policies."[27] The board would act primarily through correspondence, with only infrequent meetings, in order to save time and money.[28]

The LCCR represented the leadership of the American legal profession, a very thin veneer of the bar. The co-chairmen paid a great deal of attention to choosing the Executive Committee. A nationally prominent, biracial, nonpartisan group of men were screened and selected to represent the professional stature and prestige of the LCCR.[29]

As the month of July wore on, the need for a support staff was becoming apparent. Requests for legal assistance, educational materials, and professional advice were coming in from around the country. The requests were handled on an ad hoc basis. Members of the LCCR who were known to have knowledge or contacts were put in touch with the problem areas. They handled it from there, either by themselves, within their law firms or by consultation with other LCCR members. Following are a few examples of the types of issues coming into the committee.

A committee member in Florida requested help with theater integration in Tampa. Another needed help with a potentially explosive situation in the schools outside of Philadelphia, while aid in finding black lawyers in the South was sought by some of the minority members of the committee. The Urban League wanted help with getting in to see someone in the board of education in Philadelphia. The committee also responded to misleading or incorrect articles about legal issues that appeared in the press. One such article was written by David Lawrence opposing the President's right to enforce court orders. The reply to the Lawrence article is illustrative of the general method of committee operation. In that case, Oberdorfer called Shestack with the suggestion that something should be done to answer the piece that appeared in the *New York Herald Tribune* on July 15, 1963. Shestack contacted

---

27. *Id.* § 4.01.
28. Harrison Tweed & Bernard G. Segal to Bruce Bromley, Letter, Aug. 1, 1963, Records of the LCCR, Board of Directors File, Washington, D.C.
29. The original Executive Committee consisted of two minority members, William T. Coleman, Jr., of Philadelphia and William R. Ming of Chicago. There were no women. And the rest were white males from New York: Harrison Tweed, Bruce Bromley, former Attorney General William P. Rogers, and Judge Samuel Roseman; Bernard G. Segal from Philadelphia; Cecil E. Burney from Corpus Christi, Texas; James C. Dezendorf from California; Dean John Wade of Vanderbilt Law School in Tennessee: and William L. Marbury of Baltimore, Maryland.

the dean of the Vanderbilt Law School, John Wade, who was busy. Wade volunteered to ask a former professor of constitutional law at Columbia University, Elliot Cheatham. But time was essential, and Shestack called the dean of Catholic Law School, Vernon X. Miller, who agreed to reply to Lawrence's article.[30] Shestack and his office staff were bearing a good part of the work burden: "We have kept one or two secretaries busy full time. Consideration should be given to this problem."[31]

Relations with the Civil Rights Movement

In the summer of 1963, the purposes and policies of the LCCR were uncertain. The presidential charge to the White House Conference was to engage the bar in the mediation of the civil rights problems in the South. No understanding that the bar would engage in legal activity to forward the goals of the civil rights movement came from the meeting, nor was there any hint of such a proposal, which would have splintered the fragile coalition before it could accomplish anything. In an effort to respect the foundation of the LCCR, the co-chairmen were careful not to associate the new organization too closely with the goals of the civil rights movement and of the black community. Two incidents in the committee's first weeks illustrate this point.

After the White House meeting on June 21, Harrison Tweed and Bernard Segal were contacted by Roy Wilkins, the executive director of the NAACP, and invited "to a conference of civil rights leaders in New York on July 2." On the same day that the LCCR was created at the White House, black leaders in New York announced plans for a massive demonstration in Washington later that summer. The July 2 meeting was a planning and information meeting for the civil rights community. The co-chairmen were invited to discuss a role in the demonstration. At a committee board meeting, the Wilkins invitation was discussed. The record of that meeting states, "We heard that plans for a march on Washington re-Civil Rights legislation might be on the agenda. It was decided that HT and JJS (for BGS) would appear to make contact with Wilkins and leave. (This was done)." The LCCR did not officially take part in the

---

30. Shestack to Tweed, Memorandum, Civil Rights, July 17, 1963. Records of the LCCR, 1963 File, Washington, D.C.

31. Letter, July 1, 1963, Jerome J. Shestack, Memorandum to Harrison Tweed and Bernard G. Segal, re: LCCR, July 19, 1963, Records of the LCCR, 1963 File, Washington, D.C., at 7: "Executive Director: 1. A staff director is obviously needed. That problem awaits Segal's return. Names suggested for staff personnel are George Schermer . . . Pauli Murray . . . Lois Forer. . . . 2. Another idea is to borrow a young law professor on a year's leave of absence. . . . 3. Should the Executive Director be a lawyer?"

March on Washington. A future co-chairman, John Douglas, who was assistant attorney general at the time, coordinated the security for the demonstration and was the government's liaison with the leaders of the march.[32]

The committee faced another interesting question at one of its first board meetings in July. "Should the LCCR set an example and appoint a Negro vice-chairman?" The records of the meeting reveal that Harrison Tweed was in favor of the idea. A number of prominent candidates were suggested. However, Segal believed that it would make the administration of the committee "cumbersome." Others objected on the grounds that such an appointment would appear "too studied." Two of the candidates, William T. Coleman, Jr. and William R. Ming, were subsequently appointed to the Executive Committee.[33]

Financing the Committee

In its first few weeks of existence, the expenses incurred by the LCCR were absorbed by Harrison Tweed, Bernard Segal, and the small group of other volunteers and their law firms. As the requests for assistance grew, the financial needs became greater as well.

Harrison Tweed proved to be an enthusiastic fund-raiser. In the first part of July, he began soliciting $10,000 from 10 law firms.[34] Using the "old boy network," he successfully solicited donations from the largest Wall Street law firms. The requests were made personally to his friends and colleagues who were senior partners in the firms.[35] By the first of August, $4,000 had been

---

32. Interview with John Douglas, former Assistant U.S. Attorney General, Civil Division, March 2, 1995.

33. Jerome J. Shestack, Memorandum to Harrison Tweed and Bernard G. Segal, July 19, 1963, at 8. Suggested names were: "William Coleman of Philadelphia; Assistant Attorney General of California (Williams?); William Ming of Chicago, and James Nabritt, President of Howard University."

34. Minutes of Meeting of July 2, 1963, Present: Harrison Tweed and Jerome J. Shestack (for Bernard G. Segal) and Louis F. Oberdorfer and Ed Smith of the Department of Justice. Records of the LCCR, Washington, D.C.

35. Letter to Morris Abram, Aug. 6, 1963, from Harrison Tweed: "At the meeting in Philadelphia on July 24th it was agreed that we would try to get $1,000 from each of the following New York law firms, listed below with the contact partner: Cravath, Bromley; Shearman & Sterling, Knight; Sullivan & Cromwell, Dean; White & Case, Marden; Breed Abbott, Wm. Breed Jr.; Cahill Gorder, Cahill; Debevoise Plimpton, Debevoise; Dewey Ballantine, Laporte; Milbank Tweed, Tweed; Simpson Thacher, Seymour; Willkie Farr, Gallagher; Winthrop Stimson, Chanler; Chadbourne Parke; Cleary Gottlieb, Cleary; Lord, Day & Lord, Brownell and Loeb; Paul, Weiss, Garrison; Proskauer, Rose, Boetz; Roseman, Colin, Roseman; Donovan, Leisure, Leisure; Kelley, Drye, Drye. The plan is that I am to start by getting the following seven lawyers to get

received. It was felt, however, that fund-raising could not "go forward full steam" without the committee's incorporation in the District of Columbia and the securing of tax-exempt status from the Internal Revenue Service, which Oberdorfer was working on.[36]

Purposes and Policies

As the following account will show, the founders of the LCCR foresaw a discrete legal function for the new committee, distinct from the existing legal aid facilities of the American Bar Association and outside the original suggestions presented in the White House by President Kennedy. At first, this objective was vague and largely undefined, but within a short period of time the legal services function, rather than the proposed educational or the liaison with the government role of the committee, began to assume primary importance. The transition of the purpose of the LCCR took place in the context of increasing racial violence in the South, which was beginning to show signs of spreading to other areas of the country. The committee's response was gradual, nonpartisan, and conventional, to uphold the "rule of law." Changes in its original function, to involve the local bar in the defense of the legitimately aggrieved, happened only after it became clear that it was a failure. This approach accounts for the LCCR's continued acceptance by its diverse membership as well as its longevity.

Louis Oberdorfer drafted a letter of appreciation from the Administration that was signed by Robert Kennedy. It went out to the 244 lawyers one week after the East Room meeting, on June 28, 1963, asking them "to keep in touch with the LCCR which Messrs. Harrison Tweed and Bernard G. Segal undertook to lead at the President's request." In it, the President's recommendations for "affirmative action" were reiterated and each lawyer was invited to

---

$1,000 from his firm and $1,000 from two other firms. That will cover the full 21 firms, with something to spare because Sullivan and Cromwell and Milbank Tweed are already signed up. The seven are: Bromley, Dean, Seymour, Laporte, Marden, Cahill, Brownell or Loeb. It was also agreed that a little later on the following firms would be asked for $500: Cadwalader, Wickersham; Kay, Scholer; Strasser, Spiegelberg; Coudert Bros.; Curtis, Mallet-Prevost; Davies, Hardy; Fish, Richardon; Haight, Gardner; Hawkins, Delafield; Kirlin, Campbell; Mudge, Stern; Pennie, Edmonds; Stroock, Stroock; Weil, Gotshal; Webster, Sheffield; Brennan, London & Buttenwieser."

36. Bernard G. Segal to Harrison Tweed, Memorandum, July 26, 1963, Records of the LCCR, Washington, D.C.

communicate directly with the Attorney General "about any significant developments or problems."[37] The lawyers were told they could contact the Attorney General through Oberdorfer's office at the Justice Department.[38]

The letter was great public relations for the new committee. Not only did it keep the issue current in the minds of the proposed membership, but it was good balm for the ego. No matter how a person felt about civil rights and the Kennedys, to be called on to advise Washington during a national crisis as a confidant of an Attorney General of the United States was flattering. More important, it furthered the issue of membership. The Attorney General's letter implied cohesion and continuity among the 244 lawyers and it kept the door opened for follow-up contact by the co-chairmen.

The letter reflects maturing ideas about the role of the LCCR. It reiterates the President's original recommendations, which we have seen were generated at Justice by Oberdorfer. On June 21, the ideas that John Kennedy offered the group were perfectly in keeping with the conventional Legal Aid efforts of the organized bar and the ABA. The President asked the lawyers "to insure that legal aid groups . . . provide legal counsel for all." The Attorney General's letter changed the emphasis from an institutional response to an individual responsibility by calling on lawyers to meet the legal needs of the poor both "individually and as a group." The letter recommended that each lawyer "make sure that legal aid is available to all who need it on a nondiscriminatory basis."

---

37. Robert F. Kennedy, Attorney General of the United States, Letter to Lloyd N. Cutler, June 28, 1963, Records of the LCCR, Committee File, 1963, Washington, D.C.: "We sincerely believe that great good can come from your taking affirmative action now along the lines the President indicated. As he stated, we hope that those at the meeting can, individually and as a group . . . ." The eight recommendations were: (1) Initiate, help organize, and participate in local biracial committees; (2) volunteer professional services to other civil (e.g., religious, business, labor) organizations facing up to the problems at the local level; (3) eliminate any form of racial discrimination in your state and local bar association membership and activities; (4) make sure that legal aid is available to all who need it on a nondiscriminatory basis; (5) work with local government officials to eliminate unconstitutional laws and municipal and police practices, and to develop any needed affirmative legislation or programs; (6) speak out publicly to urge respect for the judiciary and the legal process; (7) speak out publicly to refute irresponsible and erroneous legal commentary by newspaper columnists and others having the ear of the public; (8) concern yourself publicly with the adequacy of local educational and recreational facilities, and particularly engage yourself this summer in efforts to combat school dropouts next autumn.

38. *Id.* Oberdorfer did not join the LCCR officially until after he resigned from the Justice Department.

At first glance, this appeared to be a small change, a nuance. But on reflection, it is the essential difference between the approach of the LCCR and the conventional system. Local, state, and national bar associations gave lip service to the institution's duty to advocate for all. In practice, however, lawyers in private practice had shifted that responsibility to the bar. Because the institutionalized bar had failed to meet that duty, those summoned to the White House recognized the necessity of the presidential call for intervention. To note its appearance in the Attorney General's letter does not suggest that Oberdorfer and the others harbored a well-defined plan in July of 1963 to turn the LCCR into a proactive legal organization. Judging by the White House suggestions for intervention, the founders of the committee held moderate views about the private lawyer's responsibility vis-á-vis the black civil rights movement. The recommendations put forward by the White House and the Department of Justice were much more in keeping with the views expressed by the ABA than with more liberal organizations such as the National Lawyers' Guild. The shift in emphasis to individual responsibility marks the beginning of a process of exploration about what the committee might do if individual lawyers and law firms could be mobilized—by no means a sure thing in 1963.

Bernard Segal's thinking about the functions of the new committee are reflected in statements he made to the press as the White House Conference ended on June 21. The committee would "act as a clearing house for lawyers and citizens with civil rights problems, and as a permanent liaison between the legal community and the White House." Its "purposes will be 'corollary and supplemental' to the American Bar Association and the state and local bars on civil rights matters." One of its functions would be to "keep the public informed on the law when constitutional controversy arises."[39]

Soon after the White House Conference, in the July issue of the *ABA Bar News*, an explanation of the functions of the LCCR was published by the ABA for its members. According to the article, "The Lawyers' Committee will function as a liaison organization between the government and the legal profession. It is expected to function under an executive committee small enough to act quickly in response to new developments on the civil rights front. It will not act in any situation where the American Bar Association or other established bar groups are authorized to act. It will function . . . as a clearing house for the ideas of lawyers and serve as an information agency for the American public, which becomes confused by all the by-play on civil rights issues."[40]

---

39. Joseph C. Goulden, *Defend Judges on Bias Rulings, Lawyers Urged,* THE PHILADEL-PHIA INQUIRER, June 23, 1963, at A-1.

40. *The ABA House Action on Civil Rights Report,* AM. BAR NEWS, July 4, 1963, at 4.

On July 1, 1963, just three days after the Attorney General's letter went out, another letter was sent to the same 244 lawyers. This time it went out under the masthead of the LCCR. The letter outlined the proposed functions of the committee and asked for contributions from the "larger firms in the major cities of the country." In this letter, the co-chairmen enlarged the committee's contemplated scope. First, it was intended to be a liaison between the government and the profession, and it would be the "central agency for the profession."

The co-chairmen then introduced the idea that the LCCR would function as a new type of legal services group, national in scope. In that capacity, the committee would "help local lawyers find lawyers 'outside' the community willing to help in civil rights cases; to obtain counsel for any individual or group unable to do so."

The committee would also provide leadership in forming biracial committees, mediation, and public education about legal and judicial problems. According to the letter, the purpose of the LCCR was "to marshal action by the lawyers of the nation wherever this can be helpful in resolving disputes and relieving tensions." "With your aid," the co-chairmen wrote, "we look forward to activities and achievements which will be of service to the Nation in resolving some of the difficult problems which face us. In this way, we hope to demonstrate the willingness and the ability of the legal profession to serve the public interest."[41]

A "blue book" was begun.[42] Its purpose was to refine the goals stated in the July 1 letter. The blue book was "what might be called a bible, for adoption and a certain amount of distribution by the LCCR." As Shestack wrote to Segal about the section entitled "Objectives of the Committee and the Procedures to Attain Them," "We must somehow state more comprehensively and persuasively and thoroughly than we have as yet, what it is that we are going to do and how we are going to try to get it done. Perhaps the greatest value of this will be that out of it should come a fairly definite set of suggestions and directions to bar associations, state and local, as to what they can do and how to do it."[43]

---

41. Harrison Tweed and Bernard G. Segal, Letter, To the lawyers invited by President Kennedy to the White House Conference on Friday, June 21st, July 1, 1963, Records of the LCCR, 1963 File, Washington, D.C. Also, Shestack to Bernard G. Segal, Memorandum, Aug. 1, 1963: "Mr. Tweed has now obtained contributions from: Dewey firm $1,000; Roseman firm, $ 1,000; Sullivan & Cromwell firm, $1,000; and, Milbank, Tweed firm, $1,000.

42. Jerome J. Shestack, Memorandum re. Blue Book, August 29, 1963, Shestack File, Records of the LCCR, Washington, D.C., at 6.

43. *Id.* at 7-8.

In the draft for the blue book the co-chairmen wrote, "The reason for the creation of the committee was to make use of the talents of the legal profession, and since its membership consists exclusively of lawyers, it follows that the work to be undertaken is that for which lawyers are especially qualified by training, experience and development."[44]

The early LCCR was not envisioned as a legal organization whose function was to bring about advances in minority rights through litigation. This judgment comes from assessing the areas, in the original draft for the blue book, where the committee felt it could be effective. Five areas were chosen: legal advice, representation, conciliation, education of the public on the workings of the judicial process, and public leadership.[45] First and "conspicuous among them is the giving of professional advice on questions of law and legal procedures. This is generally referred to as the preventive side of the lawyers' work. There is abundant need for the giving and accepting of such advice in the present situation."

Second, "An even more conspicuous activity in the profession is the representation of parties to legal proceedings. The committee will try to find existing professional or other organizations willing and able to meet the need, but in any case in which this proves impossible, it will undertake the obligation."

"A third area of legal activity is less well recognized by the public but is always important . . . conciliation. The greatest hope for progress towards an end to the present conflict lies in the sort of accord which can be reached only through mutual understanding."

Fourth, "moving a little further from the area of strictly legal activity, there is the work which the lawyer does . . . to bring the public to a better understanding of the theory and operation of the judicial process. This calls for informed and expert oral and written refutation designed to educate the public to understand the principles involved in the administration of justice."

And finally, "One more demand made by professional standards lies in furnishing leadership in civic and educational and other public matters."[46] To carry out each of these goals, a subcommittee would be established and presided over by a member of the Executive Committee.

In light of the fact that within two years the LCCR would open a litigation office in Jackson, Mississippi, it is interesting to note that when it became necessary in the winter of 1963 to hire a full-time person to handle the affairs of the committee, Shestack questioned the need for hiring a lawyer.[47] If the

---

44. *Id.*
45. *Id.*
46. *Id.* at 3-5.
47. Shestack, *supra* note 31.

committee was not meant to be a litigation group, then a nonlawyer could perform the duties associated with a headquarters, as did a lay staff at the ABA, as well as a person with legal training.

The LCCR's First General Meeting

By August 1963, the LCCR counted 136 official members, not including Lou Oberdorfer, and other government lawyers like Assistant Attorney General for Civil Rights Burke Marshall, who felt they could not join while in government service.[48] Bylaws had been written[49] and five subcommittees created whose names and functions followed the "various areas of the committee's work" described above.[50] The process for applying for a tax-exempt status was on track.[51] Oberdorfer hoped that it would be granted by August for announcement at the ABA annual convention in Chicago when the LCCR planned to hold its first general meeting.

At the end of July 1963 when Bernie Segal returned from Europe, he decided that the committee should hold a Board of Directors meeting in conjunction with the annual convention of the American Bar Association in Chicago. Segal saw the chance for a public relations coup. Hundreds of lawyers attend the annual convention of the ABA, which is the most prestigious professional gathering in the country. The two-day meeting draws a broad cross-section of government and private lawyers and elected officials. Segal's plan was to introduce the LCCR to the profession at large.[52] Acceptance at the convention was yet another imprimatur for the LCCR. Ironically, decisions made at the August convention would help move the committee closer to becoming a civil rights litigation group.

---

48. *Id.* Also, Interview with Louis Oberdorfer.
49. Shestack, *supra* note 42, at 5-6: "Incorporation—We have discussed this back and forth and Mr. Tweed has consulted frequently with Lloyd Garrison. Mr. Tweed's man in Washington has prepared a draft of the articles. . . . There are a number of unanswered questions such as who are to be members, officers, directors, etc."
50. Harrison Tweed and Bernard G. Segal, Letter to the Members of the LCCR, July 18, 1963, Records of the LCCR, Washington, D.C.
51. Shestack, *supra* note 31, at 5: "The Tax Ruling—The request was prepared and Mr. Tweed and I met . . . with Mitchell Rogovin, Esquire, Assistant Commissioner of Internal Revenue. He made some suggestions and indicated we would obtain a favorable ruling as a charitable organization. (The decision was made not to seek a professional expense deduction.) The request was redrafted, reviewed and sent to Mr. Grindle of Mr. Tweed's firm and Rogovin in Washington. We should get the ruling shortly."
52. *Id.* at 13. The question of whether the LCCR would offer membership to those ABA members who apply during the convention was discussed.

Like any large organization, the program for the ABA annual meeting was set well in advance. It would be hard, if not impossible, to find space for a luncheon room and to get the board meeting on the official agenda. But Segal had worked closely with the Chicago headquarters of the ABA for many years and had friends who were able to arrange the last-minute inclusion of the committee's board meeting. Harrison Tweed, who was as well connected within the ABA as Segal, convinced the ABA staff to carry a story, which Tweed wrote, in the *ABA Journal* on the creation of the LCCR. Meanwhile, Bernard Segal persuaded them to publish another piece on the LCCR in the ABA newsletter that reached 5,000 to 6,000 members.[53]

In Chicago, in the Conrad Hilton Hotel on August 13, 1963, Deputy Attorney General Nicholas Katzenbach and 22 board members attended the first general meeting of the Board of Directors of the LCCR. Katzenbach brought with him President Kennedy's greetings. Katzenbach, now the number two lawyer at Justice, was not Segal's first choice. Robert Kennedy had been asked to address the LCCR Board. However, the Attorney General was unable to attend, and he sent Katzenbach in his stead. Katzenbach's attendance was a further signal to the bar of the Administration's support for the LCCR.

At the meeting, the co-chairmen announced that $12,000 in contributions had been accepted, and that the committee's Articles of Incorporation had been filed in the District of Columbia. Also, informal notification of the tax exemption had been received,[54] and the committee now had an office in Washington, D.C., thanks to Lloyd Cutler, who gave the committee housing in his law firm. The appointment of a 12-member, biracial Executive Committee was also announced.[55]

Further, it was resolved that the Executive Committee would act on behalf of the board of directors between meetings of the board. The decision was made to continue to pursue a tax exemption despite the fact that the committee would have to forgo lobbying for legislation. It was felt that an

---

53. *Id.* at 7.
54. Letter dated Nov. 15, 1963, from John W. Littleton, Director, Tax Rulings Division, U.S. Treasury Department, Internal Revenue Service, Washington, D.C., to LCCR, Records of the LCCR, Tax File, Washington, D.C. The LCCR received a 501(c)(3) of the Internal Revenue code of 1954 as a charitable organization.
55. Minutes of the Meeting of the Board of Directors of the LCCR held on Aug. 13, 1963, at the Conrad Hilton Hotel, Records of the LCCR, Board of Directors File, Washington, D.C., at 3. The Executive Committee consisted of Bruce Bromley, Cecil E. Burney, William T. Coleman, Jr., Lloyd N. Cutler, James C. Dezendorf, William L. Marbury, William R. Ming, William P. Rogers, Samuel I. Roseman, Bernard G. Segal, Harrison Tweed, and John Wade.

exemption would be the most desirable way to solicit funds and that it was the only way private foundation grants could be sought. The first committee volunteer in Mississippi, J. Robert Lunney, reported to the board on his experience, followed by a general discussion.

The August meeting was a defining moment in the evolution of the LCCR. During the discussion about the nature and scope of the committee's activities, William Ming of Chicago, one of the minority members of the board, returned to the subject of Mississippi and Robert Lunney's experiences. Ming pointed out the difficulty of obtaining lawyers in civil rights cases in that state. He opened Pandora's Box—that is, the question of how to best utilize the talents and resources of the LCCR. This led to the question of whether or not the local bar in Mississippi would provide counsel. The conclusion of the discussion was that the committee should supply counsel for groups such as the National Council of Churches, the group Lunney had represented, rather than to individuals. The board concluded that the LCCR should generally act in test cases only, and then in "none but cases falling within the committee's expressed objectives."

Another debate ensued about giving the LCCR's list of lawyers to the Inc. Fund and other civil rights litigation groups in Mississippi. This was a list of men and women who would be willing to act as counsel in civil rights controversies. The fact that many of these lawyers were white was considered by some at the meeting to be a problem. Would the white Mississippi lawyers have agreed to be on the LCCR list if they had been told that it might be given to the NAACP or other activist groups? Before reaching any conclusion, it was decided that Ming should contact the various civil rights groups to see if they wanted the committee's help. Further, a new subcommittee on liaison with civil rights groups was established. Ming took the floor again and suggested that the committee write legal briefs in cases where important principles were involved and where the lawyers handling the matter required help and reinforcement. Another minority board member, William Coleman, Jr., was appointed co-chair of a new subcommittee on research and briefs.[56]

This meeting was the first time since the White House that the lawyers had met as a group. It was a marker in the process of building a structure and purpose for the committee. A few months later, in a Report to the Membership, the committee's purposes and policies are succinctly outlined in the section that describes the order, and function, of the six standing committees.

1. *Committee on Cooperation With Bar Associations.* Cecil E. Burney, chairman. This committee will seek to: (1) stimulate local and state

---

56. *Id.*

Bar Associations to play an active role in their localities in working on civil rights problems; (2) encourage such associations to establish biracial committees which will formulate programs seeking solutions of civil rights problems, including the elimination of any discrimination in their own organizations; and (3) help local and state Bar Associations carry out their responsibility to see that all persons in civil rights controversies can obtain competent legal counsel and that lawyers are supported against unjust criticism or attack because of representation of unpopular clients or causes.

2. *Committee on Mediation and Conciliation.* Judge Samuel I. Roseman, chairman. This committee will seek to utilize the special skills of its members in negotiating appropriate solutions to civil rights controversies and to bring conflicting parties together in face to face discussions in which differences can be resolved in an atmosphere of understanding and cooperation.

3. *Committee on Representation and Advice.* Judge Bruce Bromley, chairman. This committee will seek to encourage local individual lawyers to help in civil rights trials and appeals in those states where assistance is needed and requested. As a general proposition, this committee will not undertake to duplicate or supplement the work which other experienced groups are now doing competently in providing counsel. In important test cases, the committee will try to enlist the help and participation on a volunteer basis of outstanding lawyers of prestige and competence.

4. *Committee on Research and Briefing.* William T. Coleman, Jr. and John W. Barnum, co-chairmen. This committee will provide research and briefing help for cases selected by the LCCR for active support and will also study important legal problems common to pending or potential controversies in this area. This committee will also provide legal research for other of the standing committees as may be required.

5. *Committee on Relations with Other Organizations.* Morris B. Abram, chairman. There are many other organizations concerned with civil rights problems. The Standing Committee will establish liaison with such groups, inform them of the LCCR's objectives in securing adherence to the rule of law and in assuring equal rights to all citizens, and render professional advice where appropriate.

6. *Committee on Public Information.* Vernon X. Miller, chairman. This committee will urge respect for the judiciary and adherence to the rule of law by all citizens, will speak out to refute irresponsible legal

commentary in this field and seek to further public understanding of the judicial and legal processes in civil rights controversies.[57]

Civil Rights Mediation

Individual members did offer their services as mediators in a number of racial disturbances. For example, Bernard Segal volunteered to handle the negotiations between the Negro community and the state of Pennsylvania over conditions in the schools in Foxcroft, Pennsylvania, a suburb of Philadelphia. As a result of prompt action, the committee was credited with having helped avert serious violence. The NAACP acknowledged Segal's influence in the settlement of the problem. "Without a doubt, it was your influence and intervention which brought Walter Alessandroni, Attorney General of Pennsylvania, into the crucial situation in Foxcroft, Pennsylvania. We who were in the Bakers' house that night might not have lived to tell the story if it weren't for your interest and immediate help."[58] A few weeks later the small town of Cambridge, Maryland, erupted in racial violence. The LCCR board member William Marbury played a behind-the-scenes role to help bring the two sides together. "In these activities the committee eschews publicity, preferring to remain in the background wherever possible and leaving public expressions to the state and local bar associations, or the individual lawyers acting in the particular case."

The co-chairmen conjectured, "As the committee becomes better known, it is expected that its members will be called upon with increasing frequency to exercise leadership in mediating and resolving civil rights controversies."[59] In theory, this was how the committee should work on a local level. Undoubtedly, the example of these men, prominent leaders in their respective legal communities, inspired others. But the pace of events in the South was moving so rapidly that small advances, such as the incidents related above, even multiplied many times, were swallowed up in the turbulence of the times.

Civil Rights Litigation

During its formative period, June 1963 to June 1965, the LCCR took on just two civil rights litigation cases. In both cases, the committee's stated goal of

---

57. Minutes of the Meeting of the Board of Directors of the LCCR, Aug. 13, 1963, at the Conrad Hilton Hotel, LCCR Board of Directors File, Washington, D.C. at 5-7.
58. Letter dated March 19, 1964, from Philip H. Savage, Area Secretary, National Association for the Advancement of Colored People, to Bernard G. Segal.
59. Tweed & Segal, *supra* note 8, at 19-20. In Cambridge the committee called upon William Marbury, who practiced in Baltimore. Marbury's famous ancestor left his mark on legal history in *Marbury v. Madison*.

using the resources of the local bar to obtain competent counsel proved unrealistic. For the first time, the committee turned to pro bono counsel. The effectiveness of this approach was a blueprint for the future, an example of how to effectively utilize the formidable resources of the committee.

The first case was in Americus, Georgia, and the other was in Farmville, Virginia. The victory won in the Americus action, enjoining state officials from illegal criminal prosecutions, was a landmark decision and the first legal precedent won by the LCCR. The Farmville case involves many important legal issues, including such matters as the right of removal to a federal court; the exclusion of blacks and women from juries in Prince Edward County; the right to resist an unlawful order by police officials; the inability of the defendant to obtain local counsel; and other issues of significance. What follows is taken from a brief prepared for the Executive Committee.[60]

In September 1963, responsible sources, including the National Council of Churches, advised the committee that a racial conflict had developed in Americus, Georgia, in which a number of persons were being seriously deprived of civil rights, and asked the committee to investigate. The committee asked two of its members to visit Americus to report. As a result of that investigation, it was reported that the city of Americus, Sumter County, Georgia, was a segregated community that barred blacks from places of public accommodation, such as restaurants, hotels, and the local theater. This pattern of public discrimination extended even to publicly supported institutions, such as schools and the public library. Despite the fact that blacks constituted more than 50 percent of the population of Sumter County, no black ever sat on a grand or petit jury. The physical facilities of the county courthouse, such as seats, washrooms, and water fountains, were segregated. Less than 10 percent of blacks Sumter County of voting age were registered to vote.

About nine months prior to the investigation, a number of local citizens, both black and white, joined together in the Sumter County Movement. One of the major goals of this movement was the registration of additional black voters and the instruction of black citizens in their civil rights, including the right to vote. Beginning early in 1963, representatives of the Student Nonviolent Coordinating Committee (SNCC) and the Congress of Racial Equality (CORE) came to Americus to assist in the attainment of these objectives. Starting in March 1963, both SNCC representatives and local blacks were arrested and peaceful demonstrations protesting discrimination were broken up, often by the use of force. During the months of July and August 1963, over 300 people were arrested for the alleged violation of various state and local laws. To make the penalties more onerous, an

---

60. *Aelony v. Georgia* Report, Jan. 31, 1964.

ordinance was passed requiring persons arrested in these demonstrations to pay the cost of their board in the local jails and detention camps. In August 1963, several young men, black and white, were arrested and charged with violating the Georgia Insurrection Statute and the Unlawful Assembly Statute of the Code of Georgia. Since the insurrection law carried the penalty of death, the defendants were held without bail. The Insurrection Statute under which the defendants were imprisoned was clearly unconstitutional and had been so held by the Supreme Court of the United States in *Herndon v. Lowry* in 1937, the only reported case in which Georgia had sought to enforce it. The Unlawful Assembly law was also held unconstitutional, and the Supreme Court of the United States, in *Wright v. Georgia*, in 1963, reversed a conviction under that statute.

Morris B. Abram, one of the lawyers who was sent to investigate the case on behalf of the LCCR, was formally asked by the parents of one of the defendants, Zev Aelony, to represent him. Abram was a member of the Board of Directors of the of the LCCR, was formerly general counsel of the Peace Corps, and practiced in Georgia before joining the firm of Paul, Weiss, Rifkind, Wharton & Garrison in New York. Since the intervention of the LCCR had been requested, and since the case involved important legal principles, Abram was asked if he would undertake the representation and the committee would help him. Abram agreed and he worked with C.B. King, a black member of the Atlanta bar, who played an active role in defending persons in Americus.

On behalf of Aelony, a suit was instituted in the U.S. District Court of the Middle District of Georgia seeking to enjoin various officials of the state of Georgia from enforcing or executing the Insurrection and Unlawful Assembly provisions of the Code of Georgia on the ground that such statutes are unconstitutional. The complaint alleged that the officials had arrested and imprisoned Aelony and others under statutes they knew to be unconstitutional and that they had acted for the purpose of depriving those arrested of rights guaranteed under the Constitution. One of the officials admitted that prior to the commencement of the injunction action, he did not even intend to call Aelony's case to trial and that if Aelony would leave the state, he would consent to his admission to bail and release him from jail.

Hearings were held in early November 1963 before a three-judge court consisting of Judge Elbert P. Tuttle of the U.S. Court of Appeals for the Fifth Circuit, and Judges Lewis Morgan and J. Robert Elliott, both of the U.S. District Court in Georgia.

Judges Tuttle and Morgan (with Judge Elliott dissenting) held that the Georgia Insurrection and Unlawful Assembly statutes were unconstitutional and void, and they enjoined any further prosecution or detention by virtue of those statutes. Judges Tuttle and Morgan also found that proof had been adduced in support of the contention that the remaining prosecutions were being conducted with the intent, and for the purpose of, depriving the plaintiffs of rights guaranteed to them under the Constitution of the United States. However, since Georgia officials requested additional time to prepare and present proof in support of their contention that no such intent or purpose existed, the court did not restrain proceedings under the remaining Georgia statutes provided that the Georgia officials established bonds, which would not exceed $500 for each misdemeanor charged and $1,000 for each felony charged.

The second case was not as dramatic. Fred Wallace, a black graduate of Amherst College and a second-year law student at the Harvard Law School, spent the summer of 1963 working in the law office of two black lawyers in Richmond, Virginia. His duties brought him to Farmville, the county seat of Prince Edward County. The day Wallace was in Farmville, a Sunday, was one of racial unrest. There had been demonstrations in the town. Wallace went to the courthouse to deliver a message to the attorney for whom he was working and who was meeting with a judge on the third floor. As he was going from the second to the third floor, he was accosted by a police official who questioned his presence in the courthouse. From there, the stories differ widely. One thing is clear, that in due course he found himself on the floor of the sheriff's office, held by a number of police officers ostensibly in order to search him. In the melee that followed, while he was being searched, blood was drawn from the finger of one of the police officers, who also said he had been kicked. This was the basis for charging Wallace with the felony of wounding with the intent to maim, disfigure, disable, or kill. A person convicted of this felony is subject to imprisonment for not less than three nor more than twenty years. There were also misdemeanor charges.

The Lawyers' Committee was asked by Erwin N. Griswold, dean of the Harvard Law School and a member of the board of directors, to help Wallace obtain a white lawyer in Virginia to represent Wallace in association with his former employer, S.W. Tucker. After consultation with Dean F.D. Ribble, a member of the Lawyers' Committee, and after discussing the case with Tucker, the co-chairmen called upon George Edward Allen, Sr., a distinguished Virginia lawyer and a former president of the Richmond Bar Association, a man 70 years of age and of vast court experience. Allen readily undertook the representation without a fee. The Lawyers' Committee wrote briefs and did research for the case.[61]

The LCCR and Mississippi: 1963-1964

Racial incidents similar to those in Georgia and Virginia were playing out all

---

61. *Aelony v. Georgia* Report, Jan. 31, 1964. The summary of the *Aelony* case was taken from the Records of the LCCR, *Aelony v. Georgia,* 1963, File.

over the South. The summer of 1963 was long, hot, and filled with racial discontent. In the South, it began on the night of June 11 when Medgar Evers was assassinated in Jackson, Mississippi, and ended with the bombing in September of a black church in Birmingham, Alabama, that left six young girls dead. Evers' murder turned Mississippi into the epicenter of the black revolution and civil rights activity. The NAACP, for whom Evers worked, the Inc. Fund, the ACLU, SNCC, CORE, and Martin Luther King's SCLC all intensified the pressure for change in Mississippi.

The concentration on Mississippi by civil rights organizations and the magnification of black protest resulted in the arrests and unjust imprisonment of hundreds of activists who attempted to exercise their rights of free speech and association. Local lawyers refused to represent black activists. Despite the growing need for lawyers in Mississippi, the LCCR remained on the periphery of the struggle. Robert Lunney was the committee's sole representative in the state in 1963, and he went at the behest of the National Council of Churches.

In the winter of 1964, the travesty of justice that was taking place in Mississippi resulted in the call for another committee of lawyers to handle the criminal defense of the activists. The new group was called the Lawyers' Constitutional Defense Committee (LCDC). LCDC, whose creation will be discussed later, was formed by groups that shared a more liberal ideology than the LCCR. Though asked, the LCCR chose not to join the LCDC. It wasn't until the summer of 1964 that the LCCR chose to send 18 volunteers to Mississippi, and then for the sole purpose of assisting ministers from the National Council of Churches in the event that they ran into legal difficulties. By then, Mississippi was burning.

The LCCR's mission in 1963-1964 was to the bar. It was organized on power, not ideology. Its membership was chosen not on the basis of demonstrated commitment to civil rights but by virtue of professional stature and reputation. What united the committee was a respect for the rule of law and the right to be represented by lawyers. Segregation was legal in 1963-1964, and a decision by the leadership of the committee to join with organizations more radically oriented, or to dedicate the committee to the reform of the southern system of segregation, would have had the result of fracturing the young organization, diluting its power—a unique asset—to affect the bar. It was the passage of federal civil rights legislation in the spring of 1964 and the Voting Rights Act in August 1965 that cast the civil rights problems in the South in new terms. The legislation struck down the pillars of segregation and discrimination and gave lawyers, for the first time, the standing to challenge state-sponsored discrimination in the courtroom. After 1965, the LCCR was reacting to legally cognizable grievances, and its experiences with the refusal of the Mississippi bench and bar to uphold the law and defend black rights changed the committee.

Mississippi: 1964-1965

The struggle that brought the LCCR to Mississippi began with a young black activist from New York, Robert Moses, who joined the Southern Christian Leadership Conference (SCLC) in 1960. Moses believed that blacks had to win their right to vote. He began working toward that goal in Mississippi in 1961. With little more than the blessing of the SCLC (which was not active in Mississippi), Moses began to organize rural blacks to register to vote. Moses worked with volunteers from the Student Nonviolent Coordinating Committee (SNCC). Simultaneously but unconnected to Moses, Medgar Evers launched a sit-in drive in the state capital, Jackson, to win economic concessions. For two years, 1961-1963, the rural black voter registration campaigns and the sit-ins and mass demonstrations in Jackson raged on, by and large without help from the bench or bar, the federal government, or the traditional civil rights organizations.

The Bench and Bar in Mississippi

The bench and bar in Mississippi mirrored prevailing white prejudices. In June 1961, William Harold Cox, an unrepentant racist, was appointed to the Federal District Court of the Southern District of Mississippi. He was a known apologist for segregationist policy in Mississippi. His appointment was approved by the Senate Judiciary Committee, whose chairman was James Eastland, the senior U.S. senator from Mississippi.[62] Senator Eastland, a former classmate of Judge Cox, occupied a key position in the Senate. His cooperation was important to the Kennedy Administration. Cox was the first federal court nomination of the Kennedy Administration. His appointment to the district court was a disappointment to the civil rights movement. If any changes in voting registration practices in Mississippi would come through the legal system, they would have to be won in the courts. Judge Cox would be in a position to block change and did.[63]

Robert Ostrow, a committee volunteer lawyer who went to Mississippi in 1964, observed: "Mississippi is a wasteland of lost and troubled souls, white and black. Mississippi is not a part of the United States, and if she is to join the other 49 states in the Union, she must be rehabilitated and democratized in the same fashion that Germany and Japan were democratized—through

---

62. Bernard Segal was chairman of the ABA Committee on the Federal Judiciary when the Cox nomination was approved,
63. JOHN DITTMER, LOCAL PEOPLE: THE STRUGGLE FOR CIVIL RIGHTS IN MISSISSIPPI (Pantheon Books 1965). "When Judge Cox's name had been submitted to the American Bar Association's Standing Committee on the Federal Judiciary, he had received its highest recommendation—the 'exceptionally well qualified' rating."

use of an army of occupation. . . . There is no law in Mississippi. Federal and state judges are perpetrators of injustice and are co-conspirators with peace officers, the Ku Klux Klan, and White Citizens' Counsel hoodlums in the most monstrous conspiracy to deny human rights to any group of persons since Hitler's Germany."[64]

There were only three black Mississippians practicing law in the state in 1963.[65] "We have next to no lawyers to defend our rights in Mississippi," a black Mississippian complained to an LCCR volunteer. "There are no white lawyers and only three Negro lawyers that will handle civil rights cases. These Negro lawyers are just about totally overburdened. Out-of-state lawyers are generally barred from practicing, including the federal district courts. The present legal setup is inadequate."[66]

The bar in Mississippi was white, and, with the exception of a very few and very brave men—for example, Bill Higgs and Francis Stevens, who practiced in Jackson—white lawyers refused to take part in civil rights cases.[67]

The state bar association was opposed to "outside interference" in the struggle. Referring to the Justice Department's attempts to enforce federal court decisions in the South, the Mississippi State Bar declared that "it does not in any way approve of nor lend its support to the present unwarranted invasions of the reserved powers of the Several States of the United States of America . . . but on the contrary expresses its conviction that the present process of erosion of the Constitution of the United States constitutes a serious threat to the freedom of the individual citizens of this nation."[68]

Another volunteer, Jack Oppenheimer, a lawyer from New York who went to Mississippi in 1964, said, "The unwillingness of the white Missis-

---

64. Robert W. Ostrow to Berl I. Bernhard, Executive Director of the Lawyers' Committee for Civil Right Under Law, Oct. 30, 1964; Jackson, Mississippi File, Records of the LCCR, Washington, D.C.

65. DITTMER, *supra* note 63, at 81: "They were Carsie Hall and Jack Young . . . (and) Jess Brown," all three of whom practiced in Jackson, the state capital.

66. Robert Hunter Morley, Dictated Notes, March 3, 1964, from the personal file of J.J. Shestack, Philadelphia, Pennsylvania.

67. Interview with the Honorable James Robertson, U.S. District Court, former chief attorney of the Jackson, Mississippi, office of the Lawyers' Committee for Civil Rights, Sept. 18, 1996, Washington, D.C. *Also see* DITTMER, *supra* note 63, at 230, who names New Yorker William Kunstler as an early volunteer with SNCC. Jack Young, Jess Brown, and Carsie Hall had been receiving some aid from the NAACP Inc. Fund since 1961.

68. Statement of the Board of Bar Commissions of the Mississippi State Bar, June 19, 1963; Jackson, Mississippi File, 1963, Records of the LCCR, Washington, D.C.

sippi bar to furnish legal assistance to Negro citizens . . . explains the invasion of Mississippi by northern lawyers volunteering their services."[69]

The Voter Registration Campaigns

The heart of the Mississippi law that allowed whites to legally disenfranchise blacks was the "understanding clause" of the state constitution. This provision allows county registrars to determine who will be permitted to vote in Mississippi. Its most flagrant abuse was in the small town of Hattiesburg.

Hattiesburg was home to a "400-pound mountain of a man who was not a lawyer by profession"—Theron C. Lynd, who became registrar of voters in February 1959. The county had an adult voting age population of 30,000, of whom 25 percent were black. Less than 3 percent of the blacks had been certified eligible to vote in 1960, in contrast to 75 percent of the whites. For two years Moses and SNCC clashed with Lynd, but they failed to make any progress.

Shortly after the 1960 Voting Rights Act went into effect, the federal government began to investigate Lynd because of his policy of "personally and exclusively handling all Negro applications," because he said "the girls don't want to deal with them." The federal government sought to prove that "no blacks had been registered in the county during his term" nor had any blacks "even been permitted to attempt to register." Lynd could do what he wished in Hattiesburg because he had the protection of the courts. The Justice Department case came before Harold Cox. Judge Cox heard the case and demanded that the Justice Department produce written proof that blacks were denied the right to register. At the same time he refused to do anything to force Lynd to give the Justice Department the records that they requested. Lynd refused to hand over the required information. In February 1962, Judge Cox dismissed the case "for the production of records."[70]

The Justice Department succeeded in having a portion of the case that was before Judge Harold Cox consolidated with other voting cases, which was heard in New Orleans by the Fifth Circuit Court of Appeals. The court found for the Justice Department, which immediately charged Lynd with both "criminal and civil contempt of court."

A panel of the court of appeals convened, as a trial court, in Hattiesburg under Judges John R. Brown, John Minor Wisdom, and Griffin B. Bell in mid-September 1962. According to the government, Lynd continued to refuse registration to at least 19 blacks, one of whom was a schoolteacher who held two

69. Jack Oppenheimer, *The Abdication of the Southern Bar,* in SOUTHERN JUSTICE, Leon Friedman ed. (Pantheon Books 1965), at 128.

70. FRANK T. READ & LUCY S. McGOUGH, LET THEM BE JUDGED: THE JUDICIAL INTEGRATION OF THE DEEP SOUTH (Scarecrow Press, Inc. 1978) 293-95.

master's degrees. The court found Lynd in contempt and ordered him to register qualified black applicants.[71] Lynd continued to defy the federal court.

The National Council of Churches and Mississippi

After the appeals court decision that Lynd refused to honor, Robert Moses intensified the voting registration campaigns in Hattiesburg. The national attention that was created by both the white and black actions in Hattiesburg attracted out-of-state aid. People and money began flowing into Mississippi. One of the groups that came to the aid of Moses and the voter registration campaigns was the National Council of Churches.

Like the bar, the attitude of the churches in the United States was adjusting to the social demands for change.[72] A later study of the National Council of Churches chronicled its entrance into the struggle in Mississippi.

> During the summer and fall of 1963, the commission staff seemed to focus its attention increasingly on events taking place in Mississippi . . . . In early August 1963, the commission began to offer legal aid to embattled civil rights workers and their local supporters in Mississippi . . . . Seventeen civil rights protestors had been arrested for their activities and sent to the Mississippi state penitentiary at Parchman, known for its brutal treatment of prisoners, especially blacks. By this time the commission had on its staff a full-time lawyer who was also a recent graduate of Union Theological Seminary. Because in 1963 there were literally no

---

71. *Id.* at 298-99.

72. JAMES F. FINDLAY, JR., CHURCH PEOPLE IN THE STRUGGLE: THE NATIONAL COUNCIL OF CHURCHES AND THE BLACK FREEDOM MOVEMENT, 1950-1970 (Oxford Univ. Press, 1993), at 34. On June 7, 1963, the General Board of the National Council of Churches (NCC) announced the formation of a new Commission on Religion and Race, designed to allow the NCC to become involved in the "day-to-day" racial struggle, and to establish "the churches' presence in Washington as well as in the hinterlands." The new committee was given a budget more than 10 times the previous budget for race relations, "$175,000 for the rest of 1963, and $275,000 for 1964." The chairman of the NCC, J. Irwin Miller, had been selected by President Kennedy "to chair" and to "oversee efforts at follow-up" from another White House conference, the White House Conference for Religious Leaders, which was held on June 17, 1963, in the East Room, just four days before Kennedy met with the lawyers. As a result of the philosophical commitment behind the Commission on Religion and Race and Miller's assignment from the President, the NCC began to lobby for passage of the civil rights bill and to aid the black movement in the South.

local lawyers in Mississippi willing to take civil rights-related cases, Jack Pratt was sent there by the commission to help.[73]

Clarksdale, Mississippi

It was at the request of Jack Pratt that the LCCR first became involved in Mississippi. Jack Pratt had just returned from Itta Bena, Mississippi, where the National Council of Churches had posted bond for a group of demonstrators, most of them in their teens. They were arrested when 45 people marched into Itta Bena to protest the fire-bombing of their church to the town marshal. A voter registration meeting had been held in the church.[74] A prohibitively high bond was set, which the blacks could not pay. The group, including the teens, were sent to Parchman Prison. Two months later, in the summer of 1963, they were finally freed when Pratt paid the fines. Jack Pratt had seen the refusal of the local bar to become involved in the black struggle.

When Pratt decided to take a group of ministers to Clarksdale, Mississippi, to join the voting registration demonstrations, he knew that if the ministers were arrested while aiding demonstrators in voting registration marches, the local Mississippi bar would refuse to defend them. It was suggested to Pratt that he contact the LCCR for assistance. He talked to Oberdorfer. The situation in Mississippi was of particular concern to Louis Oberdorfer, a close advisor to the Attorney General, and Burke Marshall, the Assistant Attorney General for Civil Rights.[75] Oberdorfer suggested that Pratt contact Robert Knight, the partner who represented the National Council of Churches in the New York law firm of Shearman & Sterling. Knight, a Republican who had served in the Eisenhower Administration, had attended the White House Lawyers' Conference on June 21. Pratt asked Knight for his help in finding someone who would be willing to go with the delegation to Mississippi. Knight discussed the situation with Harrison Tweed.[76]

---

73. *Id.* at 78-79.

74. Letter dated Feb. 12, 1964, from John M. Pratt, Counsel to the Commission, National Council of Churches, to Robert F. Kennedy, Attorney General of the United States. The Federal Bureau of Investigation, National Council of Churches File, 100-50869, FBI Reading Room File, Washington, D.C.

75. Interview with the Honorable Louis F. Oberdorfer, U.S. District Court, June 1994, McLean, Va. Judge Oberdorfer recollected his early-morning walks with then-Assistant Attorney General Marshall when they served at the Justice Department. The men would arrive early and walk the grounds to have some private time. Oberdorfer, a Southerner from Birmingham, Alabama, felt he "spoke the language" of the Southerner and had an understanding of the southern mentality that could not possibly be appreciated by those who did not grow up in the South.

76. The account of the Pratt-Knight meeting is from an interview with Robert Knight.

It was decided that Shearman & Sterling would send a young associate, J. Robert Lunney, to Mississippi, at the firm's expense, to assist the National Council of Churches.[77] Robert Lunney went to Mississippi as a representative of the legal establishment. He came from a major New York law firm. His role with the National Council of Churches, a legitimate client of his firm, was a conventional one, legal counsel.[78] He did not represent any social agenda for change. For the few days while Lunney was in Clarksdale, he had a number of occasions to represent members of the ministers' group in judicial proceedings. When he reported on his experiences in Mississippi to the first general board meeting, he told the board, among other things, that the members of the Mississippi bar treated him "cordially."[79] He remembers that "I treated the judges and lawyers with respect, and they treated me the same." Lunney thought that the white lawyers in Mississippi cooperated with him because he wasn't "an agitator." He felt that there were moderate lawyers in Mississippi who would cooperate with LCCR lawyers. He also reported on the need for counsel.[80] The board took encouragement from Lunney's experiences with the local bar. An attitude of cooperation was in keeping with their belief that the local bar would respond to legitimate requests for help.

Hattiesburg, Mississippi

In Hattiesburg, Lynd was still refusing to register qualified blacks. Lawrence Guyot, a young SNCC volunteer and future committee staff member, was coordinating an effort to find applicants to present themselves for registration in a large group at Hattiesburg's courthouse. The group registration day was to be January 22, 1964, Hattiesburg's Freedom Day. As the day approached, civil rights activists from around the country gathered in Hattiesburg to support the applicants and marchers who would accompany them to the courthouse. Despite the federal order to Lynd, everyone expected that it would prove to be a violent confrontation. In anticipation of his arrest in Hattiesburg, Robert Moses sent a telegram to the Attorney General:

> Tomorrow morning, hundreds of Hattiesburg's citizens will attempt to register to vote. We request the presence of federal marshals to protect them. We also request that local police interfering with constitutional rights be arrested and prosecuted.[81]

---

77. Interview with Robert Knight, Shearman & Sterling, New York, Feb. 15, 1993.
78. Interview with J. Robert Lunney, White Plains, New York, Oct. 1994, former Lawyers' Committee Volunteer in Mississippi, 1963 and 1964.
79. Minutes of the Board, Aug. 13, 1963, at 5.
80. *Id.*
81. Howard Zinn, SNCC: The New Abolitionists (Beacon Press 1964), at 104.

Jack Pratt had organized a large delegation of clergymen from the National Council of churches to fly into Hattiesburg for the demonstration. Again Pratt was joined by Robert Lunney from the LCCR. The night before Freedom Day, Pratt told an audience at a church rally that the National Council of Churches is "here to prod the Justice Department a bit."[82] Lunney met with some of the local lawyers "just to chat," but they offered no assistance.[83]

True to expectations of the civil rights activists, the Hattiesburg police arrested Robert Moses and other demonstrators outside of the county courthouse. Jack Pratt immediately contacted the Attorney General. He wrote, "On January 23, 1964, Robert Moses was convicted in the Justice of the Peace Court of the City of Hattiesburg on charges of obstructing a sidewalk and refusal to obey the lawful command of an officer."[84] Historian Howard Zinn counts the Hattiesburg Freedom Day as a tremendous success, because "a few Negroes" out of more than 100 who came to register completed the process.[85]

Along with Robert Moses, Oscar Chase, a recent graduate of Yale and a SNCC volunteer, was arrested and beaten to unconsciousness. Pratt wrote to the Department of Justice that "Mr. Chase has alleged that the beating was done in the presence and with the encouragement of the jailer and two or three members of the Hattiesburg Police Department." Chase and Moses were prosecuted by the Hattiesburg authorities and Pratt and "Robert Lunney of the LCCR . . . defended" them.[86]

The events in Hattiesburg signaled an alignment of National Council of Churches with the goals of Robert Moses and SNCC. This meant "direct involvement in SNCC's efforts to nurture grassroots, community-based programs." In January and February 1964, Robert Lunney and the SNCC people who were in Hattiesburg were told about SNCC's idea to recruit workers from northern colleges for a summer project. The project was conceived "in part to attract widespread public and media attention to the terrible racial situation in Mississippi."[87] Lunney informed the Executive Committee of the

---

82. *Id.* at 105.
83. Interview, *supra* note 78.
84. Pratt, *supra* note 74, at 2
85. ZINN, *supra* note 81, at 105, 117.
86. ZINN, supra note 81, at 117; and Pratt, *supra* note 74, at 3.
87. Findlay, *supra* note 72, at 7. Also DOUG MCADAM, FREEDOM SUMMER. (Oxford Univ. Press 1988) at 77-78. Voter registration was the cornerstone of the Summer Project but was not necessarily the most important part of the project. It was the success of the Freedom Vote Campaign in the fall of 1963 that led SNCC and COFO to approve Bob Moses's plan for an even more ambitious political project the following summer. As long as the state Democratic party was effectively closed to blacks, it was unclear how beneficial the simple registration of voters would be. To address this problem,

LCCR about SNCC's summer project, which today is referred to as "Freedom Summer." The LCCR was asked to send volunteers.[88]

A Request for Help in the South from the Attorney General

The need for lawyers to defend the criminal charges lodged against the civil rights protestors in the South was tremendous. Attorney General Kennedy approached the committee for help, particularly in Mississippi and Alabama. At a meeting at the Justice Department in October, Kennedy said "that perhaps the most discouraging aspect of the problem (in the South) was the failure of persons in positions of leadership to speak up." He expressed the view that no solution would be found until "the underlying difficulties of employment and education" could be solved. It was "not sufficient to provide attorneys for particular cases" to the Attorney General, but "more had to be done to change the climate in the South."

Kennedy's assistant, Burke Marshall, pointed out that, "in opposing the extension of civil rights for the Negro, many local officers in the South had corrupted the legal procedure. . . . Everyone involved, the judge, jury, local officers, and townspeople," were involved in the legal sham. Marshall stressed "the debilitating effect upon respect for law caused by such corrupt use of the legal process."[89]

The Attorney General had the support of the co-chairmen, Louis Oberdorfer, and a number of leading members of the Executive Committee. But as the minutes for the Executive Committee meeting on October 21, 1963 show, "One basic unresolved point was the extent to which the Committee should provide counsel for civil rights cases. Members of the Committee expressed differing viewpoints."[90] The committee was not ready to abandon the belief that the local lawyers in the South would respond.

SNCC spearheaded the establishment of the Mississippi Freedom Democratic Party (MFDP) at a meeting held in Jackson on April 26, 1964.

88. David Stahl, Minutes of the Meeting of the Board of Directors, LCCR, New York City, May 13, 1964: "The National Council of Churches has asked the Lawyers' Committee to provide a group of lawyers who would be available to render legal advice to ministers acting as counselors or chaplains to the many students expected in the South this summer, and where necessary to protect the rights of ministers or students in the courts. Under the guidance of the Committee on Representation and Advice, an attempt is being made to secure lawyers for this purpose."

89. Minutes of the Meeting of the Board of Directors of the LCCR, Washington, D.C., November 14, 1963, at 6-9.

90. Memorandum, To the Members of the Executive Committee, unsigned and attached to Meeting of the Executive Committee at the Association of the Bar of the City of New York at 11:00 A.M., Oct. 21, 1963.

The Response of the LCCR

In January 1964, the LCCR began a project "to enlist the aid of state and local Bar Associations in emphasizing the application, to the civil rights area, of one of the most important canons of the legal profession: that no fear of public disfavor should restrain them from their duty to represent unpopular clients or causes, in accordance with the standards of their profession." In 1953, in 1962, and again in 1963, the American Bar Association called upon state and local bar associations to implement those principles. The committee's project was executed because "in many southern states Negroes cannot obtain white lawyers to represent them in civil rights controversies because a white lawyer who becomes involved in civil rights litigation representing Negroes faces loss of clients, impairment of social status, public criticism, and often threats to him and his family."

The committee planned to meet with state and local bar associations in the South, and those meetings would be handled by a southerner, Texan Cecil E. Burney, chairman of the Standing Committee on Cooperation with Bar Associations.[91]

A Request from the Attorney General to Join in Civil Rights Litigation

Meanwhile, the Attorney General wanted "to turn over" to the LCCR the "function that would be performed by the Department of Justice under Title III of the (as yet unpassed) Civil Rights Legislation."[92] Title III would give the Attorney General the right to sue for the desegregation of local and state public facilities, that is, parks, swimming pools, libraries, hospitals, etc. In a memo for the co-chairmen responding to the Attorney General's request, Shestack advised them that the committee should concentrate on the work with local bar organizations. He argued that the committee could not become a litigating organization in the South:

> For one thing, we do not have the money, second, we do not have the manpower, and third, we would be getting in antagonisms with

---

91. Harrison Tweed & Bernard G. Segal, co-chairmen, Report to the Members of the LCCR, Jan. 31, 1964, at 15-16, Board of Directors File, Records of the LCCR, Washington, D.C.

92. Title III of the Omnibus Civil Rights Act had to do with the desegregation of public facilities, that is, state or local government-owned parks, swimming pools, libraries, hospitals, etc. It would give the Attorney General the right to sue for their desegregation.

other groups who are presently handling such suits, and fourth, we would be getting antagonisms every time we turned down a case. Beyond that, our getting into a broad variety of cases, rather than special ones of great moment, does not advance the ultimate solution to the problem at all. The real attack on the problem seems to me to get southern lawyers into the frame of mind where they would be willing to handle these unpopular causes.[93]

Shestack thought the committee might be able to persuade southern bar associations to appoint panels of lawyers who would handle the civil rights cases. He argued that if southern lawyers were involved, it would change the climate with respect to handling unpopular causes and it would build a network of lawyers who would be sympathetic to the minority viewpoint in the civil rights controversies. "Since these civil rights cases take up time" and since many of the lawyers would be young and unable to afford the time, Shestack suggested that the committee apply for a grant to the Ford Foundation to pay the attorneys' fees. "Hence, what I contemplate is a situation whereby the LCCR would undertake the job of persuading the bar associations to go along with the plan, and the Ford Foundation would provide the financing." He believed that ground rules would have to be established, but that "the southern bar association might be willing to go along with cases involving school plans, voting rights, police brutality, excessive bail, and certain other of the more important categories"; however, they most likely would not agree to defend every demonstrator who was arrested.[94] Funding was not sought from the Ford Foundation, and the co-chairmen did not act upon Shestack's plan, nor the suggestion from the Attorney General.

A Request from Other Lawyers for Help in the South

There were other white lawyers willing and eager to go to Mississippi to work in the civil rights movement. Many of them went on their own as volunteers for SNCC and the other national groups. Searching for some structure, these lawyers rallied behind another legal organization, the Lawyers' Constitutional Defense Committee (LCDC), which was created during the winter of

---

93. J.J. Shestack to B.G. Segal, Memorandum, Oct. 29, 1963, Shestack File, Records of the LCCR, Washington, D.C.

94. *Id.* Shestack discussed his idea about Ford funding with Paul Yivisacker, "who was quite receptive to it . . . I discussed it with William Pincus, Esquire, of the Ford Foundation. Pincus was quite receptive to the idea . . . the key, of course, was our persuading some southern bar associations to go along with the idea."

1964. The LCDC was formed by a coalition of legal groups in New York to address more specifically the immediate consequences of the bar's failure in Mississippi. The LCDC was organized by Melvin Wolf of the American Civil Liberties Union.[95] It was the brainchild of a "coalition of the chief legal officers of several major New York based human rights organizations, including CORE, the American Civil Liberties Union, the NAACP Legal Defense Fund, the American Jewish Congress, and the National Council of Churches," and it became an outlet for younger, more liberal lawyers who wanted to become actively involved in litigation in the South.[96]

The LCDC was a civil rights organization whose members were united by an ideology and professional purpose that was not in character with the goals of the committee in 1964. The committee continued to see its role as nonpartisan, working within the bar to affect legal practices in the South. Because of the differences between the goals of the groups, the committee decided not to join the LCDC. But the pressure for some response from the committee to the problems with the administration of justice in the South, particularly in Mississippi, was mounting. At the LCCR Executive Committee meeting on March 25, 1964, the subject of joining the LCDC was discussed and a decision to meet with representatives of the Mississippi Bar was made:

> One of the functions of the LCCR . . . is to assist in obtaining legal representation of individuals who are unable to secure counsel to defend human and civil rights secured by law. . . . From time to time, the Executive Committee has discussed ways in which this purpose could be implemented in those communities where local counsel is generally unavailable. The matter was raised again at this meeting because other organizations are in the process of seeking volunteers for legal work in many southern areas this summer. Representatives of CORE, ACLU and other groups recently asked the LCCR to join in a combined effort to secure lawyers. In order to enable the Committee to gain a firsthand account of the problems in the area of legal representation, we invited to the meeting John McKee Pratt . . . and J. Robert Lunney. . . . Mr. Lunney's activities have been in behalf of the LCCR as well as the National Council of Churches. Mr. Lunney . . . stressed the importance of having counsel present in an advisory capacity as a moderating influence which can often prevent or, at least, reduce tension and conflict. . . . Mr. Pratt talked about the moral issue inherent in the failure of local

---

95. DITTMER, *supra* note 63, at 230.
96. FRANK R. PARKER, BLACK VOTES COUNT: POLITICAL EMPOWERMENT IN MISSISSIPPI AFTER 1965 (Univ. of North Carolina Press 1990), at 81.

lawyers to provide representation. . . . He asked the LCCR to recruit lawyers who would be willing to perform the same kind of services as Mr. Lunney. . . . Plans were made to set up a meeting with the Mississippi bar in the very near future, one of the objects of the meetings to be to seek local representatives for persons involved in civil rights controversies by the establishment of an assignment scheme or other arrangement to make lawyers available for this purpose.[97]

On April 2, 1964, the LCCR sent a representative to the meeting in New York to discuss the LCDC. The representative was not a member of the board or the Executive Committee, but staff. David Stahl, the executive director of the LCCR, attended for the LCCR. "Present at the meeting were: Melvin Wolf, general counsel of the ACLU; Carl Rachlin, general counsel for CORE; Jack Greenberg, director of the NAACP Legal Defense and Education Fund; Leo Pfeffer, American Jewish Congress; and Harry Fleishman, representing the American Jewish Committee."

Stahl was told that the planning group would adopt a two-part plan. First, they would disseminate a letter on behalf of the organizations that they represented to more than 1,000 northeastern lawyers and law firms asking for volunteers to spend part of the summer in southern communities to work directly with the various active civil rights organizations requesting legal assistance. The letter would be signed by, and on the stationery of, Robert J. Drinan, dean of the Boston College Law School. Second, they proposed to incorporate a nonprofit organization, to be called the Constitutional Rights Defense Fund, that would seek a tax exemption for the purpose of providing an agency to receive contributions to carry out the volunteer lawyer program.

Stahl reported to the co-chairmen, "In response to a query as to the role of the LCCR, I stated that while we also recognize the urgent need for having lawyers available this summer, we preferred not to join in the letter which Dean Drinan would sign nor in the formation of the new corporate organization. I indicated further that we planned to initiate a 'recruiting' drive of our own among New York, and possibly other, city law firms."[98] The committee had decided to

---

97. Meetings of the Executive Committee, LCCR, Washington, D.C., March 25, 1964. David Stahl, a professor of law at the University of Pittsburgh, was granted a leave of absence to work with the LCCR. He assumed the post in January 1964. Preceding Stahl, Jerome J. Shestack unofficially filled the role of executive director from June 1963 to December.

98. David Stahl to Co-Chairmen Cecil Burney, Lloyd Cutler, Cody Fowler, Jerome J. Shestack, Memorandum, April 6, 1964, Mississippi Meeting, Jackson, Mississippi File, Records of the LCCR, Washington, D.C.

take a two-pronged approach to Mississippi. It would sponsor a group of volunteers, recruited from the large law firms, to advise the National Council of Churches group working with Freedom Summer, and members of the board would meet with officers of the state bar of Mississippi to work out a plan for a joint effort between local lawyers and committee volunteers in the state. For the LCCR, David Stahl and his successor as executive director, Berl Bernhard, met with civil rights groups, while the co-chairmen and the board met with representatives of the state and local bars.

The LCCR was criticized by civil rights activists in Mississippi for its choices—that is, working closely with the Mississippi bar over affiliation with LCDC and other civil rights groups. It could be said that many of the early civil rights lawyers in Jackson, Mississippi, questioned the LCCR's commitment.[99] In Mississippi in the early 1960s, the LCCR was seen as "old line"—that is, an extension of the ABA—and many activists were dubious about the extent of the LCCR's dedication to minority rights.[100]

---

99. Records of the LCCR, Board of Directors File, Minutes, Meeting of the Board of Directors, Jan. 27, 1965. The minutes reflect a meeting held in Morris Abram's office between representatives of the Lawyers' Committee and the LCDC. At this meeting, Abram "urged that the two groups seek to formulate a joint program in Mississippi . . . Mr. Abram mentioned a conversation with Jack Greenberg who told him he would welcome the Lawyers' Committee's assumption of primary responsibility in Mississippi because of deficiencies in the effectiveness of the LCDC program in the past. . . . Mr. Abram reported that he had encountered a 'flareback' from LCDC as a result of these conversations. He found that the LCDC officers were dubious of the Lawyers' Committee's commitment to the substantive civil rights struggle. They entertained the fear that our lawyers' efforts would not be consistent with the thrust of our clients' activities."

100. Interview with Armand Derfner, former lawyer for the Lawyers' Constitutional Defense Committee in Jackson, Mississippi, and former staff member of the LCCR, Charleston, South Carolina, November 1996. It is from Derfner's recollections, in part, and from Morris Abram's comments in the following note that the author takes the above conclusions about the committee's standing in the early days of Jackson, Mississippi. Derfner relates a story whose point is to show that the Lawyers' Committee was not considered part of the inner circle of civil rights activists in Mississippi. Accompanying Al Bronstein, the head of the LCDC in 1966, to New Orleans, Derfner, who had left the Washington law firm of Covington Burling to work in Jackson, Mississippi, was mistaken for a Lawyers' Committee volunteer. After he was rudely ignored throughout a meeting, it became clear that Derfner was from the LCDC, not from the LCCR. "Oh, I'm sorry, I thought you were from the President's Committee," said the lawyer who had been ignoring his presence.

The Decision to Go to Mississippi

The *Ten Year Report of the LCCR* recounts the committee's entry into the state this way:

> Mississippi was where the civil rights action was. Not only clergy, but college students and organizations . . . poured into the state in the summer of 1964. The Justice Department could not protect all of them . . . . The committee sent eighteen volunteers from leading law firms in New York, Philadelphia and Washington. They went for two-week periods, not as activists, but rather as missionaries to the Mississippi bar, which the committee believed would shoulder its responsibility and begin to represent civil rights workers. Acting on that conviction, members of the committee met with leaders of the Mississippi bar during the Spring of 1964 and encouraged them to provide legal services to black Mississippians.[101]

The LCCR believed that real change could only be accomplished by changing the culture and that would be done by change at the local level. In their view, the good will of the ABA was important to establishing common ground with the local legal establishment with whom they hoped to work.

In August 1964, at the second general meeting of the committee, Alfred J. Schweppe, chairman of the ABA Committee on Civil Rights and Racial Unrest, spoke. He said:

> I have explained on various occasions, and again yesterday in the House of Delegates, that there is complete collaboration and coordination between our Committee and this Committee. . . . I think the work that this Committee has done has been phenomenally effective, and I know it has the . . . blessings of the Association. . . .[102]

The LCCR could not align itself with Alfred Schweppe and Robert Moses and keep the respect of either group. The coalition of lawyers that made up the committee continued to be united by an appreciation of the bar's responsibility to uphold the law and to make legal counsel available for legitimate grievances, whether they agreed with the cause or not. How far they were willing to go to support those responsibilities was a question. The leadership of the committee in 1964 continued to hope that through its mediation and urging, the bar in Mississippi would uphold the tenets of the profession.

---

101. *Id.* at 28.
102. Minutes of Membership Breakfast Meeting, LCCR, Aug. 13, 1964.

The request for volunteers for Freedom Summer that was brought to the committee by Robert Lunney was considered by the co-chairmen and the Executive Committee. The board decided to send volunteers to Mississippi to aid the National Council of Churches volunteers, but not to affiliate itself with SNCC. The committee reasoned that because of the formation of the Lawyers' Constitutional Defense Committee, "it would be sufficient to make between 15 and 20 lawyers available to the National Council of Churches, and that the role of these lawyers should be limited to advice and possible representation of the ministers working in Mississippi communities this summer."[103] The Executive Committee's feeling was "that any lawyers going to Mississippi or elsewhere under the auspices of the LCCR should not become associated directly with any one of the civil rights organizations." It was decided "that where no local counsel was available as a base of operations, the out-of-state lawyers could work as an advisor to the ministers or staff members of the National Council of Churches. . . . It should be emphasized, of course, that the other organizations . . . will no doubt . . . work directly with civil rights organizations regardless of the way we may decide to operate."[104]

In keeping with its objective of working with the local bar, the LCCR "sought to recruit lawyers whom it felt would be capable of working objectively in situations involving an emotionally-charged atmosphere," for the work with NCC and Freedom Summer. The committee's decision in Mississippi was to "fill a vacuum often left unfilled by other civil rights groups as well as local bar associations in Mississippi, i.e., objective legal assistance and negotiations." The lawyers selected would remain in Mississippi for a period of two weeks each, and there would be at least two lawyers in Mississippi at all times during the summer.

The lawyers had five general objectives: first, to advise the ministers sent to Mississippi by the NCC; second, to defend clergymen supervising or staffing the community centers; third, to confer with local white lawyers in an effort to encourage them to undertake representation of persons involved in civil rights controversies in their localities; fourth, to investigate any incidents arising in the area, such as charges of police brutality, economic reprisals, etc.; and finally, to maintain contact with appropriate local, state, and federal law enforcement agencies. Ultimately 18 volunteers were chosen for the project; the first two left in early July for Mississippi and the

---

103. Minutes of the Meeting of the Executive Committee, LCCR, New York City, June 16, 1964.

104. Stahl Memo, *supra* note 98, at 4.

rest left at two-week intervals throughout the months of July, August, and September.[105]

Acting on the hope that the Mississippi Bar would assume its civic responsibilities, the LCCR sent representatives to the state to talk to the Board of Bar Commissioners of the Mississippi State Bar about providing legal services to blacks. "The LCCR's Committee on Cooperation with Bar Associations was headed by Cecil Burney, a southerner from Corpus Christi, Texas. He set up meetings with the leaders of the Mississippi Bar, the first one in New Orleans.[106] One of the objects of the meetings to be to seek local representation for persons involved in civil rights controversies by the establishment of an assignment scheme or other arrangement to make lawyers available for this purpose."[107]

In May 1964, a month after the passage of the Civil Rights Act by Congress, Bernard G. Segal, Cody Fowler of Florida, and Cecil E. Burney met with the president of the Mississippi Bar Association, Earl Thomas; the president-elect, Orma R. Smith; and several past presidents, including John Satterfield, a former president of the American Bar Association and member of the ABA Board of Governors. They urged that in light of the new law, "steps be taken to assure representation by local attorneys in civil rights cases."[108] The discussions took place in private on and off for the next month.[109]

The LCCR representatives were sensitive to the pressures that the southern lawyers faced in their home state. Segal explained, "Needless to say, we do not work in the public press. That is because it was a friendly interchange of views. . . . They have to work with their local officials. In many cases when it comes to representation they need the help of the court, they need the protection of judicial appointment. We can be helpful in working out with each

---

105. Berl I. Bernhard, Executive Director, and John H. Doyle III, Assistant Executive Director, LCCR, Draft Report on the Mississippi Summer Project, Oct. 20, 1964, Mississippi File, Records of the LCCR, Washington, D.C. The 18 volunteers were: Robert Ostrow, New York; Stephen Hopkins, New York; John Doyle III, New York; John Bodner, Jr., Washington, D.C.; William Messing, New York; Patricia Eames, Philadelphia; L. Thomas Bryan, Jr., New York; Joseph Zuckerman, New York; Martin Spiegel, New York; J. Robert Lunney, New York; Prof. Robert O'Connell, Milwaukee; Robert Janover, New York; Morton Klevan, New York; John Lankenau, New York; Asa Sokolow, New York; Lewis Stone, New York; Bruce Sullivan, New York; John Wing, New York.

106. Interview with Jerome J. Shestack.

107. Minutes, March 25, 1964.

108. Bernard Segal & Harrison Tweed, co-chairmen, LCCR, Statement of Purpose and Activities, June 1, 1965, Yearly Reports File.

109. *Id.*

community what procedure it ought to follow, not because we are wiser than they, but because we have a greater exposure."[110]

Segal praised the bar leaders: "The reaction since the Civil Rights Act is a tribute to our fellow citizens in the South. I think it has been far less eruptive and far more cooperative than many people hoped." He went on to say, "We cannot expect Mississippi lawyers to ignore the high feelings and overturn the sentiment of the community in a moment. . . . Overall our lawyers received the cooperation of Mississippi lawyers and even state officials."[111]

On July 15, 1964, the board of the Bar Commissioners of the Mississippi Bar responded to the LCCR mediation by passing a resolution stating that all members of the bar who practice in the Mississippi state and federal courts "will continue to be faithful and true to their duties and oaths in according to every person, of high or low estate, resident or nonresident, rich or poor, popular or unpopular, respected or despised, and regardless of race, color, creed or national origin, a fair and impartial trial, with assistance and protection, where sought, of competent counsel." Further, the bar board resolved that "the president of the bar is requested to appoint a Special Committee to act as liaison committee from the membership of our bar to be available for consultation with the Courts, State and Federal, and persons within the area."[112] Undoubtedly, Mississippi lawyers would have found it hard to argue against the resolution.

Unfortunately, as the *Ten Year Report of the LCCR* reports, the bar resolution proved to be "an empty gesture." The members of the committee seriously underestimated the "depth of Mississippi's feelings about civil rights," and they didn't fully appreciate the reality of the threat of economic and physical reprisals against white lawyers who might consider stepping forward to help.[113]

Bob Ostrow, one of the committee's Mississippi volunteers, wrote about his experience in Freedom Summer. "Consultation and mediation with local Mississippi lawyers is a complete waste of time, money and effort and can only lead to furtherance of the goals of bigots in the Mississippi Bar. I submit that the Resolution passed on July 15, 1964 was not meant to be used by Civil Rights workers as a tool in obtaining counsel where otherwise unavailable. It was meant to be used as a weapon in the cases arising out of this summer and

---

110. Bernard Segal, Report to the Committee, Aug. 1964, Reports File, Records of the LCCR, Washington, D.C.
111. *Id.* at 23-24. Robert Lunney "substantiated" Segal's sentiments.
112. Resolution of the Board of Bar Commissioners of the Mississippi State Bar, July 15, 1964, Mississippi Project File, Records of the LCCR, Washington, D.C.
113. Ten Year Report of the LCCR (The LCCR 1973) at 28.

next when the Mississippi legal and judicial system comes under review by our highest court." He goes on to give graphic examples of obstruction by Mississippi lawyers and officials when volunteer lawyers tried to get them to abide by the Resolution. One was on July 30, 1964, when he was with Jack Pratt in Clarksdale. Pratt was arrested for "improper passing." In a cross-examination with the chief witness against him, the Town Prosecutor, this remark was made: "Yes, Mr. Pratt, if what you mean by that question is am I biased, I must say in all fairness that I certainly am biased against you and your kind—and all who come into our state to try to change our way of life." Ostrow thought that the LCCR should become more active in Mississippi and at one point, discussing the experiences of two other committee volunteers, Tom Bryan and Bob O'Connell, he relates hearing, "I went 'SNCC' early in the game."[114]

The LCCR and the volunteers had their eyes opened by their experiences with the Mississippi system of justice. The volunteers informed the National Office that they would be leaving the civil rights workers without protection if volunteers like themselves abandoned Mississippi. The experience of Freedom Summer made it clear that volunteers could not provide the continuity needed to carry on any but the most rudimentary defenses in Mississippi and that something more permanent was called for in Jackson. Exactly one year to the day after William Ming opened the discussion about the need for legal aid in Mississippi, at the second annual meeting of the committee on August 13, 1964, the 18 volunteer lawyers who first went to Jackson, Mississippi, urged the board of the committee to expand their activities in Mississippi "and that a permanent committee office be established in the state."[115]

At the same meeting a replacement for David Stahl, the executive director of the LCCR from January through September 1964, was named. Stahl's replacement was Berl I. Bernhard, who was a former staff director of the United States Commission on Civil Rights.

In January 1965, the LCCR announced its intention to establish a litigation office in Jackson, Mississippi.[116] The office would be staffed by at least two full-time lawyers and by volunteer lawyers recruited for temporary periods.[117] It was the hope of Bernard Segal "that the LCCR would be

---

114. Robert W. Ostrow to Berl Bernhard, Oct. 30, 1964, at 2-3. In 1963 the U.S. Supreme Court had decided *Gideon v. Wainwright,* which required legal representation in all capital criminal cases.

115. LCCR, Report on Anniversary Meeting of Members, Waldorf-Astoria Hotel, New York, Aug. 13, 1964, at 6. File on Annual Reports, Records of the Lawyers' Committee for Civil Rights, Washington, D.C.

116. Records of the LCCR, Minutes of the Board, Jan. 27, 1965.

117. Ten Year Report, *supra* note 113.

able to terminate its program in Mississippi within three years, at which time the Mississippi Bar and the NAACP Legal Defense Fund might be able to bear the full burden of responsibility for civil rights cases in the state."[118]

The mission of the Jackson Office was twofold: to provide legal defense in criminal and civil rights cases and to "institute civil actions to secure human and civil rights." This mission was a transformation of the initial purpose and procedures outlined in July 1963, which did not envision the creation of a litigation office.[119]

The committee was careful to meet with leaders of the Mississippi Bar before opening the new office and to assure them that the committee's office would function in a professional manner. They assured the Mississippi Bar that the LCCR would not divert fee-generating matters from them. On May 24, 1964, the Board of Bar Commissioners of the Mississippi State Bar passed a resolution stating:

> The Board of Bar Commissioners extends its cooperation to this committee in the discharge of its policy so pronounced, provided said committee shall require any . . . person (it represents) to present evidence sufficient to it to establish the fact that such person cannot obtain legal representation from the Mississippi Bar, and that such committee shall require evidence over and above an unsupported statement by the person involved and provided further, that if such person is able to pay for such representation, the services will be extended only where such person has been unable to obtain Mississippi counsel, regardless of compensation.[120]

If the LCCR promised to carefully screen and select its volunteers, and to brief them in Mississippi state practice, the Mississippi Bar stated that it

---

118. Minutes of the Board of Directors Meeting, January 27, 1965, p. 2

119. Letter to Membership, July 1, 1963. First, it was intended to be a liaison between the government and the profession, and it would be the "central agency for the profession." . . . The committee would "help local lawyers fund lawyers 'outside' the community willing to help in civil rights cases, to obtain counsel for any individual or group unable to do so." The committee would also provide leadership in forming biracial committees, mediation, and public education about legal and judicial problems. . . . [p]urpose of the Lawyers' Committee was "to marshal action by the lawyers of the nation wherever this can be helpful in resolving disputes and relieving tensions." Also see this chapter, at 90-91.

120. *Id.*

would not object to appearances by committee lawyers in Mississippi courts.[121]

Forty-five new volunteers were recruited, screened on the basis of their answers to the same questionnaires used to evaluate appointees to the federal bench; briefed by the Legal Defense Fund during the spring of 1965; and scheduled to begin in the Jackson office during the summer.[122] Each volunteer had to perform a minimum of one month of service.

The Jackson office was opened on June 2, 1965, and the goals of the committee in Jackson were "to lead the bar in assuming its professional responsibilities in civil rights and to provide legal services where they would be otherwise unavailable."[123]

The first chief counsel of the Jackson office was Clifford N. Carlsen, Jr., who came from the firm of King, Miller, Anderson, Nash & Yerke in Portland, Oregon. John H. Doyle III of the New York firm of Patterson, Belknap Webb served as assistant chief counsel until he joined Berl Bernhard in Washington, D.C., as assistant executive director of the national office. In September 1965, Richard E. Tuttle, who resigned as chief counsel of the California Public Utilities Commission, became the new head of the office.

Less than two weeks after the office opened in Jackson, on June 14, 1965, hundreds of peaceful demonstrators were arrested as they marched in downtown Jackson to protest the consideration of restrictive voting bills then under consideration by the Mississippi legislature. They were all charged with violating local parade ordinances and locked up without proper facilities or water supply at the county fairgrounds.

On June 19, 1965, the LCDC, the Inc. Fund, and the LCCR joined in a lawsuit. The lead counsels were John Honnold of the LCCR and Melvyn Zarr of the Inc. Fund. The suit challenged the constitutionality of the parade ordi-

---

121. Interview with Armand Derfner, September 1977, Charleston, South Carolina. Derfner explained that out-of-state lawyers could not normally appear in Mississippi state courts without being connected to a lawyer admitted and practicing in Mississippi. Of course, this limited the effectiveness of civil rights lawyers because there were few, white or black (in 1964 there were about 10 black lawyers practicing in the state), who were willing to act in behalf of such cases. The Mississippi State Bar rescinded its help to the Lawyers' Committee after it became clear that the committee had joined with the other civil rights groups' affirmative action suits. Federal courts had different rules for practice.

122. Berl Bernhard, Executive Director, LCCR, Report on the Committee Office in the South, Aug. 7 through Oct. 6, 1965, Jackson Mississippi File, Records of the LCCR, Washington, D.C. Also, from the Records of the LCCR, National Staff, Letter to Martin Luther King from Bernard G. Segal, May 4, 1965.

123. *Id.*

nances in the federal court in Jackson. The statute was challenged for vagueness. For five days, the detainees and the lawyers waited for action by the court. Finally, the group appealed in an emergency measure to the federal appeals court. In *Guyot v. Pierce*, the appeals court enjoined further enforcement of the ordinances, any further prosecution of persons previously arrested, and any other action to prevent orderly marches for the purpose of communicating political or social opinion.[124]

The mass arrests in Jackson were a baptism under fire for the new office of the LCCR. It emerged from the fight as a civil rights litigation office. In the ensuing years, the committee became a pillar of "that Farish Street Crowd" (the street where the civil rights bar was housed in Jackson, Mississippi), a name bestowed on the civil rights lawyers in Mississippi by Harold Cox.

The committee's permanent legal staff was upped to four lawyers, and in the next months the Jackson office "initiated seven new affirmative suits and . . . accepted the role of defense counsel in scores of criminal prosecutions and civil actions, involving literally hundreds of defendants. In addition, it undertook investigations into several facets of Mississippi life that demand reform." The Jackson office took on cases challenging the closing of swimming pools; educational policies; public demonstrations; and public accommodations, employing the services of "at least seven lawyers at all times."

When the Jackson office was conceived, the committee continued in its hope that it could work with the Mississippi Bar, and it was not foreseen that the staff would become involved in such complicated and time-consuming legal battles. The office's case backlog was building to the point where Chief Counsel Tuttle suggested that "one possible way to lighten the workload . . . would be to stop accepting new small or trivial cases. Much of the office time of lawyers in Jackson is spent on drop-in clients and phone calls. Our greatest contributions will be in the area of carefully selected affirmative actions of widespread impact."[125]

The LCCR's efforts at accommodation and conciliation were not totally lost on the local Mississippi establishment. On Friday, September 3, 1965, Assistant Chief Counsel John Doyle addressed approximately 50 lawyers at a luncheon meeting of the Junior Bar Association of Jackson. The address was made at the request of James C. Child, program director of the Junior Bar, who was introduced to Doyle and other committee lawyers by Sherwood Wise of

---

124. Frank T. Read & Lucy S. McGough. Let Them Be Judged: The Judicial Integration of the Deep South (Scarecrow Press 1978) at 365. *Guyot v. Pierce*, 372 F.2d 658 (5th Circuit 1965), invalidated a Jackson ordinance that required a permit issued by the City Council for all parades and other public gatherings.

125. Bernhard, *supra* note 122, at 20-23.

Jackson, a past president of the Mississippi State Bar and a member of the ABA Committee on Civil Rights and Racial Unrest. Wise, it will be remembered, was an original member of the committee who predicted "if you let a camel put his nose under the tent, he will soon get the whole thing."

Chief Counsel Tuttle reported to the national office that "John Doyle's appearance constitutes a first in recent Mississippi history. Although there have been a number of meetings between representatives of the Negro community and the white leadership over the last twenty years, this marks the first time that an organization of white business and professional people has publicly invited a person identified with the civil rights movement to address it. There can be no doubt that without the efforts of the LCCR, even these limited advances would not have occurred."[126]

At the second annual meeting of the LCCR in New York on August 13, 1964, Carl T. Rachlin, one of the founders of the LCDC, said:

> There is no doubt that the presence of lawyers of our group, plus those who have come from the Lawyers' Committee here, have had a great inhibiting effect on the illegal activities of police and other local officials in the state of Mississippi . . . . So that at present I can say from my own personal knowledge that the lawyers going south in this great migration of lawyers, the greatest migration in history of Anglo-Saxon law, has had a tremendously helpful effect despite the few incidents of violence that have taken place. Without them it would have been a disaster.[127]

In response to Rachlin, John Satterfield of Mississippi rose to speak in defense of the Mississippi Bar,[128] saying, "I had the pleasure of arranging the first meeting of Segal with the lawyers in Mississippi, and I think that we have the same sincerity and honesty in carrying out our profession as any other lawyer in the state, in the Union, and I rise to say so in this presence."[129]

What separated John Satterfield and Carl Rachlin was not a question of professional conduct but of vision and conviction. Each had a distinct view of the role of the lawyer in society. Satterfield epitomized conventional legal thinking, while Rachlin embodied the changing role of American lawyering.

For awhile in 1965, the LCCR bridged these distinct professional worlds.

---

126. *Id.* at 4-5.
127. Carl Rachlin, quoted in the Bernhard minutes, *supra* note 122, at 26.
128. Derfner, *supra* note 121. Derfner related that John Satterfield was considered to be one of the worst racists that the bar dealt with.
129. *Id.*

CHAPTER 4

The Staff—A New Symmetry

At its inception in June 1963, the mission of the ad hoc Lawyers' Committee for Civil Rights Under Law (LCCR) was to mobilize the private bar to help mediate the civil rights problems in the South. This was to be accomplished in the conventional manner—that is by uniting individual local advocates with individual local clients. When it became evident that the problems affecting the administration of justice in the United States were deeper and far more ubiquitous than first realized, the Lawyers' Committee adapted and changed. Ultimately, it matured into a public interest law group whose mission was to unite the financial and human resources of the country's largest law firms with the legal needs of the nation's minority communities. It functioned not through the part-time services of a select group of bar leaders, but through a national office and a network of local LCCR offices that were run by full-time legal staffs of dedicated civil rights lawyers

In 1964, the small group of corporate lawyers who originally formed the LCCR opened a national headquarters and hired a lawyer to run it. This national office soon became the committee's hub for communications, fundraising and program strategy. It grew in size and in significance with the work of the committee. In 1968, the mission of the committee was expanded to include problems with the administration of justice in the North as well as the South. An Urban Areas Project was launched. The LCCR established local offices in a number of the country's largest cities and staffed the new offices with at least one lawyer. Simultaneously, smaller committees were formed in urban areas to support the legal work of the national office. The local committees offered counsel and advice to clients but they were not legal

aid offices in the traditional sense. Their goal was to identify cases of significance to the lives of urban minority communities and then to involve
large law firms in those cases, taking advantages of the firms' abilities to
handle vast, complex, and expensive litigation. Staff lawyers would prepare and strategize cases brought to them by local clients, after which they
would unite the clients with a law firm that was affiliated with the LCCR.
The private firm would handle the litigation pro bono. The aim of the
committee was to facilitate social reform through litigation.[1] Ultimately,

---

1. The following account of one recent Washington Lawyers' Committee case is related
   as an example of the characteristic work of the Lawyers' Committee for Civil Rights
   Under Law [hereinafter LCCR]. This summary of the history of the *Parents United v.
   Barry* (Civil Action 92-348, *Parents United for the District of Columbia v. Marion
   Barry, Mayor, Washington, D.C.*) case came from an interview on Sept. 22, 1997,
   with the director of the Washington LCCR and Urban Affairs, 1972-1997, Roderic
   Boggs. Boggs makes the point that the suit would never have achieved the results that
   it did if it had not been for the team effort. The team was made up of three interlocking
   members: the director of Parents United, Delabian Rice-Thurston; the Washington
   LCCR Director of the Public Education Project, Mary Levy, an expert in education
   law; and the litigation team of Steptoe & Johnson, headed by Alfred Mamlet. Boggs
   believes the LCCR empowers its community clients to pursue change within the
   judicial process. At the present time the Washington LCCR is working on more than
   300 issues with the community. The Washington committee has an effective network,
   with over 90 different law firms in the city. Staff lawyers meet at least four times a
   year with the pro bono representatives from these firms to discuss the issues involved. How the cases are assigned is "a very ad hoc" thing. Some firms, according
   to Boggs, are more interested in one type of case than another. In June 1997, after
   years of litigation between a parents' group and the District of Columbia government,
   Judge Kay Christian ruled that 50 public school buildings in the District of Columbia
   were unsafe and would remain closed until ordered repairs were completed. The
   origins of this suit dated back to cuts in the District of Columbia government's budget
   of the early 1980s. Those cuts had profound effects on the public schools and the
   quality of education in the district. Many parents in lower-income areas, who had
   been fighting city hall for years for increased funding, felt the cuts fell inequitably on
   their schools. Parents in more affluent school districts believed that the Barry Administration shorted the school budget to spare other areas of the government over which
   he had more control and patronage. They, too, believed the cuts were inequitable. An
   alliance was formed between the disparate groups affected, which was known as
   Parents United. The goal of Parents United was to force the government of the
   District of Columbia to improve the situation in the schools. Years of negotiations
   between the mayor and Parents United failed to produce change. The ensuing deterioration in the District of Columbia schools was in part responsible for the exodus from
   the city by both black and white families. The city's student enrollment went from a
   near peak in 1980 of 140,000 students to under 100,000, leaving the school system
   97 percent black.

the national office began to initiate and handle minority rights litigation. In the course of this evolution, the influence and example of the committee on the professional bar resulted in the modification of the pro bono practices of private law firms—some of the nation's largest firms in particular.

In the early 1980s, the Washington LCCR initiated a Public Education Legal Services Project to help community clients who were seeking legal advice about the educational problems in the district. Parents United became a client of the LCCR. In 1990, as part of the strategy to force Mayor Marion Barry to improve the schools, staff lawyers at the Washington Lawyers' Committee, invoking the Freedom of Information Act, decided to seek materials about fire code violations in the district schools. These materials revealed dozens of violations, which were verified by on-site investigations by Lawyers' Committee staff. At that point, in 1992, having developed the facts and a legal theory for compelling enforcement of the fire and safety codes, the Washington Lawyers' Committee asked the law firm of Steptoe & Johnson to assume responsibility for representing Parents United in court in this matter. Steptoe & Johnson, a major Washington law firm associated with the Lawyers' Committee, brought a lawsuit against Marion Barry to force the government, not the school system, to enforce the fire codes and repair 50 roofs in the district's public school buildings. Alfred Mamlet, a partner at Steptoe & Johnson and a specialist in international communications, was the lead counsel for Parents United. The court ordered the district to repair the buildings. According to John Nolan, Steptoe & Johnson handled the case pro bono publico. (Interview with John Nolan, senior partner, Steptoe & Johnson, board member of the LCCR, former and original co-chairman of the Washington LCCR, former administrative assistant to Attorney General Robert F. Kennedy, and former managing partner of Steptoe & Johnson Law Firm, Washington, D.C., Sept. 30, 1997.) In 1994, with the repairs still not done, Parents United returned to court. Judge Kay Christian found that the district was not in compliance with the court order. Judge Christian assumed jurisdiction over the schools in question. In September 1997 the District of Columbia schools failed to open on time because the repairs were as yet incomplete. At that point, the district government gave extraordinary attention to resolving the code violations as quickly as possible. It was the interaction between the aggrieved local clients, the mediation, the preparation of a factual legal case by the staff lawyers, and the courtroom advocacy of the litigators that resulted in a change in the conduct of the government of the District of Columbia that improved the quality of the city's schools This vast, complex, expensive lawsuit could not have been brought, except by a major law firm that has the human and financial resources to pursue this kind of litigation. The link in bringing this lawsuit activity was the Washington LCCR. The *Parents United v. Barry* case exemplifies the type of legal activity that is currently characteristic of the LCCR. This type of cooperation between the legal establishment and public interest clients was uncharacteristic of lawyering in 1963 when the LCCR appeared.

The Leaders of the Lawyers' Committee

The development of the LCCR, like other institutions, was affected by its leadership. Increasingly, the staff joined with the board of the committee in the exercise of that leadership. The growth of the staff function will be traced in this chapter. It will chronicle the process of how the decision-making authority within the committee shifted from being the sole responsibility of a select board of practicing lawyers to become a shared enterprise between the board and its younger and more ideologically oriented staff. In the course of this evolution, the character of the committee changed. No conflict was associated with the changing balance. Rather, it occurred as a natural result of decisions made by the board to delegate its authority as the mission of the committee took on greater scope and complexity.

The key point of significance that this chapter proposes to convey is that a fundamental shift in the balance of authority began with fund-raising and the development of the docket of the Mississippi office and continued to shape the programmatic direction of the organization. More and more the LCCR began to be steered by a group of younger, more liberal professionals who shared the objectives of the board but were more in touch with other civil rights organizations and less connected to the established order.

This chapter will discuss this evolution and the development of the committee's pro bono litigation efforts by tracing the introduction of the staff function in 1964 and its growth over the following decade. From 1964 to 1974, there were five executive directors of the committee—David Stahl, 1964; Berl I. Bernhard, 1964 to 1968; Milan C. Miskovsky, 1968 to 1970; James Robertson, 1970 to 1972; and David S. Tatel, 1972 to 1974. They served under five sets of co-chairmen—Harrison Tweed and Bernard G. Segal, 1963 to 1965; Burke Marshall and Whitney North Seymour, 1965 to 1967; Arthur H. Dean and Louis F. Oberdorfer, 1967 to 1969; John W. Douglas and George N. Lindsay, 1969 to 1971; and Lloyd N. Cutler and John Doar, 1971 to 1973. Each left a distinct mark on the development of committee.

The original co-chairmen, Segal and Tweed, set the tone for many things in the life of the committee. One of their most important decisions was the choice of David Stahl, a lawyer and a peer, as the first executive director. Stahl helped to establish the character of the position. His successor, Berl Bernhard, served the committee longer than any of his counterparts. During his time as executive director, he worked closely with three sets of co-chairmen. Together they developed the national office and created the Jackson, Mississippi, office. The mission of the committee was changed to encompass the urban centers of the North. The scope of committee fund-raising was expanded. Bernhard played a leading role in all of these developments. During his tenure, the executive director became an integral part of the organization, essential to the success of the co-chairmen. Co-chairmen Oberdorfer and Dean launched the committee in a new direction in 1968 when they introduced a revolutionary plan that called for large law firms throughout the country to provide pro bono service. Dubbed the Urban Areas Project, it necessitated changes in the balance of authority in the committee that were phased in over the next four years. As a result, the tenures of the next two executive directors, Milan Miskovsky and James Robertson, were marked by the new character of the LCCR's work. Under their direction, the committee's offices, local and national, were transformed into a public interest law group. The services of these offices were enhanced dramatically in 1971 when Co-chairman Lloyd Cutler unveiled an extraordinary refinement of the pro bono activities first introduced by the Urban Areas Project. He extended this work beyond the 14 cities in which the LCCR had established offices through a program that called for the country's largest law firms to donate 1 percent of their services to civil rights and poverty law matters that were referred to them by the national and local offices of the committee. Tatel's tenure is defined by this program and the fact that, for the first time, the national office began to litigate civil rights cases.

The Political and Social Context

Three events were critical in shaping the direction of the LCCR during this period. The passage of the 1964 and 1965 Civil Rights Acts and the leadership of Lyndon Johnson; the urban race riots; and the election of Richard Nixon as President of the United States and his pursuit of a "Southern Strategy." A brief discussion of these events is necessary to place the direction of the LCCR in context.

Lyndon Johnson

On November 27, 1963, just a few days after John F. Kennedy's assassination, the nation's new leader, Lyndon Baines Johnson,[2] spoke to a joint session of Congress. President Johnson captured the mood of the country when he said: "John Fitzgerald Kennedy lives on. . . . No words are sad enough to express our sense of loss. No words are strong enough to express

---

2. Vice President Lyndon Baines Johnson was sworn in as the 39th President of the United States at 2:38 P.M., Nov. 22, 1963, in Air Force One at Love Field, Dallas.

our determination to continue the forward thrust of America that he began. Let us highly resolve that John Fitzgerald Kennedy did not live—or die—in vain."[3]

Under Johnson, the political agenda developed by Kennedy was realized.[4] He successfully brokered Kennedy's civil rights bill through Congress the following spring.[5] And, by Executive Order in June 1964, Johnson created the Office of Economic Opportunity (OEO). He appointed Sargent Shriver, John F. Kennedy's brother-in-law, to run "the war on poverty" in the executive branch. President Johnson asked the LCCR to coordinate its "activities wherever possible" with the National Citizens' Committee for Community Relations, an organization created under OEO.[6] Arthur Dean, a prominent Republican member of the LCCR's Executive Committee, was named chairman of the new Committee for Community Relations. More than 60 LCCR members volunteered their services as "conciliators" should specific controversies arise in their communities.[7]

---

3. Public Papers of the President of the United States, Lyndon B. Johnson: Containing the Public Messages, Speeches, and Statements of the President: 1963-1964 (in two books), November 22, 1963 to June 30, 1964 (United States Government Printing Office 1965), Book 1, 10- 11, entry 11, Address Before a Joint Session of the Congress, November 27, 1963.

4. *Id.* "No words are strong enough to express our determination to continue the forward thrust of America that he began. The dream of conquering the vastness of space—the dream of partnership across the Atlantic—and across the Pacific as well—the dream of a Peace Corps in less developed nations—the dream of education for all of our children—the dream of jobs for all who seek them and need them—the dream of care for our elderly—the dream of an all out attack against mental illness—and above all, the dream of equal fights for all Americans, whatever their race or color—these and other American dreams have been vitalized by his drive and by his dedication. And now the ideas and ideals which he so nobly represented must and will be translated into effective action . . . he said, 'let us begin.' Today, in this moment of new resolve, I would say to all my fellow Americans, let us continue."

5. ROBERT WEISBROT, FREEDOM BOUND: A HISTORY OF AMERICA'S CIVIL RIGHTS MOVEMENT (W.W. Norton & Co. 1990) 89-91. The U.S. House of Representatives passed the Civil Rights Act on Feb. 10, 1964, 290-130. The bill was filibustered in the Senate. On June 14 the filibuster was broken by a vote of 71-29 after Senator Everett Dirksen of Illinois supported cloture. Three weeks later the Civil Rights Act was passed and signed into law on July 2, 1964, by Lyndon Johnson.

6. In August 1964, under Title X of the Civil Rights Act, the Community Relations Service of the Department of Commerce was created. As part of that effort, the Department of Commerce sponsored a community initiative known as the National Citizens' Committee for Community Relations.

7. Records of the LCCR, Report to the Membership, 1965.

The following November, Lyndon Johnson won the presidency in his own right with 61 percent of the popular vote, the highest percentage to that point in American history.[8] Social reform was an idea whose time had come and Lyndon Johnson roused the American conscience. Under Johnson, Democrats gained two seats in the Senate and 37 in the House.[9] The conservative coalition of Southern Democrats and Midwestern Republicans that traditionally blocked reform efforts was replaced by a sympathetic Democratic majority. Johnson viewed his landslide election as a clear mandate to look to the federal government to provide solutions to the major domestic issues facing the country. In his inaugural address, he encouraged Americans to consider ". . . not only how to create wealth, but how to use it; not only how fast we are going, but where are we headed." He wanted to beautify America, to eliminate water and air pollution, to clean up the cities, provide education for the young, and medical care for the aged. He wanted to make America a "Great Society."[10] His legislative skill, coupled with the Democratic majorities, a booming economy, and a political center that was shifting to the left of center,[11] allowed for the passage of unprecedented social legislation. For the

---

8. Congressional Quarterly Guide to United States Elections, Second Edition (Congressional Quarterly Inc. 1985) 308, 361. LBJ received 61.05 percent of the popular vote, 43,126,584 votes. Senator Barry Goldwater received 38.47 percent, or 27,177,838 votes. Goldwater only took six states in the election, receiving just 52 electoral votes. LBJ received 486 electoral votes.

9. *Id.* at 1116, *Political Party Affiliations in Congress,* U.S. House of Representatives: 1961-1963, Democrats 258, Republicans 177: 1963-1965, D-263, R-174: 1965-1967, D-295, R-140. In the U.S. Senate: 1961-1963, D-65, R-35; 1963-1965, D-68, R-32; 1965-1967, D-68, R-32.

10. Public Papers, Inaugural Address, 73. "I do not believe that the Great Society is the ordered, changeless, and sterile battalion of the ants. It is the excitement of becoming—always becoming, trying, probing, failing, resting, and trying again—but always trying and always gaining. . . . In each generation . . . we have to earn our heritage. . . . If we succeed . . . it will be because of what we are . . . what we believe."

11. For a discussion of liberalism and, in particular, American liberalism and modern liberalism, *see* David G. Smith, *Liberalism, in* The International Encyclopedia of the Social Sciences (Macmillan Co. & The Free Press 1968) 9:276. Smith defines liberalism as "the belief in and commitment to a set of methods and policies that have as their common aim greater freedom for individual men." He believes that the two most important objectives of liberalism are "noninterference and enfranchisement." For a discussion of the American youth movement, the counterculture and the new left in the 1950s and 1960s, see: Hal Draper, Berkeley: The New Student Revolt (1965); David Harris, Dreams Die Hard (1984); Allen J. Matusow, The Unraveling of America (1987); Jim Miller, Democracy Is In the Streets (1987); and Theodore Roszak, The Making a of the Counter Culture (1968).

next four years, Johnson attacked the problems of segregation, poverty, health, education, and the environment. From 1964 through 1966, Johnson shepherded through Congress more significant legislation than had any other President during a comparable period of time.[12] The new legislation transformed the movement for social justice into a political and social revolution that would touch every aspect of American society by the end of the century. Great Society programs and legislation recast the cultural struggle into a legal battle. Federal legislation gave lawyers the tools to attack in the courts discrimina-

---

12. JOHN MORTON BLUM, YEARS OF DISCORD: AMERICAN POLITICS AND SOCIETY, 1961-1974 (W.W. Norton & Co. 1991), chapters 5 and 6, March 1965. The Voting Rights Act eliminated discriminatory literacy tests, provided federal officers to assist black voters in registering to vote, and established severe penalties for interference with any individual's right to the ballot. Further, whenever a county in any state failed to register 50 percent of its voting- age population, the Justice Department could suspend any test that that county applied to voters and, if necessary, use federal examiners to register those requesting the vote. Within a few years, black voters in the South reached 50 percent. In September 1965 President Johnson issued an executive order instituting a federal affirmative action policy. The president's order required federal contractors and institutions receiving federal assistance to take special steps to employ more women and nonwhites. Over time that order had a profound effect. Universities had to admit significant numbers of women, blacks, Hispanics, and Asians. In June 1965, Johnson promised to move toward equality of races. He did that on two fronts. The first was the Office of Economic Opportunity (OEO), an executive program that was created early in 1964 to coordinate the president's attack on poverty. Its director, Sargent Shriver, was in charge of overseeing community action programs, legal services corporation, and the Job Corps—all administered by the executive departments. Johnson's second attack on poverty and more effective endeavor channeled into various programs cash and services that went directly to the poor. That initiative accounted for increases in Social Security coverage, AFDC payments, and food stamps, among other things. In 1965 the Congress passed Medicare and Medicaid, which established a system of medical care for those 65 and older. Medicaid was a health care program for those on welfare of all ages that committed the federal government to bear between 50 and 80 percent of the costs of medical care to the indigent blind, disabled, and members of families with dependent children—the same groups covered by federal welfare before 1965—as well as individuals with insufficient financial needs. In 1965 Johnson put the poor and minorities on the educational agenda with the passage of the Elementary and Secondary Education Act, the Higher Education Act, and the National Defense Act. In 1966 Congress passed the Clean Water Restoration Act, the Fair Packaging and Labeling Act, and the Automobile Safety Act. In 1968 the Occupational Safety and Health Administration (OSHA) was created. LBJ persuaded Congress to subsidize the National Endowment for the Arts and the National Endowment for the Humanities as well as supporting public radio and television broadcasting.

tion of minorities, women, the elderly, and the disabled. Lawyering moved back to its natural habitat—the courtroom. Public interest lawyering emerged as an accepted type of professional practice in the mainstream bar, and the legal establishment's civil rights initiative—the LCCR—was on the cutting edge. Its professional stature and leadership within the corporate bar[13] conferred upon the emerging pro bono movement the sanction of legitimacy.

For the LCCR, the Mississippi office led the way. "The passage of the Voting Rights Act triggered a new era of voting rights litigation designed to overcome the barriers that diluted the voting strength of the newly enfranchised black voters."[14] The staff lawyers of the Jackson office helped provide the strategy and resources to mount a direct challenge to the barriers that local and state authorities threw up to block minority voting after 1965. After 1965, black activists were no longer just looking to the civil rights groups for help as criminal defendants but as plaintiffs in voting rights lawsuits seeking remedies that would enable blacks to be elected to public office.[15]

The Riots

As Robert Kennedy had warned in the East Room on June 21, 1963 ". . . the North is far from blameless. While there is dejure discrimination in the South, there is de facto discrimination in the North."[16] On August 11, 1965, just six days after President Lyndon Johnson signed into law the Voting Rights Act of 1965, the black ghettos of the North erupted into racial violence.

The rioting began in the Los Angeles neighborhood of Watts over an incident that involved arrest for drunk driving of a 21-year-old black man by a white policeman. It took 14,000 national guardsmen and several thousand local police six days to stop the arson, theft, rampaging, and sniping that followed. It left 34 people dead and caused some $45 million in property

---

13. Report to the Members of the LCCR (LCCR, March 1964) at 4. The board now numbers 45, of whom 10, together with the officers (the co-chairmen, Harrison Tweed and Bernard Segal, Lloyd Cutler, secretary, and Cecil Burney, treasurer), constitute the Executive Committee. The board includes the president and eight past presidents of the ABA, former Attorney General William Rogers, Judge Samuel Rosenman, the deans of the Law Schools of Harvard, Yale, Pennsylvania, and Vanderbilt Universities, respectively, the president of the American Bar Foundation, and other prominent lawyers.

14. FRANK PARKER, BLACK VOTES COUNT: POLITICAL EMPOWERMENT IN MISSISSIPPI AFTER 1965 (University of North Carolina Press 1990), at 9.

15. *Id.*

16. Jerome J. Shestack, *A Mass in Memory of Robert F. Kennedy: Personal Memoir* (1968), at 15.

damage. The nation was in shock.[17] Within the next two years, Chicago, Cleveland, South Bend, New York, Detroit, Newark, and Milwaukee would all be rocked by rioting.

Even more widespread and destructive race rioting followed the assassination of Martin Luther King, Jr., on April 4, 1968. In just six days, from April 4 to April 10, more than 130 cities were torn apart. By conservative estimates, some 2,600 fires resulted in property damage of more than $100 million.[18] The disorders led to 20,000 arrests and brought 130,000 troops and national guardsmen into domestic combat.[19] The hardest hit were Washington, D.C., Chicago, and Baltimore.[20] President Johnson encouraged the LCCR to examine the problems in urban areas.[21] The committee concluded that it should devote its attention to the need for cooperation, understanding, and respect between the police and the various communities that make up a city.[22] Less than two months later, on June 6, 1968, Robert F. Kennedy was assassinated while campaigning for the Democratic presidential nomination.

In response to the civil disorder, President Johnson created the National Advisory Commission on Civil Disobedience, also known as the Kerner Commission. The commission's mission was to investigate the causes of the riots. It found that, "Our nation is moving toward two societies, one black, one white—separate and unequal."[23] The LCCR responded to the need and in June 1968, the LCCR began an Urban Areas Project, an unprecedented effort whose aim was to mobilize lawyers in a response "to the summons to action issued by the Kerner Commission."[24]

Richard Nixon

By the late 1960s, the American political center was moving back to the right. Polarizing racial violence, Vietnam, inflation, and disenchantment with Great Society programs drove the national debate during the presidential election of 1968. The Republican candidate, Richard Milhous Nixon, was elected by a divided American society with just 43.4 percent of the

---

17. For a discussion of the Watts riots, *see* WEISBROT, *supra* note 5, at 158-61.
18. *Id.*
19. *See* WEISBROT, *supra* note 5, at 130.
20. The Ten Year Report: The Lawyers Committee for Civil Rights Under Law (LCCR 1973) 52.
21. Records of the LCCR, Membership Report of the LCCR (1965), Section B, Mediation and Conciliation: *Future Role of the Lawyer*.
22. Proceedings: Planning Sessions on Police-Community Relations (LCCR) 4.
23. *Id.*
24. ANNUAL REPORT: LCCR: 1968-1969 (LCCR) 2.

vote. Alabama's George Wallace drew 13.5 percent of the vote, the best showing by a third-party candidate in 44 years."[25] Nixon wanted, and felt he needed, the Wallace voters to win a second term. To win that bloc, he adopted what has become know as his "Southern Strategy."[26] As President, Nixon gave sustained attention to conservative themes, which put him in conflict with civil rights groups.

In 1968, the U.S. Supreme Court expanded the 1954 *Brown v. Board* decision in *Green v. County Board New Kent County* by requiring schools districts to prepare desegregation plans that promised "realistically to work now."[27] Further, in light of the Court's ruling, the Department of Health, Education, and Welfare changed its guidelines for compliance. The new guidelines called for "terminal desegregation" on penalty of forfeiting federal funds. The Department of Justice readied plans to implement school desegregation in Mississippi under the *Green v. Kent County* decision. Since 1954, the touchstone for the commitment of an administration to minority rights was its enforcement of school desegregation. The Nixon Administration came under tremendous pressure from both sides of the issue.

The powerful Democratic floor leader of the Senate, John Stennis of Mississippi, urged the administration not to implement the desegregation plans prepared by the Civil Rights Division of the Justice Department. When Stennis threatened Nixon with blocking his top legislative issue, the antiballistic missile system, Nixon retreated on school desegregation. This retreat created a virtual civil war in the Civil Rights Division.

Adding to the discontent over the struggle to maintain the momentum on school desegregation, Nixon nominated two southern jurists, Clement Haynsworth and G. Harold Carswell, to fill a vacancy on the Supreme Court created by the resignation of Abe Fortas. The Senate rejected both nominations. Then, in 1969, Chief Justice Earl Warren resigned. To the dismay of liberals, Nixon nominated Warren Burger to replace Warren. Burger was the chief judge of the Court of Appeals of the District of Columbia and a strict constructionist.[28]

Under Nixon, civil rights groups no longer pressed for sweeping re-

25. Congressional Quarterly Guide to United States Elections, Second Edition (Congressional Quarterly Inc. 1985) 361.

26. For a discussion of Nixon's southern strategy, see Weisbrot, Freedom Bound, and Tom Wicker, One of Us: Richard Nixon and the American Dream (Random House 1991).

27. Green v. County Board of New Kent County (Virginia), 391 U.S. 430 (1968). It was in the *Green* decision that busing was suggested as one possible means to achieve racially mixed school systems.

28. Wicker, *supra* note 26.

form legislation. Instead, they worked to save existing laws and to stave off political appointments they felt would hurt the black cause. In the summer of 1970, the LCCR petitioned the Department of Justice to enforce *Green v. Kent County*. Before the schools opened for the year, Assistant Attorney General for Civil Rights Jerris Leonard informed the committee that the Justice Department did not have enough manpower for the job, The committee responded by recruiting, training, and deploying 100 lawyers pro bono, who went throughout the South to monitor the compliance with the court order by southern public school systems.

In November of 1972, Richard Nixon won a second term in the White House with 60.7 percent of the total vote. Nixon received almost 20 million more votes than his Democratic opponent, George McGovern. The character and direction of Nixon's Civil Rights Division at Justice reflected the changing national priorities. The LCCR goal turned to enforcement of the law, which committee leaders believed was not being adequately done by the federal government. As a result, the committee's national office began to concentrate more of its attention on the initiation and managing of private litigation to advance public interests.

The Evolution of a Staff Function

Fundamentally, the original vision of the LCCR was to arouse local, state, and national bar associations to the threat to the judicial system in the South and to have them mobilize their membership to help, as a matter of professional duty, in the mediation of the crisis in the South. Its founders understood that for such a mission the committee's strength lay in its professional stature and reputation. They believed only an association of the "Barons of the Bar" could contend with the inevitable objections from other powerful forces—such as the American Bar Association, the cultural and political beliefs of many members of the bar, and practical financial concerns—and sway the legal practices of private lawyers on a subject of such controversy. They envisioned themselves as catalysts for change, professional leaders stepping into a void, not as members of a professional civil rights organization. As we have seen, no consideration was given to a paid staff for many months after the committee began. When it became clear that the administrative details of running the group were more than the committee members and their law offices wanted to handle, it was questioned whether or not a lawyer was necessary for the job.

The decision to hire a lawyer—someone of known accomplishment—was made by the first co-chairman, Bernard G. Segal.[29] It was a fateful deci-

---

29. Interview with Jerome J. Shestack, March 1996, Philadelphia, Pennsylvania.

sion that helped shape the future of the committee. The man that Segal hired in January 1964, the first executive director of the LCCR, was David Stahl. Stahl, an acquaintance of Segal's,[30] was a former city solicitor of Pittsburgh and later attorney general of Pennsylvania. At the time he was contacted by Segal, he was a professor of law at the University of Pittsburgh Law School, a position from which he took a semester's leave of absence. In 1964, the survival of the committee was still a question and a full-time permanent job was out of the question. Reality required someone who understood the position was limited in duration. The LCCR was fortunate to engage the services of someone of the caliber of David Stahl.

David Stahl

On January 15, 1964, David Stahl opened the national headquarters of the LCCR in space provided by the law firm of Wilmer, Cutler & Pickering.[31] In a letter announcing the new office, the co-chairmen reported that Lloyd Cutler "has made rooms in that firm's suite available to the committee at no cost."[32] No independent function was described for the new office other than introducing it as a central headquarters. The co-chairmen wrote to the membership that "We hope you will feel free to visit our office to meet Mr. Stahl and to discuss with him the progress of the Committee's work. We also urge you to communicate with Mr. Stahl or with either of us in order to keep us informed of what is happening in your community and state. We are particularly anxious to learn about local programs, bar-sponsored or otherwise, carrying out the stated objectives of the Lawyers' Committee."[33] The following August, Harrison Tweed told the general meeting that, "a Washington office has been established to serve as a clearing house for members of the committee, for lawyers generally, and for state and local bar associations in providing information in the area of civil rights and race relations."[34]

David Stahl ran the national office from January to September of 1964. Two things are notable about his tenure. First, he won the respect and confidence of the co-chairmen and the Executive Committee with whom he worked closely. Second, he became the committee's liaison with and representative to

---

30. *Id.*
31. Letter dated January 15, 1964, from David Stahl, Executive Director of the LCCR, to Bernard G. Segal. "I had thought you might want a 'first day' letter for framing in the future archives of the Lawyers' Committee."
32. Letter dated February 11, 1964, from the co-chairmen, Harrison Tweed and Bernard G. Segal, to Members of the Committee.
33. *Id.*
34. Minutes of Membership Breakfast Meeting: LCCR, Aug. 13, 1964, at 4.

the civil rights movement. Segal had chosen a peer for the position and Stahl lived up to his expectations. Someone younger than Stahl, with less experience, personal assurance, and stature, and less a part of the "old boy network" (such as a woman) might not have been as readily accepted by the group. From the beginning, Stahl was given a key role in committee fund-raising, which put him in contact with committee members and their firms. His positive relationship with the board laid the foundation for future relationships between the co-chairmen and the executive director.

The executive director became increasingly prominent in the hierarchical decision making of the organization. Increasingly, the board and Executive Committee began to rely on Stahl for substantive support. The two most pressing issues the committee faced in 1964 were money and the group's affiliation with the civil rights movement. Stahl played a key role in dealing with both issues.

On November 15, 1963, the Internal Revenue Service granted the LCCR tax-exempt status, which made contributions to it "deductible for income, estate, and gift tax purposes." The committee, "which now numbered approximately 200 members,"[35] decided to undertake a broad solicitation of the bar. The board explained "in order to fund the work of the Lawyers' Committee they should first seek funds from members of the bar because not until they have shown their interest and confidence can laymen and foundations be expected to contribute."[36] The LCCR's fund-raising efforts needed to be extended beyond the largest establishment law firms, which had provided the committee's support thus far. The co-chairmen reported to the membership that, "the committee cannot operate effectively without funds for salaries and office, traveling, and other expenses." A finance committee was formed to assist in the effort. Davidson Sommers, general counsel of the Equitable Life Insurance Company, was named as its chair.[37] Preceding the formation of this committee, Co-chairman Harrison Tweed had assumed the responsibility for fund-raising. Tweed held a distinct position of leadership in the American bar and, as a result, he conducted appeals for funds for the LCCR primarily through personal contacts, both his own and those of other members of the committee. It proved to be an extremely time-consuming activity. When Tweed was replaced in this role by a committee of the board, it meant that a new fund-raising system had to be devised. The fund-raising campaign that was initiated was ambitious and Stahl was given a liberal role in its execution.

The co-chairmen decided to divide the lawyers into groups based on the

---

35. Memo: LCCR, Finance Committee File, Records of the LCCR.
36. Report to the Members, March 1964, at 4.
37. *Id.* at 4-5.

size of the law firm. "A suggested scale of contributions by size of firm (counting both partners and associates), which has been the pattern on which funds have been received to date, is as follows: firms with 50 or more lawyers, $1,000; firms with 25 to 50 lawyers, $500; firms with fewer than 25 lawyers, $250; individuals, $100."[38] The country was divided as well. Prominent LCCR members were asked to direct fund-raising activities in their respective cities. The Finance Committee drafted fund-raising letters, and Stahl played an integral role in this effort. He coordinated the different elements of the program and personally communicated the gratitude of the committee to all contributors and members who worked for its success. A tentative budget of $100,000 for 1964 was considered necessary. By March, $55,000, in contributions had been received.[39]

The committee began to investigate private charitable foundations as another source of support. In November 1963, the chairman of the Board of Trustees of the Philadelphia-based Fels Foundation approached Bernie Segal and suggested the LCCR apply for a grant from the foundation. According to Segal, "that was really quite unusual, as Judge Winnet has been besieged by all of his so-called friends since he became chairman, each with hat in hand for some cause. He started the conversation by saying that this was the first time he could recall that he was suggesting a request for a grant be filed."[40] In the following years, the co-chairmen and the executive directors of the LCCR would seek support from many charitable foundations. Tweed suggested to Segal that the Fels application be handled by the Finance Committee.[41] Also, preliminary discussions were held with the Public Affairs Department of the Ford Foundation about a grant to the committee to encourage specialized training in the field of civil rights law. In order to provide guidance in formulating the application for the Ford Foundation, and to plan for supervision of the program, an education committee, chaired by Dean Jefferson B. Fordham of the University of Pennsylvania School of Law, was created.[42]

---

38. *Id.* at 2.
39. Minutes, Meeting of the Executive Committee: LCCR, March 25, 1964. The Finance Committee was concentrating its efforts on the cities of Chicago, Detroit, Los Angeles, San Francisco, and several Texas cities. The budget was as follow: Salaries, Professional and Consulting Fees—$40,000; Administrative and Overhead Office Supplies—$15,000 (postage and distribution costs, telephone and travel expenses); Legal Representation Activities—$20,000; Educational Activities (applications have been made for grants to carry on educational activities, and the program would be greatly expanded if grants are received)—$25,000.
40. Letter, Nov. 18, 1963, from Bernard G. Segal to Harrison Tweed.
41. Letter, Nov. 21, 1963, from Harrison Tweed to Bernard G. Segal.
42. Minutes, *supra* note 39, at 2.

As for the LCCR's relations with the civil rights movement, 1964 was a year of great flux. Race relations were explosive, particularly in the state of Mississippi, where criminal defense lawyers were desperately needed. Yet the committee hesitated to become too closely involved with the civil rights movement. In 1964, the committee's mission in Mississippi was to mobilize the white bar to assume its professional responsibilities within the judicial process. They went to Mississippi as "missionaries to the bar" and in the beginning concentrated their greatest efforts on changing the attitudes of the local and state bars. In 1964, the job of serving as liaison to the civil rights movement in Mississippi was given to Stahl. He met with representatives of other civil rights groups and coordinated and managed the 18 volunteers the committee sent to Mississippi.

The co-chairmen concentrated their efforts in three other areas: education of the state and local bars; the litigation in Farmville, Virginia, and Americus, Georgia; and the public policy debate surrounding the Civil Rights Act, which was before Congress.

We have already discussed the LCCR's role with the National Council of Churches and the Lawyers Constitutional Defense Committee for the "Mississippi Summer" sponsored by Student Nonviolent Coordinating Committee (SNCC). The LCCR cooperated with the NAACP's Legal Defense and Education Fund, Inc. The Inc. Fund put together a series of civil rights and law institutes. The institutes were a series of academic sessions taught by prominent law professors, who presented cases and materials to civil rights lawyers for criminal defense work. The LCCR was invited to participate in the series. Only two members of the board, William Ming and William Coleman—both minority members—joined the academic lecturers. Other committee members helped gather material for the institutes by securing personnel to prepare practice and procedure manuals for Florida, Kentucky, Louisiana, Maryland, Missouri, South Carolina, and Texas.[43]

In Washington, D.C., the committee joined with the Department of Justice in a National Conference on Bail and Criminal Justice, which was sponsored by the department. For the conference, committee members were asked to prepare a number of reports and surveys on bail practices in various parts of the country. Northern and southern cities that had recently experienced arrests on a large scale were chosen for study. In conjunction with the ABA, the LCCR

---

43. Minutes of the Meeting of the Board of Directors: LCCR, May 13, 1964. Marvin Frankel of Columbia University Law School headed the academic institutes. The faculty for the various institutes included Professors Louis Henkin and Louis Lusky of Columbia, Louis Pollak of Yale, Mark de Wolfe Howe of Harvard, Anthony G. Amsterdam of the University of Pennsylvania Law School, Robert McKay of New York University School of Law, William Ming, and William T. Coleman.

contacted the local bar associations throughout the country to urge that a discussion of the current race relations problems be included in programs marking the observation of Law Day on May 1. The letters to the local associations included materials and suggestions for programs.[44]

John F. Kennedy's civil rights bill was debated by the Congress during the winter and spring of 1964. Senators Hubert Humphrey and Thomas Kuchel asked the co-chairmen in their "individual capacity and not as co-chairmen of the committee" to comment on the constitutionality of Titles II and VII of the bill, which dealt with public accommodations and equal employment. Segal and Tweed brought together a representative group of 20 lawyers, many from the committee, and "rendered" an opinion. The group came to the conclusion that the two parts of the bill were in accordance with prior judicial decisions ruling upon the validity of similar regulatory statutes.[45] Senators Humphrey and Kuchel wrote "the opinion was most helpful and most persuasive." It helped "clarify" some of the legal issues involved in the great debates on the bill for some members of the Congress, both in the Senate and the House, with whom they talked.[46]

On August 13, 1964, the membership of the committee gathered for its second general meeting in conjunction with the Annual Meeting of the ABA in New York. The committee had come a long way since the previous summer in Chicago. The chairman of the ABA's Civil Rights and Civil Unrest Committee, Alfred Schweppe, spoke in praise of the LCCR's work, as did another guest, Judge Thurgood Marshall.[47] Stahl's leave of absence from his teaching duties was over and Segal presented him with a plaque expressing the committee's appreciation for his "leadership."[48]

---

44. *Id.*

45. Notes for the Annual Membership Meeting, Aug. 1964, at 6.

46. Minutes of the Membership Breakfast Meeting: LCCR, Aug. 13, 1964, at 20.

47. *Id.* at 12. Thurgood Marshall said, "It is the lawyer in the community that speaks with authority as to what the law is and what is right and wrong, and I submit, he is also a part of the authoritative structure that decides what is morally correct. And so if we are to get rid of much of the frustration . . . I believe that the Bar and especially the organized Bar, whether it be local, state or national, can do much. But it is for the individual lawyer who is going to have to do it. So I say that the Committee, to my mind, is important because it is a group that will go around the community so that other people will see that instead of sitting back and saying that the Chief Justice is this or that—that instead of that, if the lawyer in the community takes the leadership, I am concerned only with the fact that the rest of the community will follow the lawyer."

48. *Id.* It read, "Lawyers' Committee on Civil Rights Under Law expresses its deep appreciation and high commendation to David Stahl for dedicated and inspired leadership as Executive Director during the critical period of January to September 1964."

Berl I. Bernhard

David Stahl was invited to join the Board of Directors of the LCCR. To succeed him as executive director, the board chose a young civil rights activist, Berl I. Bernhard. Bernhard considered himself a "civil rights lawyer," something that was rare for the day.[49] He remembers that he "didn't think the committee would last too long."[50] He came to the committee when the racial struggle in the South was on the verge of being transformed into a political and social revolution. The issues and the people driving the movement were new and Berl Bernhard became the LCCR's chief liaison with the civil rights movement. During his tenure, from September of 1964 through the winter of 1967-1968, the LCCR opened a litigation office in Jackson Mississippi; responded to a presidential request to become involved in the administration of justice in the North; and enlarged its national staff. In addition, fund-raising took on a new dimension in the life of the committee. During his tenure, Bernhard worked closely with the co-chairmen and the board to adapt and modify the LCCR's goals to meet the changing needs both in the South and in the North. He attended all of the Executive Committee meetings and participated in the decision-making process.

Bernhard actually began working with the LCCR part time in the early summer of 1964 while he was still on Thurgood Marshall's staff at the State Department.[51] He worked with the 18 volunteer lawyers sponsored by the LCCR in the Students Nonviolent Coordination Committee's (SNCC) "Mississippi Summer" Project.[52] The 18 lawyers were sent to Mississippi at the request of the National Council of Churches (NCC). Their role was to aid the NCC ministers in the event that they ran into trouble with the law and were unable to secure legal assistance from the local Mississippi bar. Managing the Mississippi volunteers was Bernhard's primary responsibility at the time he was chosen as LCCR's executive director in September 1964 at the age of 33.

Bernhard was a graduate of Dartmouth University and Yale Law School and had clerked for Judge Luther W. Youndahl on the U.S. District Court for the District of Columbia. He came to the committee after having been the staff director of the U.S. Commission on Civil

---

49. Records of the LCCR, Executive Director File, Resumé, Berl I. Bernhard, 1968.
50. Interview with Berl Bernhard, March 3, 1993.
51. Bernhard Resumé, *supra* note 49.
52. Interview, *supra* note 50.
53. *Id.* Bernhard left the Civil Rights Commission in January and worked for the next six months with Judge Thurgood Marshall, who was at the Department of State, as an American Specialist to East Africa (Kenya, Tanganyika, Uganda, and Ethiopia).

Rights and a consultant[53] to Thurgood Marshall.[54] Despite his civil rights background, Bernhard was "to the manor born." He was comfortable with the group right from the beginning[55] and they with him. He moved with ease within the committee ranks. The ability to deal as an equal with the leaders of the legal establishment was an important asset, particularly when he was called upon to explain controversial social reform programs both in the North and the South. Bernhard's civil rights background, professional training, and personal temperament made him an asset for the changing times. A series of interviews with former co-chairmen and staff members makes it clear that Bernhard was a team player, a self starter, and someone who had "firsthand knowledge" and a "feel for the problems and the people" in the movement in the South.[56]

Bernhard moved quickly to enlarge the operation that he inherited from Stahl. The committee moved from the Cutler firm into independent offices.[57] John H. Doyle III, a volunteer for the LCCR in the 1964 "Mississippi Summer," was hired as an assistant executive director.[58] Bernhard and Doyle assumed a daunting workload. Under Bernhard, the national headquarters was transformed into the committee's nerve center and the role of executive director became more and more indispensable to the co-chairmen and the Executive Committee, who were, after all, part-time volunteers.

In the early years, funding the work of the committee was the job of the board and the Finance Committee. Bernhard shouldered much of the Finance Committee's responsibilities. In the early 1960s, Bernhard and his contemporaries were pioneers in developing fund-raising techniques for non-

---

54. Records of the LCCR, Executive Director File, Resume, Berl I. Bernhard, December 1965. He was nominated by President John F. Kennedy in June of 1961 and confirmed by the Senate in July.

55. Minutes, Aug. 13, 1964. When he was introduced as the Executive Director-Elect, he rose and announced that "he would be calling on committee members for their help."

56. Interviews with Jerome Shestack, Louis Oberdorfer, and Harry McPherson, 1996-1997.

57. Records of the LCCR, Announcement in Executive Director File: "Berl I. Bernhard as of September 1, 1964 became Executive Director. The Committee will move its office to Suite 1035, Universal Building North, 1875 Connecticut Avenue N.W., Washington, D.C. 20009.

58. Records of the LCCR, Executive Director File, Memorandum from Berl I. Bernhard, Oct. 15, 1964. John Doyle joined the National Staff. He "received his LL.B. from Harvard Law School in 1962 and studied at the University of Paris under a Fulbright Grant in Jurisprudence during the academic year 1962-63. He has been an associate attorney at Patterson, Belknap & Webb in New York City since June 1963, and will serve in his position with the Lawyers' Committee under a leave of absence of one year from his firm."

profit organizations and in writing project grant applications for funds from private charitable foundations. His ability was rewarded with the respect of the co-chairmen, who sought his opinions on substantive issues. He became in effect, if not in fact, a member of the Executive Committee.

When Bernhard was introduced as the new executive director at the August meeting, one of the volunteers from the "Mississippi Summer," Robert Ostrow voiced a concern about the LCCR's withdrawal of the students and ministers from Mississippi. He believed that this would result in the isolation of the Negro leadership. Ostrow postulated that people who cooperated with the committee ". . . are in an exposed position. Because of this, the work of the Lawyers' Committee should be a continuing responsibility."[59] In a subsequent report on the LCCR 's experiences in Mississippi in 1964, Bernhard said:

> As you will note, the report recommends that the Lawyers' Committee undertake responsibility for an adequate program of representation and mediation in that State. In recent weeks the Lawyers' Committee has consulted with several representatives of foundations and other persons familiar with the crisis posed in Mississippi and interested in contributing to its solution. We have found widespread support for such an undertaking by the Lawyers' Committee.[60]

Despite the LCCR's efforts to seek support from state and local bars, the white bar in Mississippi continued to refuse to represent legitimate minority grievances. To Ostrow and others who had worked in Mississippi, it was becoming clear that as "missionaries to the bar" the LCCR was not succeeding. Nonetheless, the board decided to continue its efforts in that direction. The committee decided to staff and open an office in the state to further encourage Mississippi lawyers to accept responsibility for the equitable administration of justice in their state.

At the board meeting on January 27, 1965, it was resolved that the LCCR establish an office in Jackson, Mississippi, "to be staffed by at least two full-time attorneys and volunteer lawyers to be recruited from throughout the country."[61] The minutes of that meeting reveal that "the ultimate

---

59. Minutes of the Aug. 13, 1964 Meeting, at 25.
60. Records of the LCCR, Board of Directors File, Memorandum, Jan. 22, 1965, From Berl Bernhard to the Board of Directors, p. 2.
61. Records of the LCCR, Board of Directors File, Resolution of the Board of Directors January 27, 1965. Attached to the Minutes, Meeting of the Board of Directors, Jan. 27, 1965.

purpose of the project would be to bring about the full assumption of responsibility for representation on the part of the Mississippi Bar."[62] Segal expressed the hope that the LCCR would be able to withdraw its program within two or three years, at which time the Mississippi Bar and the NAACP Legal Defense Fund might be able to bear the full burden of responsibility for civil rights cases in the state.[63] A liaison arrangement was made through Earl Thomas, president of the Mississippi State Bar Association, with the hope that when the committee ran into trouble finding local counsel, the association would help.[64] At the direction of the board[65] in June 1965, the Mississippi office was opened and staffed.

The office quickly experience a baptism by fire. On June 14, 1965, less than two weeks after the office opened, hundreds of demonstrators were arrested in Jackson for peacefully marching in protest of bills under consideration by the Mississippi legislature. The LCCR became involved in the litigation of the mass arrests and imprisonments of civil rights activists in Jackson.[66] The Jackson office and the leadership of the LCCR were unprepared for the committee's new role. The focus of the organization shifted to the Jackson litigation office. Shuttling back and forth, Bernhard and Doyle spent a great deal of time in Mississippi.[67]

---

62. Records of the LCCR, Board of Directors File, Minutes, Meeting of the Board of Directors, Jan. 27, 1965, at 2.

63. *Id.*

64. *Id.*

65. Minutes, Board Meeting, Jan. 7, 1965. In attendance at the Board Meeting that authorized the Jackson, Mississippi, office were: Harrison Tweed, Bernard Segal, Lloyd Cutler, Morris Abram, Bruce Bramble, John Buchanan, James Dezendorf, Nathan Goodnow, David Maxwell, Samuel Pierce, Jr., Eugene Rostow, Whitney North Seymour, Jerome Shestack, Arthur Shores, Davidson Sommers, John Wade, Berl Bernhard, and John Doyle III.

66. Ten Year Report, *supra* note 19, at 30. Natchez, Mississippi, was the scene of demonstrations against city officials who had closed a city park and swimming pool rather than integrate them. A mass demonstration was sparked by the closing and subsequent car bombing of a NAACP worker's car. Hundreds of blacks were arrested. There were no bail bondsmen and property bonds were refused. The arrested were first herded into the civic auditorium and then sent 200 miles north to the Mississippi State Penitentiary at Parchman. There they were forced to strip naked, take cold showers, and drink laxatives. Many were beaten. No medical help was available. Days later they were released and given no assistance in returning to their homes. The LCCR filed suit in federal court to enjoin further enforcement of the parade and leafleting ordinances and the Fifth Circuit declared them unconstitutional.

67. Interview with Berl Bernhard, March 3, 1993.

When the Mississippi Project was approved at the board meeting in January, the ability of the LCCR to attract good recruits was one area seriously underestimated. The board had great faith in the willingness of the private bar to support the Jackson office. One board member, Morris Abram, compared it to the Peace Corps. He said that the proposed program would be "as a Peace Corps . . .which would draw upon the best young legal talent from all sections of the country."[68] The committee board proposed to contact "leading law firms to request that they donate the time of younger associates to the Lawyers' Committee projects," which would be publicized through bar associations.[69] One year later to the day, January 27, 1966, the Jackson office chief counsel, Richard Tuttle, came to the board meeting. Because he felt unable to properly handle the case load, he brought his letter of resignation. He wrote that, in his opinion, the Jackson office has been staffed inadequately by volunteers and, as a result, the work has not been of a quality with which he would like his name associated. The litigation undertaken as a result of demonstrations in Jackson and later in Natchez, Mississippi, that resulted in the mass arrests was only part of a huge case load that had begun to accumulate. Tuttle told the board that his office was involved with clients all over the state, "mostly in criminal defense matters but also in cases involving complaints of violations of public accommodations section of the Civil Rights Act of 1964." He and his staff met regularly with a liaison man assigned by the Mississippi Bar, but no help was forthcoming from Mississippi lawyers.[70] Bernhard and Whitney North Seymour, a member of the Board of Directors and a former president of the American Bar Association, were in charge of recruiting for the Jackson office. They told the meeting of the "extreme difficulty" they encountered in recruiting volunteers. The response to Seymour's recruiting efforts in New York was "disappointing" and the executive director, who had contacted all the major law schools, had been turned down "flatly."[71]

The committee's relations with the state bar deteriorated. In December 1966 the Mississippi State Bar complained of violations of the agreement under which the LCCR opened its office. The state bar withdrew its consent for committee lawyers to practice in Mississippi courts. In 1967, the U.S.

---

68. Records of the LCCR, Board of Directors File, Minutes of the Board of Directors Meeting: LCCR, Jan. 27, 1965.

69. *Id.* at 3.

70. *Id.* at 31.

71. Records of the LCCR, Board of Directors File, Memorandum to the Executive Committee, Jan. 27, 1966, from Berl Bernhard, 1-4.

District Court for the Southern District of Mississippi adopted new rules of practice designed to bar out-of-state civil rights lawyers from appearing in that federal court. Committee lawyers promptly challenged the rules in a mandamus action. The Fifth Circuit invalidated the rules on the ground that they abridged the rights of civil rights litigants to seek relief in federal court.[72]

Louis Oberdorfer, who was at the meeting when Tuttle tendered his resignation, put forward a revolutionary suggestion for enhancing the litigation work of the Mississippi office. Oberdorfer proposed that the large East Coast firms represented by the LCCR accept pro bono civil rights litigation. He suggested a plan be instituted that would operate as follows:

> A person in Mississippi aggrieved by private persons or public officials would, as in the past, bring his or her problem to the Mississippi office. Where the problem required legal services on a continuing basis . . . a lawyer in the Mississippi office would provide the needed services. In other cases, the Lawyers' Committee representative would retain one of the firms in Washington, New York, Philadelphia, or some other metropolitan area, experienced in handling cases in other jurisdictions by associating with local counsel. The firm would take the matter as a firm responsibility and would provide the manpower to meet that responsibility. It would be handled like any other matter except that the firm would pay any expenses for travel, telephone, etc. and no fee would be charged. He pointed out that this plan would provide the Mississippi Bar with much more convincing evidence of the national Bar's strong commitment to assure equal justice under law.[73]

Oberdorfer's suggestion was like throwing seeds in the wind. As was discussed in Chapter 1,[74] it was not the conventional practices of law firms to offer this kind of pro bono aid and where the "seeds" might fall and what might grow was anybody's guess that day. But the group that it was offered to had some ability to influence the direction of their law firms. Further, pro bono legal aid was an honored tradition of the American bar.[75] Over time, a number of the board members and their firms did offer their assistance to

---

72. Sanders v. Russell, 401 F.2d 241 (5th Cir. 1968).
73. Memorandum, *supra* note 71, at 7.
74. For a discussion of legal services offered by the American legal profession prior to 1960, see chapter one, *infra*.
75. *Id.*

the Jackson office, particularly with the complex federal litigation in Mississippi.[76] When Oberdorfer became co-chairmen in 1967, he adapted this model and used the idea of the large law firms pro bono resources and litigation services as the basis for the LCCR's Urban Areas Project. This project changed the course of the committee and will be discussed at length later in this chapter.

After some discussion, Tuttle offered to remain in Jackson as chief counsel until a replacement could be found. John Doyle, Berl Bernhard's assistant executive director in the national office, moved to Jackson to take over the position. Another lawyer, Robert Nelson, was hired as Doyle's replacement in Washington. Doyle, too, had his hands full in Jackson and was replaced within the year by Dennison Ray, a litigator from the New York firm of Cravath, Swaine & Moore.[77]

Understaffed, the Jackson office was contending with an overwhelming case load. Frank R. Parker in the Jackson office was beginning to take test cases challenging the attempts of the Mississippi legislature to block the effects of the Voting Rights Act. The act swept away the primary legal barriers to black registration and voting in the South, eliminating the literacy tests and the poll taxes, and allowing the Justice Department to dispatch federal registrars and poll watchers to insure the integrity of the voting process. Yet in the years that followed, despite tremendous increases in black registration, blacks found that they were unable to elect more than a few candidates to public office. Southern legislatures adopted a strategy of dilution of black voting strength. "Immediately after the act was passed, southern states, led by Mississippi, adopted massive resistance strategies designed to nullify the impact of the black vote. Devices such as at-large elections, racial gerrymandering of district lines, abolishing elective offices and making them appointive, and increasing the qualifying requirements for candidates running for public office were instituted."[78] In 1965, Mississippi became the testing ground for southern resistance to efforts to empower black voters. As a result, the first court cases challenging the new dilution of black voting strength were brought in Mississippi.[79] The LCCR's

---

76. Interview with James Robertson (October 1997) and Armand Derfner (September 1997), former litigator for LCDC in Jackson, Mississippi, and former director of the LCCR Voting Rights Project, Washington, D.C. Also, when Oberdorfer became co-chairman in 1967, he adapted this model and used the idea of the large law firms' pro bono resources and litigation services as the basis for the LCCR Urban Areas Project—a project that changed the course of the committee.

77. Interview with Berl Bernhard, March 3, 1993.

78. PARKER, *supra* note 14, at 1.

79. *Id.*

office played an important part in this battle. Frank R. Parker, a staff attorney hired as a litigator for the Jackson office, was a key figure in solidifying the committee's role as a leading player in the struggle for voting rights reform. According to a former chief counsel of the Jackson office who worked with Parker, "Frank Parker, who came from the Civil Rights Commission, was the only one of us who knew what he wanted to do. He wanted to work on voting rights."[80] As Parker writes in his book *Black Votes Count*, an account of black political empowerment after 1965:

> . . .given the enormous amount of time and expense involved in complex federal litigation, most of the major civil rights reform litigation after 1965 was handled by three national civil rights reform organizations, which maintained offices in Jackson—the Lawyers' Committee for Civil Rights Under Law, the Lawyers' Constitutional Defense Committee (LCDC); and the NAACP Legal Defense and Educational Fund, Inc. . . . Given the Inc. Fund's specialization in school related cases, the law suits contesting Mississippi's political massive resistance legislation were handled by either the Lawyers' Committee or the Lawyers' Constitutional Defense Committee. During the early 1960s . . . these two groups litigated almost all the voting rights cases in Mississippi.[81]

The LCDC office in Jackson closed down in 1971. Armand Derfner and Mary Frances Derfner, the voting rights litigation team for LCDC, continued reform work with the LCCR.

Supporting and supervising the work of the Mississippi office was a major role of the national office and a major part of Bernhard's duties. However, the committee's growing commitment in Mississippi was joined by a second priority—the administration of justice in the North—at the request of President Johnson. Bernhard remembers that "everything was moving very fast in those days,"[82] and the pace picked up after the riot-torn summer of 1965. That September, President Johnson asked the committee

---

80. Interview in April 1997 with the Honorable James Robertson, U.S. District Court, Washington, D.C., former chief counsel of the Jackson, Mississippi, office of the LCCR, 1969-1970. Judge Robertson remembers that "Frank Parker was the only one who came to the Jackson Office with a particular mission—voting rights."

81. *Id.*

82. Interview with Berl Bernhard, March 3, 1993.

83. Letter dated Sept. 9, 1965, from Lyndon B. Johnson, President of the United States, to Whitney North Seymour, co-chairman of the LCCR, reprinted in the Statement of Purpose and Activities: LCCR, Whitney North Seymour and Burke Marshall, co-chairmen, 1966.

"to play a more vigorous role in the large cities of this country."[83]

In August 1965, at the LCCR's Board of Directors meeting, which was again held in conjunction with the ABA's annual meeting, Harrison Tweed and Bernard Segal stepped down as co-chairmen. In the tradition of the White House Conference at which the committee was created, President Lyndon Johnson asked Burke Marshall and Whitney North Seymour to serve as the new co-chairmen.[84] Former Assistant Attorney General for Civil Rights. Marshall had left the Justice Department and was serving as general counsel to IBM. Seymour was a founding members of the LCCR, a leader of the New York City bar, a former president of the ABA, and the senior partner in the Wall Street law firm Simpson, Thatcher & Bartlett. A few weeks later, on September 9, 1965, President Johnson wrote a letter to the co-chairmen formally asking the LCCR to become involved in the urban centers of the North, as well as acting in the South.[85] The co-chairmen agreed to act on the President's request. It was in the large northern cities, acting as lawyers in defense of minority rights, that the LCCR found its distinct role in the American civil rights revolution.

President Johnson's September 9 letter to the new co-chairmen was written during the aftermath of the Watts riots in Los Angeles. In the "Statement of Purpose and Activities" that Marshall and Seymour issued, they reported, "The committee at once embarked on the needs of these areas. It concluded that two broad types of programs are mandatory. One, to fulfill the President's request for strengthening respect for law and order (in) the existing crisis of police/community relations. The other is responsive to the Presidential request for the protection of the legal rights of economically deprived slum dwellers. It is a legal assistance program that is concerned with basic social reform."[86] However, when they met officially for the first time, the minutes of that meeting stated, "It was agreed that the President's letter should be answered, but there was some uncertainty as to just how it should be done." The job of working up a proposed program of committee activities in the urban areas was given to Marshall. Bernhard was asked to prepare a "draft policy statement for committee's representation efforts." Seymour, with the help of Bernhard, was assigned the chief responsibility for fund raising and

---

84. Biennial Report: 1967-1968, LCCR.

85. LCCR Statement of Purpose and Activities, 1966.

86. *Id.*; *see* section entitled "A Program for Urban Areas."

87. Records of the LCCR, Board of Directors File, Meeting of Co-Chairmen, Sept. 23, 1965. Further, it was decided that the board would meet semiannually and that the Executive Committee would meet quarterly. The officers would meet on the first Monday of every month at the Bar Association of the City of New York from 12:00 to 3:00

increasing membership, particularly in the South.[87]

At an Executive Committee meeting in January 1966, Marshall said that he and Bernhard "had devoted a great deal of time to considering the various types of programs the Committee could design for the urban areas in response to the President's request." They had considered two main qualifications. First, the programs should be in areas in which lawyers have some specific competence and, second, the program should be in areas where few other lawyers' or citizens' groups were working. The two concluded that a police/community relations program met both of these qualifications and that the need in this area was considerably greater than in any of the other areas considered.[88]

Undoubtedly, their deliberations were influenced by the fact that on December 8, 1965, Bernhard reported, "I also spoke briefly last week with Chris Edley of the Ford Foundation about our possible entry into the urban areas. He was particularly interested in having the committee in the field of police and community relations, and believed that the Ford Foundation itself might be interested in sponsoring such a program." In the same report, Bernhard noted that the head of the Legal Services Division of the Poverty Program, Clinton Bamberger, "was very interested in the Committee's urban program and intimated that financing could be obtained from the Poverty Program for specific programs of a representational nature."[89]

The board of the LCCR voted to proceed with an experimental police/community relations project. Three cities would be selected based upon their demonstrated need for such a program. A description of the key elements of the new project can be found in the records of the board meeting. The board believed that the pivotal job in the program would be that of the voluntary coordinator. He would have to be an outstanding lawyer from among the committee's membership who would be willing to undertake the task of visiting with the bar in the three experimental cities. "Acting informally and quietly," he would create an autonomous committee of lawyers in each city. The autonomous committees would be funded by the LCCR. These committees would be assisted by a staff from the Washington office. One lawyer would be

---

in the Carter Room. They would be luncheon meetings. The committee membership was approximately 200. By 1968, it was almost 300. It would take the next three years to develop fully what has become known as the committee's Urban Areas Project. The first step was the creation of the LCCR's Police-Community Relations Project.

88. Records of the LCCR, Board of Directors File, Memorandum to the Executive Committee from Berl Bernhard, Jan. 27, 1966.

89. Records of the LCCR, Foundation Groups File, Memorandum from Berl Bernhard to Messrs. Seymour, Marshall, Tweed, Segal, Burney, and Oberdorfer, Dec. 8, 1965.

assigned to each city and would be responsible for evaluating the local situation and determining the problems and needs of the individual cities. After this was done, the staff would work with consultants from the International Association of Chiefs of Police and the U.S. Conference of Mayors and elsewhere to develop a specific program for each city that would be responsive to that city's needs, taking into account its political and social structure and history. At the same time, the consultants and staff would prepare and distribute a looseleaf police/community relations manual and a model human relations training curriculum."[90]

The Police/Community Relations Project was funded under a grant from the Office of Law Enforcement Assistance Administration. Atlanta, Detroit, and Seattle were chosen as the three experimental cities. "Funds from a Ford Foundation grant subsequently made possible the establishment of an office and staff in each city to carry out the mandates of the local committees."[91] This project, coupled with the earlier contacts created by the Committee for Community Relations, under the chairmanship of Arthur Dean, was helping to build a network of professionals who shared the LCCR's objectives within the legal communities of the largest cities.

The expanded commitments of the LCCR were becoming much more expensive. Originally, the members of the committee relied on the large law firms to fund their work, which was limited in scope. From June 1963 through September 1964, the LCCR had raised approximately $70,000 toward an estimated budget for 1965 of $100,000.[92] When Bernhard joined the national office, the committee's first application for a grant from a private charitable foundation, the Fels Foundation, was in the process of being finalized. It had taken practically the entire tenure of Stahl, working with the Finance Committee, to write and submit the Fels Foundation application. Due to the length of time the application was "in process,"[93] it was believed that foundations could not be a vital source for funding committee activities. That was about to change.

The board estimated that in 1965 the budgetary needs of the committee

---

90. *Id.*

91. Biennial Report, 1967-1968, of the LCCR (LCCR, August 1968) at 16.

92. Records of the LCCR, Foundation Grants File, Letter dated Sept. 24, 1964, from Berl I. Bernhard to Dale Phelan, Executive Director, Samuel S. Fels Fund. "1. The present working budget for the year 1964, approved by our executive committee on March 25, 1964, is . . . $100,000."

93. Records of the LCCR, Foundation Grants File, Application to the Fels Foundation of Philadelphia for a Grant to the LCCR, July 1964. The application asked for $25,000 to support a project "to promote understanding and acceptance of the Civil Rights Bill and to urge compliance after its enactment." $10,000 was granted to the LCCR in November 1964.

would more than triple. The Jackson, Mississippi, office alone would require $200,000 in its first year and $100,000 to $150,000 a year thereafter.[94] With the board's decision to assume responsibility for establishing projects in the North, the budget projections for 1966 quickly rose to $500,000.[95] Bernhard spent much of his time learning how and where to raise funds. In the process, the board and executive director came to understand a great deal about the relationship between mission and money,

Bernhard took the initiative to develop some new areas of fund raising. With the blessing of the co-chairmen, he contacted "a respectable and effective fund-raiser in New York City," Harold Oram. Oram was "recommended by Jack Greenberg, Vernon Eagle, and some others." Oram had convinced Bernhard that "he would have no trouble" raising $100,000 at a dinner for the LCCR from the New York City area alone. "This would require no work on our part," Bernhard told the co-chairmen. "To raise this amount of money," he told them, Oram "would expect $10,000."[96] The co-chairmen decided to follow Bernhard's advice and the dinner was the first of many successful fund-raising events of this type.[97]

Money was becoming a key priority. In 1965, the job of going "hat in hand" to the foundations, as Segal had put it, fell increasingly on Bernhard, who had the complete support of the co-chairmen, the Executive Committee, and the other board members. During 1965, eight private charitable foundations gave $155,000 to the LCCR.[98] However, new sources of income had to

---

94. Records of the LCCR, Fundraising File, Letter dated March 8, 1965, from Berl Bernhard to Grenville Clark. *Also see* March 15, 1965 Draft of Memo to Selected Local Lawyers Who Will Organize Fund Raising for the LCCR in Their Respective Cities.

95. Records of the LCCR, Executive Director File, Program, Dinner in Honor of the Honorable Nicholas deB. Katzenbach, Attorney General of the United States, given by the LCCR, Wednesday, May 4, 1966.

96. Records of the LCCR, Correspondence File, March 17, 1965, Letter from Berl Bernhard to Bernard Segal.

97. Records of the LCCR, Correspondence File, April 27, 1965, Letter from Berl Bernhard to Harold Oram. *Also see* Memorandum, May 10, 1965, from Berl Bernhard to Harrison Tweed. The money raised at the dinner was to be split 50/50 "between the Mississippi project and general funding of the committee's operation until such time as we are assured of full and adequate financing for the Mississippi project."

98. Records of the LCCR, Foundation Groups File, Memorandum from Margaret North, Dec. 8, 1965, to Bernard G. Segal. They were the Field Foundation, $50,000; The New World Foundation, $25,000; The Taconic Foundation, $25,000; The Twentieth Century Fund, $25,000; The Fels Foundation, $10,000; The Apple Hill Foundation, $10,000; The Overbrook Foundation, $5,000; and the New York Foundation, $5,000.

be found if the committee was to grow. It was decided to concentrate on three areas: the large foundations, such as the Ford Foundation, the Rockefeller Foundation, and the Carnegie Corp.; multimillion-dollar corporations; and the organized bar. Whitney North Seymour and Berl Bernhard handled the solicitation of the bar. They divided the country up by large cities and recruited committee members of stature—board members, if available—in their local areas to further allocate the solicitation responsibilities. The effort was expected to fund one-third of the committee's needs.[99]

The LCCR had many close ties with the corporate community. A Corporate Fund-Raising Committee was established. It consisted of Lloyd Cutler in Washington, D.C., Co-Chair Burke Marshall, general counsel of IBM, and Bruce Bromley in New York. The committee was also charged with covering one-third of the LCCR's expenses. As Cutler wrote to the chairman of Xerox, committee member Sol Linowitz, the "business community is really a national community, so we have to turn to national companies." The "communications-business machines industry" was to be the starting point for this type of solicitation, since "so many of our Executive Committee members have ties to that industry." They hoped to establish regular annual contributions from the corporations such as Xerox, IBM, CBS, RCA, and others. They approached the car industry as well. "All four passenger car manufacturers and Kaiser Jeep Corporation contributed more than $30,000 in cash and autos."[100] The lawyers in the Jackson, Mississippi, office had use of the cars.

In the 1965-1966 fiscal year, the Ford Foundation and the other 15,000 private foundations in the United States gave away some $1.1 billion for public purposes. Ford alone gave some $250 million around the world.[101] A sizable grant from just one of these foundations could provide the LCCR with financial security, at least for a period of time.

The grant process at the Ford Foundation was "bureaucratized" and applications took a very long time to wend their way through the system. "Ford grants usually carry a long internal history," according to an article about the organization. "Every grant must work its way through a 'discussion paper' prepared for the staff officers in a particular program, such as education. The

---

99. Records of the LCCR, Correspondence File, March 15, 1965, Draft of Memo to Selected Local Lawyers Who Will Organize Fund Raising for the Lawyers' Committee in Their Respective Cities, Course of Action, Finances.

100. Records of the LCCR, Correspondence File, Letter dated Oct. 3, 1966, from Lloyd Cutler to Sol Linowitz.

101. *The American Way of Giving*, NEWSWEEK, March 14, 1966, at 87.

next step takes it to all the officers and, finally, through the president to the trustees. Trustee approval of programs of projects is far from automatic."[102] The LCCR's requests for project funding were not approved by the Ford Foundation until June of 1966 when the foundation granted the committee $600,000. In 1966, McGeorge Bundy left the Johnson Administration to head the Ford Foundation. Bundy who was in John F. Kennedy's Administration and served Lyndon Johnson as National Security Advisor, knew Burke Marshall, Louis Oberdorfer, and a number of others on the board of the committee.[103] He was acquainted with the committee's history with the Kennedys and Lyndon Johnson's request that the committee become involved in the urban areas. He had reason to respect the personal accomplishments and professional judgment of its members. Bundy had confidence in the ability of the committee and in the leadership of Burke Marshall.[104] In announcing the general purposes grant to the LCCR, Bundy said, "If the law is to fulfill its role as a great binding force for civil peace in our country, it must be readily at the service of all, the poor as well as the rich."[105]

The LCCR and the Ford Foundation numbered among the country's establishment organizations that were trying to respond to an explosive situation within the nation. In the summer of 1967, the United States witnessed the worst rioting in its history. Arthur Schlesinger described it as "a contagion of riots, marked by arson, looting, and sniping, began in the South in May, spread to the North in June and reached an awful climax in July." Twenty-six people were killed in Newark, New Jersey, in disorders lasting from July 12 to July 17. On July 23 the greatest violence of all exploded in Detroit,

---

102. *Id.* at 89.
103. Interviews with Harry McPherson, September 30, 1997; Berl Bernhard, March 3, 1993; and Lou Oberdorfer, January 1994.
104. Fred P. Graham, *Five-Year Study Due of Arrests Here: $1 Million Ford Grant Will Set Up 3-Part Program Under Burke Marshall,* June 3, 1966, THE NEW YORK TIMES, at 1. Graham reported that, at the same time the LCCR grant was announced, the Ford Foundation announced a $1.1 million grant to a new civic group, the Vera Institute of Justice, for a five-year study in New York City of police handling of confessions, alcoholics, and the early release of arrested persons. The chairman of the board of the new institute was Burke Marshall, co-chairman of the LCCR. THE NEW YORK TIMES reported that "[t]he Vera Institute of Justice, a new organization, will replace the Vera Foundation and operate the program.

   "The Vera Foundation was established in New York City in 1961 by Louis Schweitzer . . . the Ford Foundation has agreed to make the grant but is withholding its formal grant letter until the charter of the new institute is registered with the state. The expansion was necessary because the Ford Foundation does not make direct grants to family-controlled foundations."
105. Graham, *supra* note 104.

where 43 people died in four days of rioting. Governor George Romney called out the National Guard. "Later that night Johnson sent tanks and paratroopers into Detroit."[106]

The American people were troubled. As noted earlier, one of the most significant responses to the riots was President Johnson creation of a Commission on Civil Disorders, chaired by Governor Otto Kerner of Illinois. The commission issued a report in February 1968 that portrayed the United States as a nation moving toward "two societies, one black, one white—separate but unequal" 'The White House," Daniel Patrick Moynihan wrote, "would not receive it.'"[107] The LCCR's response to the riots in the North changed the character and scope of its activities.

Like the country, the committee faced a crossroads. It had been formed in June 1963 during a racial crisis in the South to mobilize the private bar to help mediate immediate problems. Its original goal was to educate lawyers through the offices of the organized bar to assume some responsibility for the equitable administration of justice in communities. When it became evident that the original goal of the LCCR was unattainable, the committee modified its "missionaries to the Bar" stance and altered its practices to become actively involved in civil rights litigation aimed at securing social reform and compliance with the law in Mississippi. Its experiences in the Jackson, Mississippi, litigation office affected its approach in 1968 when President Johnson requested the committee's help in the solution of the racial problems in the North. By that time, the members of the LCCR had come to see that not only were minorities and the poor facing social, economic, and political inequities but they also had to contend with an even more invidious problem—the breakdown of the American system of justice. Building on LCCR experiences in Mississippi and in the Police/Community Relations Project, in 1968 the new co-chairman of committee laid out a new direction for the organization and for the establishment bar. Not only did individual lawyers need to assume responsibility for the administration of justice in the United States, but the nation's largest law firms did as well. Because of their size and power, both financial and human, the LCCR devised a plan to mobilize their services pro bono in a unique effort to provide some balance to the justice system for the poor. The committee stands out as a leader of this new legal aid movement because its Urban Areas Project, launched in 1968, led the way for the institutionalization of a pro bono bar in the United States.

---

106. Arthur M. Schlesinger, Jr., Robert Kennedy and His Times 337 (Houghton Mifflin 1978) at 797.

107. *Id.* at 846.

In August of 1967, Louis Oberdorfer and Arthur Dean were asked by President Johnson to take over the co-chairmanship from Burke Marshall and Whitney North Seymour.[108] Former Assistant Attorney General Oberdorfer had returned to his law practice at Wilmer, Cutler & Pickering in Washington, D.C. Dean, the former U.N. negotiator at Panmunjan in Korea who had negotiated the peace settlement for the Eisenhower Administration and the Nuclear Test Ban Treaty for President Kennedy, practiced law in New York with the Wall Street firm of Sullivan & Cromwell. Co-Chairmen Oberdorfer and Dean assessed the situation in the United States and laid out their vision for the future of the LCCR. In a letter to the membership in November 1967, they wrote, "The disturbing events of last summer in the cities from coast to coast have impressed on your Executive Committee the imperative need to reassess and then redirect the activities of the Lawyers' Committee." They assured the membership that they intended to continue the committee's activities in the South. But the events of the past summer illustrated that many problems that the committee was attempting to deal with in the South were limited to that region of the country. These problems included people arrested without charges, held without bond, abused by police officers without recourse, and tried and convicted without representation by counsel. The co-chairmen saw a great need for additional "Negro personnel" for service as police "as a means of reassuring Negroes of the even-handedness of law enforcement and as a specific deterrent to mob violence." They intended to expand the Police/Community Relations Project and saw "the resultant necessity for more funds."

Two new projects were going to be undertaken "to contribute to reducing tensions in the cities." Former Assistant Attorney General John Douglas would organize a committee to cooperate with the Department of Defense "in the recruitment and training of Negro personnel." The Executive Committee would contact committee members in the major cities who would work to find employment in their cities for veterans as police officers. The second committee would be chaired by former Under Secretary of Defense Cyrus Vance. Vance had been an observer of the justice system during the race riots in Detroit. He reported to the committee about the virtual "breakdown of the administration of justice" in that city. Police arrested hundreds of people and judges set very high bail for them. As a result, there was a large number of cases and defendants than could be processed by the then available judges, prosecutors, and detention facilities. Vance's committee

---

108. Records of the LCCR, Reports File, Biennial Report, 1967-1968 of the LCCR, August 1968.

would develop an emergency plan for the administration of justice, which will "be farmed out to members of our Committee in various large cities in the hope that it will serve to prevent repetitions of the collapse of the judicial powers which occurred in riot tom cities." To meet the commitments in the South and the expanded responsibilities in the urban areas, the committee estimated expenditures of approximately $500,000 during the year with an increase to $600,000 for 1968. The co-chairmen requested that "each member, or his firm," consider establishing an annual contribution to the LCCR. "While lawyers' contributions are no longer the mainstay of the Committee financially," they wrote, "the foundations insist, as a condition of their support, that we maintain an 'earnest' of contributions by lawyers." In 1966 the committee received $56,250 in contributions from individual lawyers and law firms. "This work is a major responsibility of the Bar. We cannot neglect it." In November 1967, the committee had raised only $1,105 and was $75,000 short.[109]

Co-Chairmen Oberdorfer and Dean turned to the Ford Foundation for a grant. In 1968, the foundation awarded the committee another grant of $950,000 for the Urban Areas Project. The project-specific grant was to cover the formation of local lawyers' committees in 25 cities. The goal of the local committees was to respond to the specific needs of minority clients. The Executive Committee hoped to establish subcommittees in each of the cities, which were to be made up of at least three lawyers. When possible, the subcommittees were to include a senior leader of the bar, a younger lawyer

---

109. Records of the LCCR, Correspondence File, Letter, November 1967, from Louis F. Oberdorfer and Arthur H. Dean, co-chairmen of the LCCR, to the Members of the Lawyers' Committee. Listed on the letterhead were the names of the 60 members of the board. An asterisk designated the Executive Committee members. The Board of Directors consisted of *Morris B. Abram; Eugene D. Bennett; Henry Brandis, Jr.; *Bruce Bromley; John G. Buchanan; Kenneth J. Burns, Jr.; Clifford Carlsen, Jr.; Warren M. Christopher; Archibald Cox; Walter E. Craig; *Lloyd N. Cutler; *James T. Danaher; Charles W. Davis; James C. Dezendorf; *John W. Douglas; Jefferson B. Fordham; *Cody Fowler; Eugene H. Freedheim; Harold J. Gallagher; *Lloyd Garrison; *Gerhard A. Gessell; Nathan B. Goodnow; William Gossett; Erwin N. Griswold; Albert E. Jenner, Jr.; W. Page Keeton; David W. Kendall; Robert E. Lillard; Sol M. Linowitz; Arthur Littleton; Ross L. Malone; *William I. Marbury; *Orison S. Marden; David F. Maxwell; *Robert B. McKay; Robert W. Meserve; William R. Ming; James M. Nabritt, Jr.; *William H. Orrick; Samuel R. Pierce, Jr.; Louis H. Pollack; John D. Randall; Charles S. Rhine; William P. Rogers; *Samuel I. Rosenman; Eugene V. Rostow; Barnabas F. Sears; *Jerome J. Shestack; Arthur D. Shores; Sylvester C. Smith, Jr.; Davidson Sommers; *Theodore C. Sorensen; *William B. Spann, Jr.; *David Stahl; Gary Thoron; *Cyrus R. Vance; James Vorenberg; *John W. Wade; *Bethuel M. Webster; Herbert Wechsler.

experienced in public affairs, and a Negro lawyer. A small staff would be employed full time. The staff director of the LCCR would be responsible for designing programs and coordinating the work of each local committee.[110]

Milan C. Miskovsky

It was during this period that Harry McPherson, White House counsel to Lyndon Johnson, "convinced" Bernhard to take a six months leave of absence from the LCCR. McPherson wanted Bernhard to head up the White House Conference on Civil Rights.[111] Bernhard decided to take the position and assumed the title of counsel to the LCCR. After serving with the White House Conference on Civil Rights, Bernhard decided that the time had come to return to the private practice with the young firm of Verner, Lipfert & Bernhard. He was succeeded by Milan C. "Mike" Miskovsky, who brought to the committee different talents and experiences.

Co-Chairman Oberdorfer asked Miskovsky to join the LCCR. While Assistant General counsel of the Central Intelligence Agency, Miskovsky had been the chief liaison officer with the Department of Justice. He became acquainted with Assistant Attorney General Oberdorfer and Robert Kennedy when their respective agencies worked together to obtain the release of prisoners taken at the Bay of Pigs. Miskovsky, who was assistant general counsel of the Treasury Department, had taken a leave of absence to become the Director of Investigations for the Kerner Commission. He was serving in that position when he was recruited by Oberdorfer.

Miskovsky, according to those who knew him and worked with him at the time, was "easy to get along with," a good administrator and problem solver, who functioned well in unstructured situations.[112] His experience with the Kerner Commission gave him credibility among the lawyers who were being asked to help establish local LCCR committees. His experience with the commission also gave him a knowledge of the basis of anger in the inner cities that went beyond an appreciation of systemic discrimination. He brought to the committee an understanding of what the inner-city problems were that gave him the sensibilities needed to deal well with minority community groups. One of Miskovsky's early initiatives was to hire Sam Peters, the first black

---

110. The description of the Urban Areas Project was taken from the LCCR's Biennial Report, 1967-1968, at 4.

111. Interview with Harry McPherson, partner in Verner, Lipfert, Bernhard, McPherson & Hand, former counsel to President Lyndon B. Johnson, Sept. 30, 1997.

112. Interviews with Louis Oberdorfer, June 1994, and Peter Connell, October 9, 1997.

113. Kirkland Taylor was the first director of the New York LCCR in 1968. Taylor was the sole black local staff director during that period. Throughout the period under discussion, the national staff and the local staffs are, with few exceptions, white. Also,

staff lawyer to join the LCCR.[113]

Miskovsky came to the LCCR when it had grown to a position of rec-ognized leadership within the legal establishment. During its less than four years of existence, a litigation office in Mississippi had been established and an urban areas program was begun. No longer would it be possible for the part-time leadership of the committee to manage its complex and costly operations. The new direction of the committee necessitated that it expand and decentralize decision-making authority. In the next few years, a new chain of command developed. This process did not happen immediately. It evolved during the tenure of Miskovsky (1968 to 1970), and his successor, James Robertson, who served from 1970 to 1972

In 1968, the new team at the helm of the LCCR, Co-Chairmen Oberdorfer and Dean, and Executive Director Miskovsky had their work cut out for them. The year was one of immense social division and political upheaval that would challenge the "rule of law" in the United States. In March 1968, Robert Kennedy, who was then a U.S. Senator from New York, announced his intention to run for the Democratic nomination for President of the United States, challenging the incumbent, Lyndon Johnson. Two weeks later, on March 31, Lyndon Johnson, beleaguered with problems at home and with the war in Vietnam, announced that he was out of the race. Within the week, on April 4, 1968, Martin Luther King, Jr. was assassinated. Black anger and frustration erupted spontaneously all over the country. King's assassination was followed by the most destructive race riots in the nation's history. There were riots in 110 cities. Thirty-nine people were killed and more than 2,500 were injured. More than 75,000 national guardsmen and

---

Interview with Clifford Alexander, former White House Assistant to McGeorge Bundy, and the first black lawyer named a partner in a major Washington establish-ment law firm. Alexander notes the lack of black lawyers hired by the law firms of the members of the LCCR in the 1960s and 1970s.

114. Interview in April 1996 with the Honorable James Robertson, District Court of the District of Columbia; former chief counsel, Jackson, Mississippi, 1969-1970; former director, National Office of the LCCR, 1970-1972. The day after King's death, a future head of the national staff, Jim Robertson, walked out of his office at Witmer, Cutler to smell tear gas. He remembers that "something happened to me when I smelled the tear gas." Robertson, who had never been in a courthouse before . . . "because in those days the 'better firms' didn't do much litigating" walked directly to the D.C. Court of General Sessions and volunteered to represent anyone who needed a lawyer. That evening his law partner, Lou Oberdorfer, called and asked him to join other partners from the firm, including Lloyd Cutler and himself, at the courthouse. Witmer, Cutler took 50 or 60 cases that night, and followed them thereafter. Robertson remembers that he knew a LCCR existed. Within a few months, he left Witmer, Cutler to join the staff of the Jackson office.

federal troops were on duty in the streets of America.[114] On June 6, 1968, Robert Kennedy was assassinated in California. Louis Oberdorfer, who headed Kennedy's campaign in Washington, D.C., remembered that his death had the effect of "resolving" those who shared his vision for American society to work even harder for the fulfillment of the principles of justice that Robert Kennedy's life represented.[115] After the first series of urban riots, Co-Chairmen Oberdorfer and Dean had unveiled their plan for an LCCR response to the needs in the inner city, the Urban Areas Project. Now, after the tumult of the spring and summer of 1968, they resolved to immediately engage the profession.

All during the summer and fall of 1968, Oberdorfer and Miskovsky traveled to the nation's largest cities to explain and recruit leading lawyers and law firms for the LCCR. Committees were begun in 14 cities: Atlanta, Cleveland, Indianapolis, Los Angeles, Philadelphia, Oakland, New York City, Seattle, Baltimore, Chicago, Kansas City, Boston, San Francisco, and Washington, D.C.[116] Five years later, nine were still in operation: Atlanta, Boston, Cleveland, Chicago, Indianapolis, Kansas City, Philadelphia, San Francisco, and Washington, D.C. The others were closed due to insufficient funds and a lack of local volunteers.[117]

Six new staff lawyers, administrative personnel, and a full-time accountant[118] were hired by Miskovsky to help direct, coordinate, and design programs for the Urban Areas Project.[119] Each of the local committees retained at least one full-time lawyer, staff volunteers, and clerical staff. Miskovsky was assigned the title director, Robert Nelson became the executive director, and a new position of assistant executive director was filled by Peter Connell, who was recruited by Miskovsky from the general counsel's office of the Treasury Department. The choice of the personnel and the organizational development of the national office were left to Miskovsky.

---

115. Interview with Louis F. Oberdorfer
116. Records of the LCCR, Executive Committee File, Minutes, Nov. 18, 1968, Attachment of Report on the establishment, staffing, and organization of the local committees in Atlanta, Cleveland, Indianapolis, Los Angeles, Philadelphia, St. Louis, Pittsburgh, Milwaukee, Oakland, New York City, Seattle, Baltimore, Chicago, Gary, Memphis, New Orleans, Kansas City, and Denver.
117. Ten Year Report, *supra* note 19, at 53.
118. The brother-in-law of Jerome J. Shestack, Leonard Feldman, CPA, of Feldman & Feldman in Philadelphia, had previously supplied his services, mostly pro bono, to the LCCR. Feldman continues to this day to consult with the LCCR.
119. Minutes, Nov. 18, 1968. Attachments: Peter Connell, Sharon White, Harvey Friedman, Samuel Peters, Errol Miller, and Jacques Feuillan.

Miskovsky, who spent a great deal of his time establishing local committees, in turn delegated authority for administration to Nelson and program
development to Connell.[120]

Miskovsky's first priority was to help the Executive Committee in the
formation of the local committees. In addition, working with individual local
offices, the national office was to create an inventory of the urban problems
in that city and the local and federal resources and programs under way or
available in each city. The local subcommittee was to undertake programs to
stimulate and assist in the implementation of ongoing programs and efforts.
For example, the national office had a police/community relations program
that the local committees were urged to replicate. The local committees were
responsible for initiating—by themselves or with other groups such as the
local Urban Coalition—additional programs as appropriate.[121]

At the end of the Urban Areas Project's first year, the LCCR announced
that the 14 operating committees had engaged about 300 volunteer lawyers
from 150 firms to work on 266 projects. The local committees litigated,
worked for legislative and administrative reform, and became involved in
extra-legal projects, such as developing a recruitment program for minority
lawyers and working to set up neighborhood dispute settlement center.[122] The
Ford Foundation expressed some concern about the lack of specific areas of

120. Interview with Peter Connell, October 9, 1997.
121. *Id.*
122. Records of the LCCR, Urban Areas Project File, Monthly Report on New Matters,
     June 1969. Of the 266 projects, 41 involved litigation and 24 legislative or administra-
     tive reform. Forty-two were extralegal. The remaining 159 (60 percent) involved the
     provision of general legal counsel. The projects span the range of problem areas as
     follows: legal services, 10; law enforcement and police community relations, 14; ad-
     ministration of justice in lower criminal courts, 21; administration of justice under
     emergency conditions, 1; structures for grievance mediation, 3; jobs and training, 19;
     economic development, 88; consumer assistance, 10; housing, 38; education, 23; health,
     5; food assistance, 2; transportation, 2; community development, 18; and other, 12.
123. Records of the LCCR, Executive Committee File, Minutes, Dec. 2, 1969. In the calen-
     dar year of 1970, the Ford Foundation granted a supplement of an additional $600,000
     for operations. These funds would be divided into $400,000 for local city support and
     $200,000 for headquarters support. However, there would be a matching requirement
     whereby Ford would provide two dollars for every one dollar raised from other sources
     by the committee. The co-chairmen reported they, along with Messrs. Vance, Marshall,
     and Miskovsky, had met with Bundy and representatives of the foundation concerning
     the request for supplemental funds. Ford officials were interested in the level of volun-
     teer services and the appearance of a lack of focus by the local committees on specific
     areas of concern, e.g., administration of justice, housing, etc. The co-chairmen ex-
     plained that the role of the local committees was to respond to specific requests of the
     cities and indeed these often covered many different areas.

focus, but it continued to be the principal support of the project.[123]

Supporting the project was not the only concern of Miskovsky and the national office. The LCCR was responsible for the oversight of the Jackson, Mississippi, office as well. LCCR's Washington staff had the responsibility for the coordination of the pro bono lawyers from the large law firms who volunteered to handle the complex cases that grew out of the work in Mississippi. They also handled fund raising and public relations.

The complexity of the growing body of substantive civil rights law, distance, and the demands of the enlarged commitments on the time of Miskovsky, the co-chairmen, and the Executive Committee, necessitated that they place great reliance on the judgment of the chief counsel of the Jackson office. Unfortunately, the Jackson office had gone through a series of chief counsels, none of whom had gotten "control" of the administration of the office.[124] In three years, 1965 to 1968, there had been four chief counsels: Richard Tuttle, John Doyle, Dennison Ray, and Larry Aschenbrenner. Ray, who came to Mississippi from the New York firm of Cravath, Swaine & Moore, was replaced because of personality conflicts.[125] He was succeeded in 1968 by Aschenbrenner, who had been a volunteer and a staff attorney in the Jackson office. In a historical symposium, convened to discuss the evolution of the civil rights movement in Mississippi, he describes the intensity of the pace and docket of the office:

> In 1965 the Lawyers' Committee's primary emphasis continued to be criminal defense, simply because there were an awful lot of arrests going on. But gradually, as months and years progressed, the emphasis of the Lawyers' Committee turned from being primarily defensive to affirmative in nature. As a result, every possible kind of discriminatory case you can think of was brought by the committee with the exception of school desegregation cases. The latter were exclusively LDF, their lawyers, who were the experts in school cases, referred their criminal and many other kinds of cases which they didn't have time to handle to us, and we referred all our school desegregation cases to them. That's how the split of the work between our two firms worked out.[126]

---

124. Interview with James Robertson, April 1996 and Louis Oberdorfer, January 1994.

125. Interview with James Robertson, former chief counsel of the LCCR Jackson, Mississippi, office, April 1996.

126. *Collection on Legal Change*, Guide to the Microfilm Edition of Southern Civil Rights Ligation Records for the 1960s, Clement E. Vose ed., Lawyers Constitutional Defense Committee, LCCR, NAACP Legal Defense Fund, Inc. (Wesleyan University), 38-39.

Aschenbrenner described the period from 1967 to 1969 as follows:

> We emphasized affirmative jury discrimination cases. We challenged the juries in 13 of the 82 counties in Mississippi . . . Each of these cases was a federal case, brought against the officials of the particular county to insist that blacks be represented on the jury in proportion to their percentage of the population. We filed a few public accommodation cases involving hotels, motels, and restaurants, although there weren't that many needed at that time. A number of Title 7 employment discrimination cases were filed, several of which went to the Fifth Circuit . . . . we also filed a large number of S 1983 damage suits for killings and beatings against the White Knights of the Ku Klux Klan, chiefs of police, sheriffs, majors, and the Superintendent of the State Penal Farm.[127]

To another forum he related the following facts:

> The Jackson office was reputed to have more federal court civil cases pending than any law office in the United States, with the exception of the U.S. Department of Justice in Washington, D.C. For the first two months in 1969 our docket showed 61 cases pending in federal courts: 4 in the U.S. Supreme Court; 2 in the 5th Circuit; 28 in the Northern District; and 27 in the Southern District. In addition we had 61 cases in the State courts including 6 in the Mississippi Supreme Court. And all these cases were handled by six lawyers plus the critical, albeit intermittent, volunteers. In 31 years of practice I've never seen any law office that could hold a candle to this case load.[128]

When Miskovsky took over the national office, the Jackson office was staffed by five lawyers: Chief Counsel Aschenbrenner, Frank Parker, Robert Fitzpatrick, Larry Ross, and Martha Wood Jenkins. All were active in

---

127. *Id.*

128. Larry A. Aschenbrenner, chief counsel of the LCCR, Jackson, Mississippi, 1968-1969, *as quoted in* The Lawyers' Committee: The First Twenty-Five Years, Edith S.B. Tatel & Florence B. Isbell eds. (LCCR 1988), at 11. *Also see* Records of the LCCR, Executive Committee File, Minutes, March 3, 1969, Attachment, Docket as of Feb. 28, 1969, LCCR, 233 North Farish Street, Jackson, Mississippi.

challenging private and public institutions that maintained segregated policies[129] and in litigating employment discrimination cases,[130] cases insuring a
fuller participation in the democratic process[131] and in the administration of

129. Annual Report: LCCR: 1968-1969 (LCCR 1969), 15-16. The LCCR filed suit in the
District of Columbia seeking to remove a tax-exempt status of segregated private
schools established to avoid meaningful integration of the public schools; filed suit
against a totally segregated hospital receiving federal funds; filed against the governor
of Mississippi alleging a violation of Title VI of the Civil Rights Act of 1964 in
appointments made to the State Planning Commission created pursuant to the Omnibus Crime Control and Safe Streets Act of 1968; successfully challenged the constitutionality of a Mississippi statute that gave the governor absolute discretion to allow
or deny the issuance of a corporate charter; (this statute had been used to deny charters
to Negro or civil rights-oriented organizations with a consequent loss of many thousands of dollars in federal and private grants, which depended upon incorporation;
the governor of the state must now issue a corporate charter to any organization that
meets the legal requirements of the application); and threatened legal action that
resulted in the integration of "private" membership swimming pools in Meridian,
Mississippi.

130. *Id.* at 16. The LCCR settled one of its first employment discrimination cases in which
the defendant corporation agreed to eliminate the effect of past discrimination by
hiring Negroes on a preferential basis, and to pay lost wages of $4,000 to the plaintiff;
filed four suits involving seven different corporations challenging discriminatory
hiring practices under Title VII of the Civil Rights Act of 1964; and filed 10 complaints with the Equal Employment Opportunity Commission.

131. *Id.* at 16-17. In 1969 there are 91 elected Negro officials in Mississippi. In 1967 there
was one. The LCCR has provided affidavits and legal counsel to the biracial Loyal
Democratic Delegation to the National Democratic Convention in Chicago (the delegation, headed by Charles Evers, Lawrence Guvot, Aaron Henry, and Hodding Carter III,
unseated the almost all-white regular delegation; as a result, the Democratic Party in
Mississippi is now controlled by the biracial loyalists); participated in the argument
before the United States Supreme Court in the case of *Allen v. Board of Elections et al.*,
in which the Court construed Section 5 of the Voting Rights Act of 1965 to embrace
practically every change of the state's voting statutes affecting the Negro franchise,
whether direct or indirect. Companion cases, *Fairley v. Bunton* and *Patterson,* were
argued by staff lawyers. Subsequently the Attorney General objected to and thereby
rendered unenforceable two Mississippi statutes, the purpose and effect of which was
to dilute Negro voting strength, and prepared and conducted seminars for newly elected
Negro officials on their official obligations under Mississippi law.

132. *Id.* at 17-18. Staff lawyers obtained a preliminary injunction enjoining the state judges
and prosecutors of Sunflower County, Mississippi, from bringing to trial without state-
appointed counsel indigent juveniles or indigent adults charged with misdemeanors
(this injunction, which has been made permanent, may result in the involvement of

justice,[132] and in cases seeking civil damages under the Civil Rights Acts.[133] Though Aschenbrenner did an estimable job at a critical and difficult period in the Mississippi office, administration was not his strong suit.[134] Miskovsky realized that closer control of the Jackson office and its rapidly changing docket was needed. Co-Chairman Oberdorfer asked his law partner, James Robertson, to move to Jackson to become the next chief counsel[135] and Robertson agreed.

When Robertson arrived in Jackson in the spring of 1969, the office was completing its fourth and most successful year of operations. Many of the cases prepared and filed in 1965, 1966, and 1967 came to trial. Robertson assumed the leadership of a group of litigators from Ivy League schools and establishment firms who were committed to advancing the cause of civil rights.[136] According to those who worked him and oversaw his progress, he did a "terrific job."[137] Robertson's professional training and judgment inspired the confidence of the co-chairmen and the board. According to Robertson,

---

lawyers in large numbers of juvenile and misdemeanor cases, which could be a significant deterrent to harassing and frivolous arrests of Negroes involved in civil rights activities); successfully challenged the court rule barring lawyers not admitted to the Mississippi Bar from appearing in more than one case per year (which allowed the Jackson office to file, try, and dispose of cases in ever-increasing numbers. The rule could have been employed to limit the appearance of many civil rights lawyers in the federal courts); and brought an affirmative jury suit in the U.S. District Court for the Northern District of Mississippi, in which the court enjoined the prosecution of all Negroes and women in Grenada County until such time as the jury selection procedures produce a representative cross-section of the community. In February 1969, six more jury suits were filed in Leake, Kemper, Marion, Yazoo, Choctaw, and Winston Counties. Favorable consent orders have been entered in two of these cases, while a total of 13 cases are still pending. The staff lawyers also obtained a reversal by the Mississippi State Court of the murder conviction of a 75-year-old Negro woman. The court extended *Miranda v. Arizona* in reversing the conviction.

133.   *Id.* at 18. Lawyers obtained a jury verdict and final judgment of $1,022,500 against the White Knights of the Ku Klux Klan and three knights for the murder of an elderly Negro and obtained an $85,000 judgment against the sheriff of Leflore County. The plaintiff was a 14-year-old Negro boy, blinded while in custody by a shotgun blast by an armed trustee. The federal court found that the youngster's civil rights were violated in that he was subjected to cruel and unusual punishment.

134.   Interview with Jim Robertson, April 1996.

135.   *Id.*

136.   *Id.* Frank Parker, a Harvard lawyer, came from the Commission on Civil Rights; Larry Ross came from Dewey Ballantine; Martha Wood Jenkins came from White & Case; Bob Fitzpatrick came from a Washington law firm.

137.   Interview with Lloyd Cutler, February 3, 1997.

he became the "middleman" between the lawyers and the board. He remembers that he "spent a lot of time negotiating" with them (the board) about the type of lawsuits the Jackson office was bringing. Under Robertson's guidance, more time was devoted to civil suits seeking affirmative relief in federal courts to change or eliminate practices of major institutions responsible for unequal treatment of a large number of citizens of Mississippi. The Jackson office started to file Title 7 cases, also called "pocketbook cases" because they carried monetary penalties for discrimination. He emphasized "taking the offensive," and looking for cases "that would make a difference."[138] The office was handling cases in the area of welfare,[139] housing discrimination,[140] and in the development of the law.[141] In Jackson, Robertson, learned a great deal about leadership, litigation, civil rights strategy, and the substantive issues confronting blacks.

138. Interview with James Robertson, April 17, 1996. Robertson became the chief counsel of the Jackson office after Larry Aschenbrenner moved to Cairo, Illinois, in September 1969. In 1966, Richard Tuttle resigned as chief counsel over the staff and volunteer situation. He was succeeded by Dennison Ray, from the New York law firm of Cravath, Swaine & Moore. Denny Ray managed to outrage just about everyone and was fired. Larry Aschenbrenner, a prosecutor from Oregon, replaced Ray. Aschenbrenner was not a good administrator, and the board was concerned about the types of lawsuits that the LCCR was becoming involved in. Jim Robertson's mission was to bring some control to the Jackson office.

139. *Id.* at 19. The staff filed a suit seeking to overthrow the so-called 30 percent provision, which provides that recipients of Aid to Families with Dependent Children receive only 30 percent of subsistence needs, while recipients of other categories of public assistance receive nearly 100 percent. Over 90 percent of the recipients of AFDC are Negro children. If successful, the case will add 16 million dollars to the amount available to children in the category.

140. *Id.* A suit was filed against eight land development corporations in Mississippi and Alabama seeking to enjoin the advertisement and sale of real estate lots on a "white only" basis. This was the second case in the country to be brought under the Civil Rights Act of 1968. The defendants agreed to a consent order that enjoined discrimination in advertisement and in the future sale of lots.

141. *Id.* The staff obtained a ruling from the U.S. Court of Appeals, Fifth Circuit, that a district court may enjoin a state proceeding that threatens to, or actually does, infringe First Amendment rights. The Fifth Circuit's opinion appears to be the first unequivocal holding that 28 U.S.C. 2283 must yield when First Amendment rights are at issue. The suit arose when a Mississippi state court enjoined picketing, marching, or distribution of leaflets in support of a civil rights boycott against white merchants. Also, a suit was brought under sections 1981 and 1982 of the Civil Rights Act of 1866 against a dress shop, alleging discrimination in contractual relationships. The dress shop in question does not allow Negro customers to use the dressing room provided to white customers.

In the summer of 1969, the LCCR was undergoing another change in leadership. As had become the tradition, the co-chairmen served for two years. Louis Oberdorfer and Arthur Dean turned over the co-chairmanship to John W. Douglas, a former assistant attorney general for the Civil Division who was practicing with the Washington, D.C., law firm of Covington & Burling, and George N. Lindsay, an international lawyer and senior partner in the New York firm of Debevoise, Plimpton, Lyons & Gates. The new co-chairmen took over at a very interesting time in the evolution of the committee. The LCCR was no longer a small elite group whose initiatives were supported by a small professional staff. The creation of the Urban Areas Project shifted this balance. It transformed the committee into an organization primarily concerned with minority rights litigation, national in reach, with literally hundreds of law firms in more than a dozen cities handling major legal matters in housing; employment, education, the administration of justice, voting rights, and minority business ventures.[142] This, in turn, altered the respective responsibilities of the board and the staff.

The board, having established the fundamental objectives of the committee, delegated more and more of its authority to local committees that were meant to be programmatically and financially independent. By virtue of the size and complexity of the new arrangement, the board necessarily delegated more autonomy to the director of the national office, who for the same reasons delegated increasing authority to this professional staff to initiate ideas for legal reform projects, which would be replicated by the local committees. By 1969, the national office was developing into a professional organization whose corporate leadership was represented by the co-chairmen, and whose mission was to mobilize the resources of the private bar, particularly the largest law firms, for the private enforcement of civil rights in minority communities. According to the committee's *Annual Report for 1968-1969*, the organization's mission was to use the legal process to advance the objectives of "those who are seeking the full range of economic and social opportunities."[143]

---

142. The purpose of this book is to chronicle a process not to record the litigation achievements of the LCCR, which are many. The significant achievements of the committee during this period in each of the areas mentioned are cited in the Ten Year Report, *supra* note 19.

143. Annual Report: Lawyers Committee for Civil Rights Under Law: 1968-1969 (LCCR, 1969) 1-2. From the Report to the Members of the LCCR, Jan. 31, 1964, by Harrison Tweed and Bernard G. Segal, 111, The General Objectives of the Committee. The philosophy of the committee, as it appears in a report on "Policy and Program" prepared by a subcommittee of which Judge Samuel I. Roseman was chairman and approved by the Board of Directors is: "We believe that in the solution of the present problem in the field of racial civil rights, lawyers are especially equipped by education,

James Robertson

Co-Chairmen John Douglas and George Lindsay assumed the leadership of the committee in 1969 at a time of transition in the character of the organization and in the nature of the civil rights struggle in the United States. From 1968 to 1970, Miskovsky oversaw the enlargement of the national office. He functioned as the chief liaison between the board and the national office. His replacement, James Robertson, served as chief liaison as well, but, in his own view, he functioned as a "middleman" between two worlds that shared common objectives but were growing, for a number of natural reasons, more distinct.[144] The transition between Miskovsky, who left for private practice in 1970, and Robertson, who moved from the Jackson office to head the national office in 1970, was smooth.

During this period, two incidents exemplified the growing confidence of the LCCR in the legitimacy of its mission and in its ability to mobilize lawyers quickly and effectively. The first was a civil rights conflict in Cairo, Illinois, in the summer and fall of 1969 and the second was the committee's challenge to the Nixon Administration over its school desegregation policy in August and September of 1970.

The episode in Cairo is notable for two reasons. It was an example, in microcosm, of the ability of the LCCR to bring to bear the resources of the bar in defense of minority rights. Second, it was a pivotal experience for three young staff members—James Robertson, Peter Connell, and David Tatel—who would help shape the future direction of the committee. They came away from Cairo with a new appreciation of the unique asset that the committee had in its membership; a firsthand lesson in the difference that competent legal advocacy could make in maintaining the "rule of law," and

---

professional training, experience and skills to play a leading role; and are under a special responsibility boldly to assume and carry out that role. More than any other single group, lawyers must always stand ready to fight lawlessness and defiance of court decisions. It is their duty to encourage and, if need be, to compel all of our citizens to obey the law and the public officials to enforce it. All our human and property rights depend upon a system of laws which are to be obeyed. Otherwise there can be only chaos and anarchy. The logic, skill and dispassion of members of the legal profession must be enlisted to solve and prevent the dangerous emotional outbreaks which racial conflicts present. Because of their experience in negotiations, lawyers can help keep open the local avenues of communication in disputes between races, and make smoother and easier the road to racial peace."

144. Interview in April 1996 with James Robertson, former Executive Director of the LCCR, 1970-1972.

the importance of the careful selection of test cases for the advancement of minority rights.[145] It was a baptism by fire for the three white men from Princeton, Yale, and the University of Chicago, who had little firsthand experience with discrimination, prejudice, or poverty. All three were approximately 30 years old at the time, had joined the committee within the year, and did not think of themselves as civil rights lawyers. They all had been recruited and had no previous knowledge of the LCCR. Robertson and Tatel had practiced corporate law with major establishment law firms—Robertson with Wilmer, Cutler & Pickering in Washington, D.C., and Tatel with Sidley, Austin in Chicago—before joining the committee. Connell had come from the general counsel's office of the Treasury Department. They were students when the LCCR was founded and their experience with the civil rights movement differed from those of the founders. In 1969, the civil rights issues facing the country were becoming more difficult and hitting all Americans closer to home. When the LCCR became involved in Mississippi, Louis Oberdorfer believes that the issues were such that "reasonable minds could not differ."[146] In 1969, the politics of the Nixon Administration reflected great differences in attitudes about further advancement of minority rights in the United States. All three men played active roles in the solution of the Cairo crisis.

Cairo had a character much like a Mississippi town of the early 1960s. Located at the confluence of the Mississippi and Ohio Rivers at the southern tip of Illinois, in 1969 it was a city of 6,300 that had once been a center for riverboat traffic but now was economically depressed. Blacks made up 38 percent of the population. Their demands for equal protection of the law were growing more insistent. By the time the LCCR was contacted in 1969, the racial situation in Cairo had been completely polarized. What appeared to be an intractable problem for the black community was mediated through the judicial process by the intervention of the committee.[147]

The LCCR was first alerted to the need for lawyers in Cairo through a personal request made to the committee's executive director, who, at the time, was Peter Connell (Bob Nelson had left the committee to join Bernhard's firm). Connell was contacted by the Reverend John Adams, who worked with a coalition of ministers that was attempting to mediate the racial problems in Cairo, which had erupted in a classic civil rights struggle during the summer.

Increasingly serious confrontations began between the black and white communities in Cairo when a local civil rights group, the United Front of

---

145. Interviews with James Robertson, April 1996; Peter Connell, Oct. 9, 1997; and David Tatel, Sept. 13, 1997.

146. Interview with Louis Oberdorfer, January 1994.

147. Ten Year Report, *supra* note 19, at 90-95.

Cairo, was organized in the black community. Whites organized a local affiliate of the Citizens Councils of Mississippi; they called themselves the United Citizens for Concerned Action, known locally as the "White Hats." In reaction to the formation of the White Hats, the United Front called for a boycott of all stores in Cairo and demonstrations in the business district to publicize the boycott. This led to weekly confrontations between black demonstrators, the local police, and the white citizens. Nightly gunfire and sniping became commonplace. Arsonists caused heavy damage throughout the city. A large contingent of state police was sent to Cairo to help maintain order. The state government tried unsuccessfully to mediate the dispute, which had become national news.

It was this situation that caused the Reverend Adams to contact the LCCR. Connell contacted the Reverend Charles Koen of the United Front in Cairo and took his request for help to the co-chairmen. The co-chairmen directed the national office to sort out the problems in Cairo and to determine if the committee could be helpful in solving those problems. The office was also asked for ideas about where to find funding for a Cairo project.[148]

The co-chairmen decided to send the former chief counsel in Jackson, Larry Aschenbrenner, to Cairo to assess the situation. A local white lawyer in the city, Robert Lansden, offered his services to the committee. Lansden agreed to sign pleadings for the committee lawyers and offered his office as a base of operations. In addition, Tatel arranged for Chicago law firms associated with the committee to help.

Upon evaluating the situation, Aschenbrenner immediately filed a series of suits to enjoin the enforcement of local ordinances and state laws arbitrarily used by the police to prevent demonstrations and marches. James Robertson and Larry Ross came up to Cairo from Jackson to help him. The first suit was filed less than a week after the committee arrived. Robertson remembers watching Neil Armstrong take his historic "first step for mankind" on the moon while sitting in a Catholic convent in Cairo. Across a levee, he and the nuns could hear intermittent gunfire: "We felt we were in a war."[149]

The LCCR's suit sought to declare unconstitutional two city ordinances and the mayor's civil emergency proclamation, which required any gathering of more than three people to obtain approval from the chief of police. The regulations effectively prohibited all parades, picketing, and other peaceful assemblies. Five days later, the federal court issued a temporary restraining

---

148. Interview with the former Executive Director of the LCCR, Peter J. Connell, Rock Hall, Maryland, Oct. 9, 1997.
149. Interview with James Robertson, Oct. 14, 1997.

order. Subsequently, the court permanently enjoined use of the ordinances and proclamation, holding them to be unconstitutional on their face and ordering all pending criminal cases dismissed.

Undaunted, officials continued to prohibit demonstrations by relying on state statutes regulating the use of highways. The LCCR filed suit in October seeking to declare these laws unconstitutional as applied in Cairo. That same day a federal judge heard oral argument and issued a temporary restraining order by telephone to Cairo authorities at 4:45 p.m., just as a group of black marchers was less than 1,000 feet from the point of confrontation with 150 Illinois state police officers and 18 Cairo policemen.

Local lawyer Lansden was vilified by the white community for providing assistance to the LCCR. He acted as the outside general counsel for one of the two banks in Cairo. The White Hats organized a run on that bank to put pressure on Lansden. Lansden called Connell in Washington, who contacted the co-chairmen and Oberdorfer. Oberdorfer agreed to make some calls and he suggested that the head of the local committee in Chicago, Richard Babcock, be notified of the situation. Babcock, a senior partner at Sidley & Austin, and others on the Chicago committee represented major businesses, which they contacted for help. Inland Steel and Sears, Roebuck & Company quickly responded to a request to deposit money in the Cairo bank to stop the run, as did Adlai Stevenson, who at the time was Treasurer for the state of Illinois. The state government, the corporations, and some large New York banks that were contacted by the co-chairmen infused over $1 million into Cairo by day's end. The "overnight money," much more than had been withdrawn, was left in Cairo on a continuing basis.[150] The run on the bank was stopped.

The LCCR's ad hoc set-up in Cairo was handling a case load that was staggering—two federal cases, 49 state criminal cases, two juvenile cases, three employment discrimination cases, and 31 misdemeanors. By early 1970, it was clear that Cairo needed a permanent legal services program. The LCCR lacked the resources to support such an operation and the church groups that had financed the work to that point could not do so indefinitely. The committee sought and obtained an Office of Economic Opportunity grant to support the operation of the Cairo office for one year. The committee moved Martha Jenkins from the Jackson office to Cairo.

The OEO grant prohibited the staff from taking on any additional criminal cases In 1970, legal representation in criminal matters was resumed when a state-funded public defender's office was established in Cairo. The

---

150. Interviews with Peter Connell, Oct. 9, 1997, and David Tatel, Sept. 13, 1997.

establishment of the office freed the LCCR to concentrate on traditional legal aid and civil rights matters.[151] A committee report on Cairo recounts the following:

> When the Lawyers' Committee first entered the civil rights struggle in Cairo almost no blacks were sitting on local juries. The Committee requested jury trials in all criminal cases. The lack of adequate representation of blacks on the juries was cause for complaint to the court by the Committee. As a result, all jury trials were suspended while local judicial personnel established a more representative selection process. Biracial juries began to appear in the county courthouse regularly. Faced with high quality, full-time legal counsel and more representative juries, the state's attorney began to drop frivolous and ambiguous criminal prosecutions—cases that normally would have been tried or at least been a basis for a bargained plea. The state's attorney received heavy criticism from Cairo officials because of the turn of events, but what had actually happened was that the system of criminal prosecution had finally become an adversary system of justice and black defendants were no longer railroaded through at the whim of local officials. The requirements of due process of law became a part of the local legal system.

The LCCR also brought traditional legal aid to the region:

> For the first time in Cairo, people with everyday legal problems, such as divorce matters, consumer problems, landlord-tenant difficulties, real estate matters and public aid difficulties, could obtain skilled legal assistance. One of the most interesting developments was that an increasing number of white citizens of Cairo began coming to the Lawyers' Committee office for legal assistance. By May 1971, half of the 146 cases on the Lawyers' Committee docket concerned white clients."[152]

---

151. Ten Year Report, *supra* note 19, at 93-94. A suit was brought against the State's Attorney for Alexander County (Cairo, Ill.) seeking damages and injunctive relief on the grounds that investigators and two state judges all systematically applied the state criminal laws to discriminate against blacks. This suit, which went to the Supreme Court, was argued by lawyers from the Chicago committee, which established a close relationship with the Cairo office. Other suits were filed seeking damages from the Cairo police and state police for unconstitutional mass searches of homes in Cairo's all-black housing project.

152. Ten Year Report, *supra* note 19, at 94-95. By 1972, most of the committee's activities

By 1972, most of the committee's activities concerned traditional legal services. For this reason it was decided to merge the Cairo office into a unified legal services program for all Southern Illinois.

The second key initiative of Robertson's tenure, the challenge to the Nixon Administration, began in the late Summer of 1970.

It was a period when the atmosphere in the country concerning civil rights was changing. Robertson remembers the "issues [such as busing, employment and education quotas] were hitting closer to home, and Americans were choosing sides." The election of Richard Nixon in 1968 and his adoption of a Southern Strategy to win re-election in 1972 affected the nature of the relationship of the LCCR with the Department of Justice, Robertson recounts:

> Overnight we [the Committee] became something like the "Loyal Opposition." We found ourselves opposed to the government's policy a great deal of the time. At one point, the Department of Justice was defending more civil rights cases than they were bringing. We spent a good deal of our efforts "calling out the Government," that is requiring them to deal with things.[153]

One issue that the committee "called out" the Nixon Administration on was school desegregation. Two years had passed since the 1968 decision of the Supreme Court in *Green v Kent County*, which required school districts to prepare plans for immediate desegregation. Southern school districts, particularly in rural areas, were failing to implement the order in a timely manner, or in some cases at all.[154] The LCCR and other civil rights organizations working in the South had been in court challenging efforts by some of the larger southern districts whose integration plans, in the committee's view, were inadequate. For example, many white schools were seriously overcrowded because of the refusal of white districts to use previously all-black school facilities, citing such problems as "inadequate toilet seats" in the black buildings.[155] Many schools that did integrate created a new "separate but equal"

---

concerned traditional legal services, and for this reason it was decided to merge the Cairo office into a unified legal services program for all Southern Illinois. On May 1, 1972, the Land of Lincoln Legal Assistance Foundation was opened and the committee's Cairo office became part of it.

153. Robertson, *supra* note 150.

154. Interview with David Crossland, former director of the Atlanta LCCR, Oct. 28, 1997.

155. Interview with James Skiles, former staff lawyer, National LCCR, Oct. 13, 1997.

student life in the schools. They formed all-black and all-white student councils, after-school clubs, and sports teams in an effort to moderate the mixing of the races in the schools.[156] In Washington, the LCCR kept pressure on the Nixon Administration and the Department of Justice. When asked, board members would testify before Congressional Committees about conditions in the South and in private and public forums they would speak out about the law and the lack of oversight by the government. The committee filed an amicus curia brief in the desegregation case of *Alexandria v. Holmes County, Mississippi* with the Supreme Court in opposition to the Department of Justice.[157]

As the opening of the new school term approached in the summer of 1970, the activity intensified. Robertson, at the request of the board, had formally asked Attorney General John Mitchell to supply Justice Department lawyers to monitor desegregation plans throughout the South.[158] In August, Assistant Attorney General Jerris Leonard informed the committee that because of "budget considerations" the Department of Justice did not have the personnel to send at this time. In response, Robertson volunteered the services of 100 LCCR lawyers. The Attorney General declined the offer. The board decided that the committee would go ahead with the plan to send volunteer lawyers to monitor the opening of schools in the South.

This series of events coincided with the annual American Bar Association meeting in New Orleans, which was attended by a large number of the LCCR board members. It had become a tradition to hold a general board meeting of the committee at the ABA annual convention. Co-Chairman John Douglas called a press conference to announce Attorney General Mitchell's refusal of the committee's offer and the board's decision to continue with its plan to send "100 lawyers to the South" to monitor the compliance of the schools with the law of the land. David Crossland, a native of Birmingham, Alabama, and the director of the Atlanta Lawyers' Committee for Civil Rights, remembers the meeting. He was at a table with John Douglas and other committee people, including Randolf Thrower, the board member who volunteered two years before to organize a local committee in Atlanta. (Thrower was to join the second Nixon Administration as chief of the Internal Revenue Service.)[159]

---

156. Crossland, *supra* note 155.

157. Robertson, *supra* note 150. Robertson remembers that in the court John Satterfield from Mississippi, who was a member of the committee and former president of the ABA, shared the defense table with Jerris Leonard, assistant attorney general.

158. *Id.*

159. Crossland, *supra* note 155.

Robertson asked Crossland to coordinate the committee plans in the South with the other civil rights organizations who were interested in joining the project. Atlanta became the staging point for "100 Lawyers South."[160]

Robertson's office in Washington had general responsibility for implementing the plan. A new lawyer, Jim Skiles, a former VISTA Volunteer who came from the Civil Rights Division of Health, Education and Welfare (HEW), was hired for the national office.[161] Skiles remembers that when he was interviewed he was told the committee needed someone "right away" to help coordinate the 100 Lawyers South project. "I wasn't hired just for the project," but the "timing" of his employment hinged on the "immediate need." At HEW, Skiles had worked for Ruby Martin, the first head of the Civil Rights Division at HEW who had left the Nixon Administration over the government's refusal to implement the Supreme Court's integration decision.[162] She joined Marion Wright Edelman at the Washington Research Project, the precursor of the Children's Defense Fund. The Washington Research Project, the NAACP Legal Defense Fund, along with John Lewis of the Southern Research Council and the Lois Green of the American Friends Service Committee, joined with the committee in the monitoring project.[163]

The committee recruited lawyers from law firms across the country. According to Skiles, the LCCR board stepped up to the request from the co-chairmen. "The senior partners in the largest firms were contacted."[164] John Douglas and George Lindsay "put pressure on their firms to send two volunteers each." The co-chairmen and others on the board "personally" called senior partners whom they knew and "told them they had to send someone." The committee "volunteers numbered over one hundred" lawyers, "mostly young white men," They were sent by their firms to Atlanta. "The whole thing took about 10 days maybe two weeks." David Crossland had arranged for the use of a highrise building "that should have been condemned years ago" for a headquarters and where orientation sessions were conducted for the volunteers A checklist of what the lawyers should look for was put together "mostly by the other groups." The volunteers went through a "three- or four-hour course" before they fanned out across Georgia, South Carolina, and Mississippi. Violence was a fear in the beginning, but those fears proved to be unwarranted.

The following year, the committee, the Washington Research Group, and

---

160. Robertson, *supra* note 150.
161. Skiles, *supra* note 156.
162. *Id.*
163. Records of the LCCR, Implementing School Desegregation in the South.
164. Skiles, *supra* note 156.

the American Friends Service Committee issued a joint report, "Implementing School Desegregation in the South." The importance of the project was not its effect on the school systems, for it had little quantifiable influence, "a few lawsuits resulted but not many." Its value lay, according to Crossland, "more in educating the lawyers . . . more in making the bar and the country aware of the circumstances in the South."[165] "It helped get the issue into the news," remembers Skiles, and it brought in new volunteers.[166] Further, in a society based on the "rule of law," the legal profession was vigilant. The LCCR's actions had shown the Department of Justice and the President— whose job it was to enforce judicial decisions and to uphold the constitutional system—that the committee was watching and cared. The stature of the LCCR made it impossible for the Nixon Administration to dismiss or ignore its actions.

The shift between the authority of the board and co-chairmen and the director of the national office became more apparent during the two years that Robertson ran the national office. In part, the acceleration of the changes had to do with funding the work of the Urban Areas Project and, in part, with the quality of the lawyers brought on to run the program. As one director of the national staff said, "If you wanted to attract good lawyers you had to give them the authority to make decisions."[167] No new initiatives could be realistically contemplated without finding the money to run them.

Outside of the major grants that sustained the committee, the question of locating money was more and more left up to individual staff lawyers to explore independently. As a result, staff lawyers/project managers, began to think without constraint about what projects—for example, prison reform, administration of justice, and educational reform—would be appealing to which foundations or government agencies. The leadership of the committee and the staff shared common objectives and, in the natural evolution of the committee the co-chairmen, had deliberately delegated increasing authority to the national and local offices. By 1970, the co-chairmen and the board had set the fundamental goals and how they were carried out had become the work of the staff.

Robertson stood at the center of the changing committee from 1970 to 1972. He had a distinct perception of his authority and of his relationship with the board. During the Cairo crisis, a major lesson that he took away with him was that "the greatest asset the committee had" was the stature and power

---

165. Crossland, *supra* note 155.

166. Skiles, *supra* note 156.

167. Interview with the Honorable David S. Tatel, U.S. Court of Appeals, Washington, D.C., former director of the LCCR, 1972-1974, Oct. 3, 1997.

of its membership. His age, professional experiences, and training helped him assume a "middleman" role in Washington.[168] He remembers, "When the [civil rights] issues got more difficult, the civil rights movement ran into a rock. As the steam went out of civil rights, as the level of outrage began to diminish, the board became less of a factor."

Under Robertson, the caliber of the professional staff was upgraded, a process that had begun under Miskovsky. Staff lawyers were expected to provide less backup for the local committees, which were programmatically independent by 1970. Robertson did not envision the national office as a "think tank" and people who were acting more like "social scientists" were let go.[169] The national office turned its energies to devising legal reform projects that combined both long-term strategy and professional resources. On their own initiative, his staff members were expected to develop law reform projects for specific areas of focus, such as education, housing, health care, and the administration of justice. They were also expected to develop the funding to administer the projects. Sarah Carey, who came to the committee as assistant director shortly before Robertson, led that effort.[170]

In the few years that Carey had been out of law school she had been one of the first female associates with the law firm of Arnold & Porter, had worked on the Kerner Commission, and had led the Law and Government Section of the National Urban Coalition. Some of projects she was responsible for—reform in the areas of health care, housing discrimination, and education—envisioned systemic changes. The legal projects were developed with the intention that they could be replicated by local committee offices and other organizations, such as the Office of Economic Opportunity's Legal Services office, the Inc. Fund, the Southern Research Council, and the Washington Research Project, to name a few.[171]

Along with the legal strategy, the new projects introduced other innovative steps. Steven Browning, who was hired by Carey to run an education financing reform project, started a newsletter that reported on cases, research, and resources that would be of help to others interested in the field. Significant litigation resulted from these projects. Major law firms affiliated with the committee were engaged by the staff lawyers to take the cases on a pro bono basis.

Robertson brought people up from Mississippi. They had, unlike many

---

168. Robertson, *supra* note 150.

169. *Id.*

170. Interview with Sarah Carey Reilly, Oct. 18, 1997. She served as assistant director of the LCCR from 1970 to 1972.

171. *Id.*

others on the local and national staffs, firsthand experience with civil rights issues. When the LCDC office closed in Jackson in 1971, Armand Derfner[172] and his wife, Mary Frances, who had been concentrating on the development of voting rights law in Mississippi, were asked to continue their work with the LCCR's office. Francis Stevens, a member of the Mississippi bar who had come forward in 1963 to aid the LCCR, joined the staff, as did Larry Guyot, a young black lawyer who was also working with LCDC and who served time in Parchman Prison for his work with the SCLC voting registration campaigns, He later represented the Mississippi Freedom Democratic Party at the 1964 Democratic Convention. These individuals helped to associate the LCCR with the goals of the civil rights movement. Stevens and Guyot began a program in Mississippi for young black lawyers to provide a guaranteed retainer in return for assistance on committee cases. This helped to reduce the workload of the Jackson office, gave the participating young lawyers access to technical assistance and consultation, and, most important, began building a black bar in the state.[173]

Robertson hired good people and gave them latitude. He and his staff discussed their ideas for new law reform projects, but the key consideration was finding funding for the projects. Any project was only as good as its grant. "A process began," according to Robertson, "of chasing grants. . . . Money began to shape the mission of the Lawyers' Committee." The million-dollar grant from the Ford Foundation for the Urban Areas Project was almost gone in 1970 and the relationship between the national office and Ford was "almost adversarial."[174] The grant officer at Ford, Leonard Ryan, who was responsible for the LCCR, required that the bar itself provide a greater percentage of project financing. Foundation grant proposals became the key factor in the selection of issues and projects. Once a project reached the stage where funding was a good possibility and, in the judgment of Director Robertson was worthy of the committee efforts, it was advanced to the co-

---

172. PARKER, *supra* note 14, at 11: In 1969 the U.S. Supreme Court decided *Allen v. State Board of Education*, which struck down Mississippi's effort to switch at-large elections of county supervisors, appoint county school superintendents, and increase the qualifying requirement for independent candidates, resulting in the doubling of the number of black county supervisors. At 181: In 197 1, Armand Derfner, in Mississippi working for the LCDC, won a decision in the Supreme Court, *Perkins v. Matthews*, which upheld Alien and held that changes in polling place locations, municipal annexations, and a change from ward to citywide elections of municipal aldermen in Canton, Mississippi, all were changes affecting voting that were subject to federal preclearance.

173. The Lawyers' Committee: The First Twenty-Five Years.

174. Robertson, *supra* note 150.

chairmen and the board for approval or disapproval, Only one project was disapproved by the board while Robertson was director and that was one of his own design, a project to reform large lot zoning, or "snob zoning," in exclusive suburban communities.[175]

David S. Tatel

During the two years that Robertson ran the national office there were two sets of co-chairmen, John Douglas and George Lindsay from 1969 to 1971 and Lloyd Cutler and John Doar from 1971 to 1973. Cutler was one of the founding members of the LCCR and senior partner in the Washington, D.C., firm of Wilmer Cutler & Pickering. Doar was Burke Marshall's successor as Assistant U.S, Attorney General for Civil Rights—a position Robert Kennedy persuaded him to leave[176] to become the director of the Bedford-Stuyvesant Development and Services Corporation in 1967.

In the summer of 1971, David S. Tatel, who was director of the Chicago committee, moved to the Washington office. He was assigned to work with the new co-chairmen on an unprecedented pro bono initiative, which was conceived by Cutler and became known as the 1 Percent Program. Tatel became director of the committee when Robertson returned to Wilmer, Cutler & Pickering the following year. "A transition," according to Tatel that, "was seamless."[177]

After graduating from the University of Chicago School of Law, Tatel had joined the Chicago firm of Sidley & Austin, whose senior partner, Richard Babcock, was a member of the LCCR. Tatel first heard about the committee in 1968 from Alison Davis, a black lawyer who was a guest at a dinner party the Tatels were attending. At age 28 he was interested in doing something to help ameliorate the civil rights problems erupting in the country. He decided to take the position as the first director of the Chicago office of the committee. Richard Babcock was the Chicago committee's chairman.[178] Tatel, who opened the Chicago office in June, was immediately thrown into the civil rights litigation fray.

During his time in Chicago, Tatel learned a good deal about the importance of "carefully chosen test cases for the defense of the minority communities' interests."[179] While he was responsible for establishing the local office, the Chicago committee office became the command center for the

---

175. *Id.*

176. SCHLESINGER, *supra* note 106, at 788.

177. Tatel, *supra* note 168.

178. *Id.*

179. *Id.*

city's law firms that were recruited to help with the litigation that arose from the Cairo project. Compounding this "baptism by fire" for the Chicago committee, the Democratic Convention was held in Chicago the same summer. David Tatel and the Chicago committee defended Fred Hampton and the Black Panther case.

When he moved to Washington, he was put in charge of the 1 Percent Program. He chose "cases that could make a difference" for the volunteers. He remembers that it was a period of expansion "and of increased efforts to prevent the Nixon Administration from erasing the gains of the past."[180]

The 1 Percent Program was launched by Lloyd Cutler, the co-chairman of the LCCR. Its aim was to include large cities with no local offices of the committee in the pro bono efforts of the committee. Under Cutler's 1 Percent Program, law firms located in cities without local committees were asked to "commit themselves to devote at least one percent of their resources to civil rights and poverty law cases referred to them by the Lawyers' Committee. . . ." Firms in 45 cities made that commitment. Each firm agreed to accept cases on a fully professional, but uncompensated basis and to handle them as firm matters, supervised by partners and sharing equal dignity and importance with the other work of the firm.[181] Co-Chairmen Cutler and Doar put enormous time and energy into contacting and persuading lawyers to participate.[182] The 1 Percent Program expanded the volunteer resources of the committee substantially. The program advanced LCCR's mission of mobilizing the resources and skills of the private bar on behalf of minority rights. The co-chairmen "left the running of the national office" to David Tatel.[183]

By Tatel's tenure, the committee was a recognized leader in the civil rights struggle. Litigation was important but not the committee's only tool. "Monitoring administrative agencies actions, participating in agency proceedings, analyzing and drafting legislation, writing research reports, and keeping client groups informed about their legal rights and remedies" were all techniques employed by the committee.[184] As director, Tatel remembers that he spent most of his time "managing the Committee, fund raising, and on Mississippi." The Ford Foundation continued to provide major support for the committee.[185]

---

180. *Id.*
181. *Id.*
182. *Id.*
183. *Id.*
184. The LCCR: Fifteenth Anniversary Report, 1978, at 27.
185. Tatel, *supra* note 168.

"The Washington staff,'" according to Tatel, "became lawyers and . . . most of the legal work came from three places."

First, work was generated by the Mississippi office, whose new chief counsel was Tex Wilson, the first minority lawyer to assume that post. This work included Frank Parker's voting rights project and a number of discrimination cases.

The second source of legal work came from the 1 Percent Program and the third source was the school finance and the voting rights projects of the Washington office. Tatel's staff utilized the lawyers and firms associated with both the Urban Areas Project and the 1 Percent Program, The national staff "initiated and handled" litigation and other activities on behalf of committee clients and served "as resources for . . . other civil rights and poverty law organizations."[186]

Tatel met regularly with representatives from the civil rights community. He and the staff were responsible for creating novel strategies and theories, both in the development and application of civil rights law, which other groups could use and at the same time they could draw upon the committee's growing legal experience in specific fields.

Tatel was a litigator. Under his direction, for the first time in the history of the national office, he and his staff became directly responsible for reform litigation—that is, they went to court as litigating lawyers.[187] Tatel took part in an education finance reform lawsuit in conjunction with a Washington law firm, Hogan & Hartson, which was affiliated with the committee. John Fannen, a partner at Hogan & Hartson, worked with him on the case for nearly two years.

In 1974, Tatel was considering a return to Chicago. He had come to Washington in 1971 on a one-year leave from his firm. The practice of law, particularly in the largest firms, was changing, in large part due to the example of the LCCR and the pro bono programs it sponsored. In the mid-1970s, large law firms were beginning to institutionalize the provision of pro bono services to the minority and poor communities. Many of the largest law firms, particularly in Washington, were on the cutting edge of this movement. The amount of time and resources volunteered by the firms was considerable. In an effort to bring some cohesion and direction to the work, a number of the largest firms had designated a pro bono partner to coordinate the pro bono work.[188] The arrangement varied among the law firms. In

---

186. Ten Year Report, *supra* note 19, at 54.
187. Interview with David Tatel, Sept. 13, 1997.
188. Interviews with Lloyd Cutler, Feb. 3, 1994; John Nolan, Oct. 3, 1997; and James Robertson, all of whom are former managing partners of their law firms.

some, like Hogan & Hartson, the decision was made to hire a lawyer to manage the firm's commitment, its strategy, and resources on a full-time basis. John Fannen asked Tatel if he would consider becoming Hogan & Hartson's first pro bono partner. Tatel accepted the position.

CHAPTER 5

The Lawyers' Committee and South Africa

In 1997, Judge David Tatel,[1] who was appointed by President William Clinton to the United States Court of Appeals for the District of Columbia, recounted in a speech to the State Bar of California the following story about the pro bono bar:

> One day last year I took my place on the bench to hear what I expected to be three fairly routine cases: a prisoner's habeas corpus petition, a community organization's challenge to the Federal Reserve Board's administration of the Community Reinvestment Act, and a Vietnam war veteran suffering from posttraumatic stress disorder who was seeking correction of his military records. Listening to the arguments, I suddenly realized that all three lawyers—for the prisoner, the community organization, and the veteran—were serving pro bono. Successful partners in major law firms all were contributing their time without charge. What a superb illustration of the legal profession at its very best.
>
> Through the pro bono services of those lawyers, this profession opened the doors of the legal system to each client. And even though the three clients were disadvantaged in many ways, through their lawyers they stood before the court on equal terms with all three powerful, well-represented government agencies, present-

---

1. David Tatel was director of the Lawyers' Committee for Civil Rights Under Law [hereinafter LCCR] from 1972 to 1974.

ing their claims of abuse of government authority to a tribunal empowered to provide a complete remedy. The rule of law was alive and well that day in the D.C. Circuit. As a lawyer and judge, I was proud to be a member of the legal profession."[2]

The type of pro bono representation described by Judge Tatel was not a standard practice before 1963 in the United States. Founded in 1963, the Lawyers' Committee for Civil Rights Under Law (LCCR) led the bar in the promotion of pro bono legal assistance by private lawyers and law firms. Its innovative leadership and the example of its members is in large part responsible for the acceptance of a duty to provide pro bono legal services by American lawyers, particularly in the country's largest firms. In one generation in the latter portion of the twentieth century, the professional practices of the legal profession in American were transformed. The LCCR stands out in this process.

To its added distinction, the committee stands out as a leader in another area of significance. This chapter will discuss the LCCR's role in the anti-apartheid[3] movement, a movement that, in 1994, helped bring to an end the political oppression of more than 30 million black South Africans[4] and in which the LCCR alone organized the services of the American bar in support of the rule of law in South Africa. This leadership by the committee also helped to further the transformation of the role of lawyering in the United States.

In 1967, the LCCR's involvement with apartheid began in a very modest ad hoc way. Beginning in 1970, its involvement took on a structure and a prominence within the operations of the committee that made it one of its

---

2. Remarks of Judge David S. Tatel: Alexander F. Morrison Lecture, Annual Meeting of the California State Bar, San Diego, California, Sept. 13, 1997.
3. APARTHEID IN PRACTICE (The United Nations, 1969), Unit on Apartheid: Department of Political and Security Council Affairs, ST/PSCA/SER.A/9, at 1: "The purpose of the 200 statements in this book is to provide a clear and accurate description of apartheid. Since the present Government came to power in South Africa in 1948, a vast body of legislative enactments has come into existence designed to give effect to the new policy of apartheid. Hundreds of laws have been passed by Parliament; thousands of regulations, proclamations and Government notices have been issued under those laws. In addition there are numerous bylaws made by the municipal councils of cities and towns throughout the country. All these combine to constitute the legal apparatus which regulates the daily lives of more than four fifths of the population of South Africa, i.e., the 15 million non-whites."
4. Thirtieth Anniversary Commemorative Program, 1963-1993: Forging a Path to Equal Justice Under Law (LCCR, 1993), at 7.

three principal activities.[5] In that year, the committee financed and instructed lawyers in every major human rights trial in South Africa, and there were scores of them.[6] In the United States, the committee litigated on behalf of the anti-apartheid movement[7] and on behalf of the Congressional Black Caucus.[8] In one case in the early 1970s, the committee was instrumental in securing a commitment from the government of South Africa to desegregate all South African airlines flights, including all purely internal flights, as well as all air, connecting rail, and other transportation systems in South Africa.[9] The significance of the LCCR's efforts in South Africa led eventually to its accepting requests to organize and manage the international election monitoring upon the independence of Namibia and the first democratic elections in South Africa.[10]

The LCCR adopted the position that just as certain legal and human rights transcend political boundaries so too does the responsibility of lawyers to assist in the protection of those rights. This policy, though a reflection of the

---

5. The other two were the Mississippi Litigation Office and the Urban Areas Project.

6. Interview with Peter J. Connell, former executive director of the National Office of the LCCR, 1968-1973, architect of the Southern Africa Project, 1970. *Also see* STEVE BIKO: BLACK CONSCIOUSNESS IN SOUTH AFRICA (Millard Arnold ed., Random House 1978). Mr. Arnold was the director of the LCCR Southern Africa Project, 1978-1980. He directed the Lawyers' Committee's participation in the Steve Bantu Biko inquest, after which he published BIKO, donating all proceeds to the Biko family.

7. Diggs v. Schultz, 470 F.2d. 461 (D.C. Cir. 1972), *and* New York Times Co. v. City of N.Y. Comm'n on Human Rights, 349 N.Y.S.2d 940, 76 Misc. 2d 17 (1973).

8. Goler Teal Butcher, *Southern African Issues in United States Courts*, No. 2, 26 HOWARD L. J. 1983, 601-43. "Domestic litigation on Southern Africa issues in order to enforce United States legal obligations under the United Nations Charter and relevant domestic law began in the early 1970s," and n.1: "The legal counsel was primarily provided by the Lawyers' Committee for Civil Rights Under Law (Southern Africa Project) . . . ."

9. Diggs v. Civil Aeronautics Board, 516 F.2d 1248 (D.C. Cir. 1975).

10. Gay J. McDougall, director of the Southern Africa Project of the LCCR from 1980 to 1995, was the only American and one of only three non-South Africans chosen by Nelson Mandela to serve on the Independent Electoral Commission that organized and supervised the first free elections in the history of South Africa. Ms. McDougall was given the further honor of accompanying Nelson Mandela to cast his historic vote. As he did so, she stood at his right side. In Namibia, Ms. McDougall and the Southern Africa Project of the LCCR was commissioned by the United Nations to manage an international monitoring committee for the elections. The United States Ambassador to the United Nations, Donald McHenry, and Ms. McDougall worked together on oversight of the elections.

culture's changing expectations of justice, was ahead of its time. The position adopted by the LCCR in 1967 was unique within the organized legal profession. The committee's acceptance of an obligation to offer assistance to lawyers in South Africa who were defending those opposed to apartheid helped to clarify the need for, and the direction of, change in the bar's attitude about racial justice outside of the United States. For this reason, the committee stands out as a leader of the bar and as a leader in the history of the anti-apartheid movement, both in the United States and South Africa.

The LCCR was drawn into the apartheid issue in large part because its members were perceived as public leaders and as Americans who had demonstrated an openness and a willingness to aid social change. Anti-apartheid activity was not a fit with the work of the committee in the United States. It did not begin as a committee initiative. Charles Runyon, the Assistant Legal Advisor for Africa at the U.S. Department of State, chose to involve the committee when Joel Carlson, a South African lawyer, approached him for aid for defendants charged under that country's newly enacted Terrorism Act.

Support of the "Rule of Law"[11] in South Africa: 1967-1969

In 1967, the laws that gave definition to the policy of apartheid, which began in South Africa in 1948, denied fundamental human rights to the then 17 million nonwhites who constituted more than 80 percent of the population of the country. Black Africans were denied any participation whatsoever in the political process; they were denied the right to travel freely within their own country; the right to assemble peaceably; the right to a decent education; the right to speak their minds; the right to bargain collectively; the right to a decent living wage; and, in some cases, the right to trial before incarceration. Nowhere in the world was racial discrimination and exploitation institutionalized to the extent that it was in South Africa. Literally millions of people were suffering severe subjugation and deprivation simply because of their

---

11. Records of the LCCR, South Africa File, Arthur Suzman, Q.C., *South Africa and the Rule of Law, reprinted from* THE SOUTH AFRICAN L. J., vol. LXXXV 261, August 1968. Quoting from a South African government publication, Suzman gives the definition of the "rule of law" that was officially accepted. "The rule of law may mean different things to different people, but there is general agreement that it requires that a person on trial be accused in open court; be given an opportunity of denying the charge and of defending himself; and that he be given the choice of a counsel. These rights are at all times assured by the South African courts, also in the case of persons charged under the Terrorism Act." For white South Africans, the rule of law did exist; for black Africans the rule of law existed at the discretion of the government.

race.[12] There was very little systematic opposition in the United States to apartheid. The nation's foremost opponent of apartheid was the nonprofit American Committee on Africa, a predominantly white organization That organization was a pressure group that worked through public education, information dissemination, and lobbying.

It was Robert Kennedy in June 1966 who focused American public attention on the injustices of the apartheid system in South Africa. During a highly publicized and emotional trip, he visited the country at the invitation of the anti-apartheid National Union of South African Students (NUSAS).[13] In what is considered by some to be his greatest speech, he challenged the students at the University of Cape Town, and by implication all people of principle, to act:

> Each of us can work to change a small portion of events, and in the total of all those acts will be written the history of this generation. It is from numberless diverse acts of courage and belief that human history is shaped. Each time a man stands up for an ideal, or acts to improve the lot of others, or strikes out against injustice, he sends a tiny ripple of hope, and crossing each other from a million different centers of energy and daring those ripples build a current which can sweep down the mightiest wall of oppression and resistance.[14]

There were a number of members of the bipartisan board and Executive Committee of the LCCR who shared Kennedy's opposition to apartheid. Also, there was a natural reservoir of support among the committee members for the courageous lawyers who were defending unpopular causes and minority rights in South Africa. Like the work of the committee in the United States, the South African lawyers were on the cutting edge in the fight to uphold the rule of law. Many on the board were clearly disposed to do what they could if the occasion arose. In October 1967, it did.

---

12. Records of the LCCR, Ford Foundation File, Request for Financial Support for the Southern Africa Legal Assistance Program, 1971.

13. ARTHUR M. SCHLESINGER, JR., ROBERT KENNEDY AND HIS TIMES 337 (Houghton Mifflin 1978) at 743: "A fortnight before his arrival, the government placed Ian Robertson (the president of National Union of South African Students) under ban (house arrest), excluding him from political and social life for five years. Then it denied visas to forty American newspaper and television correspondents assigned to cover the trip." When Kennedy flew into Capetown, he immediately went to visit Ian Robertson and gave him a copy of PROFILES IN COURAGE, inscribed by Jacqueline Kennedy.

14. *Id.* at 746.

Joel Carlson

The preceding June, the South African Parliament had passed the Terrorism Act,[15] which provided for unlimited pretrial detention for the purposes of interrogation. The act condoned the use of torture and made a capital crime of actions that tended "to embarrass the administration of the affairs of State"[16]— that is, to criticize the government.[17] It shifted the burden of proving innocence beyond a reasonable doubt to the defendant. The South African Parliament unlawfully applied the act to Namibia, an international territory.[18] Seven days after the passage of the act, 37 Namibians—the first prosecuted under the draconian law—were arrested and charged ex post facto.[19] While being held incommunicado by the South African security police, the Namibians were brutally tortured.

---

15. Arthur Suzman, supra note 11, at 268-69. The Terrorism Act "designed to deal with terrorists . . . contains provisions for the detention and interrogation of persons suspected of terrorist activities or of withholding information relating to terrorists. . . . Any commissioned police officer of or above the rank of lieutenant-colonel, if he has reason to believe that any person is a terrorist or is withholding from the police any information relating to terrorists or to offences under the Act may, without warrant, arrest such person or cause him to be arrested. Such persons may be detained for interrogation until the Commissioner of Police orders his release when satisfied that he has satisfactorily replied to all questions at the interrogation, or that no useful purpose would be served by his further detention, or until his release is ordered by the Minister. . . . No person—other than the Minister or an officer in the service of the State acting in the performance of his duties—shall have access to any detainee, or shall be entitled to any official information relating to or obtained from any detainee. . . . No court of law may pronounce upon the validity of any action taken under the section or order of any detainee."

16. *Id.*

17. For a discussion of the arrest, detention, and torture of the 37 Namibians see JOEL CARLSON, No NEUTRAL GROUND (Crowell, 1973). Mr. Carlson was the South African lawyer for the case and an early activist in the anti-apartheid movement in South Africa. He was eventually banned, had his passport removed, and fled the country to take up residence in the United States.

18. Butcher, *supra* note 8, at 605: Namibia was the former German South West Africa. The supervision of the territory was given to the Union of South Africa but was removed from South Africa's control by a resolution of the United Nations General Assembly on Oct. 27, 1966, G.A. Res. 2145, deciding that "the Mandate conferred upon His Britannic Majesty to be exercised on his behalf by the Government of the Union of South Africa is therefore terminated, that South Africa has no other right to administer the territory and that henceforth South West Africa comes under the direct responsibility of the United Nations."

19. For a detailed account of the period and of the trial of the Namibians, see CARLSON, *supra* note 17.

Their defense was being handled by Joel Carlson, a South African lawyer. In South Africa, "the role of attorney is central in providing an adequate defense since it is his responsibility, as it is that of the solicitor in the United Kingdom, to find, brief, and pay able—and expensive—advocates (barristers) who must actually present the case in court. It is crucial that the attorney be brought in at an early stage in order to provide investigation and careful preparation of the case."[20] In Carlson's opinion, the trial of the Namibians was a "political trial" that was going to result in the death by hanging of the 37. Carlson's professional services had been secured for the Namibians by a London firm, but Carlson had never met Lord Campbell, the benefactor of the trial, or anyone in the firm through which he received his "instructions" in the case. As the trial neared its conclusion, and because of the impression left by Robert Kennedy, Joel Carlson decided to go to New York to seek the aid of the United Nations and the U.S. government in pressuring South Africa not to impose the death penalty.[21] The 42-year-old Carlson—who was "one of the very few attorneys" who were willing and able to serve in cases involving persons detained, tried or imprisoned under South African security legislation—knew little of American politics or of its legal establishment.[22] He remembers that he "thought his prospects of finding the kind of support I was looking for in London seemed less likely than in the home of the United Nations and of the Kennedys." As a result, Carlson, an expansive man, undeterred by personal doubts or other obstacles,[23] flew to New York. "I made the trip 'blind'"—that is he didn't know anyone in New York except two friends who had fled South Africa, Michael and Jennifer Davis.

The Davises had been activists in the South African anti-apartheid movement. In New York, they joined the American Committee on Africa (ACA). The Davises hosted a gathering in their apartment to introduce Carlson to some ACA members "who would be particularly interested." A dozen or so people, among them George Hauser, ACA president, were at the gathering.

---

20. Records of the LCCR, South African File, The Case for a Further Grant to the Lawyers' Committee for Civil Rights Under Law for Use in South Africa, 1969.

21. Interview with Joel Carlson, Great Neck, New York, March 28, 1993. This interview is the basis of the account of Mr. Carlson's visit to the United States in October 1967. Also, interview with Charles Runyon, former dean, Yale Law School, former assistant legal adviser for Africa, U.S. Dept. of State, April 1993. Also, interview with Burke Marshall, former Assistant Attorney General of Civil Rights.

22. Carlson, *supra* note 21. Also, Introduction to The Case for a Further Grant to the Lawyers' Committee for Civil Rights Under Law for Use in South Africa, 1969, Records of the LCCR, South Africa File.

23. This is the opinion of the author, who had known Mr. Carlson and his family since 1970.

From that meeting, Hauser put Carlson in touch with Wayne Fredericks at the Ford Foundation. It was Fredericks, the former Deputy Assistant Secretary of State for African Affairs, who had urged Robert Kennedy to go to South Africa in June of 1966 because, " South African liberals needed all the encouragement the outside world could give." He met with Carlson and Burke Marshall at Marshall's office at IBM headquarters in New York.[24] Marshall, who was IBM's general counsel, had just handed over the co-chairmanship of the LCCR to Louis Oberdorfer and Arthur Dean. Carlson explained his reasons for coming to the United States and showed the documents that he had smuggled out of South Africa—the defendants' affidavits of torture. Fredericks and Marshall agreed to try to get Carlson in to see Robert Kennedy. In the meantime, while he was still in New York, they arranged for him to talk to Arthur Goldberg, the former Supreme Court Justice and member of the LCCR who was then U.S. Ambassador to the United Nations. Carlson met with the ambassador then flew to Washington, D.C.

In Washington, he was met at National Airport by Charles Runyon,[25] the Assistant Legal Advisor for Africa of the United States Department of State. For the next few days, Carlson was "debriefed" at the State Department. He was taken "to meet Robert Kennedy, Senator Edward Kennedy, and a number of other Congressmen and Senators." He remembers the period as being exhausting, "I talked nonstop and in the evenings I watched television until all hours. You see I had never seen a TV before," as they were excluded from South Africa. His final visit was with Under Secretary of State Nicholas Katzenbach, who asked him, "'What do you want us to do?' Which I thought meant he was going to do something." He told Katzenbach that he sought a demonstration of support for the anti-apartheid movement and asked that a representative of the U.S. government speak to the South Africa's ambassador to the United States concerning the death penalty. He further asked that he and others who were under constant surveillance by the South African security police be given the privilege of sending and receiving correspondence through diplomatic pouch and that those involved in legitimate opposition to South African policies be given permission to read the international journals and newspapers that were available the American consulate in South Africa, but were banned elsewhere in the country.

Carlson never learned officially if anything came of his discussions at the

---

24. Interview with Burke Marshall, former Assistant Attorney General for Civil Rights and former co-chairman of the Lawyers' Committee, September 1995.

25. Charles Runyon is a modest, self-effacing man who was an early and consistent opponent of apartheid. He is one of the unsung heroes of the anti-apartheid movement.

State Department or with Katzenbach, but he believed that the attention his visit focused on the trial was instrumental in saving the lives of the defendants. In South Africa, all 37 Namibians were found guilty but none was sentenced to death. When he returned home, he became "great friends" with Thomas Reiner, the American Consul General in Johannesburg and Pretoria who "accorded him every courtesy," which Carlson also attributed to his visit to Washington. And, according to Runyon, information and correspondence to and from Carlson was sent through diplomatic pouch regularly.[26] His visit did, however, have other significant results

Before Carlson returned to South Africa, Runyon suggested that he meet with Louis Oberdorfer, the co-chairman of the LCCR. He also took him to the committee's national office and introduced him to Executive Director Robert Nelson. Runyon explained to Carlson that the LCCR was involved in the struggle against discrimination in the United States and that he thought it might be useful to talk to them. Runyon, a former assistant dean of Yale Law School, believed that "there was a natural basis for cooperation between the legal traditions in the United States and South Africa. They both respected the concept of the rule of law."[27]

Other than filling a few hours of time before Carlson left for South Africa, there was no substantive reason for his visit to the LCCR office. At no point during Carlson's other visits with the leaders of the government and legal establishments did anyone suggest that he meet with the anyone associated with the committee staff. His meetings with Robert Kennedy, Burke Marshall, Arthur Goldberg, and Nicholas Katzenbach were all independent of their connection to the Lawyers' Committee. Carlson's main purpose in coming to the United States was to garner support for opposition to the imposition of the death penalty. He hoped to persuade people of influence to bring political pressure to bear on the South African government. Carlson was directed to prominent leaders who logically might be sympathetic to the South African problems and who, by virtue of their positions, might be able to help. Taking Carlson to meet with the LCCR staff on the day of his departure was the spontaneous idea of Runyon. The two men had some time to spare and Carlson remembers, "I had never heard of the Lawyers' Committee before Charlie suggested that I talk to them. I didn't know what to talk about but I thought it would be good to get some legitimate contact started. I had no idea where it might go."

Carlson explained to Nelson that there was no pro bono legal aid tradi-

---

26. Runyon, *supra* note 21. Also, the Records of the LCCR, South Africa File, contain copies of information with the State Deparment stamp.

27. Runyon, *supra* note 21.

tion in South Africa and that the government provides pro deo counsel—advocates, not lawyers—only in capital cases. There were three major sources of legal assistance for victims of repressive and discriminatory legislation: the underfunded United Nations Trust Fund, established in December 1965; a South African philanthropy group, Defense and Aid, which was banned in 1966; and very limited support from overseas, particularly from England. Also, the policies of the South African government received wide support from the country's lawyers, who, in turn, exerted tremendous financial and peer pressure on colleagues who take and represent "anti-government" cases.[28]

The Board Accepts Responsibility

When Nelson reported on Carlson's visit to the Executive Committee meeting in December 1967, many of those present were already familiar with the issue. At that meeting, it was decided that the board would undertake a South African Assistance Program.[29] Goldberg volunteered to help raise private funds "to support the independence of the judicial system from the political system in South Africa."[30] In early 1968, the committee secured a $10,000 grant from the Field Foundation for the "purposes of expenses and fees of counsel." For the next two years, the LCCR board helped raise money to provide legal counsel in defense of those arrested under the Terrorism Act. The committee "instructed" Carlson in the case of the 37 Namibians and "in the case of Mbindi, a South West African detainee under that Act who . . . was allegedly brutally assaulted by the South African Special Branch."[31]

From 1967 to 1969, the committee's commitment, which was undertaken by a few board members, was limited to working in South Africa almost exclusively through Carlson, with assistance from Runyon, who served as Assistant Legal Advisor for Africa in the Department of State under both Lyndon Johnson and Richard Nixon.[32] The committee's legal assistance, though significant, was limited to responding to a few specific legal cases and it only

28. Carlson, *supra* note 21.
29. Records of the LCCR, Executive Committee File, Minutes, Dec. 14, 1967.
30. *Id.*
31. Records of the LCCR, South Africa File, The Case for a Further Grant to the Lawyers Committee for Civil Rights Under Law for Use in South Africa, at 1.
32. Secretary of State William Rogers was an original member of the LCCR. Undersecretary of State Elliott Richardson continued to support Charles Runyon, as had Undersecretary of State Nicholas Katzenbach, who served under President Johnson. Mr. Richardson and Mr. Katzenbach both became members of the Lawyers' Committee upon leaving government service.

involved a few lawyers in both countries. The board's involvement was separate from the work of the national office.[33]

In the grant application to the Field Foundation requesting continued support of the South African Assistance Program there is an overview of the LCCR's goals:

> Carlson is in need of further financial and moral support from respectable sources overseas. Unless he and a few other lawyers who continue to handle politically sensitive cases are so supported, many African and other victims of current South African repressive legislative and policies will not have proper legal representation What is urgently proposed is a modest grant to the Lawyers' Committee of something in the neighborhood of $25,000 for 1969 to permit it to accomplish the following ends: 1) Help Joel Carlson and other lawyers to stay in business; 2) Maintain the principle that assistance is available for persons who may otherwise be deprived of good legal help and whose need for such help arises out of the operation of any of the myriad South African statutes and regulations which (a) impose burdens on the basis of race, and (b) impose on individuals regardless of race, obstacles to judicial relief, burdens before the courts, or vulnerability to abuses at the hands of police and other authorities that are clearly in contradiction of the rule of law. 3) Maintain the principle that help in such cases is premised on right to counsel, regardless of the 'political' importance of a case, and thus hold open a channel of nonpolitical professional concern to which open and direct approaches can be made by lawyers and others in South Africa. 4) Be prepared, when opportunity is presented, to secure legal help promptly to South West Africans as well as South Africans held or charged under the Terrorism Act.

At the LCCR Executive Committee meeting on March 3, 1969, Goldberg praised Carlson and indicated that with additional financial support more lawyers in South Africa could be expected to provide legal counsel.[34]

Runyon, who was at the meeting, told the Executive Committee that:

---

33. Interview with Peter Connell (Oct. 9, 1997) former executive director of the National LCCR, 1968-1972, and James Robertson, former director of the National LCCR, 1970-1972. The staff was aware of the board's interest in South Africa but was not involved.

34. Records of the LCCR, Executive Committee File, Minutes, March 3, 1969.

On behalf of the Legal Advisor, I am here to present the views of the Department of State . . . . the Department of State desires to encourage and assist efforts of the American Bar to provide the moral and financial support needed. It considers by such support in the Tuhadeleni and Mbindi matters in 1967-68 the Bar, and in particular, the Lawyers' Committee . . . performed a substantial and important public service in the international field.[35]

The Creation of the Southern Africa Project of the Lawyers' Committee

From 1967 to 1969, the tacit acceptance of an obligation by the LCCR—to uphold principles of justice that were seen to transcend political boundaries—was the first step in the organization of a regular program of legal assistance for lawyers who were defending those who were resisting apartheid in South Africa. By 1969, the LCCR efforts in South Africa had sensitized the bipartisan leadership of the committee, which was made up of recognized leaders of the establishment bar. It had sensitized them to the fact that black citizens in South Africa were being deprived of their civil rights and made them aware of what lawyers could do to help alleviate the situation. Committee leaders had also come to recognize the need to provide public support and approbation to the lawyers on the frontlines who were honoring the most noble traditions of the bar through their help to those struggling for civil rights. This growing awareness among committee leaders led to the development of a major new staff project, the Southern Africa Project.

The Southern African Project proposed a novel, supplemental, purpose—to challenge apartheid both in the United States and in South Africa.[36] Proposing to bring the struggle against apartheid into the courts in the United States was new. For 28 years, the LCCR's Southern Africa Project was a major force in the struggle for racial justice.[37] The project, the Mississippi litigation office, which was started in 1965, and the Urban Areas Project, which was created in 1968, are the three major elements that defined the mature character of the LCCR. The committee was committed to no other elemental goals. From 1970 to the present, all of its work was rooted in those three commitments.

---

35. Records of the LCCR, Executive Committee File, Statement of Charles Runyon, Assistant Legal Adviser For Africa, U.S. Dept. of State, March 3, 1969.
36. After the massacre at Sharpville in 1960, the U.S. government and the United Nations offered aid to Africans. A number of individual lawyers offered financial and professional support at that time.

The conception and promotion of the Southern Africa Project came about as the direct result of the efforts of George Lindsay and Peter Connell following their exposure to the human degradation and racial injustices caused by apartheid. Their determination and commitment to supporting those South African lawyers engaged in the struggle against apartheid made the Southern Africa Project a reality and assured its continuation into the future. After returning from separate trips to South Africa, both men resolved to strengthen the South African activities undertaken by the committee.

In July of 1969, Lindsay, a senior partner in the New York law firm of Debevoise, Plimpton, Lyons & Gates, was asked by LCCR Co-Chairman Arthur Dean to go to South Africa in an effort to lend the support of the American bar to Carlson, whose passport had been taken away by an executive order of the South African authorities. The committee was "afraid that this was the first step in possibly a banning order or house arrest, as had been the case with some other lawyers who had handled political cases."[38]

Carlson's passport was removed after the Lawyers' Committee had sent Dr. Alan R. Moritz, a leading pathologist and an authority in electric torture, to testify in an inquest into the death of James Lenkoe, who had been detained under the Terrorism Act. Lenkoe died while in detention. Moritz testified that "beyond any reasonable doubt, the man had been subjected to electric torture on his toes within less than 12 hours of death." Shortly after that had happened, the South African government took away Carlson's passport. The Lenkoe inquest was abruptly ended and the magistrate declared the case a suicide.[39]

---

37. Southern Africa Project: 25th Anniversary, *South Africa—Can Negotiations Succeed?*, Oct. 14, 1992 (LCCR, 1992): "Over the past twenty-five years the Southern Africa Project has: financed the defense of thousands of political prisoners in South Africa and Namibia; assisted the families of prisoners who died of torture in detention to have legal representation at the inquests; and financed civil lawsuits brought against the security forces when they have opened fire on peaceful demonstrators . . . established the Commission on Independence in Namibia, a bipartisan group of distinguished Americans who monitored Namibia's transition to independence . . . produced annually a series of briefing papers analyzing legal and political developments in South Africa and Namibia . . . organized a series of international conferences held in South Africa on constitutional options for post-apartheid South Africa which involved experts from countries worldwide; and produced series of studies used by participants in the multi-party negotiations with the South African government, which presented a comparative analysis of steps taken in other countries undergoing a transition to democracy."

38. Records of the LCCR, South Africa File, Testimony of George Lindsay to "Working Group" of the Commission on Human Rights, New York, July 1969.

39. *Id.*

Lindsay's trip to South Africa was officially undertaken in response to a request from Under Secretary of State Elliot Richardson to Arthur Dean, an active Republican and a prominent international lawyer.[40] In an effort to reinforce the impact of foreign interest in South African system of justice, Dean contacted Lord William Shawcross, chancellor of Sussex University in England, to ask for a leading British barrister to lend support to Lindsay. Shawcross wired Dean that he did not believe that any British barrister could be found to go to South Africa, but, after some hesitation, Edward Lyons, a member of Parliament who represented the International Commission of Jurists, agreed to accompany Lindsay.[41] Their trip received conspicuous notice in the South African press.[42]

When Lindsay returned to the United States, he was a committed supporter of the anti-apartheid movement, a cause to which he dedicated himself for the next 25 years.[43]

Not long after Lindsay returned from South Africa, 22 South Africans, including Winnie Mandela, were arrested under the Terrorism Act and "held incommunicado for over a year and have been tortured during that time."[44] The defendants in the "Trial of the Twenty-Two" had been acquitted in February 1970 of substantially identical charges and rearrested while in the dock.[45] Charles Runyon suggested that the LCCR send an observer to the trial, which was being handled by Carlson and a defense team led by Sidney Kentridge, one of South Africa's most prominent lawyers.[46] The trial was scheduled to

---

40. Records of the LCCR, South Africa File, Letter dated July 6, 1969, from Elliott L. Richardson, Undersecretary of State, to Arthur H. Dean, Sullivan & Cromwell.

41. Records of the LCCR, South Africa File, Telegram to Lord Shawcross, July 7, 1969, from Arthur Dean. Reply from Lord Shawcross to Arthur Dean, July 8, 1969: "Thank you for Telex. Will do my best but think it difficult to find any barrister of standing able to go to South Africa at this time."

42. Records of the LCCR, South Africa File, George Lindsay's Trip to South Africa. In the file on Mr. Lindsay's trip there are 14 press clippings, a number from the front page and some that included pictures.

43. George Lindsay was chosen by Gay McDougall, director of the LCCR Southern Africa Project, to serve as an official election monitor in both the Namibian elections and the first free elections in South Africa in 1995.

44. Records of the LCCR, South Africa File, Memorandum, July 4, 1970, to James Robertson from Peter Connell re.: The Future Role of the Lawyers' Committee in South Africa.

45. *Id.*, Request for Financial Support.

46. Ten Year Report of the Lawyers' Committee for Civil Rights Under Law (LCCR, 1973), at 97: In the case of the Trial of the Twenty-two, the defense entered a plea of autrefois acquit and included in their argument U.S. case law on double jeopardy

begin on August 3, 1970.[47] Peter Connell, the LCCR executive director, was sent as an observer of the trial.[48]

In the weeks preceding the trial, James Robertson and Peter Connell had discussed the future role of the committee in South Africa. They found that the committee would have "$50,000 to support this work."[49] From 1967 to 1970, the committee's efforts in South Africa had relied heavily on the availability and professional contacts of Carlson and the assistance of Runyon. That arrangement provided limited contact with the South African bar and could not be counted on to last indefinitely.[50] It was becoming clear that new arrangements would be necessary if the LCCR was going to continue to provide legal assistance in South Africa. In a memo to Robertson, Connell said that "Charles Runyon suggested. . . that the Lawyers' Committee take steps to place itself directly in touch with Joel Carlson and other attorneys (solicitors) in South Africa, who might be persuaded to provide legal assistance, on our instructions, in those cases in which we may have an interest. Obviously this cannot be done by mail."[51] It was apparent that Connell was not going to South Africa simply as a trial observer. In the same memo, Connell said "if a decision is made to send someone from the Committee to South Africa to accomplish the purposes described above, that mission should coincide with the beginning of the trial."

Connell was the only lawyer observer at the trial in Pretoria and was received with courtesy by the judge, Justice Viljoen. The committee acted on

---

furnished by the Lawyer' Committee. The defense in this case was successful. However, two weeks after accused were freed, they were placed under banning orders (i.e., house arrest) by the Minister of Justice.

47. Records of the LCCR, South Africa File, Clipping, Sept. 6, 1970, SUNDAY TIMES, JOHANNESBURG, at 2: "Mr. Connell arrived in South Africa on Aug. 23, 1970 for the trial's opening."

48. *Id.* Peter Connell represented both the LCCR and the American Bar Association at the trial in the Transvaal Provincial Division of the Supreme Court of South Africa, in Pretoria.

49. Records of the LCCR, South Africa File, Memo, /222July 4, 1970: "$25,000 from the Ford Foundation; $5,000 from the United Nations Trust Fund for South Africa; $3242.50 from the private bar; and $3242.50 from the Field Foundation."

50. Records of the LCCR, George Lindsay's Trip, Memo from Charles Runyon, June 24, 1969, to George Lindsay: "The attached informal summary may prove a useful recapitulation of the crisis confronting Joel Carlson and those who have been supporting his legal defense work. Since it was written we have learned that, through harassment, Carlson's office staff is down to a bookkeeper and messenger and that his attorney correspondent in Pretoria is bowing out. . . ."

51. Memo, *supra* note 49.

the belief "that while the rule of law had been steadily eroded in South Africa, the judiciary had managed to cling to its tradition of independence, and lawyers had increasingly come to recognize their professional responsibility to safeguard the rudiments of due process of law."[52] According to Connell, if the LCCR hoped to work with the bar inside South Africa, it would have to eschew inflammatory rhetoric.[53] "You couldn't denounce the government and work with the lawyers whose position was already quite vulnerable."[54] His mission, in August 1970, was "to learn at firsthand of the legal procedures and institutions of this country and further the exchange of views between the bar in the United States and our counterparts in South Africa."[55]

During his two weeks in the country, Connell learned a great deal about the mechanics of apartheid, such as the practices of banning, pass laws, and home lands,[56] and had the opportunity to speak with many anti-apartheid activists and government officials."[57] From jail, Winnie Mandela wrote him:

> I am so sorry I was unable to speak to you in Court. In my Country prisoners do not speak to anyone else except his defense and the police. Your presence in our trial meant a great deal to us. It is inspiration from organizations like yours and people like you who give us the courage to go on fighting no matter how difficult this might be. Please give our gratitude to your friends . . . . We hope you will

---

52. Records of the LCCR, South Africa File, 1.

53. Records of the LCCR, South Africa File, Memorandum, July 4, 1970, from Peter Connell to James Robertson re.: The Future Role of the Lawyers' Committee in South Africa.

54. Connell, *supra* note 6. Also, the Lawyers' Committee was aware of the difficulties that faced lawyers who worked with anti-apartheid groups.

55. Peter Connell, *U.S. Lawyers Show the Way in Civil Rights Fight*, the SUNDAY TIMES, Johannesburg, Sept. 6, 1970, at 1.

56. For a detailed discussion of apartheid practices, see the U.N. publication APARTHEID IN PRACTICE.

57. Records of the LCCR, South Africa File, Southern Africa Project, Memo dated Dec. 16, 1970, from Peter Connell to George Lindsay; Draft Letter to Mrs. Kentridge from Mr. Lindsay; Memo from Peter Connell to George Lindsay, Dec. 16, 1970. While in South Africa, Peter Connell was invited to speak to the student body and the faculty at the University of Witwatersrand Law School. At that time he suggested a program in which lawyers might litigate selected cases coming to the attention of the Black Sash Advice Centers, legal advice centers run by upper-middle-class white women who had been trained in selected areas of the law, particularly urban removal laws and the pass laws. A clinical program for law students who evinced an interest in a program to become active at these centers was undertaken by Mrs. Sidney Kentridge, who taught at the Law School.

continue your interest in our struggle for human dignity. My colleagues join me in wishing you a safe journey back home. . . ."[58]

He, too, was converted by his experiences in South Africa. He remembers that he was "inspired by the words of Robert Kennedy" to the students at
Cape Town and he knew from the Cairo, Illinois, experience "that we can
make a difference." "I realized that we [the Lawyers' Committee] were just
dabbling" in South Africa and that if any real progress was to be made some
organizational structure and direction for the work had to be created.[59] Upon
his return from the "Trial of the Twenty-Two," he proposed the creation of a
Southern Africa Project.

Connell returned from South Africa with the names of lawyers who had
expressed an interest in cooperating with the committee's work.[60] Under apartheid, the lip service[61] that South Africans gave to the rule of law in their
country accorded some procedural rights to defendants, even those prosecuted
under the Terrorism Act. One of the goals of the Southern Africa Project was
to make sure they were honored in practice. When considering possibilities
for the project with Lindsay, he wrote:

> The major problem in South Africa is that the rule of law has been
> supplanted by the delegation of vast, unchecked authority designed
> to be used in furtherance of the policy of apartheid. Therefore, I
> think our basic goal should be to use the legal process in South

---

58. Records of the LCCR, South Africa File, Letter from Winnie Mandela to P.J. Connell,
undated.

59. Connell, *supra* note 6.

60. Records of the LCCR, South Africa File, Memo, Nov. 12, 1970, from Peter J.
Connell to George N. Lindsay, re.: South Africa Program: "Joel Carlson is clearly
the leading attorney in South Africa in providing the kind of representation we seek
to foster. . . . If our financial position becomes such that we must choose among
cases brought to our attention by different attorneys, we should elect to fund Joel's
case even if it may not appear as important as others. We owe him that." Other
lawyers identified were Henry Brown (Capetown), Hymie Berriadt (Capetown),
David Dallas (Capetown), Raymond Tucker (Johannesburg), and Gerald Mallinick
(Capetown).

61. The South African judicial system gave defendants in criminal trials, even blacks,
the right to engage counsel. However, black defendants were without funds to pay
lawyers, the bar, by and large, refused to defend blacks, and there was no pro bono
legal aid tradition in South Africa. When in capital cases the South African government provided counsel it was without the services of a lawyer, who was a necessary
component for an adequate defense.

Africa in order to hold government officials there legally responsible in their own courts-morally accountable to world public opinion-for the way they exercise or abuse the broad authority accorded them under the law. Hopefully this kind of exposure and pressure will serve to curb abuses of authority (torture of detainees) and in some instances deter the full exercise of unquestioned legal authority (e.g., redetention of acquitted defendants).[62]

For the project, which would be run out of the LCCR's Washington offices, he proposed a two-pronged attack. In South Africa, the committee would broaden its contacts with the bar and would continue to be involved in instructing lawyers, providing expert witnesses to testify at trials in that country, and preparing memoranda of law on issues where American and South African common law principles were similar.[63] In response to a request from Lindsay that they develop some guidance for lawyers in South Africa, three suggestions were offered: "(1) focus attention on particularly reprehensible practices . . . (2) we could recommend challenges to specific statutes . . . (3) we could articulate the goals we seek to accomplish through litigation and the elements which would be found in cases furthering those goals."[64] Connell favored the third suggestion, which was chosen. He believed that the first option "could unduly narrow our areas of concern" and result in missing solid opportunities The second "would involve the committee in devising hypothetical challenges on the basis of a cursory familiarity with South African law; our suggestions could appear naive and therefore diminish the confidence in us; and even if we focused on a particular statute, there would remain the problem of locating a plaintiff. I believe we must begin the formulation of our goals with the recognition that, given the state of law in South Africa, we cannot confine our selection to cases which we believe we would have a good chance of winning. To do this would . . . require an overly conservative

---

62. Memo dated Dec. 16, 1970, from Peter J. Connell to George N. Lindsay, re.: South Africa Litigation.

63. The situation in South Africa was difficult and at times dangerous for lawyers who undertook the representation of unpopular cases. Sensitive to the needs of the South African lawyers, and concerned that the South African government could arbitrarily ban the Lawyers' Committee from working within the country, Mr. Connell decided that it would be in the best interests of the anti-apartheid work to keep a very low profile in South Africa—they were there as lawyers, not as political activists. The Lawyers' Committee was scrupulous about its practices, giving the government no cause to act against them or the lawyers who cooperated with the committee.

64. Memo, *supra* note 61.

selection of cases. In addition, we must be wary of placing ourselves in the position of simply trying to provide legal services for hardship cases since they are ubiquitous in South Africa."[65]

In the United States, the committee would join forces with other parties and organizations interested in opposing apartheid. In the United States. The project would create and execute a strategy to challenge—in American courts, with the public, and with the U.S. government—the racially discriminatory policies of the South African government that were contrary to American law. It was unlike anything the committee had been doing and it was an extraordinary initiative for the times.

The concept of a Southern Africa Project was not universally accepted by the board and the Executive Committee. Berl Bernhard, committee counsel, recalled that he opposed it on the grounds that the committee needed to stay on mission, to dedicate its limited resources to solving racial discrimination problems in America, not spread itself thin in an effort where they could not hope to make a real difference.[66] Nonetheless, with the backing of Co-Chairmen George Lindsay and John Douglas the establishment of the Southern Africa Project was approved by the board.

Throughout its 25 years of its existence, the Southern Africa Project was able to accomplish much because of its leadership and the consistency of its goals. In an introduction to a *Howard Law Journal* article, "Southern African Issues in United States Courts," Gay J. McDougall, the project's director from 1980 to 1995, wrote:

> The Southern Africa Project's program of litigation in U.S. courts has sought to further human rights in southern Africa through the application of U.S. law or international law which should be enforceable in U.S. courts. The novel approach taken by the project's program of domestic litigation has met with some successes over the years. It has helped to focus the attention of the U.S. public, particularly the bar and the judiciary, on the abuses of apartheid and, on occasion, it has forced a change in U.S. governmental policy and established new precedents with regard to the legal interest of U.S. citizens in foreign matters.[67]

According to Connell, the Southern Africa Project "merely advanced a

---

65. *Id.*
66. Interview with Berl I. Bernhard (Sept. 30, 1997), former executive director of the LCCR.
67. Introduction to Butcher article, *supra* note 8, Gay J. McDougall, director of the Southern Africa Project, LCCR.

better, more decisive way of opposing apartheid"[68] and James Robertson, the director of the national office, approved of that concept. However, like all new staff projects, the axis upon which the Southern Africa Project would turn was money. To secure adequate funding, Connell believed he would have to commit himself officially to the project. For the next two years, Connell dedicated himself to establishing the project, even turning down the offer to become the LCCR director.

Good ideas had to be backed by good direction and organization. The Ford Foundation, which had given $25,000 to the board's initiative the year before,[69] was one of the few foundations capable of granting long-term resources, but it was hesitant to fund the ambitious goals of the Southern Africa Project. It did not commit funds to the project until the spring 1973. It, too, was concerned about what the committee could realistically expect to accomplish.

Over the next two years, Lindsay and Connell had a series of discussions with Ford Foundation representatives Wayne Fredericks, William Herman, and Chris Edley, Sr. about what the LCCR might do to oppose apartheid.[70] The Ford officials "were intrigued, and clearly wanted to do something." They recognized the seriousness of the deprivation of rights in South Africa and realized that the South African courts could be used as a forum to expose the system of detention and torture. They believed the LCCR could help defend rights, limited though they may be, in the South African judicial system. Nonetheless, in the final analysis, they were troubled by the system of apartheid. It was executed through the law and the legal system was "stacked against these people." To the extent that the committee was helpful and participated in the process by which those laws are enforced "you may simply make it appear that the rule of law prevails in South Africa." The work of the Lawyers' Committee wouldn't be changing the underlying system of apartheid. The question that became a stumbling block was, "Given that the laws are stacked against the Blacks in South Africa, unlike in the American South, the issue of 'specifically what the Committee hoped to accomplish' had to be addressed" in the application for funding.[71]

In his application to the Ford Foundation for a two-year grant in February 1973, Connell responded as follows:

---

68. Connell, *supra* note 6.
69. Memo, *supra* note 43, at 1.
70. Remarks by Peter J. Connell, November 1995, at the Washington, D.C., ceremony commemorating the Lawyers' Committee's contributions in South Africa upon the conclusion of the South African Elections.
71. *Id.*

We believe our cooperation is important because it lends support to those lawyers in South Africa who have refused to "cave in" and whose work constitutes a living affirmation of the spirit of man. That spark of integrity may or may not develop to the point at which it can light the way to reform, but we feel that we have a responsibility to what we can do to keep it alive. . . . If racial justice does come to Southern Africa, it will be followed shortly by a painful analysis of the history of racial subjugation, exploitation, and cruelty. The question will then be asked of the world—as it was after World War II—"What did you do to stand up for the fundamental human rights of these oppressed people?" The Lawyers' Committee intends to have an answer.[72]

The continuation of the project rested on adequate funding and the staff, which had concentrated its hopes on Ford, anxiously waited for word from the foundation. The committee's expectation was that Ford would fund the project fully for the first year at $50,000. In April, the foundation announced that it would grant $100,000 to fund the Southern Africa Project for two years. The amount and length of the grant was a surprise and great relief. By receiving backing for two years, it must be assumed that the staff and the board of the Ford Foundation were convinced that the goals of the project, as well as the proposed works, were valuable and worth the foundation's support.

In South Africa, the project concentrated on the Robert Sobukwe case,[73]

---

72. Records of the LCCR, South Africa File, Grant Application from the Lawyers' Committee for Civil Rights Under Law to the Ford Foundation for a South Africa Project, Feb. 2, 1971, 19-20: "The question remains of course, as to the efficacy of the use of the legal process in a non-democratic, repressive system of government such as that which prevails in South Africa. We offer four observations in support of the Lawyers' Committee's Legal Assistance Program for South Africa: 1. The Black, Coloured and Indian clients who needed the legal assistance which we helped make possible have told us that they highly value this support; 2. The program is fully consistent with U.N. General Assembly Resolution adopted on November 2, 1971 by a vote of 109 to 2 which 'appeals to national and international associations of jurists to take appropriate steps' to combat inhumane treatment of opponents of apartheid and to promote the cause of justice in South Africa; 3. We believe our cooperation is important because it lends support to those lawyers in South Africa who have refused to 'cave in' and whose work constitutes a living affirmation of the spirit of man. . . ."

73. *Id.* at 8-9. "Banning orders are a form of punishment without trial permitted by South African security laws; they are not subject to Judicial review. A question arose, however, as to whether banned individuals could exercise a common law right to leave the country. The case in point involved Mr. Robert Sobukwe, the leader of the

the "Trial of the 13,"[74] the trial of the Ovambo strikers,[75] and cases arising out

---

Pan African Congress, which was summarily outlawed in the early 1960s. Mr. Sobukwe was imprisoned for his part in a nonviolent protest against the Pass Laws. Each year for five years the Parliament passed a special statute authorizing his continued detention for yet another year. When he was finally released he was banned to the inland town of Kimberley. In 1970, Mr. Sobukwe was offered a professorship at the University of Wisconsin and arrangements were made to admit him and his family to the United States for permanent residence—if they could leave South Africa. An exit permit was granted—as required by law—by the Minister of Interior. Contemporaneously, the Minister of Justice summarily denied Mr. Sobukwe permission to travel to the airport to exercise his 'absolute right' to leave. At that point, the Lawyers' Committee financed a legal challenge to the authority of the Minister of Justice in this regard. An adverse decision was handed down by the Supreme Court, Transvaal Provincial Division on June 22, 1971. The decision was affirmed by the Appellate Division."

74. *Id.* at 9-12. "On August 2, 1971, two trials under the Terrorism Act began. In one the defendant was the Rev. ffrench-Beytagh, the dean of the Anglican Cathedral in Johannesburg. It was decided not to allocate funds for the dean because 'we believed (correctly)' that funds for his defense would be easier to secure. The other defendants in the case were 13 Black, Coloureds and Indians who were members of the Unity Movement legal political organization whose 'Ten Point Program' was considered considerably less radical than the U.S. Bill of Rights. The 13 were represented by several South African attorneys of Indian extraction with whom we wished to establish a cooperative relationship. The prosecution based its case against the 13 on evidence which the security branch had secured from individuals who had been in detention for months in a remote forest camp. One of the detainees, Mr. Cutshela, died in detention. One of these detainees, who was induced to sign a statement incriminating the defendants, repudiated that statement in court and testified that it had been coerced. When he left the witness stand, he was arrested and charged with perjury. During the presentation of the State's case, it became evident to the defense that a major challenge should be mounted against the interrogation techniques and practices of the security branch. One of the advocates, Mr. Harry Pitman, came to the United States in November of 1971 to consult with the staff and the Board of the Lawyers' Committee. This consultation led to the decision to introduce evidence in the trial establishing a pattern of interrogation methods used by the security branch, which would be followed by expert psychiatric testimony challenging the credibility of evidence secured by the application of those interrogation methods. For its part, the Lawyers' Committee identified a leading American psychiatrist, Dr. Louis West, who had treated American POWs held and interrogated by the Chinese during the Korean War. He has authored many articles for professional journals on the psychological and physiological effects of various interrogation techniques. Lawyers' Committee staff briefed Dr. West extensively on South Africa law, detention practices and the details of the instant case. The staff also provided defense counsel with memoranda on U.S. case law governing the circum-

stances of detention and interrogation which have been held by the U.S. Supreme Court to be so inherently coercive as to require the exclusion of evidence secured under those circumstances. Defense counsel then went to England and secured a score of affidavits from expatriate South Africans who had been detained and interrogated by the security branch. Arrangements were made for Dr. West's transportation to South Africa and a senior advocate, Mr. Muller, Q.C., was retained by the defense to challenge the reliability and admissibility of evidence secured from detainees. On February 8, 1972, one of the South African attorneys called to report that the Supreme Court at Pietermaritzburg refused permission for the defense counsel to lead evidence which was to have formed the foundation of the psychiatrist's testimony. He asked that the psychiatrist not be sent. All 13 accused were convicted, but given relatively light sentences. The convictions were appealed on the ground, inter alia, that the Court erred. . . . In addition, . . . the defense attorney in this case filed an action seeking damages against the Minister of Police on behalf of 12 of the tortured detainees."

75. *Id.* at 12-14. "On Dec. 13, 1971, Black workers in Namibia began an unprecedented and historic general strike to protest the contract labor system. Under the system, Black men who seek employment must contract with a central government agency (SWANLA) which grades them according to physical fitness. They are then dispatched to distant locations, without families, for 12-18 months. Minimum wages for a 50-hour work week range from $1.50 per week to $11.70 per week; actual weekly wages paid average $6.65. The employers' lack of technical 'ownership' of the workers may be said to distinguish this system from slavery. The strike closed most of the country's mines and seriously disrupted the economy, which is heavily dependent on mining. Under South African Law, collective bargaining by Blacks is unlawful; so is striking. In an effort to break the strike, 13 Ovambos were arrested; their trial was set for January 25, 1972. Twelve of the defendants had no lawyers and could afford none. On January 13, 1972, the Lawyers' Committee staff telephoned Anglican church officials in Namibia and asked that they convey to the defendants the Lawyers' Committee's belief that the accused should have counsel and the Committee's willingness to provide financial support toward that end. On the basis of that undertaking, attorneys were secured and an advocate, Mr. Brian O'Linn, was briefed. The International Commission of Jurists sent observers to this trial on three separate occasions, and it is perhaps worthy of remark to note that two days before the arrival in Windhoek of U.N. Secretary General Waldheim, the prosecutor asked for, and received, a two-week recess of these proceedings and consented to the release of all accused on bail for that two-week period. Most observers of the South Africa scene believe that this trial was postponed because it was viewed by the South African government as a source of serious embarrassment, in that it provided a forum for exposing to public view the extraordinarily harsh conditions of servitude which prevail in Namibia. On June 5, 1972, the court issued its judgment. All 12 accused had been charged on three counts: striking, inciting others to strike and intimidating others to strike. Four of the accused were acquitted of all charges and the remaining eight were acquitted on two out of three of the counts. They received suspended sentences and each fined 25 rand. . . . As a result

of the students protests in June 1972.[76] In the United States, the work of the committee was not governed by the same constraints or goals. The project's aim was to oppose apartheid in a multitude of arenas, to publicize the atrocities of the apartheid system to the American people, and to challenge the U.S. government to insist that the South African government uphold the rule of law.[77] In the period under discussion, the project was involved in three major legal cases in the United States—a complaint against the *New York Times* for publishing employment adds for "all white" positions in South Africa; a case challenging the application by South African Airways for a route between Johannesburg and New York; and, a case that sought to prevent the importation of Southern Rhodesian chrome into the United States. This resourceful initiative was a new twist in the fight against apartheid and one that would lead to other creative challenges against apartheid in the United States."[78]

----

of the strike and the revelations at the trial concerning the grievances of the Ovambo workers, an agreement was negotiated between Ovambo leaders and the government of South Africa. This agreement . . . provides some modest protection for Ovambo workers not previously available, including provisions for an employee's terminating a contract, and taking home leave during the contract period."

76. *Id.* at 17. "During the nationwide student-police clashes in June of 1972, a total of 618 students were arrested. The demonstrations by White students which gave rise to these arrests were primarily directed at protesting discrimination in education in South Africa, and triggered by protests by Black university students. . . . The major clashes with police took place on the steps of St. George's Anglican Cathedral in Capetown, where 57 students were arrested. Fourteen persons, including 10 students, were charged under the Riotous Assemblies Act and brought to trial in August 1972. Because of the limited nature of our legal defense resources and because we assumed (correctly) that those charged had access to sufficient funds to provide for their own defense, the Lawyers' Committee did not contribute directly to that action. However, in concert with the International Commission of Jurists and the World Council of Churches, the Lawyers' Committee sent an Australian law professor to Capetown to serve as an observer at the trial. His report . . . was carried widely by the press around the world. . . . The convictions of the defendants in that case were appealed to the South African Supreme Court. On October 19, 1972 the Supreme Court reversed the convictions . . . also of those who had not appealed.

77. APARTHEID IN PRACTICE 45. The Preamble states: "Whereas it is essential, if man is not to be compelled to have recourse, as a last resort, to rebellion against tyranny and oppression, that human rights should be protected by the rule of law."

78. The Southern Africa Project gave advice and counsel to the anti-apartheid groups as well as representation. George Hauser, the head of the American Committee on Africa, was a leader in the field of economic divestment in South African companies. With the counsel of the LCCR, he prepared a strategy for individual stockholders of large corporations that were active in the anti-apartheid movement. He even participated individually when, upon occasion, the American Committee on

The Southern Africa Project's first legal bullet against apartheid was fired in New York City at an administrative hearing. In 1971, the *New York Times* regularly carried employment advertisements placed by South African companies and the South African government. Connell filed a petition on behalf of the American Committee on Africa, the African Heritage Studies Association, One Hundred Black Men, and William H. Booth of the New York City Commission on Human Rights, which was chaired by Eleanor Holmes Norton.[79] The petition asked that the newspaper "cease and desist" from this practice because it was unlawful under New York City law. It was argued that despite the fact that the advertisements did not specifically say "no blacks need apply," the advertisements were placed by employers that "expresses directly or indirectly," such limitations and, under New York administrative law, was unlawful."[80] After a hearing, the commission ordered the *Times* to cease and desist from publishing advertisements of employment opportunities in South Africa on the grounds that these advertisement violated the city's antidiscrimination law prohibiting any racial qualifications. The case took more than five years to work its way through the appeals process. The decision was overturned on appeal.[81] The court said that "a city agency could not make foreign policy; state courts by virtue of the act of state doctrine, cannot sit in review of laws of a sovereign state or inquire into 'its righteousness'; federal power should not be interfered with in the area of foreign policy or political questions; and this is not a matter for proper state concern."[82]

In 1972, South African Airways (SAA)[83] petitioned the U.S. Civil Aero-

---

Africa would purchase shares of, say, Ford, General Motors, or Westinghouse. At annual meetings, individual stockholders would try to raise issues concerning employment practices in South Africa and call for reports about the conditions to be met at the following annual meeting. In time these challenges became a national movement.

79. Peter Connell and Eleanor Norton had been classmates at Yale Law School.

80. New York Times Co. v. Human Rights Comm'n, N.Y.C. ADMIN. CODE § B 1-7.0 sub. 6.

81. New York Times Co. v. City of N.Y. Comm'n on Human Rights, 349 N.Y.S.2d 940, 76 Misc. 2d 17 (1973), *order vacated and relief sought by petitioner granted,* 363 N.Y.S.2d 321, 79 Misc. 2d 1046 (1974), *aff'd,* 41 N.Y.S.2d 312, 361 N.E.2d 963 (1977).

82. Butcher, *supra* note 8, at 629-30.

83. South African Airways is totally owned and controlled by the South African government.

nautics Board (CAB) for a permit[84] to become a foreign air carrier with a route from the New York to Johannesburg. The application was opposed by Connell, representing the chairman of the United States House of Representatives Foreign Affairs Subcommittee on Africa; the Congressional Black Caucus, chaired by Charles Diggs; a South African group (SWAPO); the American Committee on Africa; the Black United Front of Washington, D.C.; the African Heritage Studies Association; and others.[85] The opponents presented evidence to the CAB that the applicant was not in compliance with the statutory requirement under the Federal Aviation Act (FAA) that prohibited discrimination by a foreign air carrier. The opponents wanted to give testimony that SAA discriminated against black American citizens both in trans-Atlantic and continuation flights in South Africa and in South African airport facilities.[86] Though the administrative law judge substantially refused to admit the evidence, the LCCR presented the argument, based on U.S. case law,[87] that trans-Atlantic travel does not begin and end at international airport facilities but does, in fact, include connecting flights and auxiliary forms of transportation They argued that since SAA was a wholly owned and controlled facility of the South African government, as were the other forms of public transportation in South Africa, it was within the power of the South African government to desegregate these facilities for American citizens traveling in South Africa. In order to secure the permit from the CAB, the South African government agreed to desegregate all internal flights (all international flights had already been desegregated) whether or not they were part of an international itinerary, as well as desegregating all terminal facilities, rail, bus, and other state-owned travel facilities for American citizens.[88] The application was endorsed by the CAB and approved by President Richard Nixon under another section of the FAA law that gave him authority in matters affecting international transportation. Under the law, his decision to approve the application was not reviewable by the courts. Notwithstanding, the Southern Africa Project and the petitioners sought review on the grounds that the board failed to present the President a complete record on the issues relating to racial discrimination against American citizens and that its failure was a constitutional infirmity requiring judicial review and remand. They were not seek-

---

84. South African Airways and the Civil Aeronautics Board first entered into an agreement in 1947 allowing South African Airways a route from South Africa, Rio de Janeiro, and New York.
85. Butcher, *supra* note 8, at 612.
86. *Id.* at 613.
87. *South African Airways*, CAB No. 24944, at 3-4 (D.C. Cir. Sept. 5, 1973); also, petition for review at 25, Diggs v. CAB, 516 F.2d 1248 (D.C. Cir. 1975).
88. *Id.*

ing review of the presidential authority. The appeals court ruled that it was deprived of jurisdiction by explicit statutory language.[89]

Finally, in 1972, after Joel Carlson had been forced to leave South Africa,[90] he met with Congressman Charles Diggs and Thomas Franck at the New York University Law Center. Diggs asked the men if the center would begin research on a possible test of the United States' intention to import chrome from Southern Rhodesia.[91] In 1963, the United Nations, with the support of the United States, had imposed an arms embargo on Rhodesia and South Africa, which had been effectively honored throughout the years. In 1972, the U.S. Senate was debating a national security provision[92] for the Strategic and Critical Materials Stockpiling Act, that would allow for, according to Diggs, the illegal importation of Rhodesian chrome. The Southern Africa Project took on the challenge to the chrome importation, with the support of Diggs; the Congressional Black Caucus; the Zimbabwean African National Union; the Council for Christian Social Action of the United Church of Christ, which had been expelled from Rhodesia; the American Committee on Africa, whose chairman, George Hauser, had been banned from Southern Rhodesia; the Southern Africa Committee, an organization of Southern Rhodesians who would be banned if they returned home; Gore Vidal, who was suing for himself and 50 other authors whose books had been banned in the country; Thomas M. Franck, a scholar who was refused entry to Rhodesia to do scholarly work; the Southern Christian Leadership Conference; the Episcopal Churchmen for South Africa; and others with ideological interest in the litigation.[93] The courts found against the LCCR. They lost the appeal on substantive grounds as well, but the appeals court found that a number of the plaintiffs who had been denied entry to Rhodesia or access to their country did have standing to sue in U.S, courts. This was a considerable victory because the traditional hurdle to suits seeking to litigate the validity of governmental action is standing.

---

89. *Id.*, petition for review.
90. Carlson, *supra* note 21. Joel Carlson's anti-apartheid activities led to his banning in 1971. Alerted of the proposed state action, Carlson, with the help of the United States Consulate, fled the country without his wife, Jeanette, and their four young children. With the help of George Lindsay, he was offered a teaching position at New York University. When his family was able to obtain travel permits, they joined him. Today they live in Great Neck, New York. Carlson returned to South Africa for the 1994 election.
91. Butcher, *supra* note 8 at 608, n.14.
92. West Virginia Senator Byrd had added an amendment to the Armed Forces Appropriations Authorization, Pub. L. No. 92-156 & 503, 85 Stat. 423 (1973).
93. Diggs v. Schultz, 470 F.2d 461 (D.C. Cir.) 1972), *cert. denied*, 411 U.S. 931 (1973).

By the spring of 1973, the Southern Africa Project had been funded, a staff and organization was in place, and its program was underway, both in the United States and South Africa. Connell wanted to "move on" from the LCCR and he knew that lack of money wasn't the only reason good projects flounder. The lack of leadership and support were other important reasons for failure. "I had seen too many good projects die" for lack of institutionalized support. "I wanted to establish a permanent organizational structure to carry on the work long term." For that reason, Connell conceived of the idea of establishing a permanent South Africa Subcommittee of the LCCR, which would give South African issues a distinct and regular place in the proceedings of the board and Executive Committee meetings. "The active participation of the membership and of their firms was an important element in the success of the project and, I wanted to keep the Board abreast of the issues." The creation of a subcommittee would mean that a report from the Southern Africa Subcommittee would be on the agenda of every board meeting.

Without the cooperation and leadership of George Lindsay, the Southern Africa Subcommittee would never have materialized. Lindsay recruited a group of lawyers who reflected the stature of the LCCR and the board's commitment to the goals of the Southern Africa Project. In May 1973, the first subcommittee of the LCCR was constituted with Lindsay as its chair. Joining Lindsay were Cyrus Vance, Eli Whitney Debervoise, Whitney North Seymour, Sr., John Douglas, Ramsey Clark, Theodore Sorensen, and Bethuel Webster. When Connell left the committee that year, he was elected to the board and joined the Southern Africa Subcommittee. For the next 22 years, the subcommittee vigorously supported the increasingly significant work of the Southern Africa Project. Eschewing rhetoric, the subcommittee alone continued uninterrupted in its legal activities in South Africa, which had a profound impact in the history of the South African liberation movement and in South Africa's nation building. In 1992, shortly after his release from prison, Nelson Mandela personally thanked the Southern Africa Project on the occasion of its 25th anniversary.[94] Mandela expressed his appreciation for the LCCR's significant and steadfast work in the pursuit of racial justice in South Africa. In particular, he commended Gay J. McDougall, who served as project director from 1980 to 1995.[95] The work of the project helped secure reforms that made nonracial democratic elections possible in both Namibia and South

---

94. Nelson Mandela, Oct. 14, 1992, Transcript of Taped Remarks, Washington, D.C.
95. Directors of the Southern Africa Project were Peter J. Connell, 1970-1973; Douglas Wacholtz and Roderic Boggs, 1973-1975; Michael Peay, 1975-1977; Millard Arnold, 1977-1980; and Gay J, McDougall, 1980-1995.

Africa.[96] In a demonstration of his appreciation and respect, Mandela chose McDougall to stand with the South African people in their pursuit of freedom, democracy, and justice as they prepared for the first free elections in the country's long and troubled history. McDougall was the only American and one of only three non-South Africans appointed to the 18-person Independent Electoral Commission, whose task it was to organize, manage, and run the elections. In April of 1994, with a mix of awe and apprehension, the world awaited the outcome of this historic process. Mandela chose to cast his vote with McDougall by his side[97] and, while the election process was plagued with problems, it was nevertheless declared free and fair after four days of astonishing tranquility.

---

96. The Lawyers' Committee for Civil Rights Under Law, Annual Report 1993-1994 (LCCR 1994) 41-46.
97. *Id.* The picture of Mr. Mandela with his vote being placed in the box, with Ms. McDougall at his side, can be seen on p. 41.

EPILOGUE

It goes without saying that no one group alone can change an institution as vast and complex as the American bar. In the second half of the twentieth century, the Lawyers' Committee for Civil Rights Under Law (LCCR) stands out because it helped show the way for the bar during a critical juncture in the relatively young history of the nation's experiment with democracy. In 1963, American lawyers, like other leaders in society, were confused by the social changes that were being demanded by the poor and voiceless in America. The need for fundamental change in traditional ways of doing things was not clear at the time, nor was it clear which direction the country would choose to follow. Leaders arose to guide the nation and its key institutions. One of those leaders was the LCCR. In June 1963, the committee sent out a call to the organized bar to meet the challenges being presented by honoring the fundamental principles of their calling that for too long had been respected in word only.

This book began with a history of legal aid in America. It showed how the bar in the South—particularly in Mississippi—and, in fact, the American Bar Association, failed to respond to a perceived responsibility of the institution. From its inception, the LCCR sought to establish within the organized bar the principle that lawyers had a unique responsibility to the life of the nation. Committee members tried to bring this message home, first to lawyers in Mississippi, with very limited success. Later in the 1960s, the principle was extended to the major urban areas where the largest law firms showed that lawyers could make a difference in advocating for the poor and minorities. And, in the early 1970s, the committee took upon itself the responsibility

227

for supporting the beleaguered bar in South Africa, as those lawyers sought to meet elevated professional standards of responsibility. Ultimately, influenced by the call to lead the bar, members of the LCCR were instrumental in moving the American Bar Association to establish the Section on Individual Rights and Responsibilities to help the ABA itself adjust to the demands of a transforming America.

In ending this book, it is appropriate to mention the impact on other areas of the profession by LCCR members who were influenced by the committee's distinct vision of lawyers as public advocates. Because of the work the committee did in South Africa and because of its educational effect on members of the bar, other groups followed it. Erwin Griswold, former dean of Harvard Law School, and Lloyd Cutler, senior partner in the law firm of Wilmer Cutler & Pickering, as members of the LCCR Executive Committee, became familiar with the situation in South Africa and the role lawyers could play in the amelioration of injustices there. They worked with lawyers in South Africa to establish the Southern Africa Legal Services and Legal Education Program (SALSLEP). Half of the members of the board of that organization were members of the Executive Committee of the LCCR. SALSLEP has raised several million dollars from American law firms and foundations to fund domestic public interest law firms in South Africa, Namibia, and Zimbabwe, which are still being funded and are active. In addition, SALSLEP was instrumental in inducing American law firms to provide law school scholarships for black South African students studying in that country.

Similarly, because of the seminal experience of the leaders of the LCCR in mobilizing the private bar in the American civil rights struggle, other committee members mobilized to modify the practices of the American Bar Association by establishing a new institutional format "to enhance its opportunity to deal with the significant legal problems which face American society."[1]

Despite the emergence of the LCCR, the ABA remained uniquely suited to influence the conduct of the American bar. The committee was never meant to be a permanent organization. Early in 1964, a movement began within the ABA to create a new section of the association for the purpose of helping "lawyers deal more effectively with their responsibility to represent the cause of individual liberty and equality of treatment under law."[2] The call for the ABA to assume an institutional responsibility for the American system of

---

1. Shestack File, Need for a Section of Individual Rights In the American Bar Association.
2. Jerome J. Shestack, File on the Section on Individual Rights and Responsibilities, 1963-1966, Letter to Present and Prospective Members of the American Bar Association, March 1964, Jefferson B. Fordham, Chairman, Organizing Committee, Phila-

justice was a fundamentally altering initiative, a break with the accepted view of the institution and with the history of lawyering in the twentieth century. Like SALSLEP, the movement grew out of the LCCR experience. The success of the movement resulted in a basic revision of the goals of the organized bar in the United States and gave the ABA a new dual role as an advocate for both the profession (its historic role) and an advocate for the public.

The ABA was created in 1878 "to advance the science of jurisprudence, promote the administration of justice and uniformity in legislation. . . uphold the honor of the profession. . . and encourage cordial intercourse among the members of the American Bar."[3] It took the association almost 50 years to accept any responsibility for providing legal assistance to the poor in the United States and then its Standing Committee on Legal Aid, created in 1920, remained only a marginal function of the ABA.

Jefferson B. Fordham, the dean of the University of Pennsylvania Law School and an original member of the board of the LCCR, led the effort to reform the ABA. Jerome J. Shestack, one of the committee's founders, a partner in the Philadelphia law firm of Schrader, Harrison, Segal & Lewis, who later served as president of the ABA, gave himself unstintingly to the cause, as did other members of the committee board. Out of the original 18 members of the organizing committee for the Section on Individual Rights, 11 were members of the LCCR.[4] In March 1964, this committee conceived the strat-

---

delphia, Pennsylvania: "The recent striking growth of the ABA broadens its responsibility, and enhances its opportunity, to deal with the significant legal problems which face American society. One of these problems—both pervasive and stubborn—has been the role of the law in preservation of individual rights from excessive and unfair exercise of governmental power. Parallel to this is the responsibility of the individual and of the organized bar to preserve the rule of law when confronted with objections to controversial legislation or court decisions. Individual fights, of course, relate to property interests as well as those associated with the person and mind and the spirit of man. Today the issue as to individual fights has reached critical proportions in several areas, which include the right to equality of treatment, freedom of expression and belief, and fairness in criminal procedure. This is a proposal that the American Bar Association's capacity to deal with these and related problems be strengthened by the creation of a Section on Individual Rights."

3. KERMIT L. HALL, THE MAGIC MIRROR: LAW IN AMERICAN HISTORY (Oxford University Press 1989) 651.

4. Shestack, File, *supra* note 2. The Organizing Committee consisted of the following LCCR members: Frederick Ballard, Cecil Burney, Grenville Clark, Arthur Freund, William Gray, Erwin Griswold, Orison Marden, Eugene Rostow, Jerome Shestack, and John Wade. Others on the committee were William Fuchs, Joseph Harrison, Rufus King, Frank Newman, J. Vernon Patrick, and Michael Schatz.

egy and led the effort that resulted in the creation of the Individual Rights and Responsibility Section of the ABA in August 1966.[5]

In 1964, the ABA could be so changed in only one way, through a two-thirds vote of the organization's governing body, an elected House of Delegates that met twice a year. In order to receive a hearing by the House of Delegates, the organizing committee would have to proceed by presenting its proposal for a new section to the Board of Governors, the appointed body that actually controlled and administered the association. The Board of Governors was drawn from a small pool of lawyers who had served the ABA for many years and were well known to each other. It was an essentially conservative body and slow to change. In fact, the LCCR came into existence in 1963 because of the board's failure to act.

The proposed section was clearly aimed at dealing with the country's growing problems. Its organizing committee chose to stimulate interest in its formation before proceeding with the board and the essential vote in the House of Delegates. Each of the 18 members of the organizing committee were to send out 500 letters with the various proposal documents to ABA members and possible new members (who were young lawyers primarily)[6] along with a form for prospective members of the Section on Individual Rights to sign and return if they were interested in joining.

To the membership of the ABA, the organizing committee stressed the size of the association, which then had more than 120,000 members and,

---

5. *Id.* Proposed Name and Statement of Objectives and Jurisdiction of American Bar Association Section Concerned With Individual Rights: "The name of this Section is 'Section of Individual Rights,' its purposes are: a) to provide a common meeting ground and forum for members of the profession for consideration of problems with respect to the recognition and enjoyment of individual rights within the American constitutional system; b) to further lawyer and public understanding of individual rights through the holding of meetings for the presentation of points of view and exchange of information, the making of studies and reports and the distribution of information as to legal and related developments bearing upon individual rights; c) to nurture a sense of responsibility on the part of lawyers, individually and as a group, in the recognition and enforcement of individual rights and the meeting of individual responsibilities under the rule of law; d) to encourage greater vigilance with respect to the subject of individual rights within the framework of state and local bar associations; and e) to recommend appropriate steps for the protection of individual rights against the arbitrary exercise of power at any level of government."

6. *Id.* Letter dated June 15, 1964, from Jerome J. Shestack to Jefferson B. Fordham: "Enclosed are 500 copies of the statements I have had run off with respect to the Section of Individual Rights."

therefore, its increased responsibility and opportunity to deal with the significant problems that faced American society. They believed that the greatest of those problems was the role of the law in the preservation of individual rights from the excessive or unfair exercise of governmental power and the defense of the rule of law when confronted with objections to controversial legislation or court decisions.[7] The issue of individual rights was to be addressed in several areas—the right to equality of treatment, freedom of expression and belief, and fairness in criminal procedure. "This is a proposal," that would strengthen "the American Bar Association's capacity to deal with these related problems."

As to the question of why, three reasons were offered.

1. The profession beliefs about a lawyer's responsibility to uphold the rule of law applies to the organized bar as well, particularly the ABA. The organized bar has a special competence and a strategic position to promote public understanding of contemporary issues as to individual rights.

2. The ABA is not structured so that it can make a significant contribution in this area. The work of the several standing committees and special committees, which have responsibility in human rights "falls far short of the product to be expected from sustained attention to problems of individual rights and responsibilities."[8]

3. Due to the size of the ABA, what is needed is a unit "which is concerned with individual rights broadly and which is designed to encourage active participation by many members of the profession, who are representative of all parts of the country and of widely varying points of view," Within the ABA framework the appropriate unit appeared clearly to be a section. A Section would provide major lawyer involvement the country over; had the potential to sustain attention to the problems within a range of interest in terms research, study, and discussion, and of effective communication to the rest of the profession and the community at large.[9]

---

7. *Id*. Added was a single sentence that stated, "Individual rights, of course, relate to property interests as well," which recognized the profession's more conventional concerns for property.

8. *Id*. at 2. The groups include the standing committees on American Citizenship and Bill of Rights and the special committees on Civil Rights and Racial Unrest, Defense of Indigent Persons Accused of Crime, and Individual Rights as Affected by National Security.

9. *Id.* at 3.

Unfortunately, for the hopes of the organizing committee, the response to the recruitment drive was poor. Less than 400 names were listed after three months[10] and the organizing committee never succeeded in signing up more than 800 prospective members. Dean Fordham wrote to the organizing committee, "The total is not nearly so great as I had hoped it would be at this stage, but there is no occasion for discouragement. I am confident that with the exertion of the necessary effort we can have 1,500 prospective members by mid-fall."

Clearly, there were concerns among the membership of the ABA about the proposed functions of the Section on Individual Rights. This can be seen in one response by a Dallas, Texas, lawyer to an appeal to join the proposed Section:

> I have reviewed with interest the material relating to the proposed formation of a Section of Individual Rights . . . and I have signed and forwarded a copy of the statement of intention to apply. . . . I must say, however, that I am not without misgivings as to the new section. Certainly there could not be a more commendable task for the American Bar Association than to encourage higher standards of reason, moderation, and restraint in the continuing curtailing of personal freedom by the government under the guise of fostering "equality." Unlike most modern liberals, I have always considered freedom to be a much worthier goal than equality and from the very brief and general statement of objectives of the new section, I am not at all sure that my philosophy will turn out to be compatible with that of the organizers.[11]

In August, members of the organizing committee attended the annual meeting of the ABA in New York. At that meeting, the second general meeting of the LCCR was held. Subsequently, Fordham reported to the organizing committee, "The central thought . . . in New York . . . was that we need a very compelling list of prospective members, a list which should, numerically run into the thousands. I intend to take the lead with the utmost zeal. . . ."[12] The organizing committee continued to work to recruit prospective members of the section but it had decided to switch tactics.

---

10. *Id.*, Aug. 6, 1964, List of Prospective Members of Proposed Section of Individual Rights of the American Bar Association. There were, according to the tabulation from Dean Fordham, 374.

11. *Id.* Letter dated May 29, 1965, from George Slover, Jr. to Jerome J. Shestack.

12. *Id.* Letter dated Aug. 19, 1964, from Jefferson B. Fordham to Jerome J. Shestack.

Obviously, the establishment of a Section for Individual Rights did not yet appeal to the rank and file of the ABA who were concerned with the growing disregard demonstrated in sections of the South toward the responsibilities of citizenship. They would have to plead the merits of the case with the Board of Governors.

Under the by-laws of the ABA, a submission for a vote by the House of Delegates has to be made at least six months prior to the meeting of the House of Delegates at which action was to be taken."[13] As a result, despite a continued low sign-up rate for the new section[14] Chairman Fordham advised his committee, "the list is not so large as we should have liked, but it is certainly long on quality. I think it is good enough to justify our making the submission to the American Bar Association now."[15] With just 650 prospective members signed up, the proposal was submitted to the secretary of the ABA for consideration by the Board of Governors on January 26, 1965.[16] The organizing committee members began to lobby the board.[17]

The Board of Governors referred the proposal to a three-man committee of the board for consideration and report.[18] This committee was not ready to send the project forward.[19] Committee members called for comment from the special committees and standing committees of the ABA. The organizing com-

---

13. *Id.* Letter dated Jan. 13, 1965, from Jefferson B. Fordham to Jerome J. Shestack. Dean Fordham lists the proposed committees for the Section. They were: "1. Freedom of Speech and the Press. 2. Freedom of Religion; church and state. 3. Freedom of assembly and petition. 4. Freedom of movement. 5. Equal protection of the law—Equality of opportunity. 6. Governmental responsibility for and intergovernmental relations with respect to individual rights."

14. *Id.*, Dec. 1964, List of Prospective Members of Proposed Section of Individual Rights of the American Bar Association. Alaska, South and North Dakota, Nebraska, and Montana were not represented.

15. *Id.*

16. *Id.* Letter dated Jan. 26, 1965, from Jefferson B. Fordham to Gibson Gayle, Secretary, America Bar Association.

17. *Id.* Memo, Jan. 30, 1965, from Jefferson Fordham to Jerome Shestack.

18. *Id.* Memo, March 11, 1965, from Jefferson B. Fordham to "My Colleagues on the Organizing Committee of the Individual Rights of the American Bar Association." The three-man committee was made up of the president-elect, Edward W. Kuhn, of Memphis, Tennessee; Chairman of the Board Glenn M. Coulter of Detroit, Michigan; and Telford B. Orbison, of New Albany, Indiana.

19. *Id.* Letter dated March 30, 1965, from Jefferson B. Fordham to Edward W. Kuhn. Also, Memo, July 15, 1965, from Jefferson B. Fordham to "My Colleagues on the Organizing Committee for a Section of Individual Rights in the American Bar Association."

mittee requested a hearing before the whole Board of Governors. It was granted for October 15 at the next scheduled meeting in Chicago.[20] In preparation, the name of the proposed section was changed during the summer to Section of Individual Rights and Responsibilities.[21] The change reflected the understanding that in a voluntary system not only do citizens have rights under the constitutional system but responsibilities as well.

Jefferson Fordham, who represented the organizing committee before the board, pleaded the case for the new section and then responded to questions about the section. To him, the issue was clear—the promise of America could not be fulfilled without the support of the organized bar. He told the board that:

> The highest values in our society are associated with the integrity and the fulfillment of the individual personality. We of the Bar can have no higher responsibility than the safeguarding of individual liberty. The organized Bar has a tremendous responsibility as such in the field of individual rights. It is disturbing . . . that the stated objectives of the American Bar Association do not even mention individual liberty. I refer to this . . . in order to point to an acute need, namely the need of effective official recognition . . . of our responsibility in this field. I dismiss the jurisdictional point, We must not let great problems of our times, concerned with the first order of human values, pass us by."[22]

He further contended that in an organization of 120,000 lawyers the only way to provide for effective participation by interested people was in a division or section. Though he was not seeking public approbation, he believed the creation of the section would meet with a favorable response. "It would be a very compelling indication that the American Bar Association is alive to the great problems of human rights which exist in these complex and fascinating times." Anyone concerned with the public image of the profession should consider the creation of the section as one way of improving

---

20. *Id.* Statement by Jefferson B. Fordham Before the Board of Governors of the American Bar Association on Behalf of the Organizing Committee for a Section of Individual Rights and Responsibilities in the American Bar Association.

21. *Id.* Attachment 11, The Need for a Section of Individual Rights and Responsibilities, at 1: ". . . In August 1965, the Organizing Committee changed the name to Section of Individual Rights and Responsibilities."

22. *Id.* at 1-3.

it. It would be particularly attractive to younger lawyers and would draw their participation in the ABA.[23]

As for the jurisdictional problems, they could easily be handled. There had been problems in the past when each new committee or section was created; there would be problems to come, but with good will they would be overcome if people see a reason to cooperate.[24]

The great unspoken question that surrounded the proposal was that some people were troubled about the possibility "that the proposed section, once established, would be a divisive influence in the ABA." The section would be open to all points of view on individual rights and free expression of ideas would be healthy. "Surely, we are not looking for conformity as a desideratum. Was the concern expressed by some that there won't be sustained interest in the section a valid concern or did it stem, as he thought, from the 'tendency to associate the proposed section with the civil rights problems which we face at the present time.'" To the Board of Governors he said, "Let me make it unmistakably clear that this section would not be a civil rights unit." Its interests would be much broader. The task of reconciling government with civil liberty is likely to grow more difficult rather than the converse.[25]

In the long run, the decision to propose the approval of the Section on Individual Rights and Responsibilities was made not on the petitions from the membership, which had proven so few, or on the presentation of Jefferson Fordham, but rather on the decision of the individual members of the Board of Governors to accept the organizing committee's basic proposition that the ABA should recognize a responsibility to help lawyers deal more effectively with their duty to represent the cause of individual liberty and equality of treatment under law. The efforts of Jefferson Fordham and his colleagues were responsible for forcing the board to focus on that concern in 1965.

Nonetheless, it was not an immediate turnaround. After assessing the mood that day, Fordham decided not to press for a decision. He wrote to his colleagues on the organizing committee, "Our reading of the total situation on October 15th was that the basic issue was in doubt in the Board of Governors and that a close vote in favor of the proposal would have left it with poor prospects in the House of Delegates.[26]

When the Board of Governors did issue a response, it included specific recommendations for changes in the by-laws of the new section. The president of the ABA was granted the right to appoint one-third of the sections'

---

23. *Id.* at 3.
24. *Id.* at 4.
25. *Id.* at 5-10.
26. *Id.* Memo, Oct. 25, 1965.

board. Other changes clarified the issue of rights and corresponding responsibilities. Fordham told the organizing committee, "I think the changes . . . are not so great as to compromise our purpose" and he recommended they be accepted.[27]

The suggestions were incorporated in the by-laws of the section and the board brought the proposal up for consideration at the first quarterly meeting in 1966. At that meeting, the board's recommendation for approval was presented.[28] It was decided that three committees—American Citizenship, Bill of Rights, and Civil Rights and Racial Unrest—were in opposition to the creation of a new section and would be supplanted by the Individual Rights and Responsibilities Section.[29] With the "wholehearted support" of ABA President Edward Kuhn and of the President-Elect Orison Marden,[30] a member of the organizing committee, the Section of Individual Rights and Responsibilities was approved on August 8, 1966, by the House of Delegates with "not a dissenting vote cast." As Fordham wrote to his committee, "One could not

---

27. *Id.* Memo, March 12, 1966, from Jefferson B. Fordham to Members of Organizing Committee re.: Board of Governors Action.

28. *Id.* Undated, "To Present and Prospective Members of the American Bar Association: The changes requested are found in Attachment 1, Name and Purpose: a) to provide an opportunity within the Association for members of the profession to consider issues with respect to recognition and enjoyment of individual rights and responsibilities under the American constitutional system; b) to encourage public understanding of the rights and duties of American citizenship and of the correlative nature of both rights and duties; c) to further public and lawyer understanding of rights and duties under the Constitution and the Bill of Rights with respect to freedom of speech, freedom of religion, freedom of assembly, freedom of movement, enjoyment of property, fair trial, and equality before the law; d) to encourage public respect for law and due process and an appreciation that the vindication of rights must be accomplished by lawful and orderly means; e) to nurture a sense of responsibility on the part of lawyers, individually and as a profession, in the recognition and enforcement of individual rights and duties and in the discharge of their responsibilities with respect to assuring fair trial and equality of justice for all persons; f) to study and recommend method of maintaining a proper balance between the rights of those accused of crime and the rights of the general public to be protected in life, person, and property; g) to study the need and recommend appropriate action for the protection of individual rights against the arbitrary exercise of power at any level of government; h) to aid and seek the aid of state and local bar associations in achieving the purposes of the Section; i) to cooperate with and assist other Sections and Committees of the Association with responsibilities in associated or related activity."

29. *Id.* Memo, *supra* note 27.

30. *Id.*

ask for a clearer indication of approval for this exceedingly important step.[31] Clearly, this step, this particular choice of direction for change, was chosen by the ABA because of the work and insights of the organizing committee, which was following in the footsteps of the Lawyers' Committee for Civil Rights Under Law.

Ultimately, because of the distinct work of the Section on Individual Rights and Responsibility with the private bar, its members, many of whom were members of the LCCR, sponsored an unprecedented new public service standard for legal practice. It became part of the Code of Professional Responsibility when it was passed by the House of Delegates of the ABA in August 1975. The resolution endorsed a new duty for American lawyers to provide regular pro bono public service in their practices, in the fields of civil rights and the rights of the poor in America.[32] It "confirmed the basic responsibility of each lawyer engaged in the practice of law to provide public interest legal services without fee or at a substantially reduced fee, in one or more of the following areas." Five distinct areas were defined: poverty law;[33] civil rights (including civil liberties)[34] law; public rights law;[35] charitable organizations representation;[36] and the administration of justice.[37] This resolution of the ABA illuminates the change in the private practice of law in the United States in the latter half of the twentieth century from what was considered acceptable at mid-century.

---

31. *Id.* Letter from Jefferson B. Fordham to Dear Colleagues (prospective members of the Section of Individual Rights and Responsibility of the American Bar Association), September 1966.

32. *Implementing the Lawyer's Public Interest Practice Obligation*, An Informational Report for Discussion Purposes by the Special Committee on Public Interest Practice of the American Bar Association (ABA 1977), Introduction.

33. *Id.* at 1: "1. Poverty Law: Legal services in civil and criminal matters of importance to a client who does not have the financial resources to compensate counsel."

34. *Id.* "2. Civil Rights (including civil liberties) Law: Legal representation involving a right of an individual which society has a special interest in protecting."

35. *Id.* "3. Public Rights Law: Legal representation involving an important right belonging to a significant segment of the public."

36. *Id.* "4. Charitable Organizations Representation: Legal service to charitable, religious, civic, governmental and educational institutions in matters in furtherance of their organizational purpose, where the payment of customary legal fees would significantly deplete the organization's economic resources or would be otherwise inappropriate."

37. *Id.* "5. Administration of Justice: Activity, whether under bar association auspices or otherwise, which is designed to increase the availability of legal services, or otherwise improve the administration of justice."

The ABA is a voluntary professional association that, by convention not law, has become the self-appointed arbiter for the legal profession in America. In fact, the vote in the House of Delegates in 1975 was but a confirmation of the changes that had taken place in the professional offices of private lawyers and law firms since 1963.[38] The ABA has little power to regulate. Its authority rests in its stature and prestige within the profession in the United States. In the annals of the profession, the public service resolution of the House of Delegates recognized the profound and fundamental transformation in the legal practices of American lawyers in the latter portion of the twentieth century. It did not cause the change nor could it enforce its adoption.

The change in the perception of the American bar's responsibilities to the public welfare was a historic transformation that took place in the span of a single generation. It was first called forth under the storm clouds of racial revolution and on the impetus of an American President. In 1963, the vessel that was molded by the legal establishment in America to carry this call for change was the LCCR. Over time, its many parts proved greater than the whole.

---

38. BURTON A. WEISBROD, Study Director, in collaboration with JOEL F. HANDLER & NEIL K. KOMESAR, PUBLIC INTEREST LAW: AN ECONOMIC AND INSTITUTIONAL ANALYSIS (University of California Press 1978), Introduction. "The term public interest law is new to the language as is the institution known as the public interest law firm. Within the last decade . . . a new institutional form embodied in law firms that characterize their activities as partly or wholly 'public interest' law have proliferated. . . . With the appearance of financial support from a number of private foundations, and more recently, with the official blessing of the American Bar Association, Public Interest Law activities have multiplied." Also, at 76: In just 15 years the private bar in America was transformed. Public interest law became a legal industry with the formation hundreds of public interest groups: ". . . the major producers in the PIL (public interest law) industry . . . are a total of 166 organizations . . . with positions for nearly 1,000 lawyers and over 500 non-lawyer professionals. The total income of the industry exceeds $45 million, and the estimated total income devoted to financing PIL and PIL-like activities exceeds $29 million. . . . Voluntary sector PINL (public interest non-law) organizations dwarf the total PIL industry with over 30 times as many organizations and nearly 70 times the total income."

President John F. Kennedy

Robert F. Kennedy

In the East Room of the White House on June 21, 1963, President John F. Kennedy, along with Vice President Lyndon B. Johnson and Attorney General Robert F. Kennedy, call upon 244 of America's prominent lawyers to advance the struggle for civil rights through the Rule of Law.

On June 11, 1963, in Tuscaloosa, Alabama, Governor George Wallace raises his hand to stop U.S. Deputy Attorney General Nicholas deB. Katzenbach from enrolling two African Americans, Vivian Malone and James Hood, into the University of Alabama.

On June 21, 1978, President Jimmy Carter invited the Board of the Lawyers' Committee to the East Room of the White House to reissue President Kennedy's call on the bar to advance equal justice under law.

APPENDIX A

Sources Consulted

Primary Sources

Significant research for this dissertation is based on three primary sources: the unpublished records of the Lawyers' Committee for Civil Rights Under Law; the private files of Bernard G. Segal and Jerome J. Shestack; and personal interviews conducted by the author with key participants in the events that surrounded the formation and development of the Lawyers' Committee from 1963 to 1974. The records of the committee are divided between two depositories: the Collection on Legal Change at Wesleyan University, which holds 55 containers of records from 1963 to 1968; and the records of the Lawyers' Committee, which are archived in Washington, D.C., and accessible through a "Description of the Archives" available at the national office of the Lawyers' Committee in Washington. They are records from the committee's earliest years to the present, and are divided by subject and year. They include committee statements of purpose and activities; official documents such as the By-Laws, Incorporation in the District of Columbia, and Federal Tax Exemption; correspondence; interoffice memoranda; fund-raising activities; Minutes of Executive Committee meetings; Minutes of Board of Directors Meetings; internal committee business; correspondence with bar associations; relations with other organizations; personal files; accounting files; newspaper clippings and other organizations' publications; the Urban Areas Project; the Mississippi office; the Southern Africa Project; special projects; press coverage; miscellaneous files; speeches; and numerous files of collected materials and secondary articles.

The personal files of Bernard G. Segal and Jerome J. Shestack, founding members of the Lawyers' Committee, are located in Mr. Shestack's law firm of Wolf, Block, Schorr & Solis-Cohen in Philadelphia. The dozens of boxes of files which cover the 34-year history of the Lawyers' Committee are a particularly rich source of information about the founding of the organization. It was Mr. Segal and Mr. Shestack who put together the Lawyers' Statement of June 10, 1963, which was the precursor to the call for the Lawyers' Committee on June 21, 1963. The records of this period—and of the following six months, which saw the creation of the Lawyers' Committee—retained by Mr. Segal and Mr. Shestack are the sole existing source of recorded information about a number of seminal events in the life of the committee. Files and memoranda on the development of the committee's goals, fund-raising objectives, correspondence with members, the development of the Executive Committee, the board of directors, and the organization of the committee itself are distinct to this collection. Further, the files mirror the records of the Lawyers' Committee in all areas except internal business. Also unique to this collection are files of correspondence with members of the Lawyers' Committee concerning the activities and development of the American Bar Association. Both Mr. Segal, who became president of the American Bar Association, and Mr. Shestack, who is the current president, were active in the movement to reform the operations and goals of the American Bar Association.

Oral interviews with key participants in the events that surrounded the founding and creation of the Lawyers' Committee, the development of its goals and policies in the South, its acceptance of responsibility to aid the administration of justice in the North, the evolution of pro bono litigation services secured by the committee from the nation's largest law firms, and assumption of a role in the defense of human rights in South Africa provide information about the Lawyers' Committee's motivation in these events. These interviews were conducted with the men and women listed below.

Alexander, Clifford, assistant to former National Security Advisor McGeorge Bundy, 1967. Interviewed October 2, 1997, Washington, D.C.

Bamberger, E. Clinton, Jr., first head of the Office of Economic Opportunity Legal Services and Board Member of the Lawyers' Committee. Interviewed June 7, 1997, Chevy Chase, Maryland.

Bernhard, Berl I., Director of the National Office of the Lawyers' Committee, 1964-1968; Board Member; and Counsel of the Lawyers' Committee. Interviewed March 3, 1993, Washington, D.C.

Boggs, Roderic, former National Office staff lawyer, 1972; former co-director of the Southern Africa Project, 1973; Director of the Washington,

D.C. Lawyers' Committee for Civil Rights Under Law. Interviewed September 29, 1997.

Carlson, Joel, first South African attorney instructed by the Lawyers' Committee in 1967. Interviewed March 28, 1993, Great Neck, New York.

Citrin, Gloria. secretary to the Counsel to the President, Theodore Sorensen, June 11, 1963. Interviewed February 5, 1994, Great Falls, Virginia.

Connell, Peter J., former Assistant Director of the National Office of the Lawyers' Committee, 1968-1973; first Director of the Southern Africa Project of the Lawyers' Committee, 1970; Board Member. Interviewed October 9, 1997, Rock Hall, Maryland.

Crossland, The Honorable David, first Director of the Atlanta Committee of the Lawyers' Committee, 1969. Interviewed October 28, 1997, La Hoya, California.

Cutler, Lloyd, founding member of the Lawyers' Committee; Co-Chairman 1971-1973. Interviewed February 3, 1994, Washington, D.C.

Derfner, Armand, former staff lawyer for the Lawyers' Constitutional Defense Committee, 1965-1971; former staff Director for the Voting Rights Project of the Lawyers' Committee for Civil Rights Under Law, 1971-1983. Interviewed November 11, 1996, and September 6, 1997, Charleston, South Carolina.

Dolan, Joseph, Deputy to Robert Kennedy, Attorney General of the United States, 1961-1965. Interviewed March 8, 1995, and April 2, 1995, Seattle, Washington.

Douglas, John, former Assistant U.S. Attorney General, Civil Division; former Co-chairman of the Lawyers' Committee for Civil Rights Under Law, 1967-1969. Interviewed March 13, 1996, Washington, D.C.

Katzenbach, Nicholas deB., former Deputy Attorney General of the United States; former Attorney General of the United States; former Under Secretary of State; member of the Board of the Lawyers' Committee. Interviewed September 16, 1994, Summit, New Jersey.

Knight, Robert, former Assistant Secretary of the Treasury; law partner, Shearson & Sterling; member of the Board of the Lawyers' Committee. Interviewed February 15, 1993, New York.

Lunney, J. Robert, the first Lawyers' Committee volunteer to be sent to Mississippi, 1963-1964; associate, Shearson & Sterling; member of the Board. Interviewed March, 1993, White Plains, New York.

Marshall, Burke, former Assistant Attorney General for Civil Rights, 1961-1965; former Co-chairman of the Lawyers' Committee, 1965-1967; member of the Board. Interviewed September 1995, New Haven, Connecticut.

McDougall, Gay J., former Director of the Southern Africa Project of the Lawyers' Committee for Civil Rights Under Law; member of the South African Independent Electoral Commission, 1994. Interviewed March 17, 1993, Washington, D.C.

McPherson, Harry, former White House Counsel to President Lyndon B. Johnson; member of the Board of the Lawyers' Committee; partner, Verner, Lipfert, Bernhard, McPherson. Interviewed September 30, 1997, Washington, D.C.

Nolan, John, former assistant to Robert Kennedy, Attorney General of the United States, 1962-1965; member of the Board of the Lawyers' Committee; first Chair of the Washington, D.C. Lawyers' Committee, 1969; managing partner, Steptoe & Johnson. Interviewed October 3, 1997, Deer Valley, Utah.

Oberdorfer, The Honorable Louis F., founding member of the Lawyers' Committee for Civil Rights Under Law, former Co-chairman, 1967-1969; creator of the Urban Areas Project, 1968; former Assistant U.S. Attorney General for Tax, 1961-1966; former partner, Wilmer, Cutler & Pickering; judge, U.S. District Court for the District of Columbia. Interviewed January 22, 1994, and June 1994, McLean, Virginia.

Reilly, Sarah Carey, former Assistant Director of the National Office of the Lawyers' Committee for Civil Rights; former Director of the Urban Areas Project. Interviewed October 18, 1997, Steptoe & Johnson, Washington, D.C.

Robertson, The Honorable James, former Director of the Lawyers' Committee's Mississippi litigation office, Jackson, Mississippi, 1969; former Director of the National Office of the Lawyers' Committee, 1970-1972; managing partner Wilmer, Cutler & Pickering; former Co-chairman of the Lawyers' Committee, 1986-88; judge, U.S. District Court for the District of Columbia. Interviewed September 18, 1996, April 7, 1996, and October 14, 1997, Washington, D.C., and St. Michaels, Maryland.

Runyon, Charles, former Assistant U.S. Legal Advisor for Africa; former member of the Board of the Lawyers' Committee. Interviewed March 5, 1993, Ocracoke, North Carolina.

Shestack, Jerome J., Co-coordinator of the Lawyers' Statement of June 10, 1963; founding member of the Lawyers' Committee for Civil Rights Under Law; original member of the Executive Committee and of the Board of the Lawyers' Committee; Board member. Interviewed November 1995; March 4, 1996; April 10, 1996; and May 19, 1996, Philadelphia, Pennsylvania.

Skiles, James, former staff member of the National Office of the Lawyers'
    Committee for Civil Rights Under Law. Interviewed October 13, 1997,
    Washington, D.C.
White, Lee, former Assistant White House Counsel to President John F.
    Kennedy, 1963, and White House Counsel to President Lyndon B. Johnson,
    1964. Interviewed January 24, 1994, Washington, D.C.
White, Mary, former secretary to Theodore Sorensen, White House Counsel
    to President John F. Kennedy, 1960-1963. Interviewed January 23, 1993,
    Washington, D.C.

Other primary sources consulted for this paper include the collection at the
John F. Kennedy Memorial Library in Cambridge, Massachusetts, and the
Public Records of the Federal Bureau of Investigation at the FBI Building in
Washington, D.C.

Secondary Sources

The Alabama Lawyer. 1955-1963. Library of Congress. A publication of the
    Bar of the State of Alabama.
The American Bar News. "The ABA House Action on Civil Rights Report."
    July 4, 1963.
Auerbach, Jerold S. *Unequal Justice: Lawyers and Social Change in Modern
    America.* New York: Oxford University Press, 1976.
Beard, Charles, and Mary Beard. *The Rise of American Civilization.* Vol. 1.
    New York: Macmillan, 1930.
Berle, A. A. "The Modern Legal Profession." *The International Encyclope-
    dia of the Social Sciences,* vol. 9.
The Birmingham News. Birmingham, Alabama, June 8, 1963.
Bloomfield, Maxwell. *American Lawyers in a Changing Society: 1776-1876.*
    Cambridge: Harvard University Press, 1976.
Blum, John Morton. *Years of Discord. American Politics and Society: 1961-
    1974.* New York: W.W. Norton, 1991.
Bradway, John S., and Reginald Heber Smith. *Growth of Legal Aid Work in
    the United States.* Washington: United States Department of Labor Bul-
    letin, No. 607.
Brauer, Carl M. *John F. Kennedy and the Second Reconstruction.* New York:
    Columbia University Press, 1977.
Brisbane, Robert. *Black Activism.* Valley Forge: Judson Press, 1974
Brown, Ester Lucille. *Lawyers and the Promotion of Justice.* New York: Russell
    Sage Foundation, 1938.

Brownell, Emery A. *Legal Aid in the United States: A Study of the Availability of Lawyers' Services for Persons Unable to Pay Fees.* Foreword by Harrison Tweed; Introduction by Reginald Heber Smith. New York: The Lawyers Co-Operative Publishing Co., 1951.

Burns, James MacGregor, and Stewart Burns. *The People's Charter: The Pursuit of Rights in America.* New York: Alfred A. Knopf, 1991.

Butcher, Goler Teal. "Southern African Issues in United States Courts." *26 Howard Law Journal* No. 2 (1983), 601-43.

Cahn, Edmund. "Justice," in *International Encyclopedia of the Social Sciences* vol. 9. David L. Sills, ed. New York: Macmillan and The Free Press, 1968.

Calhoun, John C. "Letter to James Hamilton, Governor of South Caroline." August 28, 1932. In *John C. Calhoun.* Cralle ed. 6 Works (1863).

Cappelletti, Mauro, and James Gordley. *Toward Equal Justice: A Comparative Study of Legal Aid in Modern Societies. Studies in Comparative Law,* No. 13. Milano: Dott. A. Giuffre, ed., 1975.

Christensen, Barlow F. *Lawyers for People of Moderate Means: Some Problems of Availability of Legal Services.* Chicago: The American Bar Foundation, 1970.

Chroust, Anton-Herman. *The Rise of the Legal Profession in America.* 2 Vols. Norman: University of Oklahoma Press, 1965.

———. "The Right to Counsel in Civil Litigation." *Columbia Law Review* 7 (Nov. 1966), 1326.

Commitment to Public Interest Law. No. 4 in a Series of Bar Activation Monographs. Chicago: American Bar Association, Division of Bar Services, 1980.

Day, Alan. "Lawyers in Colonial Maryland 1660-1715." 17 *American Journal of Legal History* (1973): 145-63.

Dittmer, John. *Local People: The Struggle for Civil Rights in Mississippi.* Chicago: University of Illinois Press, 1994.

Donovan, Robert J. "Racial Crisis—The Official View." *The New York Herald Tribune*, June 6, 1963, at 1.

Evers, Medgar. "Why I Live in Mississippi." *Ebony* (September 1963), 142-44.

Faircloth, Adam. *To Redeem the Soul of America: The Southern Christian Leadership Conference and Martin Luther King, Jr.* London: The University of Georgia Press, 1987.

Fairman, Charles. "The Supreme Court 1955 Term: Foreword: The Attack on Segregation Cases." *Harvard Law Review* 70 (November 1956), 83.

Finkleman, Paul, ed. *Race, Law, and American History, 1700-1990, The African American Experience. An Eleven Volume Anthology of Scholarly Articles*, Volume 10. New York: Garland, 1992.

Findlay, James R., Jr. *Church People in the Struggle: The National Council of Churches and the Black Freedom Movement, 1950-1970.* New York: Oxford University Press, 1993.

Fleming, Donald, and Bernard Bailyn, eds. *Law in American History.* Charles Warren Center for Studies in American History. Boston: Little, Brown & Co., 1971.

Franklin, John Hope, and Genna Rae McNeil, eds. *African-Americans and the Living Constitution.* Washington: The Smithsonian Institution Press, 1995.

Freund, Paul. A. "Umpiring the Federal System." *Columbia Law Review* 54 (1954), 578.

Friedman, Lawrence M. *A History of American Law.* New York: Simon & Schuster, 1973.

——. "Notes Toward a History of American Justice," in Lawrence Friedman and Harry N. Schreiber, *American Law and the Constitutional Order: Historical Perspectives.* Cambridge: Harvard University Press, 1988.

Friedman, Leon, ed., with a Foreword by Mark DeW. Howe. *Southern Justice.* New York: Pantheon Books, 1966.

Fuller, Helen. "Southerners and Schools-III" and "The Segregationists Go North." *The New Republic* 140 (February 6 and 9, 1959).

Gerwalt, Gerard, W., ed. *The New High Priests: Lawyers in Post Civil War America.* New York: 1948.

Ginger, Ann Fagan, and Eugene M. Tobin. *The National Lawyers Guild: From Roosevelt through Reagan.* Foreword by Ramsey Clark. Philadelphia: Temple University Press, 1988.

Guthman, Edwin O., and C. Richard Allen. *RFK Collected Speeches.* New York: Viking Press, 1993.

Hall, Kermit L. Edited, with Introduction. *Civil Rights in American History: Major Historical Interpretations.* The United States Constitutional and Legal History Series. New York: Garland Publishing, Inc., 1987.

——. *The Magic Mirror: Law in American History.* New York: Oxford University Press, 1989.

——. William Weicek, and Paul Friedman. *American Legal History: Cases and Materials.* New York: Oxford University Press, 1991.

Handler, Joel F. *The Lawyer and His Community: The Practicing Bar in a Middle-Sized City.* Madison, Wisconsin: The University of Wisconsin Press, 1967.

Harkey, Ira B., Jr. *The Smell of Burning Crosses: An Autobiography of a Mississippi Newspaperman.* Jacksonville, Illinois: Harris-Wolfe & Co., 1967.

Haar, Charles Monroe, ed. *The Golden Age of American Law.* New York: George Braziller, 1965.

Haskins, George L. *Law and Authority in Early Massachusetts: A Study in Tradition and Design.* New York: Macmillan, 1960.

Himes, Joseph S. "A Theory of Racial Conflict." 50 *Social Forces* (September 1971), 53-60.

——. "Functions of Racial Conflict." 45 *Social Forces* (September 1966), 3-5.

Holt, Len. *The Summer That Didn't End.* London: Heinemann, 1966.

Holt, Wythe, ed. *Essays in Nineteenth-Century American Legal History.* Contributions in American History, No. 60. Westport, Connecticut: Greenwood Press, 1976.

Hurst, James Willard. *The Growth of American Law: The Law Makers.* Boston: Little, Brown & Co., 1950.

Implementing The Lawyer's Public Interest Practice Obligation. Chicago: ABA Special Committee on Public Interest Practice, June 1977.

Jacob, Herbert. *Justice in America: Courts, Lawyers, and the Judicial Process.* Boston: Little, Brown & Co., 1972.

Jack, Robert L. *History of the National Association for the Advancement of Colored People.* Boston: Meador, 1943.

Johnson, Earl, Jr. *Justice and Reform: The Formative Years of the OEO Legal Services Program.* New York: The Russell Sage Foundation, 1974.

Johnson, Lyndon Baines. *Public Papers of the President of the United States: Lyndon B. Johnson: Containing the Public Messages, Speeches and Statements of the President, 1963-1968.* Book 1. Washington, D.C.: U.S. Gov't Printing Office, 1965.

Journal of the American Bar Association. Chicago: ABA, 1959-1963.

Katz, Stanley, and John M. Murrin, eds. *Colonial America: Essays in Politics and Social Development.* New York: 1983.

Kellogg, Charles Flint. *A History of the National Association for the Advancement of Colored People.* Vols. I and 2. Boston: Johns Hopkins University Press, 1967.

Kelly, Alfred H., Winfred A. Harbison, and Herman J. Belz. *The American Constitution: Its Origins and Development.* Sixth Edition (1983).

Kennedy, John F. *The Public Papers of the President 1963* (Washington, D.C., 1964).

King, Martin Luther, Jr. *Stride Toward Freedom: The Montgomery Story.* New York: Harper & Row, 1958.

——. Interview in *Playboy* magazine (January 1965).

Kluger, Richard. *Simple Justice: The History of Brown v. Board of Education and Black America's Struggle for Equality.* New York: Alfred A. Knopf, 1976.

Kommers, Donald. "Reflections on Professor Chroust's 'The Rise of the Legal Profession in America.'" 10 *The American Journal of Legal History* (Philadelphia), 202.

Lamson, Peggy. *Roger Baldwin: Founder of the American Civil Liberties Union, A Portrait.* Boston: Houghton-Mifflin, 1976.

Lawrence, David. "Today in National Affairs: Wallace Attitude Called Challenge, Not Defiance." *The New York Herald Tribune,* June 6, 1963.

Lawyers' Committee for Civil Rights Under Law, Annual Report: 1968-1969. Washington, D.C.: Lawyers' Committee for Civil Rights Under Law, 1969.

Leflar, David. "Segregation in the Public Schools—1953." 67 *Harvard Law Review* (1954), 377.

Mandela, Nelson. Transcript of Taped Remarks on the Occasion of the Twenty-fifth Anniversary of the Lawyers' Committee for Civil Rights Under Law Southern Africa Project. Washington, D.C., October 14, 1992.

Marks, F. Raymond, with Kirk Leswing and Barbara A. Fortinsky. *The Lawyer, The Public, and Professional Responsibility.* Chicago: The American Bar Foundation, 1972.

McAdam, Doug. *Freedom Summer.* New York: Oxford University Press, 1988.

McKay, Robert B. "With All Deliberate Speed: A Study of School Desegregation." *New York University Law Review* (June 1956).

McMillan, Neil R. "Black Enfranchisement in Mississippi: Federal Enforcement and Black Protest in the 1960s." 3 *Journal of Southern History* (August 1977), 52.

Mills, Nicolaus. *Like a Holy Crusade: Mississippi 1964—The Turning of the Civil Rights Movement in America.* Chicago: Ivan R. Dee, 1992.

Morris, Richard. *Studies in the History of the American Law: With Special Reference to the Seventeenth and Eighteenth Centuries.* Second Edition. New York: Octagon Books, Inc., 1964.

Morrison, Minion K.C. *Black Political Mobilization: Leadership, Power, and Mass Behavior.* New York: State University of New York Press, 1987.

NAACP Annual Report, Forty-Eighth Year. *New Threat to Civil Liberties 1956.* New York: National Association for the Advancement of Colored People, 1956.

Navasky, Victor. *Kennedy Justice.* New York: Atheneum, 1971.

New York Herald Tribune, June 1, 1963, June 3, 1963, June 6, 1963.

"The Southern Manifesto." *The New York Times*, March 12, 1956, at 1.

O'Connor, Karen, and Lee Epstein. *Public Interest Law Groups: Institutional Profiles.* New York: Greenwood Press, 1989.

Parker, Frank R. Foreword by Eddie N. Williams. *Black Votes Count: Political Empowerment in Mississippi after 1965.* Chapel Hill: University of North Carolina Press, 1990.

Payne, Charles M. *I've Got the Light of Freedom: The Organizing Tradition and the Mississippi Freedom Struggle.* Berkeley: University of California Press, 1995.

Peltason, J.W. "Judicial Process." *International Encyclopedia of the Social Sciences.* Vol. 8. David L. Sills, ed. New York: Macmillan and The Free Press, 1968.

Pound, Roscoe. *The Lawyer from Antiquity to Modern Times: With Particular Reference to the Development of Bar Associations in the United States.* St. Paul, Minnesota: American Bar Association, 1953.

Proceedings: Planning Session on Police-Community Relations. Washington, D.C.: Lawyers' Committee for Civil Rights Under Law, 1966.

Rabin, Robert L. "Lawyers for Social Change: Perspectives on Public Interest Law." 28 *Stanford Law Review* (1976), 207-6 1.

Read, Frank T., and Lucy S. McGough. *Let Them Be Judged: The Judicial Integration of the Deep South.* London: Scarecrow Press, Inc., 1978.

Reeves, Richard. *President Kennedy: Profile of Power.* New York: Simon & Schuster, 1993.

Reinsch, Paul Samuel. "English Common Law in the Early American Colonies." *Selected Essays in Anglo-American Legal History.* Vol. 1 (1899). Boston: Little Brown & Co., 1907.

Rostow, Eugene. "The Lawyer and His Client," Part 1. 48 *ABA Journal* (January 1962), 25.

——. "The Lawyer and His Client," Part 2. 48 *ABA Journal* (February 1962), 146.

Rutherford, M. Louise. *The Influence of the American Bar Association on Public Opinion and Legislation.* Philadelphia: University of Pennsylvania, 1937.

Salter, John R., Jr., with a Foreword by Rev. R. Edwin King, Jr. *Jackson, Mississippi: An American Chronicle of Struggle and Schism.* New York: Exposition Press, 1979.

Salzburg, Stephen A. "Adversary System." *International Encyclopedia of the Social Sciences,* vol. 9. David L. Sills, ed. New York: Macmillan and The Free Press, 1968.

Satterfield, John C. "Law and Lawyers in a Changing World." The President's Annual Address. 48 *ABA Journal* (October 1962), 922.

Schlesinger, Arthur M., Jr. *Robert Kennedy and His Times.* Boston: Houghton-Mifflin, 1978.

Schlei, Norbert. "Comments of the Vice-President on the Civil Rights Legislative Proposal." June 4, 1963. *Robert F. Kennedy Papers.* AG File 1963. Located in the John F. Kennedy Memorial Library, Cambridge, Massachusetts.

Schweppe, Alfred. "Enforcement of Federal Court Decrees: A 'Recurrence to Fundamental Principles.'" 44 *ABA Journal* (February 1958).

Seymour, Whitney North, and Burke Marshall, Co-chairmen. *Statement of Purposes and Activities.* Washington, D.C.: Lawyers' Committee for Civil Rights Under Law, 1965.

Shestack, Jerome J. *A Mass in Memory of Robert F. Kennedy: A Personal Memoir.* Philadelphia: Jerome J. Shestack, 1993.

Sidlo, Thomas L. "Lawyer Referral Service: A Code of Basic Principles." 36 *ABA Journal* (March 1950), 197.

Silverstein, Lee. *Defense of the Poor in Criminal Cases: A Field Study and Report.* Volume One: National Report. Chicago: American Bar Foundation, 1965.

Sitkoff, Harvard. *The Struggle for Black Equality: 1954-1980.* The American Century Series. New York: Hall and Wang, 1981.

Smith, Reginald Heber. *Justice and the Poor.* New York: The Carnegie Foundation, 1919.

———. *Justice and the Poor: A Study of the Present Denial of Justice to the Poor and of the Agencies Making More Equal Their Position Before the Law.* With Particular Reference to Legal Aid Work in the United States. Reprinted from the third edition. New Jersey: Patterson Smith, 1972.

Sorensen, Theodore C. *Kennedy.* New York: Harper & Row, 1965.

Southern Africa Project: Twenty-Fifth Anniversary. South Africa: Can Negotiations Succeed?, October 14, 1992. Washington, D.C.: The Lawyers' Committee for Civil Rights Under Law, 1992.

Spear, Arnold H. "NAACP." *International Encyclopedia of the Social Sciences,* Vol. 9 (1968).

The State of Alabama Acts, No. 42 (1956), 1st Special Session.

The State of Georgia Laws (1956), Res. Act No. 130, at 642.

The State of Mississippi Laws (1956), S. Con. Res. 125.

Tansill, Charles Callan. *Documents Illustrative of the Formation of the Union of American States.* Washington: U.S. Gov't Printing Office, 1927.

———. "How Long Will the Southern Legislatures Continue to Acquiesce in the Alleged Decision of the Supreme Court on May 17, 1954?" 24 *The Alabama Lawyer* (June 1963), 372-74.

Tatel, Edith S.B. *The Lawyers' Committee: The First Twenty-Five Years.* Florence B. Isbell, ed. Washington, D.C: Lawyers' Committee for Civil Rights Under Law, 1988.

Tatel, David S. Remarks of Judge David S. Tatel. Alexander F. Morrison Lecture, California State Bar. San Diego, California: September 13, 1997.

Taylor, Arnold H. *Travail and Triumph: Black Life and Culture in the South Since the Civil War.* Contributions in Afro-American and African Studies, No. 26. Westport: Greenwood Press, 1976.

The Ten Year Report of the Lawyers' Committee for Civil Rights Under Law. Washington, D.C.: Lawyers' Committee for Civil Rights Under Law, 1973.

The Texas Bar Journal, 1955-1963. Located in the Library of Congress. A publication of the Bar of the State of Texas.

The United Nations Department of Political and Security Affairs. *Apartheid in Practice.* New York: The United Nations, 1969.

U.S. Census of the Population: 1950. Part 1. "United States Summary." U.S. Department of Commerce. Washington, D.C.: U.S. Gov't Printing Office, 1953.

U.S. Department of Justice. Videocassette. "Stand-off in Tuscaloosa: June 11, 1963."

U.S. House of Representatives. The Committee on Un-American Activities, March 29, 1944. "A Guide to Subversive Operations and Publications."

Vose, Clement, ed. "Collection on Legal Change." *Guide to the Microfilm Edition of the Southern Civil Rights Litigation Records for the 1960s: Lawyers' Constitutional Defense Committee; Lawyers' Committee for Civil Rights Under Law; NAACP Legal Defense Fund, Inc.* Middletown, Connecticut: Wesleyan University.

The Virginia Bar News, 1955-1963. Located in the Library of Congress. A publication of the Bar of the State of Virginia.

Wallace, George Corley. Inauguration Address. *Birmingham News*, January 14, 1963, at 4.

Walling, William English. "Race War in the North." *Illinois Independent*, September 3, 1908.

Warren, Charles. *A History of the American Bar.* New York: Howard Fertig, 1966.

Weaver, Richard M. "The Regime of the South." *National Review,* March 14, 1959, at 588.

Weisbrod, Burton A. Study directed in collaboration with Joel F. Handler and Neil K. Komesar. *Public Interest Law: An Economic Analysis.* Berkeley: University of California Press, 1978.

Weisbrot, Robert. *Freedom Bound: A History of America's Civil Rights Movement.* New York: W.W. Norton & Co., 1990.

Westwood, Howard C. "Getting Justice for the Freedman." 16 *Howard Law Journal* (1971), 492-537.

White, G. Edward. "John Marshall Harlan 1: The Precursor." 19 *American Journal of Legal History* (1975), 1-21.

Wicker, Tom. *One of Us: Richard Nixon and the American Dream.* New York: Random House, 1991.

Zinn, Howard. *SNCC: The New Abolitionists.* Boston: Beacon Press, 1964.

APPENDIX B

Lawyers Who Attended White House Meeting—June 21,1963

Information regarding membership in the American Bar Association (ABA), date of birth, date of admittance to the bar, higher education, and professional affiliations is taken from the four volumes of the 95th Annual Edition, 1963, of Martindale-Hubbell. The list of the names and states of the attendees is taken from the records of the Lawyers' Committee for Civil Rights Under Law (LCCR), Washington, D.C.

Following the name of each lawyer, the entries will reference:

- if a member of the ABA;
- the Martindale-Hubbell volume and page number;
- year of birth;
- year of admittance to the bar;
- schools attended;
- the address listed by the LCCR; and
- professional affiliations as of 1963.

Not all attendees could be located in Martindale-Hubbell, and this will be noted where appropriate.

Abram, Morris. ABA; 1:745; 1918; 1941; University of Georgia, Oxford, Rhodes Scholar, University of Chicago Law School; Paul, Weiss, Rifkind, Wharton & Garrison, 575 Madison Ave., New York, N.Y.; General Counsel of the Peace Corps, 1961; Partner, Heyman, Abram, Young, Hicks & Maloof, Atlanta, Ga.

Alessandroni, Walter E. ABA; 3:2916; 1912; 1939; Villanova College, Temple University Law School; 3 Penn Center Plaza, Philadelphia, Pa.

Alexander, Mrs. Sadie T. M. ABA; 3:2916; 1898; 1927; College and Law School, University of Pennsylvania; 1502 One East Penn Square Building, Philadelphia, Pa.; Chairman, Human Relations Commission.

Andre, Oscar J. ABA; 3:3476; 1900; 1929; Salem College, West Virginia, University of Virginia Law School, Charlottesville; Union National Bank Building, Clarksburg, W. Va.; Partner, Steptoe & Johnson, Clarksburg, W. Va.; President, West Virginia State Bar, 1962-1963.

Anthony, J. Garner. ABA; 1:806; 1899; 1926; Swarthmore, Harvard Law School; Castle and Cooke Building, Honolulu, Hawaii; Partner, Castle & Anthony. Board of Governors of the ABA, 1961-1963.

Arant, Douglas. ABA; 1:4; 1897; 1923; Villa Maria College, Erie, Pa., Yale Law School; 2100 Comer Building, Birmingham, Ala.; Partner, Arant, All & Rose; Member, ABA Standing Committee on Professional Grievances, 1961-1963.

Armstrong, Walter P., Jr. ABA; 3:3105; 1916; 1940; College and Law School, Harvard; 800 Commerce Title Building, Memphis, Tenn.; Partner, Armstrong, McCadden, Allen, Braden & Goodman, Memphis, Tenn.; Member of the House of Delegates of the ABA, 1952-1963.

Ash, Robert. ABA; 1:505; 1894; 1918; College and Law School, George Washington University; 1921 Eye St. N.W., Washington, D.C.; Partner, Ash, Bouersfeld & Burton, Washington, D.C.; Member, ABA Standing Committee on the Federal Judiciary, 1962-1965.

Barrett, George. ABA; 3:3117; 1926; 1957; Spring Hill College, Spring Hill, Ala., Vanderbilt University Law School; 2000 Cedar Lane, Nashville, Tenn.

Bartlett, John C. ABA; 2:1904; 1910; 1937; Stanford University, Boalt Hall, University of California; Box 566, Reno, Nevada; Partner, Vargas, Dillon & Bartlett; Vice President, State Bar of California, 1962-1963; Board of Governors, ABA, 1955-1963.

Beck, Lowell. ABA; 1:506; 1934; 1960; Bradley University, Ill., Northwestern University Law School; American Bar Association, 1120 Connecticut Ave. N.W., Washington, D.C.; Assistant Director, Washington Office of the ABA.

Bernhard, Berl. ABA; 1:507; 1929; 1954; Dartmouth College, Yale Law School; Staff Director, Commission on Civil Rights, 1701 Pennsylvania Ave. N.W., Washington, D.C.; Partner, Verner & Bernhard, Washington, D.C.

Berry, Theodore M. ABA; 2:2603; 1905; 1932; College and Law School, University of Cincinnati, Cincinnati, Ohio; 18 East 4th St., Cincinnati, Ohio.

Biddle, Francis. 1:507; 1886; 1911; College and Law School, Harvard. 1669 31st St. N.W., Washington, D.C.

Blackwell, Thomas W., Jr. ABA; 2:2528; 1913; 1936; University of North Carolina, Yale Law School; 15th Floor, Reynolds Building, Winston-Salem, N.C.; Partner, Blackwell, Blackwell, Canady & Eller; Board of Governors, North Carolina Bar, 1955-1958.

Bonet, Luis Torres. No entry. Executive Director, Bar Association of Puerto Rico, San Juan, Puerto Rico.

Brandis, Henry P., Jr. ABA; 2:2474; 1909; 1932; University of North Carolina, Chapel Hill, Columbia Law School, Chapel Hill, N.C; Dean and Law Professor, University of North Carolina Law School.

Branton, Wiley A. No listing. 41 Exchange Place, Atlanta, Georgia.

Breitel, Charles D. ABA; 2:2186; 1908; 1933; University of Michigan, Ann Arbor, Columbia Law School; 27 Madison Ave., New York, N.Y.; Court of Appellate Justice.

Brennan, R. James. ABA; 3:3067; 1928; 1955; University of Colorado, Boulder, University of South Dakota Law School; 507 1/2 Sixth St., Rapid City, S.D.

Bromley, Bruce. ABA; 2: 2188; 1893; 1920; University of Michigan, Ann Arbor, Harvard Law School; I Chase Manhattan Plaza, New York, N.Y.; Partner, Cravath, Swaine & Moore; Associate Judge of the New York Court of Appeals.

Brooke, Hon. Edward W. ABA; 2:1457; 1919; 1948; Howard University, Boston University Law School; Attorney General of Massachusetts, Boston, Mass.

Buchann, John G. ABA; 2:2961; 1888; 1912; Princeton University, Harvard Law School, 1800 Oliver Building, Pittsburgh, Pa.; Partner, Buchann, Ingersoll, Rodewald, Kyle & Burger, Pittsburgh, Pa.; Vice-President, American Law Institute, 1947-1963; President, ABA, 1949-1951.

Brownell, Herbert. ABA; 2:2189; 1904; 1928; Nebraska University, Lincoln, Yale Law School; 26 Broadway, Cunard Building, New York, N.Y.; Partner, Lord, Day & Lord; Attorney General of the United States, 1953-1957; President of the Association of the Bar of the City of New York, 1962.

Bull, Mason. ABA; 1:996; 1903; 1929; Harvard University, Northwestern University School of Law; 212 North Genesee St., Morrison, Ill.; Partner, Bull, Ludens & Potter; President, Illinois State Bar Association, 1962-1963.

Bunn, Charles. No entry. University of Virginia Law School, Charlottesville, Va.

Burney, Cecil E. ABA, 3:3164; 1914; 1938; College and Law School, University of Texas, Austin; 9th Floor, Petroleum Tower, Corpus Christi, Texas; Partner, Fisher, Wood, Burney & Nesbit; Member, ABA House of Delegates, 1952-1963; Texas State Delegate, 1961-1963; President, American Judicature Society, 1960-1962.

Burns, Howard F. ABA. 3:2626. 1888; 1917; Amherst College, Harvard Law School; 1956 Union Commerce Building, Cleveland, Ohio; Partner, Baker, Hostetler & Patterson, Cleveland, Ohio. Member, American Law Institute.

Burns, Kenneth J., Jr. ABA; 1:857; 1926; 1951; College and Law School, Northwestern University; 135 South LaSalle St., Chicago, Ill.; Partner, Thompson, Raymond, Mayer & Jenner; Chairman, Illinois State Junior Bar Conference, 1961-1962; Member, ABA House of Delegates, 1963.

Burns, Lawrence, Jr. ABA; 3:2680; 1910; 1933; College and Law School, Ohio State University, Columbus, Ohio; Coshocton National Bank Building, Coshocton, Ohio; Partner, Pomerene, Burns, Milligan & Frase, Coshocton, Ohio; Member, Ohio State Bar Council of Delegates, 1959-1963; President, Ohio State Bar Association, 1963.

Calhoun, Joseph D. ABA; 3:2904; 1907; 1933; Swarthmore College, University of Pennsylvania Law School; 218 West Front St., Media, Pa.

Carr, Honorable Charles V. ABA; 3:2627; 1903; 1930; Fisk University, Nashville, Tenn., Ohio State University, Columbus, Ohio; 8311 Quincy Ave., Cleveland, Ohio.

Carter, James J. ABA; 1:31; 1913; 1934; Jones Law School; Box 116, Montgomery, Ala.; Partner, Hill, Hill, Stovall & Carter, Montgomery, Ala.; President, Montgomery County Bar Association, 1957; Honorary Member Judicial Conference, U.S. 5th Circuit.

Carter, Robert L. 2:2195; 1917; 1945; Lincoln University, Lincoln, Pa., Howard University Law School; 20 West 40th St., New York, New York; NAACP.

Channell, Donald. ABA; 1:512; 1928; 1952; Drury College and Law School; American Bar Association, 1120 Connecticut Ave. N.W., Washington, D.C.; Director, Washington Office of the ABA.

Chuck, Walter G. ABA, 1:806; 1920; 1948; University of Hawaii, Harvard Law School; Suite 304, 1022 Bethel St., Honolulu, Hawaii; Director, International Academy of Trial Lawyers, 1955-1959; Member, Hawaii Senate, 1959-1963.

Clifford, Clark M. ABA, 1:513; 1906; 1928; College and Law School, Washington University; 1523 L St. N.W., Washington, D.C.; Partner, Clifford & Miller; Special Counsel to the President, 1946-1950.

Cogan, John F., Jr. ABA; 2:1460; 1926; 1953; College and Law School, Harvard; 60 State St., Boston, Mass.; Partner, Hale & Dorr.

Cole, David. ABA, 2:1995; 1902; 1925; College and Law School, Harvard; 45 Church St., Paterson, N.J.; Partner, Cole, Berman & Garth.

Coleman, William T., Jr. ABA; 3:2922; 1920; 1947; University of Pennsylvania, Harvard Law School; 2635 Fidelity-Philadelphia Trust Building, 123 South Broad St., Philadelphia, Pa.; Partner, Dilworth, Paxson, Kalish, Lohn & Dilks, Philadelphia.

Colley, Nathaniel. ABA, 1:286; 1918; 1948; Yale Law School; 1617 10th St., Sacramento, California.

Conyers, John, Jr. 2:1569; College and Law School, Wayne State University, Detroit, Michigan; 7376 Grand River, Detroit, Michigan.

Cooper, Grant B. ABA; 1: 177; 1903; 1927; Southwestern University Law School, Los Angeles, Cal.; 3919 Oakwood Ave., Los Angeles, Cal.; Partner, Cooper & Nelsen, Los Angeles; President, American College of Trial Lawyers, 1963.

Cooper, Jerome A. ABA; 1:6; 1913; 1936; College and Law School, Harvard; Suite 1025, Bank for Savings Building, Birmingham, Ala.; Partner, Cooper, Mitch & Crawford, Birmingham.

Coughlan, Glenn A. ABA; 1:814; 1914; 1939; College and Law School, University of Idaho; Idaho Building, Boise, Idaho; Partner, Coughlan & Imhoff; Vice President, Idaho State Bar, 1963.

Coulter, Glenn M. ABA, 2:1569; 1894; 1920; College and Law School, University of Michigan; Ford Building, Detroit, Mich.; Partner, Coulter, O'Hara & Coulter, Detroit; Member, ABA House of Delegates, 1944-1963.

Craig, Walter E. ABA; 1:54; 1909; 1934; College and Law School, Stanford University; 1st National Bank Building, Phoenix, Ariz.; Partner, Fennemore, Craig, Allen & McClennen; President-elect, ABA, 1962-1963.

Crawford, George W. ABA; 1:468; 1877; 1904; Talladega College, Talladega, Ala., Yale Law School; 205 Church St., New Haven, Conn.

Crockett, George W., Jr. 2:1570; 1909; 1934; Morehouse College, University of Michigan Law School, Ann Arbor; 1327 Nicolet St., Detroit, Mich.

Crowley, Marshall. ABA; 2:1972; 1908; 1930; Rutgers University Law School; National State Bank Building, 810 Broad St., Newark, N.J.; Partner, Toner, Crowley, Waelper & Vanderbilt, Newark.

Cutler, Lloyd N. ABA; 1:517; 1917; 1940; College and Law School, Yale; 815 17th St., Washington, D.C.; Partner, Wilmer, Cutler & Pickering; President, Yale Law School Association, 1962-1963.

Darrell, Norris. 2:2208; 1899; 1927; born St. Kitts, BWI; Law School, University of Minneapolis, Minn.; 48 Wall St., New York, N.Y.; Partner, Sullivan & Cromwell; President of the American Law Institute, 1961.

Darwin, Jay A. ABA; 1:315; 1903; 1931; City College of New York, New York University Law School; 68 Post St., San Francisco, Calif.

Davis, Ted J. ABA; 3:2783; 1930; 1957; Oklahoma A& M College, Stillwater, Okla., University of Oklahoma Law School; 2411 First National Building, Oklahoma City; Partner, Fuller, Smith, Mosburg & Davis, Oklahoma City; Chairman, Oklahoma Junior Bar Conference, 1962; Member, ABA Executive Council, Junior Bar Conference, 1962.

Dean, Arthur H. ABA; 2:4399; 1898; 1923; College and Law School, Cornell; 48 Wall St., New York, N.Y.; Partner, Sullivan & Cromwell; U. S. Representative at Panmunjon, 1953-1954; Chairman, U. S. Delegation to Geneva Conference on Law of the Sea, Nuclear Testing and Disarmament, 1958-1962; President, American Society of International Law, 1961-1962.

Dezendorf, James C. ABA; 3:2834; 1910; 1932; College and Law School, University of Oregon; 8th Floor, Pacific Building, 520 Southwest Yamhill, Portland, Ore.; Partner, Koerner, Young, McColloch & Dezendorf, Portland; Vice-Chairman, ABA Committee on State Legislation, 1959-1963; Board of Directors, American Judicature Society, 1963.

Dixon, Arthur. ABA; 1:869; 1895; 1921; Harvard University, Northwestern University School of Law; 208 South LaSalle St., Chicago, Ill.; Partner, Dixon, Morse, Nnouff & Holmes; Member of the Council of the American Law Institute, 1954-1963.

Dorsey, Hugh M., Jr. ABA; 1:749; 1912; 1935; College and Law School, Emory University; 64 First National Bank Building, Atlanta, Ga.; Partner, Hansell, Post, Brandon & Dorsey.

Drinan, Robert F., S.J. ABA; 2:1463; 1920; 1950; Boston College, Georgetown University Law School, Boston, Mass.; Dean, Boston College Law School.

Driscoll, Robert E., Jr. ABA; 3:3064; 1916; 1942; Stanford University, University of Colorado Law School, Boulder; Lead, S.D.; Partner, Kellar, Kellar & Driscoll, Lead, S.D.

Dudley, Edward R. No entry. President, Borough of Manhattan, 549 West 123rd St., New York, N.Y.

Dunn, Harry L. ABA; 1:182; 1894; 1922; University of California at Berkeley, Columbia and Harvard Law Schools; 433 South Spring St., Los Angeles, Calif.; Partner, O'Melveny & Myers, Los Angeles.

Durhan, W.J. No entry. 2600 Flora, Dallas, Texas.

Early, Bert H. ABA; 1:871; 1922; 1949; Duke University, Harvard Law School; 1155 East 60th St., Chicago, Illinois; Deputy Executive Director of the American Bar Association.

Endicott, Allen B. III. ABA; 2:1925; 1911; 1937; Colgate University, University of Virginia Law School, Charlottesville; Guarantee Trust Building, Atlantic City, N.J.; Partner, Endicott, Dowling & Endicott.

Eney, H. Vernon. ABA; 2:1402; 1908; 1929; University of Baltimore Law School; 1409 Mercantile Trust Building, Baltimore, Md.; Partner, Venable, Baetjer & Howard; Member American Law Institute; Standing Committee on Rules of the ABA; President-elect 1962-1963, Maryland State Bar Association.

Faust, James E. ABA; 3:3322; 1920; 1948; College and Law School, University of Utah; Kearns Building, Salt Lake City, Utah.

Fellers, James D. ABA, 3:2784; 1913; 1936; College and Law School, University of Oklahoma, Norman; First National Building, Oklahoma City, Okla.; ABA House of Delegates, 1947-1962; Member ABA Board of Governors, 1962-1963; American Law Institute.

Ferguson, Clyde. No entry. Commission on Civil Rights, 1701 Pennsylvania Ave. N.W., Washington, D.C.

Ferguson, William M. No entry. State House, Topeka, Kans.

Fitzpatrick, William F. ABA; 2:2440; 1902; 1927; College and Law School, Syracuse University; 1000 State Tower Building, Syracuse, N.Y.; Partner, Bond, Schoeneck & King.

Fowler, Cody. ABA, 1:726; 1892; 1914; University of Missouri, Cumberland School of Law; Citzens Building, Tampa, Fla.; Partner, Fowler, White, Gillen, Humkey & Trenam, St. Petersburg, Fla.; President, ABA, 1950-1951.

Fuchs, Ralph F. ABA, 1: 1042; 1899; 1922; Washington University, Yale Law School; Professor of Law, Indiana University School of Law, Bloomington, Ind.

Gaffney, Leo V. ABA, 1:465; 1903; 1928; College and Law School, Yale; 272 Main St., New Britain, Conn.; Partner, Brennen, Dichter & Brennan; House of Delegates, ABA, 1963; President, Bar Association of Connecticut, 1963.

Gallagher, Harold J. ABA; 2:2233; 1894; 1916; State University of Iowa City, Harvard Law School; One Chase Manhattan Plaza, New York, N.Y.; Partner, Wilkie, Farr, Gallagher, Walton & Fitzgibbon; President, ABA, 1949-1950.

Garrison, Lloyd K. ABA; 2:2234; 1897; 1923; College and Law School, Harvard; 575 Madison Ave., New York, N.Y.; Partner, Paul, Weiss, Rifkind, Wharton & Garrison; Dean of the University of Wisconsin Law School, 1932-1945; General Counsel and later Chairman, National War Labor Board, 1942-1945; Member Executive Committee, ABA, 1952-1955.

Gary, Frank B. ABA; 3:3039; 1900; 1928; The Citadel, The Naval Academy, University of South Carolina Law School; Security Federal Building, Columbia, S.C.; Member of the House of Delegates, ABA, 1954-1959; Member, ABA Committee on Military Justice, 1958-1959; Member, ABA Committee on Lawyers and Legal Services in the Defense Establishment, 1961-1963; American Law Institute.

Gates, Benton E. ABA; 1: 1044; 1904; 1927; College and Law School, University of Michigan, Ann Arbor; Farmers Loan & Trust Building, Columbia City, Ind.; Partner, Gates & Gates; Chairman, ABA House of Delegates, 1960-1961.

Gaunt, William W. ABA; 1:392; 1898; 1924; College and Law School, University of Colorado, Boulder; 25 South Fourth Ave., Brighton, Colo.; Partner, Gaunt, Byrne & Dirrim.

Gershenson, Harry. ABA; 2:1817; 1902; 1923; College and Law School, Benton College; 611 Olive St., St. Louis, Mo.; Member, ABA House of Delegates, 1954-1963; ABA Board of Governors, 1962-1964; Director, American Judicature Society, 1958-1963.

Gibbs, Delbridge L. ABA; 1:652; 1917; 1940; College and Law School, University of Florida; First Bank & Trust Building, Jacksonville, Fla.; Partner, Marks, Gray, Yates, Conroy & Gibbs; President, Florida Bar Association, 1963; Member, Board of Governors, Florida Bar, 1958-1963.

Goodnow, Nathan B. ABA; 2:1575; 1906; 1930; College and Law School, University of Detroit; 2746 Penobscot Building, Detroit, Mich.; Partner, Dykema, Wheat, Spencer, Goodnow & Trigg; First Vice-President, State Bar of Michigan; Commissioner, State Bar of Michigan, 1958-1962.

Gordon, Joseph H. ABA; 3:3458; 1909; 1935; Stanford University, University of Washington Law School, Seattle; Puget Sound Bank Building, Tacoma, Wash.; Partner, Gordon, Goodwin, Sager & Thomas, Tacoma; Member, ABA House of Delegates, 1951-1963; ABA Board of Governors, 1963.

Gray, Earl Q. ABA; 3:2761; 1891; 1912; University of Oklahoma, Norman, University of Chicago Law School; Box 149, Ardmore, Okla.; President, Oklahoma Bar Association.

Gray, Fred D. ABA; 1:32; 1930; 1954; Alabama State Teachers College, Western Reserve University Law School; 34 South Perry St., Montgomery, Ala.

Gray, William P. ABA; 1:190; 1912; 1941; University of California-Los Angeles, Harvard Law School; Rowan Building, 458 South Spring St., Los Angeles, Calif.; Partner, Gray, Binkley & Pfaelzer; Special Assistant to the U.S. Attorney, 1958-1963; State Bar of California, Member of the Committee on Judicial Selection, Tenure, and Compensation, 1959-1963; Member, ABA House of Delegates, 1953-1954; Member of the Board of Governors of the State Bar of California, 1960-1963; Board of Directors, American Judicature Society.

Greenberg, Jack. ABA; 2:2244; 1924; 1949; College and Law School, Columbia University; 10 Columbus Circle, New York, N.Y.; General Counsel, NAACP, Legal and Educational Fund, Inc.

Hackney, H. Eastman. ABA; 2:2967; Princeton University, Harvard Law School; 747 Union Trust Building, Pittsburgh, Pa.; Partner, Reed, Smith, Shaw & McClay, Pittsburgh.

Haddad, William N. ABA; 1:884; 1903; 1927; University of Oklahoma, Harvard Law School; 135 South LaSalle St., Chicago, Ill.; Partner, Bell, Boyd, Lloyd, Haddad & Burns.

Hall, Amos T. 3:2828; 1896; 1926; Unlisted school; 121 North Greenwood, Tulsa, Okla.

Hamo, Albert J. ABA; 2:1024; 1898; 1915; Dakota Wesleyan University, Mitchell, S.D., Yale Law School; Supreme Court Building, Springfield, Ill.

Hardesty, C. Howard, Jr. ABA; 3:3478; Duke University, West Virginia University Law School, Morgantown, W.Va.; First National Bank Building, Fairmont, W.Va.; Partner, Furbee & Hardesty, Fairmont; Member, Executive Council, State Bar of West Virginia, 1955-1963.

Harper, Alphonso R. No entry. 600 American Title & Trust Building, Detroit, Mich.

Havighurst, Harold C. ABA; 1:886; 1897; 1927; College and Law School, Harvard; 357 East Chicago Ave., Chicago, Ill.; Professor of Law, Northwestern University Law School.

Hayes, George E. C. ABA; 1:530; 1894; 1918; Brown University, Howard Law School; 613 F. St. N.W., Washington, D.C.; Professor of Law, Howard University Law School.

Healey, George A. ABA; 2:1872; 1905; 1929; College and Law School, University of Nebraska; Sharp Building, Lincoln, Neb.; Partner, Healey & Healey; Board of Examiners, Nebraska State Bar Commissioner, 1942-1963; President, State Bar of Nebraska, 1962-1963.

Hetlage, Robert O. ABA; 2:1819; 1931; 1954; College and Law School, Washington University, St. Louis, Mo.; 407 North Eighth St., St. Louis, Mo.

Higgs, William. No entry. 149 Putnam Ave., Cambridge, Mass.

Hill, Francis W. ABA; 1:532; 1895; 1917; St. John's College, Annapolis, Md., Georgetown University Law School; Tower Building, Washington, D.C.; Partner, Hill & Marshall; Member, ABA House of Delegates, 1942-1963.

Hodson, Leslie. ABA; 1:889; 1902; 1930; Washington and Jefferson College, Harvard Law School; Prudential Plaza, Chicago, Ill.; Partner, Kirkland, Ellis, Hodson, Chaffetz & Masters.

Hoffman, Louis. No entry. Dudley, Hoffman & McGowan, Grand Hotel Building, P.O. Box 717, Charlotte Amalie, St. Thomas, V.I.

Hollowell, Donald L. ABA; 1:753; 1917; 1952; Lane College, Jackson, Tenn., Loyola University Law School, Chicago; 8591/2 Hunter N.W., Atlanta, Ga.

Jaworski, Leon. ABA, 3:3237; 1905; 1925; College and Law School, Baylor University, Waco, Texas; Bank of the S.W. Building, Houston, Texas; Partner, Fulbright, Crooker, Freeman, Bates & Jaworski, Houston; Member, ABA Standing Committee on the Federal Judiciary, 1960-1963; ABA Special Committee on Federal Rules of Procedure, 1960-1963; Delegate, Fifth Judicial Circuit Conference, 1960-1963.

Jenckes, Joseph S., Jr. ABA, 1:893; 1907; 1930; College and Law School, University of Arizona; 910 Union Title Building, Phoenix, Ariz.; Partner, Evans, Kitchel & Jenckes.

Jenner, Albert E., Jr. ABA; 1:893; 1907; 1930; College and Law School, University of Illinois; 135 South LaSalle St., Chicago, Ill.; Partner, Thompson, Raymond, Mayer & Jenner; Member, Illinois State Bar Commission on Uniform State Laws, 1950- 1963, Chairman, 1963; Special Assistant to the Attorney General of Illinois, 1956-1963; ABA House of Delegates, 1948-1963; Vice-Chairman, Joint Committee for the Effective Administration of Justice, 1961-1963.

Johnson, Herbert. ABA; 1:754; 1901; 1928; College and Law School, University of Virginia, Charlottesville; 715 Rhodes-Haverty Building, Atlanta, Ga.; Partner, Johnson, Hatcher, Meyerson & Irvin; Member, Advisory Board, *ABA Journal,* 1961-1963.

Johnson, The Honorable Leroy. No entry. Senator of the state of Georgia, Atlanta.

Johnston, Joseph F. ABA; 1:8; 1906; 1929; Princeton University, Harvard Law School; First National Building, Birmingham, Ala.; Partner, Cabaniss & Johnston; Member, Council of the American Law Institute, 1950-1963.

Johnston, Paul. ABA; 1:8; 1908; 1933; College and Law School, Harvard; First National Bank Building; Birmingham, Ala.; Partner, Cabaniss & Johnston; American Law Institute.

Kahn, Gerald J. ABA; 3:3540; 1926; 1950; College and Law School, University of Wisconsin, Madison; 710 North Plankinton Ave., Milwaukee, Wis.: Partner, Godfrey & Kahn, Milwaukee.

Kallgren, Edward E. ABA; 1:326; 1928; 1955; College and Law School, University of California, Berkeley; 111 Sutter St., San Francisco, Calif.; Associate, Brobeck, Phleger & Harrison.

Karr, Lloyd. ABA; 1:1178; 1912; 1937; College and Law School not listed; 711 Des Moines St., Webster City, Iowa; Partner, Karr & Karr; President, Iowa State Bar, 1962-1963; Chairman, ABA Ways and Means Committee, 1960-1961.

Keith, Damon. ABA, 2:1580; 1922; 1950; West Virginia State College Institute; Howard Law School; 1380 Broadway, Detroit, Mich.

Kelleher, Harry B. ABA, 2:1354; 1909; 1933; College and Law School, Tulane, New Orleans, La.; 1836 National Bank of Commerce Building, New Orleans, La.; Partner, Lemle & Kelleher.

Kintner, Earle W. ABA; 1:537; 1912; 1938; DePauw University, Indiana, Indiana University Law School, Bloomington; 1815 H St. N.W., Washington, D.C.; Partner, Arent, Fox, Kintner, Plotkin & Kahn; 1959-1961, Federal Trade Commission; President, Foundation of the Federal Bar Association, 1957; President, Federal Bar Association, 1959; Member ABA House of Delegates, 1957-1963.

Knight, Robert H. 2:2275; 1919; 1950; Yale University, University of Virginia Law School, Charlottesville; 20 Exchange Place, New York, N.Y.; Partner, Shearman & Sterling; General Counsel of Treasury, 1961-1962.

Kuhn, Edward W. ABA; 3:3110; 1905; 1934; Catholic University of America, Washington, D.C., University of Michigan Law School, Ann Arbor; Box 123, Memphis, Tenn.; Partner, McKonald, Kuhn, McKonald, Crenshaw & Smith; State of Tennessee Delegate to the ABA, 1957-1961; Member, ABA Board of Governors Sixth Circuit, 1960-1963; Chairman, ABA Standing Committee on Legal Aid Work, 1959-1960; Board of Directors, American Judicature Society.

Laporte, Cloyd. ABA; 2:2281; 1892; 1921; College and Law Schools, Harvard; 40 Wall St., New York, N.Y.; Partner, Dewey, Ballantine, Bushby, Palmer & Wood; Chairman, Board of Ethics, City Bar of New York, 1963.

Lawson, Belford V., Jr. ABA; 1:539; 1906; 1933; University of Michigan, Ann Arbor, Howard University Law School; 1725 K. St. N.W., Washington, D.C.

Leibold, Arthur W., Jr. ABA 3:2936; 1931; 1957; Haverford College, University of Pennsylvania Law School; 3 Penn Center Plaza, Philadelphia, Pa.; Associate, Dechert, Price & Rhodes, Philadelphia.

Lillard, Robert E. ABA; 3:3122; 1907; 1936; Unlisted Schools; 3331/2 Fourth St. North, Nashville, Tenn.; Partner, Lillard & Birch, Nashville.

Lockhart, William B. ABA; 2:1681; 1906; 1933; Harvard University Law School; Dean, School of Law, University of Minnesota, Minneapolis.

Lougee, Laurence H. ABA; 2:1544; 1909; 1935; College and Law School, Howard Unversity, Washington, D.C.; 340 Main St., Worcester, Mass.; Partner, Mirick, O'Connell, DeMallie & Lougee.

Makepeace, Colin MacR. ABA, 3:3025; 1890; 1916; College and Law School, Harvard; Hospital Trust Building, Providence, R.I.; Partner, Tillinghast, Collins & Tanner, Providence.

Malcolm, Walter D. ABA; 2:1477; 1904; 1929; University of Oregon, Harvard Law School; 1 Federal St., Boston, Mass.; Partner, Bingham, Dana & Gould.

Malone, Ross L. ABA; 2:2042; 1910; 1932; College and Law School, Washington & Lee University; Roswell Petroleum Building, Roswell, N.M.; Partner, Atwood & Malone; Member, Council of the American Law Institute, 1959-1963; New Mexico Board of Bar Examiners; ABA House of Delegates, 1946-1960; President, ABA, 1958-1959.

Marbury, William L. ABA; 2:1410; 1901; 1925; University of Virginia, Charlottesville, Harvard Law School; 900 First National Bank Building, Baltimore, Md.; Partner, Piper & Marbury; Legal Advisor to the War Department, 1942-1945.

Marden, Orison S. ABA; 2:2296; 1906; 1930; College and Law School, New York University; 14 Wall St., New York, N.Y.; Partner, White & Case.

Marsh, Eugene E. ABA; 3:2827; 1900; 1923; University of Oregon, University of Washington Law School, Seattle; Box 596, McMinnville, Ore.; Partner, Marsh, Marsh, Dashney & Cushing; Board of Governors, Oregon State Bar, 1960-1963.

Matheson, Scott M., Jr. ABA; 3:3325; 1929; 1953; University of Utah, Stanford Law School; Union Pacific Building, Salt Lake City, Utah; Assistant General Attorney, UPPR Co.

Maxwell, David F. ABA; 3:2939; 1900; 1924; College and Law School, University of Pennsylvania; 1418 Packard Building, Philadelphia, Pa.; Partner, Obermayer, Rebmann, Maxwell & Hippel, Philadelphia; ABA President, 1956-1957; Director, American Judicature Society, 1951-1958; Chairman, American Bar Foundation Fellows, 1958-1959.

McCloskey, Paul N., Jr. ABA; 2:1479; 1909; 1934; Tufts University, Harvard Law School; 800 Welch Road, Palo Alto, Calif.

McKenzie, William A. ABA; 3:2613; 1909; 1935; Georgetown University, Harvard Law School; Fifth Third Bank Building, Cincinnati, Ohio; Partner, Graydon, Head & Ritchey, Cinncinati.

McLeod, Walton J., Jr. ABA; 3:3056; 1906; 1930; Wofford College, Spartanburg, S.C., University of South Carolina Law School; Jeffries Building, Walterboro, S.C.; Partner, Jeffries, McLeod, Unger & Fraser, Walterboro; South Carolina State Bar Delegate ABA; ABA House of Delegates, 1951-1963.

McTighe, Desmond J. ABA; 3:2912; 1902; 1925; University of Pittsburgh, University of Pennsylvania Law School; 11 E. Airy St., Norristown, Pa.; Partner, Duffy, McTighe & McElhone, Norristown; Vice-President, Pennsylvania State Bar Association, 1962.

Merrill, Maurice H. ABA; 3:2779; 1897; 1922; College and Law School, University of Oklahoma, Norman; Professor of Law, University of Oklahoma Law School, Norman.

Meserve, Robert W. ABA; 2:1479; 1909; 1934; Tufts University, Harvard Law School; 75 Federal St., Boston, Mass.; Partner, Nutter, McClennen & Fish.

Wes, Waldo G. ABA; 3:3353; 1911; 1937; College and Law School, Washington & Lee University, Lexington, Va.; First Federal Savings & Loan Building, Bristol, Va.; Partner, Jones, Woodward, Miles & Greiner, Bristol; Executive Committee, State Bar of Virginia, 1958-1963; Chairman, 1960-1961; President, State Bar of Virginia, 1962-1963.

Miller, Loren. 1:211; 1904; 1929; Kansas University, Lawrence, Kan., Washburn University Law School, Topeka, Kan.; 282 S. Western St., Los Angeles, Calif.; Partner, Miller, Maddox & Malone, Los Angeles.

Miller, Robert N. ABA; 1:547; 1879; 1906; Rose Polytechnic Institute, Terre Haute, Ind., Harvard Law School; 1000 Connecticut Ave. N.W., Washington, D.C.; Partner, Miller & Chevalier; Overseer, *Harvard Law Review*, 1960-1965; Executive Committee, American Law Institute.

Miller, Vernon X. ABA; 1:547; 1902; 1925; College and Law School, University of Minnesota, Minneapolis; 1323 18th St. N.W., Washington, D.C.; Dean, Catholic University of America Law School.

Millimet, Joseph A. ABA; 2:1917; 1914; 1939; Dartmouth, Yale Law School; 1838 Elm St., Manchester, N.H.; Partner, Devine, Millimet, McDonough, Stahl & Branch, Manchester; New Hampshire State Bar Board of Examiners, 1953-1960; Chairman, Yale Placement Committee, 1948-1963; President, New Hampshire Bar Association, 1962-1963.

Ming, William R. ABA, 1:914; 1911; 1933; College and Law School, University of Chicago; 123 West Madison St., Chicago, Ill.; Partner, McCoy, Ming & Leighton; 1957-1963, Board of Directors, NAACP; Member, National Bar Association.

Minor, C. Venable. ABA; 3:3354; 1900; 1924; College and Law School, University of Virginia, Charlottesville; Court Square Building, Charlottesville, Va.; Partner, Battle, Neal, Harris, Minor & Williams, Charlottesville.

Morial, Ernest N. ABA; 2:1358; 1929; 1954; Xavier University, New Orleans, Louisiana State University and A&M College Law School, Baton Rouge; 1821 Orleans Ave., New Orleans, La.

Morris, Earl F. ABA; 3:2673; 1909; 1933; Wittenberg College, Springfield, Ohio, Harvard Law School; Huntington Bank Building, Columbus, Ohio; Partner, Wright, Harlor, Morris, Arnold & Glander, Columbus; President, Ohio State Bar, 1956-1957; Member, ABA House of Delegates, 1951-1963.

Motley, Constance Baker. 2:2311; 1921; 1948; New York University, Columbia Law School; 10 Columbus Circle, New York, N.Y.; Associate General Counsel, Legal and Educational Fund, Inc., NAACP.

Mucklestone, Robert S. ABA; 3:3443; 1929; 1954; College and Law School, University of Washington, Seattle; Washington Building, Seattle, Wash.; Associate, Holman, Marion, Black, Perkins & Coie, Seattle.

Murane, Edward E. ABA; 3:3578; 1902; 1925; College and Law School, University of Michigan, Ann Arbor; Wyoming National Bank Building, Casper, Wyo.; Partner, Murane, Bostwick, McDaniel & Scott; Casper; Wyoming State Delegate to the ABA House of Delegates, 1953-1963; Member, Board of Governors, ABA, 1960-1963.

Nabrit, James M. ABA; 1:550; 1900; 1929; Morehouse College, Northwestern University Law School; President, Howard University, Washington, D.C.

Neville, Philip. ABA; 2:1684; 1909; 1933; College and Law School, University of Minnesota, Minneapolis; Partner, Neville, Honson & Thompson, Minneapolis; President-Elect, Minnesota State Bar Association.

Nichols, David A. ABA, 2:1381; 1917; 1949; Bates College, Maine, University of Michigan; Depositors Trust Building, Camden, Me.; Board of Governors, ABA, 1960-1963; Board of Directors, American Judicature Society, 1960-1963.

Norris, The Honorable Austin. Chairman, Board of Revision of Taxes, 15th Floor, Commercial Trust Building, Philadelphia, Pa.

O'Brien, Francis J. ABA: 3:3026; 1893; 1921; Brown University, Providence, R.I., Georgetown University Law School, Washington, D.C.; Industrial Bank Building, Providence, R.I.

O'Brien, James E. ABA; 1:334; 1912; 1935; College and Law School, University of California, Berkeley; Standard Oil Building, 225 Bush St., San Francisco, Calif.; Partner Phillsbury, Madison & Sutro, San Francisco.

O'Meara, Joseph. No entry. Dean, Notre Dame Law School, South Bend, Ind.

Orbison, Telford B. ABA; 1: 1094; 1901; 1924; Ohio State, Columbia Law School; Union National Bank Building, New Albany, Ind.; Partner, Orbison, Rudy & O'Connor; Board of Governors, ABA, 1962-1965; Regent, 1961-1964, American College of Trial Lawyers.

O'Brian, John Lord. ABA; 1:551; 1874; 1898; Harvard College, University of Buffalo Law School; 701 Union Trust Building, Washington, D.C.; Partner, Covington & Burling, Washington, D.C.; General Counsel, Office of Production Management, War Production Board, 1941-1944.

Parker, Addison M. ABA; 1:1138; 1916; 1940; Dartmouth, Harvard Law School; 500 Fleming Building, Des Moines, Iowa; Partner, Dickerson, Throckmorton, Parker, Mannheimer & Raife, Des Moines; Member, ABA Special Committee on Agriculture, 1963.

Pell, Wilbur F., Jr. No entry. Methodist Building, Shelbyville, Ky.

Petree, Jack. ABA; 3:3112; 1921; 1948; College and Law School, Washington University, St. Louis, Mo.; 900 Memphis Bank Building, Memphis, Tenn.; Partner, Evans, Petree & Cobb, Memphis; President, Tennessee Junior Bar Association, 1952-1953.

Pierce, The Honorable Samuel R., Jr. ABA; 2:2326; 1922; 1949; College and Law School, Cornell University, Ithaca, N.Y.; 477 Madison Ave., New York, N.Y.; Partner, Battle, Fowler, Stokes & Sheel; Ford Foundation Fellow; Lecturer Trial Practice, Yale; Assistant U.S. Attorney Southern District, 1953-1955; Judge, Court of General Sessions, New York, 1959-1960; 1961, Member, New York State Banking Board.

Pierce, William J. ABA, 2:1551; 1921; 1949; College and Law School, University of Michigan, Ann Arbor; University of Michigan Law School, Professor of Law.

Poole, William. ABA; 1:499; 1908; 1934; Swarthmore, Oxford; Delaware Trust Building, Wilmington, Del.; Partner, Berl, Poller & Anderson; Member, ABA House of Delegates, 1941-1963; Board of Governors, ABA, 1961-1963.

Posey, Webster. 3:2615; 1912; 1953; University of Cincinnati Law School, Cincinnati YMCA Schools; 3467 Harvey Ave., Cincinnati, Ohio.

Powell, Lewis. ABA; 3:3395; 1907; 1931; College and Law School, Washington & Lee University, Lexington, Va.; 1003 Electric Building, Richmond, Va.; Partner, Hunton, Williams, Gay, Powell & Gibson, Richmond.

Powell, George V. ABA; 3:3444; 1910; 1935; Princeton University, University of Washington Law School, Seattle; 1700 Washington Building, Seattle, Wash.; Partner, Evans, McLaren, Lane, Powell & Moss, Seattle.

Powers, George B. ABA; 2:1262; 1905; 1928; College and Law School, University of Kansas, Lawrence; Fourth National Bank Building, Wichita, Kan.; Partner, Foulston, Siefkin, Powers, Smith & Eberhardt, Wichita; ABA House of Delegates, 1952-1963; State of Kansas Delegate, ABA, 1960-1963; State of Kansas Bar Association, Secretary-Treasurer, 1950-1963; Board of Governors, Kansas State Bar, 1962-1963.

Pratt, John H. ABA; 1:554; 1910; 1935; College and Law School, Harvard; American Security Building, Washington, D.C.; Partner, Morris, Pearce, Gardner & Pratt.

Quarles, John R. ABA; 2:1484; 1897; 1929; University of Virginia, Charlottesville, Harvard Law School; 50 Federal St., Boston, Mass.; Partner, Ropes & Gray.

Rachlin, Carl. 2:2331; 1917; 1941; New York University, Harvard Law School; 280 Broadway, New York, N.Y.

Rain, Talbot. ABA; 3:3187; 1920; 1942; College and Law School, University of Texas, Austin; Republic National Bank Building, Dallas, Texas; Partner, Thompson, Knight, Wright & Simmons.

Ramsay, Louis. ABA, 2:1484; 1897; 1929; College and Law School, University of Arkansas; Simmons National Bank Building, Pine Bluff, Ark.; Partner, Coleman, Gantt & Ramsey, Pine Bluff.

Randall, William L. ABA; 3:3547; 1930; 1956; Dartmouth College, Hanover, N.H., University of Michigan Law School, Ann Arbor; 912 East Wells St., Milwaukee, Wis.; Partner, Zimmers, Randall & Zimmers; Milwaukee.

Reeves, Frank D. ABA; 1:556; 1916; 1943; College and Law School, Howard University; 1343 H St. N.W., Washington, D.C.

Rhyne, Charles S. ABA; 1:556; 1912; 1937; Duke University, George Washington University School of Law; 400 Hill Building, Washington, D.C.; Partner, Rhyne & Rhyne; ABA House of Delegates, 1944-1963; Chairman, 1956-1957; President, ABA, 1957-1958.

Ribble, Frederick D.G. ABA; 3:3355; 1898; 1920; College of William & Mary, Williamsburg, Virginia, University of Virginia Law School, Charlottesville; Dean, University of Virginia, Charlottesville.

Riehm, John W., Jr. ABA, 3:3188; 1920; 1947; Bradley Polytechnic Institute, Peoria, Ill., University of Michigan Law School, Ann Arbor; Dean, Southern Methodist University, Dallas, Texas.

Ris, William K. ABA; 1:414; 1915; 1939; College and Law School, University of Colorado, Boulder; Denver Club Building, Denver, Colo.; Partner, Wood, Ris & Hames, Denver; President, Colorado State Bar Association, 1962-1963.

Ritchie, John III. ABA, 1:929; 1904; 1927; College and Law School, University of Virginia, Charlottesville; Dean, Northwestern University Law School, Chicago, Ill.

Robinson, Spottswood W., III. ABA; 1:537; 1916; 1943; University of Virginia, Charlottesville, Howard University Law School; Dean, Howard University Law School, Washington, D.C.

Rockerfeller, Edwin S. ABA; 1:557; 1927; 1951; College and Law School, Yale; 808 17th St. N.W., Washington, D.C.; Partner, Wald, Harkrader & Rockerfeller; Member, National Council, Federal Bar, 1960-1963; ABA Special Committee on Association Programs for Lawyers in the Government, 1961-1963.

Rogers, Eugene F. ABA; 3:3041; 1929; 1952; College and Law School, University of South Carolina, Columbia; Barringer Building, Columbia, S.C.; Partner, Rogers & McDonald.

Rogers, William P. ABA; 2:2338; 1913; 1937; Colgate University, Hamilton, N.Y., Cornell Law School; 100 Broadway, New York, N.Y.; Partner, Royall, Koegel & Rogers; Attorney General of the United States, 1957-1961.

Rostow, Eugene V. ABA; 1:472; 1913; 1938; College and Law School, Yale; Dean, Yale Law School, New Haven, Conn.

Satterfield, John C. ABA; 2:1755; 1904; 1929; Millsaps College, University of Mississippi; Box 466, Yazoo City, Miss.; Partner, Satterfield, Shell, Williams & Buford, Yazoo City; Member, Board of Governors, ABA, Fifth Circuit, 1955-1958; President ABA, 1961-1962.

Schwartz, Louis B. 3:2949; 1913; 1935; College and Law School, University of Pennsylvania; Professor of Law, University of Pennsylvania Law School, Philadelphia, Pa.

Sears, Bamabas F. ABA; 1:936; 1902; 1926; St. Thomas College, St. Paul, Minn., Georgetown University Law School, Washington, D,C.; One North LaSalle St., Chicago, Ill.; Partner, Sears, Strait & Dreyer; ABA House of Delegates, 1952-1963; Member ABA Standing Committee on the Judiciary, 1958-1963.

Segal, Bernard G. ABA; 3:2949; 1907; 1932; College and Law School, University of Pennsylvania; 1719 Packard Building, Philadelphia, Pa.; Partner, Schrader, Harrison, Segal & Lewis, Philadelphia; Council Member and Treasurer of the American Law Institute, 1955-1963; Chairman, Pennsylvania Bar Judiciary Committee, 1957-1963; Chairman, ABA Standing Committee on the Federal Judiciary, 1956-1962; Member, Board of Regents, American College of Trial Lawyers, 1957-1963.

Shepherd, James L., Jr. ABA; 3:3248; 1893; 1916; College and Law School, University of Texas, Austin; Esperson Building, Houston, Texas; Partner, Baker, Botts, Shepherd & Coates, Houston; Member, ABA House of Delegates, 1957-1958; Member, Professional Ethics Committee, 1958-1963.

Sheridan, Charles F., Jr. ABA; 2:1912; 1928; 1951; Amherst College, Concord, N.H., Harvard Law School; 9 Capital St., Concord, N.H.; Partner, Sulloway, Hollis, Godfrey & Soden, Concord.

Shestack, Jerome J. ABA; 3:2949; 1923; 1950; University of Pennsylvania, Harvard Law School; 1719 Packard Building, Philadelphia, Pa.; Partner, Schrader, Harrison, Segal & Lewis.

Shores, Arthur D. ABA; 1:12; 1904; 1937; Talladega College, Talladega, Ala., LaSalle Extension University Law School, Chicago, Ill.; 1527 Fifth Ave. North, Birmingham, Ala.

Siegel, Jay S. ABA, 1:460; 1929; 1955; College and Law School, New York University; 49 Pearl St., Hartford, Conn.

Smith, C.H. Erskine. ABA; 1:12; 1934; 1958; Birmingham-Southern College, University of Alabama Law School; Comer Building, Birmingham, Ala.

Smith, Sylvester C., Jr. ABA; 2:1984; 1894; 1917; New York University Law School; 18 Bank St., Newark, N.J.; General Counsel, Prudential Life Insurance Co.; President, ABA, 1963.

Snyder, Gerald C. ABA; 1:1034; 1902; 1927; College and Law School, University of Illinois; 301 Washington St., Waukegan, Ill.; Partner, Snyder, Clarke, Dalziel, Holmquist & Johnson, Waukegan; Member, Board of Governors, State Bar of Illinois, 1960-1963; Member, ABA House of Delegates, 1959-1963; Board of Directors, American Judicature Society, 1959-1963.

Spann, William B., Jr. ABA; 1:762; 1912; 1935; Emory University, Harvard Law School; Citizens & Southern National Bank Building, Atlanta, Ga.; Partner, Alston, Miller & Gaines; Director, American Judicature Society, 1960-1963; Member, ABA Board of Governors, 1960-1963.

Stecker, Joseph. ABA; 1:943; 1904; 1928; Ohio Wesleyan University, Ohio State University Law School; 1155 East 60th St., New York, N.Y.; Executive Director of the ABA, New York.

Steen, Joseph. ABA; 2:1740; 1933; 1960; Tulane University, New Orleans, University of Mississippi; Box 1172, Jackson, Miss.; Associate, Satterfield, Shell, William & Buford, Yazoo City, Miss.

Stockwell, Oliver P. ABA; 2:1337; 1907; 1932; College and Law School, Louisiana State University; Box 1209, Lake Charles, La.; Partner, Plauche & Stockwell; Member, Council of the Louisiana State Law Institute, 1951-1963; President, Louisiana State Bar Association, 1962-1963.

Stoner, James R. ABA; 1:565; 1927; 1952; Franklin & Marshall College, George Washington University, Washington, D.C.; 1402 G St. N.W., Washington, D.C.; Vice-Chairman, ABA Junior Bar Conference, 1961-1962.

Strassburger, Eugene B. ABA; 3:2979; 1886; 1910; College and Law School, Harvard; 2602 Grant Building, Pittsburgh, Pa.; Partner, Strassburger & McKenna; Standing Master, Board of Governors of the Allegheny County, Pennsylvania Bar Association, 1944-1963; Member, Executive Committee of the American Law Institute, 1954-1963.

Sugarmon, Russell B., Jr. 3:3113; 1929; 1956; Rutgers University, New Jersey, Harvard Law School; 588 Vance Ave., Memphis, Tenn.

Swanson, Roy P. ABA; 2:1794; 1896; 1922; Park College, Parkville, Mo., Kansas City School of Law; Commerce Trust Building, Kansas City, Mo.; Partner, Swanson, Midgley, Jones, Blackman & Eager; President, Kansas City Bar Association, 1961-1962.

Swegle, Harry. No entry. ABA, 1155 East 60th St., Chicago, Ill.

Taft, Charles P. ABA; 3:2619; 1897; 1922; College and Law School, Yale; 1750 Union Commerce Building, Cleveland, Ohio; Partner, Taft, Lavercombe & Fox; Member, City Council of Cincinnati, 1955-1963; Member, National Academy of Arbitrators, 1947-1963; Mayor of Cincinnati, 1955-1957.

Taft, Seth. 3:2657; 1922; 1948; College and Law School, Yale; 1750 Union Commerce Building, Cleveland, Ohio; Partner, Jones, Day, Cockley & Reavis, Cleveland.

Talley, Bascom. Bogalusa, La.

Tanner, Jack. 3:3460; 1919; 1955; University of Puget Sound, Washington, University of Washington Law School; 1022 South Monroe St., Tacoma, Wash.

Taylor, Alfred. ABA; 3:3094; 1923; 1949; College and Law School, Vanderbilt University, Nashville, Tenn.; 217 1/2 East Main St., Johnson City, Tenn.; Partner, Epps, Powell, Weller, Taylor & Miller, Johnson City.

Taylor, Hobart. No entry. President's Commission on Equal Employment Opportunity, Washington, D.C.

Taylor, William L. No entry. Assistant Staff Director, Commission on Civil Rights, Washington, D.C.

TePaske, Henry J. ABA; 1: 1162; 1904; 1929; Morningside College, University of Chicago Law School; National Bank Building, Orange City, Iowa; Partner, TePaske & Rins, Orange City; J.D. County Attorney; Member, ABA House of Delegates, 1954-1963; Chairman, 1959-1961.

Terry, N. Maxson. ABA, 1:493; 1904; 1929; College and Law School, Washington & Lee University, Lexington, Va.; 48 The Green, Dover, Del.; Member, Board of Bar Examiners, Delaware, 1955-1963; President, Delaware State Bar Association, 1961-1963.

Thompson, John J. ABA; 3:3113; 1929; 1952; Southwestern College at Memphis, University of Tennessee, Knoxville, Tenn.; Columbian Mutual Towers, Memphis, Tenn.; Partner, Nelson, Norvill, Wilson & Thompson, Memphis; President, Junior Bar of Shelby County, 1959-1960; ABA Executive Council, Junior Bar Conference, 1962-1963.

Thorsness, David. President, Alaska Bar Association, Anchorage.

Trammell, Wilbur P. No entry. City Hall, Buffalo, N.Y.

Traynor, Roger J. ABA; 1:113; 1900; 1927; College and Law School, University of California, Berkeley; 2643 Piedmont Ave., Berkeley, Calif.; California Supreme Court Justice.

Tweed, Harrison. ABA; 2:2376; 1885; 1911; College and Law School, Harvard; 1 Chase Manhattan Plaza, New York, N.Y.; Partner, Milbank, Tweed, Hope & Hadley.

Tyler, Andrew R. ABA; 2:2376; 1918; 1945; City College of New York, Brooklyn Law School; 30 Vesey Building, New York, N.Y.

Vann, David J. ABA; 1: 13; 1928; 1951; University of Alabama, George Washington Law School, Washington, D.C.; 2100 Comer Building, Birmingham, Ala.; Associate, White, Bradley, Arant, All & Rose.

Wade, John W. ABA: 3:3125; 1911; 1934; University of Mississippi, Harvard Law School; Dean, Vanderbilt Law School, Nashville,Tenn.

Walden, A.T. ABA; 1:763; 1885; 1912; Atlanta University, University of Michigan Law School, Ann Arbor; 980 Westmoor Drive N.W., Atlanta, Ga.

Walsh, Lawrence E. ABA; 2:2380; 1912; 1936; College and Law School, Columbia University; 1 Chase Manhattan Plaza, New York, N.Y.; Partner, Davis, Polk, Wardwell, Sunderland & Kiendl; U.S. Judge, Southern District of New York, 1954-1957; Deputy U.S. Attorney General, 1957-1960.

Warren, William C. ABA; 2:2380; 1909; 1937; University of Texas, Austin, Harvard Law School; Dean, Columbia Law School, New York, N.Y.

Wechsler, Herbert. ABA; 2:2382; 1909; 1933; City College of New York, Columbia Law School; Professor of Law, Columbia Law School, New York, N.Y.

Weinmann, John G. ABA; 2:1363; 1928; 1952; College and Law School, Tulane University, New Orleans, La.; Hibernia Bank Building, New Orleans; Partner, Phelps, Dunbar, Marks, Claverie & Sims, New Orleans.

Wilcox, Francis. General Counsel, Department of Health, Education and Welfare, Washington, D.C.

Wilkinson, Samuel A. ABA; 2:1493; 1926; 1951; Dartmouth College, Hanover, N.H., Boston University Law School; 10 State St., Boston, Mass.; Partner, Grabill, Ley & Butterworth, Boston.

Willard, Charles H. ABA; 2:2387; 1905; 1932; Yale University, Harvard Law School; 1 Chase Manhattan Plaza, New York, N.Y.; Partner, Davis, Polk, Wardwell, Sunderland & Kiendl.

Williams, Laurens. ABA; 1:572; 1906; 1931; Hastings College, Cornell Law School, Ithaca, New York; Ring Building, Washington, D.C.; Partner, Sutherland, Asbill & Brennan.

Willis, Archie N., Jr. 3:3114; 1925; 1953; Talladega College, Talladega, Ala., University of Wisconsin, Madison; 588 Vance Ave., Memphis, Tenn.

Willy, Roy E. ABA; 3:3071; 1889; 1912; University of Michigan Law School, Ann Arbor; 602-9 Security National Bank Building, Sioux Falls, S.D.; Partner, Willy, Pruitt & Matthews, Sioux Falls; ABA House of Delegates, 1936-1963.

Wilson, J. Boone, 178 Main St., Burlington, N.C.

Wilson, William L. ABA; 2:1306; 1912; 1935; College and Law School, Washington & Lee University, Lexington, Va.; 414 Masonic Building, Owensboro, Ky.; Member, Board of Bar Commissioners, Kentucky, 1949-1962; Vice-President, 1961-1962; President-elect, 1962-1963.

Winslow, Francis E. ABA; 2:2516; 1888; 1911; University of North Carolina, Chapel Hill, Columbia Law School; 509-518 Peoples Bank and Trust Building, Rocky Mount, N.C.; Partner, Battle, Winslow, Merrell, Scott & Wiley, Rocky Mount.

Winters, Glenn R. ABA; 1:954; 1909; 1937; College and Law School, University of Michigan, Ann Arbor; 1155 East 60th St., Chicago, Ill.

Wise, Sherwood W. ABA; 2:1741; 1910; 1934; College and Law School, Washington & Lee University, Lexington, Va.; 918 Electric Building, P.O. Box 157, Jackson, Miss.; Partner, Wise, Smith & Carter, Jackson; President, Mississippi State Bar Association, 1961-1962.

Wolkin, Paul A. ABA; 3:2957; 1917; 1942; College and Law School, University of Pennsylvania; 6 Penn Center Plaza, Philadelphia, Pa.; Partner, Wolkin, Sarner & Cooper; Assistant Director, American Law Institute, 1947-1963.

Wood, Ruth L. No entry. 453 South Main St., Danville, Va.

Woolfenden, Henry L. ABA; 2:1600; 1906; 1929; University of Michigan, Ann Arbor, Detroit College of Law, Detroit; 2966 Penobscot Building, Detroit, Mich.; Partner, Dahlberg, Simon, Jayne, Woolfenden & Gawne, Detroit; Member, ABA House of Delegates, 1950-1963; Director, American Judicature Society, 1956; Member, Executive Committee, 1962.

Wright, Edward L. ABA; 1:92; 1903; 1925; Little Rock College, Georgetown University Law School; 1600 Tower Building, Little Rock, Ark.; Partner, Wright, Lindsey, Jennings, Lester & Shultz; ABA House of Delegates, 1946-1963.

Wyatt, Wilson. ABA; 2:1299; 1905; 1927; University of Louisville, Jefferson School of Law, Louisville, Ky.; 300 Marion E. Taylor Building, Louisville, Ky.; Partner, Wyatt, Grafton & Sloss, Louisville; Lieutenant Governor of Kentucky, 1959-1963.

Young, Jack. ABA; 2:1741; 1908; 1951; Jackson College, Jackson, Miss.; 115 1/2 North Farish St., Jackson, Miss.

APPENDIX C

The Lawyers' Committee's Revenues—1963 to 1974

The following excerpts are taken from the annual certified financial audits* of the Lawyers' Committee for Civil Rights Under Law, performed for the officers of the Board of Directors by the Certified Public Accounting Firm of Feldman and Feldman located at Two Central Plaza, Philadelphia, Pennsylvania. The audits are available through the office of the Comptroller of the Committee at the National Office of the Lawyers' Committee for Civil Rights Under Law, presently located at 1450 G St. N.W., Washington, D.C.

The necessary funding for the support of the Lawyers' Committee for Civil Rights Under Law for the years 1963-1964 came from individual contributions from members of the bar. Thereafter, while the support from the private bar continued, the committee's predominant support came from contributions from private foundations, corporations, churches, and public grants, with the Ford Foundation providing the most significant component of that revenue.

---

* The audit for the financial year of June 1967 to August 1968 was missing from the files.

Feldman & Feldman

ACCOUNTANTS AND AUDITORS

TWO PENN CENTER PLAZA
PHILADELPHIA, 2 PA
LOCUST 7-2110

Members
American Institute of Certified Public Accountants
Pennsylvania Institute of Certified Public Accountants

July 6, 1964

PAUL A. FELDMAN
LEONARD FELDMAN, C.P.A.
WALTER SKALER, C.P.A.
J.H. AARON, C.P.A.

Officers and Board of Directors
Lawyers' Committee for Civil Rights Under Law
Farragat Building
900 17ᵗʰ Street, NW
Washington, DC 20006

Gentlemen:

We have examined the balance sheet of the

<u>LAWYERS' COMMITTEE FOR CIVIL RIGHTS UNDER LAW</u>

(a District of Columbia non-profit corporation) as of June 30, 1964, and the related Statement of Income and Expenditures for the period August 1, 1963 (the date of incorporation) to June 30, 1964, inclusive. Our examination was made in acceptance with generally accepted auditing standards, and accordingly included such tests of the accounting records and such other auditing procedures as we considered necessary in the circumstances.

Based upon each examination, we present herewith the following described Exhibits which, together with our comments, comprise this report:

<u>Exhibit "A"</u> – Balance Sheet, June 30, 1964

<u>Exhibit "B"</u> – Statement of Income and Expenditures for the Period
/August 1, 1963 to June 30, 1964, Inclusive

In our opinion, the accompanying Balance Sheet and Statement of Income and Expenditures present fairly the financial position of the Lawyers' Committee for Civil Rights Under Law as at June 30, 1964, and the results of its operations for the period beginning August 1, 1963 to June 30, 1964, inclusive, in conformity with generally accepted accounting principles applied on a consistent basis.

Respectfully submitted,

FELDMAN AND FELDMAN

LF:ddm   By _Leonard Feldman_
                         Certified Public Accountant

Exhibit "B"

-3-

LAWYERS' COMMITTEE FOR CIVIL RIGHTS UNDER LAW

Statement of Income and Expenditures

For the Period August 1, 1963 to June 30, 1964, Inclusive

	FOR THE PERIOD		
	August 1 to December 31, 1963	January 1 to June 30, 1964	August 1, 1965 to June 30, 1964
Income from Contributions	$37,515,00 1/	$32,795,00 1/	$79,310.00 1/
Expenditures:			
Salary – Executive Director	$ -0-	$ 9,166.74	$9,166.74
Salaries – Staff	-0-	2,977.21	2,977.21
Committee Meeting Expenses	40.99	318.86	359.85
Legal Services	-0-	737.50	737.50
Office Expenses	40.35	209.01	249.36
Organizational Expense	189.41	-0-	189.41
Payroll Taxes	-0-	283.68	283.68
Postage	54.55	409.42	583.97
Stationary and Printing	188.95	2,473.50	2,662.45
Taxes – Other	-0-	1.00	1.00
Telephone and Telegraph	605.45	2,226.02	2.831.47
Travel Expenses	825.72	4,803.23 2/	5,628.95 2/
Total Expenditures	$1,983.42	$23,606.17	25,991.59
Excess of Income over Expenditures	$35,529.58	$9,388.83	$44,718.41

Note 1:   Contributions received prior to the date of incorporation, August 1, 1963, have been included as of that date.

Note 2:   Travel expenses include an air credit deposit in the name of David Stahl on hand with Northwest Airlines, Inc. in the amount of $625.00

Feldman & Feldman

Exhibit "B"

-3-

LAWYERS' COMMITTEE FOR CIVIL RIGHTS UNDER LAW
Statement of Income and Expenditures
For the Year Ended December 31, 1964

Income From Contributions	$49,467.05

Expenditures:

Salary – Executive Director	$18,750.10
Salaries – Staff	8,960.24
Committee Meeting Expenses	1,446.86
Contractual Services	1,802.50
Dues and Subscriptions	25.00
Interest and Expense	21.16
Moving Expenses of Deputy Executive Director	77.64
Office Expenses	898.05
Office Furniture Purchased	260.33 1/
Payroll Taxes	1,047.35
Postage	887.93
Rent	1,525.00
Stationery, Printing and Duplicating	5,346.32
Taxes – Other	1.00
Telephone and Telegraph	5,893.63
Travel Expenses	18,172.13 2/
Total Expenditures	$65,115.24

Excess of (Expenditures) over Income   ($15,648.19)

Note 1: The Lawyers' Committee for Civil Rights Under Law charges as an expense office furniture and equipment when purchased: therefore, no provision for depreciation is included in this Statement of Income and Expenditures.

Note 2: Travel Expenses include an air credit deposit in the name of Lawyers' Committee for Civil Rights Under Law on hand with Northwest Airlines, Inc. in the amount of $425.00.

Travel Expenses also include travel insurance premiums paid in the amount of $508.35 for accident liability and baggage loss for volunteer attorneys during assignment in Mississippi during 1964.

Feldman & Feldman

Exhibit "A"

-2-

LAWYERS' COMMITTEE FOR CIVIL RIGHTS UNDER LAW
Statement of Receipts and Disbursements
For the Year Ended December 31, 1965

	General Fund	Mississippi Project	Total
Contributions Received	$63,984.87	$161,413.45	$225,398.32
Operating Expenses:			
Salary – Executive Director	$20,000.00	-0-	$20,000.00
Other Salaries	16,921.85	22,953.02	39,874.87
Contractual Legal Services	-0-	9,347.00	9,347.00
Dues and Subscriptions	43.95	67.50	111.45
Fund Raising Expense	-0-	7,025.89	7,025.89
Heat, Light and Water	-0-	569.14	569.14
Insurance	231.85	786.00	1,017.85
Meeting Expenses	1,577.14	-0-	1,577.14
Office Expense	2,471.76	10,229.18	12,700.94
Payroll Taxes	1,029.07	373.64	1,402.71
Postage	534.26	679.64	1,213.90
Professional Services	1,250.00	-0-	1,250.00
Rent	5,400.00	1,500.00	6,900.00
Stationery, Printing and Duplicating	3,073.01	327.31	3,400.32
Taxes – Other	1.00	497.73	498.73
Telephone and Telegraph	7,853.46	7,234.71	15,088.17
Travel, Meals and Lodging	5,096.12	39,158.67	44,254.79
Total Operating Expenses	$65,483.47	$100,749.43	$166,232.90
Contributions in Excess /of Operating Expenses	($1,498.60)	$ 60,664.02	$ 59,165.42
Capital Expenditures and Other /Non-Operating Income and Expense 1/			
Books and Legal Periodicals	-0-	$ 6,699.87	$ 6,699.87
Leasehold Improvements	-0-	15,242.40	15,242.40
Office Furniture and Equipment	739.54	5,871.89	6,611.43
Interest Income Earned on Savings Account	-0-	(1,565.15)	(1,565.15)
Net Non-Operating Expenses	$739.54	$26,249.01	$26,988.55
Excess of Contributions to be /Transferred to Reserve Fund	$2,238.14	$34,415.01	$32,176.87

Note 1: For purposes of this Statement, the Committee has expensed all acquisitions of office furniture and equipment, leasehold improvements and books and legal subscriptions in lieu of a periodic depreciation of such costs.

Feldman & Feldman

-2-

LAWYERS' COMMITTEE FOR CIVIL RIGHTS UNDER LAW
Statement of Receipts and Disbursements of Committee Operations
For the Year Ended December 31, 1966

Contributions Received $242.662.15

	Washington Office	Mississippi Project	
Operating Expenses:			
Salary – Executive Director	$15,000.00	$-0-	
Other Salaries	24,603.72	67,446.12	
Contractual Legal Services	-0-	11,596.00	
Court Costs	-0-	8,671.27	
Fund Raising Expense	16,479.82	-0-	
Heat, Light and Water (Mississippi office)	-0-	1,476.33	
Insurance	55.00	2,291.50	
Interest Expense	42.34	-0-	
Meeting Expenses	1,133.99	-0-	
Moving Expenses – Mississippi Employees	-0-	5,289.78	
Office Expense	3,768.23	8,696.57	
Payroll Taxes	1,800.02	2,997.51	
Postage	393.52	851.76	
Professional Services	1,400.00	-0-	
Rent	5,070.00	2,400.00	
Stationery, Printing and Duplicating	3,024.53	1,157.04	
Taxes – Other	1.00	438.06	
Telephone and Telegraph	3,054.19	12,307.07	
Travel, Meals and Lodging	4,356.37	37,171.78	
Total Operating Expenses	$80,182.73	$162,790.79	242,973.52
Operating Expenses in Excess of Contributions			($ 311.37)
Capital Expenditures and Other /Non-Operating Income and Expense 1/			
Books and Legal Periodicals	$ 436.10	$2,944.63	
Office Furniture and Equipment	558.19	640.59	
Interest Income Earned on Savings Account	(1,081.45)	-0-	
Net Non-Operating Expenses	($ 87.16)	$ 3,585.22	3,498.06
Total Operating and Non-Operating /Expenditures in Excess of Contributions			($ 3,809.43)

Add: Committee Cash Contribution to
Police-Community Relations Project 2/   5,000.00

Total Expenditures in Excess of Contributions   (8,809.43)

Note 1: For purposes of this Statement, the Committee has expensed all acquisitions of office
furniture and equipment, leasehold improvements and books and legal subscriptions
in lieu of a periodic depreciation of such costs.

Note 2: In accordance with the terms of a Grant made by the U.S. Department of Justice,
Office of Law Enforcement Assistance, to the Police-Community Relations Project,
the Lawyers' Committee for Civil Rights Under Law is committed to make a cash
contribution to the Police-Community Relations Project totaling $20,000.00 between
the period July 1, 1966 and June 31, 1967. This is in addition to

$\mathcal{F}$*eldman & Feldman*

-3-

LAWYERS' COMMITTEE FOR CIVIL RIGHTS UNDER LAW

Statement of Receipts and Disbursements
for the Police-Community Relations Project

For the Period July 1 to December 31, 1966, Inclusive

Contributions:
U.S. Department of Justice –

Office of Law Enforcement Assistance	$25,030.25
Lawyers' Committee for Civil Rights Under Law	5,000.00 1/
Miscellaneous	50.00
Total Contributions	$30,080.25

Operating Expenses:	
Salary – Director	$5,000.00
Staff Attorneys' Salaries	6,675.90
Secretarial Salaries	5,656.99
Contractual Legal Services	960.00
Employment Agency Fees	541.23
Payroll Taxes	538,31
Postage	13.32
Rent	2,000.00
Stationery, Printing, Duplicating and Other Office Expenses	820.27
Telephone and Telegraph	792.16
Travel, Meals and Lodging	3,467.47
Total Operating Expenses	$26,465.65

Contributions in Excess of Operating Expenses	$3,614.60

Capital Expenditures and Other Non-Operating Expenses:	
Books and Legal Periodicals	$105.70
Office Furniture and Equipment	5,351.29
Total Capital Expenditures and Non-Operating Expenses	5,456.99

Total Expenditures in Excess of Contributions	($1,842.39)

Note 1:   The terms of the contribution from the Lawyers' Committee for Civil Rights Under Law are described in Note 2, Page 2 of this report.

Feldman & Feldman

ACCOUNTANTS AND AUDITORS

Suite 1920, TWO PENN CENTER PLAZA
PHILADELPHIA, PA 19102
561-0900

Members
American Institute of Certified Public Accountants
Pennsylvania Institute of Certified Public Accountants

LEONARD FELDMAN, C.P.A.
WALTER SKALER, C.P.A.
BENJAMIN KANFER, C.P.A.
MARVIN L. HOFFMAN, C.P.A.

February 10, 1969

Officers and Board of Directors
Lawyers' Committee for Civil Rights Under Law
1660 L Street, N.W.
Washington, DC 20036

We have examined the Statement of Assets, Liabilities and Fund Balance of the

LAWYERS' COMMITTEE FOR CIVIL RIGHTS UNDER LAW

(a District of Columbia non-profit corporation) as of December 31, 1968, and the related Statement of Contributions, Income and Expenses for the year then ended. Our examination was made in accordance with generally accepted auditing standards, and accordingly included such tests of the accounting records and such other auditing procedures as we considered necessary in the circumstances.

Based upon such examinations, we present herewith the following described Exhibits which, together with our comments, comprise this report:

Exhibit "A" –   Statement of Assets, Liabilities and Fund Balance
/as of December 31, 1968

Exhibit "B" –   Statement of Contributions, Income and Expenses for the
/year ended December 31, 1968

       Schedule 1 – Analysis of Contributions
       Schedule 2 – Analysis of Police Community Relations
                 Project Operating Expenses
       Schedule 3 – Analysis of District of Columbia Committee
                 On Administration of Justice Under Emergency
                 Conditions (Cutler Committee) Expenses
       Schedule 4 – Analysis of Fund-Raising Expenses

In our opinion, the accompanying Statements of Assets, Liabilities and Fund Balance and Contributions, Income and Expenses present fairly the financial position of the Lawyers' Committee for Civil Rights Under Law as at December 31, 1963, and the result of its operations for the year then ended in conformity with generally accepted accounting principles applied on a basis consistent with that of the preceding year except as described in the notes to the Financial Statement.

Respectfully submitted,

Feldman and Feldman

FELDMAN & FELDMAN
Certified Public Accountants

Exhibit "B"

Feldman & Feldman

-3-

LAWYERS' COMMITTEE FOR CIVIL RIGHTS UNDER LAW
Statement of Contributions, Income and Expenses
For the Year Ended December 31, 1960

Revenue:
Contributions received (Schedule 1) $690,052.00
Interest Income 2,069.41

Total Revenue $692,921.41
City

Operating Expenses:	Washington Headquarters	Urban Areas Mississippi	Total Project	Expenses
Director's Salary	$0	-0-	$17,403.86	$17,403.86
Executive Director Salary	11,916.49	-0-	9,333.19	21,249.68
Other Staff Payroll	29,930.37	$102,478.27	103,263.67	235,672.31
Books and Legal Periodicals	747.06	3,923.69	746.50	5,417.25
Contractual Legal Services	-0-	4,685.80	6,025.30	10,711.10
Court Costs/Litigation Expenses	-0-	10,434.57	-0-	10,434.57
Employee Welfare Benefits	1,350.99	2,042.84	2,850.19	6,244.02
Heat, Light, Power and Water	-0-	1,038.77	-0-	1,038.77
Insurance Expense	512.42	2,284.00	552.08	3,348.50
Interest Expense	-0-	52.32	-0-	52.32
Heating Expense	1,608.25	-0-	1,389.80	2,998.05
Moving Expenses – Employees	-0-	7,263.43	1,336.16	8,599.59
Office Furniture and Equipment 3/	935.36	135.64	7,739.30	8,810.30
Office Expense	5,647.98	12,277.40	6,087.77	24,013.15

Payroll Taxes	1,611.60	5,592.23	3,776.79	10,980.62
Postage	777.84	1,244.86	858.74	2,881.44
Professional Services	3,696.67	3,696.67	2,181.66	9,575.00
Rent	6,556.10	2,400.00	7,964.35	16,920.45
Stationery, Printing and Duplicating	1,398.86	454.88	5,074.77	6,928.51
Taxes – Other	6.00	680.13	-0-	686.13
Telephone and Telegraph	3,855.86	16,037.36	5,076.00	24,969.22
Travel, Meals and Lodging	8,609.21	28,155.92	20,142.27	56,907.40
Total Operating Expenses	$79,161.06	$204,878.78	$201,802.40	$485,342.24
Urban Areas Institute Expense (Net)				3,975.43
Police Community Relations Project Expense (Schedule 2)				56,679.31
District of Columbia Committee for Administration of Justice /Under Emergency Conditions (Cutler Committee) Expense (Schedule 3)				38,277.92
Fund-Raising Expense (Schedule 4)				11,138.75
Legal Aid Assistance				28,564.80
Total Expenses				$624,478.45
Net Contributions and Income in Excess of Expenses Transferred to Fund Balance				$68,442.96

See Notes to the Financial Statements on Page 8.

Feldman & Feldman

-4-

LAWYERS' COMMITTEE FOR CIVIL RIGHTS UNDER LAW

Analysis of Contributions

For the Year Ended December 31, 1968

Foundations:

Ford Foundation	$550,000.00
Field Foundation, Inc.	35,000.00
Twentieth Century Fund, Inc.	25,000.00
New World Foundation	10,000.00
Agnes Meyer Foundation (for D.C. Committee for Administration of Justice Under Emergency Conditions	10,000.00
Overbrook Foundation	5,000.00
Wollenberg Foundation	2,500.00
Various Other Foundations	1,750.00
Total Contributions from Foundations	$639,250.00
Corporations	33,231.00
Lawyers and Law Firms	17,571.00
Total Contributions	$690,052.00

See Notes to the Financial Statements on Page 8.

Feldman & Feldman   -8-

LAWYERS' COMMITTEE FOR CIVIL RIGHTS UNDER LAW

Notes to the Financial Statement

December 31, 1968

Note 1:   This financial statement has been prepared on an accrual basis taking into account all known unpaid expenses at December 31, 1968, upon receipt of written confirmation from suppliers, independent contractors and various vendors. Previous annual statements were prepared on a cash receipts and disbursements basis in conformity with the return filed with the Internal Revenue Service for a tax-exempt organization. Because of the change in financial reporting, it was not practical to compare 1968 operations with those of the preceding year. However, unpaid expenses at December 31, 1967, were determined not to have had a material effect on 1968 operations.

Note 2:   The Committee has valued automobiles at actual cost and/or donated value until their sale or exchange for a replacement vehicle. The inventory of such motor vehicles at December 31, 1968 included:

> 1965 Plymouth Fury Station Wagon
> 1965 Rambler Ambassador Hardtop Sedan
> 1967 Ford Custom Model 500 Sedan
> 1967 Kaiser Jeep Wagoneer
> 1967 Dodge Coronet Station Wagon
> 1968 Plymouth Belvedere Station Wagon

With the exception of the Dodge Station Wagon all of the vehicles were acquired in new condition.

Note 3:   It has been the policy of the Committee to expense all acquisitions of office furniture and equipment in lieu of periodic depreciation of such costs.

Note 4:   The Committee is contractually obligated to pay the project director of the District of Columbia Committee on Administration of Justice Under Emergency Conditions $2,000.00 per month during the period of the project operations. The estimated completion date of the program which began August 1, 1968, is February 28, 1969. This statement includes an unpaid salary to the director at December 31, 1968 in the amount of $10,000.00.

Note 5:   These notes to the financial statement are an integral part of, and are included in, our report dated February 10, 1969.

FELDMAN, SKALER & KANFER

Exhibit "B"
Schedule 1

-4-

LAWYERS' COMMITTEE FOR CIVIL RIGHTS UNDER LAW

Analysis of Contributions

For the Year Ended December 31, 1969

Foundations:

Ford Foundation	$892,500.00
Fund for the City of New York	25,000.00
San Francisco Foundation	10,000.00
The New York Community Trust	10,000.00
New York Foundation	5,000.00
Taconic Foundation	5,000.00
Overbrook Foundation	5,000.00
Wollenberg Foundation	3,000.00
Stern Foundation	3,000.00
Fisher Foundation	1,500.00
Mobil Oil Foundation	1,000.00
Fund for Tomorrow, Inc.	1,000.00
Various Other Foundations	4,550.00
Total Contributions from Foundations	$966,550.00
Lawyers and Law Firms	103,408.23
Corporations	39,656.70

Special Projects   -   United Methodist Church
(For Cairo, Illinois Project) $8,479.77
                    -   New York Urban Coalition
(for New York City Urban Areas
Project)   3,400.00
                                                                        11,879.77

Reimbursement of December 1968 Conference Costs
    From Urban Coalition   3,725.33

Grant from Department of Justice, Law Enforcement
    Association Administration   5,000.00

Miscellaneous Contributions   695.00

Total Contributions $1,130,915.03

See Notes to the Financial Statements on Page 8.

FELDMAN, SKALER & KANFER

Exhibit "B"
Schedule 2

- 5 -

LAWYERS' COMMITTEE FOR CIVIL RIGHTS UNDER LAW

Analysis of Legal Aid Assistance Expenditures

For the Year Ended December 31, 1969

International Defense Fund (South Africa Project)	$24,262.62
Lawyers' Constitutional Defense Committee (Contributions toward Litigation Expenses)	8,000.00
Selma, Alabama, Inter-Religious Project	5,000.00
Total	$37,262.62

See Notes to the Financial Statements on Page 8.

FELDMAN, SKALER & KANFER

-3-

LAWYERS' COMMITTEE FOR CIVIL RIGHTS UNDER LAW

STATEMENT OF RECEIPTS AND EXPENDITURES

(Cash Basis)

FOR THE YEAR ENDED DECEMBER 31, 1970

RECEIPTS:
  PRIVATE GRANTS AND CONTRIBUTIONS:

Ford Foundation	$1,032,500.00
Other Foundations	184,192.50
Lawyers and Law Firms	135,940.00
Corporate	700.00
Individuals	393.50
National Urban Coalition	33,000.00
Churches	29,850.00
Potomac Institute	20,000.00
North Philadelphia Tenants' Union	10,593.74
Miscellaneous	17,332.94
	$1,464,502.68

PUBLIC GRANTS:

Office of Economic Opportunity	114,000.00

INTEREST EARNED	11,778.77
Total Receipts	$1,590,281.45

EXPENDITURES:
  OPERATING EXPENSES:

Salaries and miscellaneous services	$ 752,043.75
Employee Benefits	56,793.12
Travel and meetings	80,180.42
Office operations	237,126.87
General and administrative	27,269.65
Grants and legal services	181,841.57
	$1,335,255.38
LOSS ON SALE OF SECURITIES	1,854.06

Total Expenditures	1,337,109.44
EXCESS OF RECEIPTS OVER EXPENDITURES	$ 253,172.01

FELDMAN, SKALER & KANFER
-2-

<u>LAWYERS' COMMITTEE FOR CIVIL RIGHTS UNDER LAW</u>

STATEMENT OF ASSETS, LIABILITIES AND FUND BALANCE

(Cash Basis)

DECEMBER 31, 1970

ASSETS

Cash	$244,169.45
Temporary cash investments	148,600.11
Marketable securities, at donated value which approximates market	5,050.00
Advances to employees for travel, etc.	1,644.80
Loan receivable – Fred Allen	1,350.00
Deferred rent charges	6,042.50
Deposits for security	925.00
Automobiles at cost or donated value (Note 2)	13,353.69
TOTAL ASSETS	$421,135.55

LIABILITIES AND FUND BALANCE

LIABILITIES:

Payroll taxes withheld	$3,566.12

FUND BALANCE:

Contributed Reserve, January 1	$164,397.42	
Add: Excess of receipts over expenditures (Page 3)	253,172.01	
Fund Balance, December 31		417,569.43
TOTAL LIABILITIES AND FUND BALANCE		$ 421,135.55

See Notes to Financial Statements on Page 4.

PROJECT ANALYSIS OF RECEIPTS AND EXPEND:

(Cash Basis)

FOR THE YEAR ENDED DECEMBER 31, 1970

	Washington Headquarters	National Projects Unit	Jackson Mississippi	Cairo Illinois	Urban Areas City Projects	New York Educational Project	Legal Assistance Funds	OEO Southern Ill. Research & Demonstration Project	OEO Urban Areas Research & Demonstration Project
RECEIPTS:									
Contributions Received:									
Unrestricted General Purposes	$ 35,903.00		$ 40.00						$ 36,023.00
Ford Foundation Urban Areas Project Grant	225,000.00				$400,000.00		$225,000.00		650,000.00
Ford Foundation Mississippi Project Grant			175,000.00				7,500.00		132,500.00
Local Matching Urban Area Project Contributions					192,018.44	137,500.00		$65,000.00*	192,018.44
Restricted Special Projects	200,000.00	$113,230.00		$18,559.00	11,193.74		12,487.50	165,000.00	317,961.24
Total Contributions	460,903.00	113,230.00	175,040.00	18,559.00	603,212.18	137,500.00	244,987.50	165,000.00	1,578,502.63
Interest Income									11,728.77
Total Receipts									1,590,231.55
EXPENDITURES:									
Salaries:									
Administration	$ 99,035.94	$ 47,258.11	$ 86,604.21	$10,283.97	$259,555.38	$ 7,832.03	$ 2,875.00	$15,282.19	$ 9,708.23
Legal Staff	22,837.28	13,907.51	32,234.26	2,662.00	77,168.06	1,130.00		5,329.59	
Office	25,030.35		2,002.25	200.00	29,819.18				
Miscellaneous Contractual Services	1,288.00								
Total	143,191.57	61,065.62	120,840.72	13,245.94	366,542.82	8,962.03	2,875.00	20,611.78	9,708.23
Employee Benefits:									
Employee Welfare	$ 2,172.68	$ 1,566.89	$ 2,961.84	$ 332.17	$11,664.09	$ 213.37	$ 118.53	$ 473.65	$ 121.89
Payroll Taxes	2,215.01	2,335.01	3,341.17	339.95	11,411.27	380.59	4.72	572.93	480.59
Moving Expense	4,465.00		840.91	232.25	29,819.18				
Total	14,363.22	6,138.92	9,143.92	1,374.67	23,404.14	594.46	123.25	1,046.58	602.48
Travel and Meetings:									
Transportation	$ 16,628.24	$ 15,840.67	$ 2,667.33	$ 1,041.46	$ 6,671.38	$ 181.00	$ 908.16	$ 1,069.45	
Meals and Lodging	7,603.01	5,303.75	1,554.35	320.14	3,387.36	196.50	577.41	48.64	
Volunteers' Lodging Expense			4,153.86						
Meetings					1,073.94	240.04			
Auto Costs and Maintenance	4,254.44	1,085.00							
Total	28,485.69	22,229.42	13,749.83	11,361.60	11,132.68	617.54	1,485.57	1,118.02	50,180.42
Office Operations:									
Office Furniture and Equipment Purchases	$ 1,959.07	$ 2,028.91	$ 1,852.85	$ 191.13	$ 4,322.81	$ 211.03	$ 2.50	$ 89.83	
Books and Legal Periodicals	1,995.19	1,236.99	5,438.32	1,048.38	1,634.25	1,663.36	14.35	227.75	
Stationery and Office Supplies	8,592.59	3,202.36	6,698.49	1,371.35	21,272.77	897.89		339.50	
Printing			104.49	1,327.09	2,846.30				
Duplication		1,769.43	1,039.33	760.09	10,874.92	330.14		955.78	
Postage		1,633.84		916.89	18,870.37	512.02	7.60	1,154.02	
Telephone and Telegraph		2,677.23	13,028.55		29,749.30	1,276.97	33.80	397.20	
Rent and Occupancy	12,766.52	6,666.97	4,002.04						
Total								3,298.81	237,126.37
General and Administrative:									
Professional Services	$ 22,126.77		$ 523.99	$ 42.48	45.72	4.79			
Taxes - Other		326.76	2,846.61		674.36				
Insurance	579.00								
Interest	99.17								
Total	22,804.94	326.76	3,370.60	42.48	720.08	4.79			27,269.65
Grants and Legal Services:									
Court Costs and Litigation	$ 2,518.90	$ 75.00	$ 15,323.07	$ 449.04	$ 2,247.37		$ 500.00	$ 284.70	
Contractual Legal Services		6,315.00	8,330.00	800.00	23,656.00		4,500.00		
Sub-Grants (Cleveland)									131,716.57
Total	2,518.90	6,390.00	24,253.07	1,249.04	25,903.37	341,017.41	5,000.00	284.70	
Sub-Grant: Erosion Grant Project									50,000.00
Miscellaneous ("Reprint")									125.00
Loss on Sale of Securities	1,854.06								1,854.06
Total Expenditures	302,495.32	125,193.71	211,020.72	23,292.03	521,640.79	359,611.64	9,347.07	226,559.94	1,431,102.44
EXCESS OF RECEIPTS OVER EXPENDITURES								110,310.71	235,172.01

*Note: The Southern Illinois Research and Demonstration Grant Project has been funded by the following grants: $54,000.00 from OEO and $11,000.00 non-federal. See Notes to Financial Statements on Page 4.

FELDMAN, SKALER & KANFER

- 2 -

LAWYERS' COMMITTEE FOR CIVIL RIGHTS UNDER LAW

STATEMENT OF CHANGES IN FUND BALANCES

(Modified Cash Basis)

DECEMBER 31, 1971

	Ford Fdn.Grant 670-00-204 (General Purpose)	Ford Fdn.Grant 570-00201 (Indochina)	Ford Fdn.Grant 670-0017A1 (Legal Services)	Ford Fdn.Grant 730-0001 (Boston Grant)	Other Legal Assis. (South Africa) Project Grant	CCU Southern Illinois Research & Demon. Grant A	OEO Southern Illinois Research & Demon. Grant B	OEO Urban Areas Research & Demon. Grant	Inquiry Into Incarcer- ation Grant	Equal Employment Oppty. Commission Grant	New York Educat. Project Grant	New York Common. School System Project Grant	New York Crime Control Planning Project Grant	National Project Grants	General Fund Unres- tricted Grants	Total
FUND BALANCE, JANUARY 1	-0-	-0-	215,762	1,27,723	112,994	198,442	-0-	249,682	-0-	-0-	122,728	-0-	-0-	149,423	1122,472	2,411,882
RECEIPTS:																
Ford Foundation	213,390		213,633	10,791	16,323	16,339	73,290	40,000	92,747	70,500	28,650	45,000	35,000	110,643	590,813	327,183
Other grants and contributions			370													1,116,342
Legal fees received from court awards, etc. in employment discrimination cases			36,500													
Interest															8,101	26,390
Net gain on sale of securities															318	8,101
Total	213,376	-0-	250,033	49,791	36,923	64,339	73,200	40,000	92,747	70,500	23,650	45,000	35,000	110,643	309,347	1,478,153
EXPENDITURES (Note 4):																
Salaries and other services	114,345		127,365	92,239												
Employee benefits	9,336		10,335	7,635												
Travel and meetings	16,391		12,348	11,355												
Office operations	30,175	34	43,736	23,359												
General and administrative	14,151	616	2,103	210												
Grants and legal services		3,500	96,150	20,233												
Allocated administrative expenses	(69,619)	1,122														
Total	121,301	5,373	296,047	164,230	33,552	73,811	33,154	30,742	55,004	46,263	33,492	3,095	11,457	176,312	420,291	1,271,406
EXCESS OF RECEIPTS (EXPENDITURES)	(39,533)	(15,383)	(11,398)	(120,529)	6,353	(37,621)	34,046	(742)	37,661	23,737	(23,753)	36,903	22,543	(63,844)	80,761	(92,252)
Transfer of Excess Expenditures Over Receipt to General Fund	39,533	13,414	---	22,774	---	---	---	---	---	---	---	---	---	14,121	(112,043)	
FUND BALANCE, DECEMBER 31	-0-	1 -0-	4,1,363	0 -0-	124,264	111,418	254,034	349,242	212,461	121,232	23,034	184,001	323,351	2 -0-	121,332	2,121,312

General Fund Unrestricted Grants include various local urban project not specifically designated.

See Notes to Financial Statement on Page 3.

FELDMAN, SKALER & KANFER

-4-

<u>LAWYERS' COMMITTEE FOR CIVIL RIGHTS UNDER LAW</u>
Notes to Financial Statements
(Modified Cash Basis)
December 31, 1971

---

1. These financial statements have been prepared on modified cash receipts and disbursements basis in accordance with the method of record-keeping employed by the Committee and in conformity with its tax return with the Internal Revenue Service.

2. The Committee has valued automobiles at actual cost or donated value until their sale or exchange for a replacement vehicle. The inventory of such vehicles at December 31, 1971, consisted of:

   > 1967 Dodge Coronet Station Wagon
   > 1969 Ford Custom Sedan
   > 1970 Ford Custom Sedan
   > 1970 For Custom Sedan

   With the exception of the Dodge Station Wagon, the vehicles were acquired in new condition.

3. It has been the policy of the Committee to expense all acquisitions of office furniture and equipment in lieu of providing for periodic depreciation of such costs.

4. The Southern Illinois Research and Demonstration Project A for the period July 22, 1970-1 was funded by the following grants: $90,000 from OEO, of which $54,000 was received in 1970 and $36,000 in 1971. During the grant period the Project expended $100,371, leaving an unexpended fund balance of $1,179.

5. The Southern Illinois Research and Demonstration Grant B for the period July 22, 1971-72 has been funded by an OEO grant in the amount of $99,000, of which $79,000 has been received to date; an anticipated amount of $10,265 from non-federal sources is to be received before the expiration of the grant.

6. The Urban Areas Research and Demonstration Project, which began September 11, 1970, has been extended to July 31, 1972, and has been funded by a $100,000 grant from the OEO, of which $60,000 was received in 1970 and $40,000 in 1971. Expenditures to date on this project total $51,053.

7. A grant of $141,000 has been awarded by the Equal Opportunity Employment Commission for the period July 1, 1971-72; of this amount, $70,500 was received in 1971.

8. A grant of $149,034 has been awarded by the New York State Office of Crime Control Planning for the period October 15, 1971-72; of this amount $35,000 was received in 1971.

9, The comments expressed in the Accountants' Report on Page 1 are an integral part of these notes and the accompanying financial statements and supplementary information.

FELDMAN, SKALER & KANFER

-3-

LAWYERS' COMMITTEE FOR CIVIL RIGHTS UNDER LAW

STATEMENT OF RECEIPTS AND EXPENDITURES

(Modified Cash Basis)

FOR THE YEAR ENDED DECEMBER 31, 1971

RECEIPTS:
  Grants and contributions (Page 5):

Private	$1,137,284	
Public	306,941	
		$1,444,225
Legal fees received from court awards, etc. in employment discrimination cases		26,500
Interest		8,101
Net gain on sale of securities		328
Total Receipts		1,479,154

EXPENDITURES:
Operating Expenditures:

Salaries and miscellaneous services	922,943	
Employee benefits	76,153	
Travel and meetings	83,884	
Office operations	281,868	
General and administrative	18,265	
Grant and legal services	187,822	
	1,570,935	
Federal excise tax paid on 1970 Investment income	471	
Total Expenditures		1,571,406
EXPENDITURES IN EXCESS OF RECEIPTS		($ 92,252)

See Notes to Financial Statements on Page 4.

FELDMAN, SKALER & KANFER

-5-

LAWYERS' COMMITTEE FOR CIVIL RIGHTS UNDER LAW

SUPPLEMENTARY INFORMATION

GRANTS AND CONTRIBUTIONS

(Modified Cash Basis)

FOR THE YEAR ENDED DECEMBER 31, 1971

PRIVATE GRANTS AND CONTRIBUTIONS:
Foundations:

Ford Foundation	$327,383	
Field Foundation	137,504	
The New World Foundation	40,000	
Carnegie Foundation	25,000	
Milbank Foundation	20,000	
Corporate and other foundations	196,185	
		$746,072

Others:

Lawyers and law firms	255,519	
Corporations	30,067	
Individuals	5,358	
National Urban Coalition	32,118	
Churches	11,000	
Schools and universities	15,015	
North Philadelphia Tenants' Union	15,765	
Miscellaneous	26,370	
		391,212
		1,137,284

PUBLIC GRANTS AND CONTRIBUTIONS:

Office of Economic Opportunity	155,200	
Equal Employment Opportunity Commission	70,500	
New York State Office of Crime Control Planning	35,000	
Narcotic Treatment Agency	19,200	
United Nations Trust Fund for South Africa	15,000	
Commonwealth of Massachusetts	7,441	
City of Boston	4,600	
		306,941

TOTAL GRANTS AND CONTRIBUTIONS $1,444,225

FELDMAN, SKALER & KANFER

LAWYERS' COMMITTEE FOR CIVIL RIGHTS UNDER LAW

SUPPLEMENTARY INFORMATION

PROJECT ANALYSIS OF RECEIPTS AND EXPENDITURES (Modified Cash Basis)

FOR THE YEAR ENDED DECEMBER 31, 1971

	General Support Staff	National Projects Unit	Jackson Miss. Operations	Urban Areas City Projects	New York Educational Project	Legal Assistance Funds	OEO Southern, Ill. Research and Demonstration Project A(c)	OEO Southern, Ill. Research and Demonstration Project B(c)	OEO Urban Areas Research and Demonstration Project (6)	Inquiry into Incarceration Project	Equal Employment Opportunity Commission Project(7)	New York Community Sch.System Project	New York City Control Planning Project(8)	Total
RECEIPTS:														
Grants & Contributions Received:														
Unrestricted General Purposes	$ 74,130		$ 390	$375,826										$ 459,346
Ford Foundation Htls. Grant	113,750		213,633											327,383
Restricted Special Projects		$151,169		50,857	$20,650	$36,823	$36,550	$79,200	$50,000	$92,747	$70,500	$45,000	$35,000	666,496
Total Grants and Contributions	187,880	151,169	214,023	426,683	28,650	36,823	36,550	79,200	40,000	92,747	70,500	45,000	35,000	1,464,225
Legal fees received from court awards, etc. in employment discrimination cases														26,500
Interest	8,101		26,500											8,101
Net gain on sale of securities	228													228
Total Receipts	196,209	151,169	240,523	426,683	28,650	36,823	36,550	79,200	40,000	92,747	70,500	45,000	35,000	1,499,154
EXPENDITURES:														
Salaries & Misc. Services:														
Legal and professional	84,937	107,208	90,494	236,957	7,583		26,175	19,294	35,944	18,823	7,936	2,217	5,417	
Office	27,613	28,342	10,324	62,734	11,777		7,775	7,546		5,296	10,651	109	1,950	
Miscellaneous services	1,769	28,178	6,551	15,434	3,256		1,996	3,282		3,282			225	
Total	114,319	167,728	107,369	315,145	22,616		35,946	30,122	35,944	25,199	18,587	2,326	7,642	922,943
Employee Benefits:														
Employee welfare	5,051	6,433	5,686	15,210	895		1,772	998	1,712	980	659	78	262	
Payroll taxes	3,474	4,768	4,211	12,440	1,279		1,816	588	1,792	923	894	115	85	
Moving Expense	601	560	938				1,812							
Total	9,126	11,761	10,835	27,650	2,174		5,521	1,586	3,504	1,903	1,553	193	347	76,153
Travel and Meetings:														
Transportation	10,204	19,392	2,934	4,607	152	1,066	4,070	1,860	918	3,513	320	5	122	
Meals and lodging	4,072	5,134	1,237	2,062	24	6	773	465	243	2,823	66		77	
Auto costs and maintenance	2,575	4,371		284		137	159							
Total	16,851	28,897	4,171	8,953	176	1,209	5,992	2,325	1,161	6,336	386	5	199	83,804
Office Operations:														
Office furniture & equipment	399	1,142	2,444	3,796	79		1,223	571		674	130		60	
Books & Legal periodicals	9,637	2,361	4,191	2,099	144	278	1,131	1,347		42	182		277	
Stationery & office supplies	12,174	11,753	9,417	20,678	1,014	342	2,298	58	44	272	67	94		
Printing	9,971	5,665	3,374	8,372	920		106			26				
Duplication	3,815	4,433	10,246	12,749	381		2,075	1,086		680		24		
Postage	1,997	2,067	4,861	4,952	1,110	36		260		255		30		
Telephone and telegraph	12,407	12,410	13,078	4,952	1,114		741	1,611		1,128		384		
Rent and occupancy	115	10,560	4,435	24,707			662	522	44	2,227		651		
Total	58,475	50,591	48,736	92,734	3,782	656	9,894	5,486	44	5,314		1,436		281,869
General and Administrative:														
Professional services	13,537													
Taxes, other than payroll				38										
Insurance	605	405	2,405	806	62		62	161	89	86	1,030	4,667	20	
Interest	9			844										
Total	14,151	405	2,405	844	62		62	161	89	86	3,478	4,667	20	19,545
Grants and Legal Services:														
Court costs & litigation		279	23,092	2,509	23,532	1,313	663	42	85	85	5,623	3,667	2,881	
Subcontract legal services					32,943	703		42	82	82				
Subcontracts							1,572			12,656				
Total		279	23,092	2,509	23,532	34,276	2,108	763		12,656	5,623	4,667	2,881	187,822
Allocated Adminis. Expenses				14,916				4,711		12,456		392		
Total Operating Expenditures	171,303	272,321	256,087	491,049	52,402	23,462	23,312	45,154	40,742	55,064	84,163	9,495	33,452	1,570,935
FEDERAL EXCISE TAX PAID ON 1970 INVESTMENT INCOME														441
Total Expenditures														1,571,376
EXPENDITURES IN EXCESS OF RECEIPTS	(12,619)													$ 92,222

FELDMAN, SKALER & KANFER

-3-

<u>LAWYERS' COMMITTEE FOR CIVIL RIGHTS UNDER LAW</u>

STATEMENT OF RECEIPTS AND EXPENDITURES

(Modified Cash Basis)

| | YEAR ENDED DECEMBER 31, | |
	1971	1972
RECEIPTS:		
Grants and contributions (Page 5):		
Private	$1,559,052	$1,137,284
Public	204,904	306,941
	1,763,956	1,444,225
Legal fees received from court awards,		
etc. in employment discrimination cases	15,000	26,500
Interest	6,124	8,101
Net gain or (loss) on sale of securities	(207)	328
Total Receipts	1,784,873	1,479,154
EXPENDITURES:		
Operating Expenditures:		
Salaries and miscellaneous services	1,082,544	922,943
Employee benefits	89,006	76,153
Travel and meetings	86,707	83,884
Office operations (Note 3)	296,715	281,868
General and administrative	30,745	18,265
Grants and legal services	218,676	187,822
	1,804,393	1,570,935
Federal excise tax paid on 1970		
investment income (Note 4)		471
Total Expenditures	1,804,393	1,571,406
EXPENDITURES IN EXCESS OF RECEIPTS	($ 19,520)	($ 92,252)

See Notes to Financial Statements on Page 4.

FELDMAN, SKALER & KANFER

-4-

<u>LAWYERS' COMMITTEE FOR CIVIL RIGHTS UNDER LAW</u>

NOTES TO FINANCIAL STATEMENTS

(Modified Cash Basis)

DECEMBER 31, 1972

---

1. The accompanying financial statements have been prepared on a modified cash receipts and disbursements in accordance with the method of record-keeping employed by the Committee and in conformity with its tax return filed with the Internal Revenue Service.

2. The Committee has valued automobiles at actual cost or donated value until their sale or exchange for a replacement vehicle. The inventory of such vehicles at December 31, 1972, consisted of:

    > 1969 Ford Custom Sedan
    > 1970 Ford Custom Sedan

3. It is the policy of the Committee to expense all acquisitions of office furniture and equipment in lieu of providing for periodic depreciation of such costs.

4. On September 27, 1972, the Lawyers' Committee for Civil Rights Under Law was notified by the Internal Revenue Service that it is not a private foundation because it is an organization described in Section 509(a)(1) of the Internal Revenue Code. In the opinion of counsel the Committee was not liable for payment of the federal excise tax imposed on private foundations for either calendar years 1971 or 1972.

5. The Committee has various leases for office space effective through 1975, which leases provide for payments of approximately $51,000 during 1973. Also in effect are leases with month-to-month terms, which if renewed through 193, will require another $20,580 in payments.

    Total payments for space rentals during 1972 amounted to $70,575.

6. Administrative expenses paid by the General Support Staff in the amount of $61,080 and various local offices in the amount of $14,133 were allocated to the following projects during the year:

National Projects	$21,965
Inquiry Into Incarceration	7,000
Equal Employment Opportunity Commission	24,633
New York Community School System	3,500
New York Crime Control Planning	10,726
School Finance (National Urban Coalition portion)	1,500
OEO Southern Illinois Research and Demonstration Grant	5,889
	$ 75,213

FELDMAN, SKALER & KANFER
-5-

LAWYERS' COMMITTEE FOR CIVIL RIGHTS UNDER LAW
SUPPLEMENTARY INFORMATION
GRANTS AND CONTRIBUTIONS
(Modified Cash Basis)

	YEAR ENDED DECEMBER 31,	
	1972	1971
PRIVATE GRANTS AND CONTRIBUTIONS:		
Foundations:		
Ford Foundation	$ 392,823	$ 327,383
The Field Foundation	129,100	137,504
Carnegie Corporation of New York	128,290	25,000
Rockefeller Brothers Fund, Inc.	112,100	13,250
The New World Foundation	90,000	40,000
Josephine E. McIntosh Foundation	66,500	
Milbank Memorial Fund	25,000	20,000
Eugene and Agnes E. Meyer Foundation	24,500	10,000
The Rockefeller Foundation	15,000	
Charles E. Merrill Trust	15,000	
Harry J. Loose Foundation	15,000	
Other	71,600	172,935
	1,084,913	746,072
Others:		
Lawyers and law firms	269,949	255,519
Corporations	55,152	30,067
Individuals	1,747	5,358
National Urban Coalition	35,232	32,118
The Potomac Institute	20,000	
Churches	48,860	11,000
Schools and universities	13,909	15,015
North Philadelphia Tenants' Union	15,765	
Miscellaneous	29,290	26,370
	474,139	391,212
Total Private Grants and Contributions	1,559,052	1,137,284
PUBLIC GRANTS AND CONTRIBUTIONS:		
Equal Employment Opportunity Commission	102,500	70,500
Office of Economic Opportunity	19,800	155,200
New York State Office of Crime Control		
Planning	53,429	35,000
Narcotic Treatment Agency	9,600	19,200
United Nations Trust Fund for South Africa	15,000	
Commonwealth of Massachusetts	17,500	7,441
City of Boston	2,000	4,600
City of Philadelphia	75	
Total Public Grants and Contributions	204,904	306,941
TOTAL GRANTS AND CONTRIBUTIONS	$1,763,956	$1,444,225

FELDMAN, SKALER & KANFER

-2-

LAWYERS' COMMITTEE FOR CIVIL RIGHTS UNDER LAW

STATEMENT OF ASSETS, LIABILITIES AND FUND BALANCES

ASSETS

	DECEMBER 31,	
	1973	1972*
Cash and U.S. Treasury bills	$489,078	$304,899
Grants and contracts receivable (Page 9)	133,797	101,342
Loan receivable	-	1,350
Travel advances to employees	640	785
Prepaid expenses and deposits	5,081	1,717
Automobiles at cost or donated value (Note 2)	5,666	5,666
	$634,262	$415,759

LIABILITIES AND FUND BALANCES

LIABILITIES:		
Accounts payable and accrued liabilities	$27,288	$35,838
Payroll taxes withheld	5,766	7,506
Grants and contracts deferred (Page 9)	270,457	265,037
Total Liabilities	303,511	308,381
FUND BALANCES (Page 3)	330,751	107,378
	$634,262	$415,759

*Restated (Note 1)

The accompanying notes are an integral part of these financial statements.

FELDMAN, SKALER & KANFER

-3-

<u>LAWYERS' COMMITTEE FOR CIVIL RIGHTS UNDER LAW</u>

STATEMENT OF REVENUES AND EXPENDITURES AND CHANGES
IN FUND BALANCES

| | YEAR ENDED DECEMBER 31, | |
	1973	1972*
REVENUES		
Grants and contributions (Page 5):		
Private	$1,700,795	$1,294,015
Public	371,680	306,247
	2,072,475	1,600,262
Legal fees received from court awards,		
etc. in employment discrimination cases	5,950	15,000
Interest and investment income	16,151	6,124
Net (loss) on sale of securities	(123)	(208)
Total Revenues	2,094,453	1,621,178
EXPENDITURES:		
Operating Expenditures:		
Salaries and miscellaneous services	1,112,418	1,083,157
Employee benefits	111,858	90,464
Travel and meetings	103,043	91,346
Office operations (Note 3)	329,653	319,049
General and administrative	17,353	31,331
Grant and legal services	196,755	223,770
Total Expenditures	1,871,080	1,839,117
REVENUES OVER (UNDER) EXPENDITURES	223,373	(217,939)
FUND BALANCES, BEGINNING OF YEAR	107,378	325,317
FUND BALANCES, END OF YEAR	$ 330,751	$ 107,378

*Restated (Note 1)

The accompanying notes are an integral part of these financial statements.

FELDMAN, SKALER & KANFER
-4-
LAWYERS' COMMITTEE FOR CIVIL RIGHTS UNDER LAW
NOTES TO FINANCIAL STATEMENTS
DECEMBER 31, 1973

1. The accompanying financial statements have been prepared on an accrual basis in accordance with the record-keeping method adopted in 1973. Accordingly, the financial information shown for 1972 has been restated from a modified cash basis to the accrual basis for comparative purposes.

2. Automobiles are valued at actual cost or donated value until their sale or exchange for a replacement vehicle. The inventory of such vehicles at December 31, 1973, consisted of:

    1969 Ford Custom Sedan
    1970 Ford Custom Sedan

3. In conformity with the practice followed by certain other non-profit organizations, the Committee has adopted the policy of expensing additions to furniture and fixtures and office equipment.

4. The Lawyers' Committee for Civil Rights Under Law is exempt from federal income tax under the provisions of Section 501(c)(3) of the Internal Revenue Code. In addition, the Lawyers' Committee has been notified that it is not a private foundation within the meaning of the Code because it is an organization described in Section 509(a)(1). Accordingly, in the opinion of foundations for either of the years 1972 or 1973.

5. The Committee has various leases for office space effective through August, 1976, which provide for payments of approximately $39,454 during 1974. Also in effect are leases with month-to-month terms, which, if renewed through 1974, will require additional payments of $26,680. Total payments for occupancy (including utility expenses) amounted to $79,937 and $70,753 in 1972.

6. Administrative expenses paid by the National Headquarters ($103,971 in 1973 and $61,080 in 1972) and by various local offices ($13,311 in 1973 and $14,133 in 1972) were allocated to the following projects:

	1973	1972
Equal Employment Opportunity	$50,969	$24,633
Public Employment	11,125	-
New York Crime Control Planning	-	10,726
Manpower	10,329	10,329
Election Law	10,307	6,046
School Finance (Ford Foundation)	7,065	-
School Finance (Other)	-	1,500
Inquiry into Incarceration	7,000	7,000
National Health and Environmental Law	6,407	-
African Legal Assistance (Ford Foundation)	3,376	-
OEO Southern Illinois Research and Demonstration Grant	-	5,889
Health and National Urban Coalition	2,875	5,590
National Institute of Education State Project	2,355	-
New York Community Schools	2,333	3,500
Revenue Sharing (October 1 to December 31)	1,874	-
Local Urban Areas	1,267	-
	$117,282	$75,213

FELDMAN, SKALER & KANFER

-5-

LAWYERS' COMMITTEE FOR CIVIL RIGHTS UNDER LAW
SUPPLEMENTARY INFORMATION
GRANTS AND CONTRIBUTIONS

	YEAR ENDED DECEMBER 31,	
	1973	1972*
PRIVATE GRANTS AND CONTRIBUTIONS:		
Foundations:		
Ford Foundation	$411,881	$377,573
The Field Foundation	141,237	89,932
Carnegie Corporation of New York	139,122	107,458
Rockefeller Brothers Fund, Inc.	112,096	4,675
Josephine E. McIntosh Foundation	72,710	47,123
The New World Foundation	45,833	83,332
General Services Foundation	30,000	-
The New York Foundation	25,000	5,000
The Rockefeller Foundation	15,000	15,000
Charles E. Merrill Trust	13,751	1,250
Harry J. Loose Foundation	13,750	1,250
Millbank Memorial Fund	-	25,000
Eugene and Agnes E. Meyer Foundation	12,000	24,500
Prospect Hill Foundation, Inc.	10,000	-
George A. and Dolly F. LaRue Trust	9,584	5,000
Edna McConnell Clark Foundation	9,443	-
Van Ameringen Foundation, Inc.	8,333	10,000
Wieboldt Foundation	7,500	-
Morris and Gwendolyn Cafritz Foundation	7,500	10,000
D.J.B. Foundation	6,000	-
Hallmark Educational Foundation	5,000	-
Overbrook Foundation	5,000	-
The Philadelphia Foundation	5,000	-
Kansas City Association of Trusts and Foundations	5,000	2,000
Other	26,750	19,183
	1,137,490	828,276
Others:		
Lawyers and law firms	369,108	269,949
Corporations	97,012	55,152
Schools and universities	78,773	13,909
Individuals	7,666	1,747
National Urban Coalition	5,750	35,232
The Potomac Institute	-	20,000
Churches	400	48,860
Miscellaneous	4,596	20,890
	563,305	465,739
Total Private Grants and Contributions	1,700,795	1,294,015

PUBLIC GRANTS AND CONTRIBUTIONS:

Equal Employment Opportunity Commission	233,560	134,654
Commonwealth of Massachusetts	68,109	34,771
National Institute of Education	36,569	-
City of New York	15,666	-
Narcotic Treatment Agency	12,776	9,600
Law Enforcement Assistance Administration	5,000	-
N.Y. State Office of Planning Services	-	105,347
Office of Economic Opportunity	-	19,800
City of Boston	-	2,000
City of Philadelphia	-	75
Total Public Grants and Contributions	371,680	306,247
TOTAL GRANTS AND CONTRIBUTIONS	$2,072,475	$1,600,262

FELDMAN, SKALER & KANFER

LAWYERS' COMMITTEE FOR CIVIL RIGHTS UNDER LAW

SUPPLEMENTARY INFORMATION

STATEMENT OF REVENUES AND EXPENDITURES AND CHANGES IN FUND BALANCE BY PROJECTS

FOR THE YEAR ENDED DECEMBER 31, 1972

- 6 -

	TOTALS	FORD FOUNDATION SCHOOL FINANCE PROJECT	FORD FOUNDATION AFRICAN PROJECT	NATIONAL HEADQUARTERS	SPECIAL NATIONAL PROJECTS	OTHER PROJECTS	JACKSON, MISSISSIPPI PROJECT	PRISON DEFENSE COMMITTEE, JACKSON	URBAN AREAS CITY PROJECTS	LOCAL ASSISTANCE PROJECTS	EQUAL EMPLOYMENT OPPORTUNITY COORD. PROJECT
REVENUES:											
Grants and Contributions:											
Ford Foundation	$411,881	$162,173	$40,700	$273,780	$5,703	$49,165	$200,000	29,000	$597,313	$20,300	$333,588
Other private contributions	1,280,914						28,840				733,560
Public grants and contributions	311,680					3,992					
Total Grants and Contributions	7,091,635	167,173	40,700	733,780	5,703	79,065	228,840	29,000	640,389	20,700	
Legal fees received from court awards, etc.	5,950	2,947		13,193							5,930
Interest and income on sale of securities	16,151								4		
Net Revenues	(113)			11		6	168				
Total Revenues	7,095,433	165,196	40,700	746,920	5,703	79,071	228,168	29,000	640,385	20,700	738,418
EXPENDITURES:											
Salaries and Miscellaneous Services:											
Legal and professional	735,001	90,840	21,276	78,635	10,896	6,742	79,322	6,250	210,232		64,989
Office	301,680	26,833	11,309	37,642	2,703	8,274	26,403	5,223	34,992		46,651
Miscellaneous services	77,212	611	818	6,011	640	2,808	166	1,488	2,861		113,111
Total	117,893	101,593	35,910	115,180	15,236	36,638	103,193	13,355	181,333		113,131
Employee Benefits:											
Employee welfare	52,431	3,719	1,680	6,113	996	5,031	4,065	607	14,639	1,902	5,715
Payroll taxes	56,247	3,951	1,889	3,466	690	993	2,013	643	17,166	21	7,046
Workmen's expense	1,129		171				166		499		
Total	116,416	7,670	3,206	11,533	1,686	6,126	6,022	1,136	31,645	1,933	13,291
Travel and Meetings:											
Transportation	46,965	9,411	3,127	9,653	752	3,283	4,065	864	6,209		2,867
Health and lodging	24,648	1,472	800	4,592	84	993	2,013	94	1,640		556
Meetings	10,236	943	8	1,992	6,060		166		499		
Total	103,863	12,337	4,095	16,178	7,166	4,126	9,027	1,111	8,378	1,301	3,861
Office Operations:											
Furniture and equipment	16,713	2,790	20	4,365	196	103	27	116	3,237		1,946
Books and legal periodicals	7,135	1,073	410	130	30	(1,316)	3,264	1,071	916		706
Stationery and office supplies	52,605	4,810	3,071	9,978	2,229	160	4,120	43	8,069		1,842
Filing	30,932	922	460	2,335	10,267	443	561	6	2,637		24
Duplication	49,498	9,613	331	3,699	606	307	6,599	167	14,200		186
Postage	17,220	2,174	335	2,339	337	390	1,359	1,175	16,744		251
Telephone and telegraph	75,682	6,010	2,926	10,103	1,797	1,633	8,297		16,744	4	2,543
Rent and occupancy	118,253	15,911	14,913	50,638	1,561	669	6,688	1,111	3,111		113,111
Total	388,033	40,303	21,666	83,587	17,222	1,689	30,713	2,758	68,127	1,111	119,031
General and Administrative:											
Professional services	13,037	699	2	8,600	28	1	2,818	40	60		340
Taxes, other than payroll	181		98	98	3						
Insurance	3,771	588	90	25	530	94	864	56	1,186	10,081	585
Total	17,191	1,051	100	9,150	211	15	1,666	111	211	111	113
Grants and Legal Services:											
Court costs and litigation	19,120	313	1,276	1,676	21,531	407	15,925	1,643	985		3,510
Contractual legal services	135,500	2,300		103,123	(45,612)	20,960	17,589	505	11,170		
Sub grants	21,451		1,570	29,782	590				18,823	718	20,148
Total	176,213	2,613	3,373	138,122	45,481	21,398	33,434	2,148	15,111	113	39,111
Allocated administrative expenses	107,578	30,941	454	(18,340)	15,707		273		39,355	14,596	31,521
Total Operating Expenditures	1,413,686	113,111	111,111	131,111	21,138	11,138	111,111	11,111	113,111	113,118	280,188
REVENUES OVER EXPENDITURES	235,335	(3,065)	434	(113,101)	1,538	13,101	114,111	1,111	13,118	14,118	19,334
FUND BALANCE, BEGINNING OF YEAR											
Transfer of fund balance on closed projects											
FUND BALANCES, END OF YEAR	$138,333	$113,888	($111,688)	$773,638	$0	$173,101	$114,111	$1,011	$14,111	$14,111	$130,743

The accompanying notes are an integral part of these financial statements.

	INQUIRY INTO INCARCERATION PROJECT	NEW YORK CRIME CONTROL PLANNING PROJECT	MASSACHUSETTS PRISONERS' RIGHTS PROJECT	ELECTION LAW PROJECT	REVENUE SHARING PROJECT (10/1-12/31/73)	N.I.E. STATE PROJECT	PUBLIC EMPLOYMENT PROJECT	MANPOWER PROJECT	NATIONAL HEALTH & ENVIRONMENTAL LAW PROJECT
	$110,318	$ 1,350 / 15,666	$ 43,109	$100,411	$ 12,743	$ 26,669	$112,096	$103,320	$ 75,973
		17,016							
	110,318	17,016	43,109	100,411	12,743	26,669	112,096	103,320	75,973
	110,318	17,016	43,109	100,411	12,743	26,669	112,096	103,320	75,973
	33,500	7,853	29,308	35,583	5,750	7,344	36,526	34,175	2,453
	16,833	8,208	14,856	18,072	2,654	3,933	9,513	9,556	1,042
	166	600	1,677	4,198		1,139	206	4,608	
	50,499	16,661	45,841	57,853	8,404	12,416	46,245	48,339	5,495
	2,501	738	2,009	2,890	556	643	2,258	1,906	336
	2,319	1,559	2,932	2,615	88	641	2,087	1,680	169
	4,820	2,297	4,941	5,505	644	1,284	4,345	3,586	505
	3,053	61	782	4,699	310	233	5,020	5,556	5,718
	2,518			2,872	286	2	1,621	2,530	1,354
	(100)								
	5,471	61	782	7,571	596	235	6,641	8,086	7,072
	(69)	(172)	(163)	696	159	9	2,016	1,431	77
	(866)	82	444	(30)	629	254	943	371	267
	20	(14)	1,007	4,168	93	1,321	2,820	2,425	1,256
	2,161	22	(26)	566	170	300	552	2,269	7
	449	25	692	3,113	188	351	1,235	1,825	2,662
	2,045	840	200	1,363	660	433	1,114	851	699
	4,030	1,311	1,956	5,203	473	987	4,204	2,968	2,279
			1,411	1,729		1,072	3,004	2,371	2,413
	9,492	2,024	5,519	18,808	2,372	4,722	15,888	13,769	9,660
	15	112	214	3	2	3	3	1,320	1
				145	(1)	(10)	192	2	4
								288	
	15	112	214	148	1	(7)	195	1,610	5
	16,375		211	765		228	1,045	23	64
			2,059				795	6,250	42,583
			2,355						
			4,625				1,840	6,273	42,647
	16,275	21,205	61,922	10,307	1,874	2,355	11,125	10,329	6,407
	7,000	(4,189)	(18,813)	100,932	13,891	21,238	86,279	91,992	71,791
	93,672	(12,989)	18,988	(546)	(1,148)	5,431	25,817	11,328	4,182
	(16,646)			(23,102)			3,671	14,172	(2,429)
	(4,848)								
	$ 11,738	($12,178)	$ 175	($23,648)	($1,148)	$ 5,431	$ 29,488	$ 25,500	$ 1,253

FELDMAN, SKALER & KANFER

-7-

LAWYERS' COMMITTEE FOR CIVIL RIGHTS UNDER LAW

SUPPLEMENTARY INFORMATION

STATEMENT OF REVENUES AND EXPENDITURES AND CHANGES IN FUND BALANCE

FORD FOUNDATION GRANT 720-0160 AND 720-0160A

SCHOOL FINANCE PROJECT

YEAR ENDED DECEMBER 31, 1973

	GRANT 720-0160 1/1 – 7/31/73	GRANT 720-0160A 8/1 – 12/31/73
REVENUES:		
Ford Foundation Grant	$87,750	$74,423
Investment income	2,105	842
Total Revenues	89,855	75,265
EXPENDITURES:		
Salaries and miscellaneous services	65,012	36,949
Employee benefits	5,318	2,351
Travel and meetings	7,894	4,633
Office operations	24,334	12,963
General and administrative	145	908
Grants and legal services	(117)	2,730
Allocated administrative expense	-	7,065
Total Expenditures	102,586	67,599
REVENUES OVER (UNDER) EXPENDITURES	(12,731)	7,666
FUND BALANCE, JANUARY 1, 1973	30,961*	
FUND BALANCE AT EXPIRATION OF GRANT	18,230	
FUND BALANCE TRANSFERRED TO NEW GRANT	(18,230)	18,230
FUND BALANCE, DECEMBER 31, 1973	$ -0-	$ 25,896

*Restated (Note 1)

The accompanying notes are an integral part of these financial statements.

FELDMAN, SKALER & KANFER

-8-

LAWYERS' COMMITTEE FOR CIVIL RIGHTS UNDER LAW

SUPPLEMENTARY INFORMATION

STATEMENT OF REVENUES AND EXPENDITURES
AND CHANGES IN FUND BALANCE

FORD FOUNDATION GRANT 730-0040 AND 730-0040A

AFRICAN LEGAL ASSISTANCE PROJECT

YEAR ENDED DECEMBER 31, 1973

	GRANT 720-0160 1/1 – 3/31/73	GRANT 720-0160A 4/1 – 12/31/73
REVENUES:		
Ford Foundation Grant	$12,569	$37,139
EXPENDITURES:		
Salaries and miscellaneous services	5,950	26,965
Employee benefits	692	3,017
Travel and meetings	592	3,412
Office operations	6,178	7,295
General and administrative	5	95
Allocated administrative expense	-	3,376
Total Expenditures	13,417	44,160
REVENUES (UNDER) EXPENDITURES	(848)	(7,021)
FUND BALANCE, JANUARY 1, 1973	453*	-
FUND BALANCE AT EXPIRATION OF GRANT	(395)	
FUND BALANCE TRANSFERRED TO NEW GRANT	395	(395)
FUND BALANCE, DECEMBER 31, 1973	$ -0-	($ 7,416)

*Restated (Note 1)

The accompanying notes are an integral part of these financial statements.

- 9 -

LAWYERS' COMMITTEE FOR CIVIL RIGHTS UNDER LAW
SUPPLEMENTARY INFORMATION
GRANTS AND CONTRACTS RECEIVABLE AND DEFERRED

PROJECT	GRANTOR OR CONTRACTOR	TERM	TOTAL GRANT OR CONTRACT	AMOUNT RECEIVABLE DECEMBER 31, 1973	1972
School Finance Grant 720-0160A	Ford Foundation	8/1/73 - 9/30/75	$387,000	$ 67,789	
Equal Employment Opportunity Contract 71-42	E.E.O.C.	9/1/73 - 74	315,700	52,633	
N.I.E. State Contract NE-C-00-3-0044	Department of Health Education & Welfare	6/27/73 - 74	53,337	13,375	
N.Y. Crime Control Planning	State of New York	10/15/71 - 1/15/73	150,910		$ 51,917
Equal Employment Opportunity Contract 71-42	E.E.O.C.	9/1/72 - 73	192,481		32,154
Massachusetts Prisoners' Legal Rights	Commonwealth of Massachusetts	9/1/72 - 5/31/73	61,980		17,271
TOTAL GRANTS AND CONTRACTS RECEIVABLE				$133,797	$101,342

PROJECT	GRANTOR OR CONTRACTOR	TERM	TOTAL GRANT OR CONTRACT	AMOUNT DEFERRED DECEMBER 31, 1973	1972
Public Employment	Rockefeller Brothers Fund, Inc.	12/15/73 - 74	112,100	$107,428	$107,428
National Headquarters	Andrew W. Mellon Foundation	1/1 - 12/31/74	50,000	50,000	
Revenue Sharing	Edna McConnell Clark Foundation	10/1/73 - 74	37,770	28,328	
Election Law	Josephine H. McIntosh Foundation	5/1/73 - 74	80,000	26,667	
Revenue Sharing	Norman Foundation	12/1/73 - 74	15,000	13,750	
National Health & Environmental Law	U.C.L.A.	9/1/73 - 2/28/74	39,710	13,237	
African Legal Assistance Grant 730-0040A	Ford Foundation	4/1/73 - 9/30/74	74,278	12,380	
National Headquarters	Prospect Hill Foundation, Inc.	1973 - 75	25,000	10,000	
Election Law	The New World Foundation	3/1/73 - 74	25,000	4,167	
Jackson, Miss.	Hugh M. Hefner Fund	1/1 - 12/31/74	2,500	2,500	
Jackson, Miss.	United Presbyterian Church	1/1 - 12/31/74	2,000	2,000	
Public Employment	Rockefeller Brothers Fund, Inc.	12/16/72 - 73	112,100		22,500
National Headquarters	The Field Foundation	10/1/72 - 73	30,000		20,832
New York Educational	Carnegie Corp. of New York	11/1/72 - 73	25,000		16,667
Inquiry Into Incarceration	The Field Foundation	10/1/72 - 6/30/73	25,000		19,376
Election Law	Josephine H. McIntosh Foundation	6/1/72 - 73	46,500		15,250
School Finance Grant 720-0160	Ford Foundation	2/1/72 - 7/31/73	225,000		15,250
Kansas City Pre-Trial Diversion	Harry J. Loose Foundation	12/1/72 - 73	15,000		13,750
Washington, D.C. Local	Charles E. Merrill Trust	12/1/72 - 73	15,000		13,750
Massachusetts Prisoners' Legal Rights	Committee of the Permanent Charity Fund, Inc.	9/1/72 - 5/31/73	15,000		8,400
New York Educational	Van Ameringen Foundation, Inc.	11/1/72 - 73	15,000		8,333
Washington, D.C. Local	Morris & Gwendolyn Cafritz Foundation	10/1/72 - 73	10,000		7,500
Election Law	The New World Foundation	3/1/72 - 73	40,000		6,668
Kansas City Pre-Trial Diversion	George A. & Dolly F. LaRue Trust	12/1/72 - 73	5,000		4,583
TOTAL GRANTS AND CONTRACTS DEFERRED				$270,457	$265,027

The accompanying notes are an integral part of these financial statements.

FELDMAN, SKALER & KANFER

-3-

<u>LAWYERS' COMMITTEE FOR CIVIL RIGHTS UNDER LAW</u>

STATEMENT OF REVENUES AND EXPENDITURES AND CHANGES
IN FUND BALANCES

| | YEAR ENDED DECEMBER 31, | |
	1974	1973
REVENUES		
Grants and contributions (Page 5):		
Private	$1,363,862	$1,700,795
Public	353,138	371,680
	1,717,000	2,072,475
Legal fees received from court awards	25,924	5,950
Reimbursement from publications	3,916	-
Interest and investment income	27,498	16,151
Net (loss) on sale of securities	(159)	(123)
Total Revenues	1,774,179	2,094,453
EXPENDITURES:		
Operating Expenditures:		
Salaries and miscellaneous services	1,035,039	1,112,418
Employee benefits	113,805	111,858
Travel and meetings	292,456	329,653
Office operations (Note 2)	91,754	103,043
General and administrative	33,620	17,353
Grants and legal services	162,753	196,755
Total Expenditures	1,729,427	1,871,080
REVENUES OVER (UNDER) EXPENDITURES	44,752	223,373
FUND BALANCES, BEGINNING OF YEAR	330,751	107,378
REIMBURSEMENT OF PRIOR YEARS' FEDERAL EXCISE TAX (Note 3)	471	-
FUND BALANCES, END OF YEAR	$375,974	$330,751

The accompanying notes are an integral part of these financial statements.

FELDMAN, SKALER & KANFER

-4-

LAWYERS' COMMITTEE FOR CIVIL RIGHTS UNDER LAW

NOTES TO FINANCIAL STATEMENTS

DECEMBER 31, 1974

1. Assets and Liabilities and Revenues and Expenditures are recognized on the accrual basis of accounting.

2, The Lawyers' Committee for Civil Rights Under Law changed its method of accounting for fixed assets effective January 1, 1974. In prior years furniture and equipment had been expensed at the time of purchase and automobiles were capitalized at their cost or donated values until replaced or sold, at which time they were expensed. Effective in the current year, furniture and equipment additions have been capitalized and are being depreciated over a ten-year period on the straight line method. Automobiles are also being depreciated on a straight line method over the estimated life of each vehicle. The cumulative effect to the Fund Balance at January 1, 1974 would not be material and therefore it has not been given effect to in the financial statements.

3. The Lawyers' Committee for Civil Rights Under Law is exempt from federal income tax under the provisions of Section 501(c)(3) of the Internal Revenue Code. In addition, the Lawyers' Committee has been notified that it is not a private foundation within the meaning of the Code because it is an organization described in Section 509(a)(1). The federal excise tax paid for 1971 pending the determination of the Lawyers' Committee status was refunded in 1974.

4, The Committee has various leases for office space effective through November 1976, which provide for payments of approximately $54,705 during 1975. Also in effect are leases with month-to-month terms, which, if renewed through 1975, will require additional payments of $8,074. Total payments for occupancy (including utility expenses) amounted to $79,038 in 1974 and $79,937 in 1973.

5. Administrative expenses paid by the National Headquarters ($73,480 in 1974 and $103,971 in 1973) and by various local offices ($11,600 in 1974 and $13, 311 in 1973) were allocated to the following projects:

	1974	1973
Equal Employment Opportunity	$36,099	$50,969
School Finance (Ford Foundation)	17,211	7,065
Public Employment	9,723	11,125
Inquiry into Incarceration	4,083	7,000
Revenue Sharing	3,891	1,874
African Legal Assistance (Ford Foundation)	3,376	3,376
Election Law	3,185	10,307
National Institute of Education Quality Education	2,961	-
National Institute of Education State Project	2,356	2,355

National Health and Environmental Law	1,203	6,407
Local Urban Areas and Other Projects	992	1,267
Manpower	-	10,329
Health and National Urban Coalition	-	2,875
New York Community Schools	-	2,333
	$85,080	$117,282

The accompanying notes are an integral part of these financial statements.

FELDMAN, SKALER & KANFER

-5-

LAWYERS' COMMITTEE FOR CIVIL RIGHTS UNDER LAW

SUPPLEMENTARY INFORMATION

GRANTS AND CONTRIBUTIONS

	YEAR ENDED DECEMBER 31,	
	1974	1973
PRIVATE GRANTS AND CONTRIBUTIONS:		
Foundations:		
Ford Foundation	$340,754	$411,881
Rockefeller Brothers Fund, Inc.	107,429	112,096
Josephine E. McIntosh Foundation	51,667	72,710
Andrew W. Mellon Foundation	50,000	-
The Field Foundation	37,825	141,237
Edna McConnell Clark Foundation	37,770	9,443
Eugene and Agnes E. Meyer Foundation	36,000	12,000
The Chicago Community Trust	33,685	-
The Norman Foundation	23,750	1,250
The New World Foundation	21,875	45,833
Jacob L. Loose Million Dollar Fund Association	20,700	-
The New York Foundation	20,000	25,000
Taconic Foundation, Inc.	15,000	-
General Services Foundation	15,000	30,000
Prospect Hill Foundation, Inc.	15,000	10,000
The Philadelphia Foundation	10,000	5,000
Connelly Foundation	10,000	-
The Hersey Foundation	7,092	-
Pettus-Crowe Foundation	6,000	-
Wollenberg Foundation	6,750	3,500
Wieboldt Foundation	5,000	7,500
D.J.B. Foundation	5,000	6,000
Carnegie Corporation of New York	-	139,122
The Rockefeller Foundation	-	15,000
Charles E. Merrill Trust	-	13,751
Harry J. Loose Foundation	-	13,750
George A. and Dolly F. LaRue Trust	-	9,584
Van Ameringen Foundation, Inc.	-	8,333
Morris and Gwendolyn Cafritz Foundation	-	7,500
Hallmark Educational Foundation	-	5,000
Overbrook Foundation	-	5,000
Kansas City Association of Trusts and Foundations	-	5,000
Other	32,240	22,000
	908,537	1,137,490

Others:

Lawyers and law firms	269,953	369,108
Corporations	105,350	97,012
Schools and universities	13,237	78,773
Individuals	7,016	7,666
National Urban Coalition	-	5,750
Churches	24,417	400
Miscellaneous	35,352	4,596
	455,325	563,305
Total Private Grants and Contributions	1,363,862	1,700,795

PUBLIC GRANTS AND CONTRIBUTIONS:

Equal Employment Opportunity Commission	288,466	233,560
Commonwealth of Massachusetts	-	68,109
National Institute of Education	47,948	36,569
Narcotic Treatment Agency	16,724	12,776
City of New York	-	15,666
Law Enforcement Assistance Administration	-	5,000
Total Public Grants and Contributions	353,138	371,680
TOTAL GRANTS AND CONTRIBUTIONS	$1,717,000	$2,072,475

The accompanying notes are an integral part of these financial statements.

FELDMAN, SKALER & KANFER

LAWYERS' COMMITTEE FOR CIVIL RIGHTS UNDER LAW
SUPPLEMENTARY INFORMATION
STATEMENT OF REVENUES AND EXPENDITURES AND CHANGES IN FUND BALANCE BY PROJECTS
FOR THE YEAR ENDED DECEMBER 31, 1974

	TOTALS	FORD FOUNDATION SCHOOL FINANCE PROJECT	FORD FOUNDATION AFRICAN PROJECT	NATIONAL HEADQUARTERS	JACKSON MISSISSIPPI PROJECT	PRISON DEFENSE COMMITTEE, JACKSON
REVENUES:						
Grants and Contributions:						
Ford Foundation	$ 340,756	$178,615	$ 37,139	$195,857	$125,000	$ 34,342
Other private contributions	1,023,108				75,000	
Public grants and contributions	353,138	500			700,000	
Total Grants and Contributions	1,717,000			195,857		34,342
Legal fees received from court awards, etc.	25,914	261				
Reimbursement from publications	261	4,092		23,326	80	
Interest and investment income	27,498					
Net (loss) on sale of securities	(133)					
Total Revenues	1,776,170	183,468	37,139	219,183	201,936	34,342
EXPENDITURES:						
Salaries and Miscellaneous Services:						
Office and professional	660,033	49,035	11,109	96,201	93,726	16,771
Miscellaneous services	293,704	39,027	7,115	32,269	25,390	16,432
Total	1,035,023	113,444	20,638	155,383	119,423	33,723
Employee Benefits:						
Employee welfare	55,900	5,475	1,086	3,315	7,388	2,022
Payroll taxes	52,585	4,612	1,289	8,879	5,071	2,025
Moving expense	5,210			4,254		
Total	113,802	10,087	2,375	18,448	12,459	4,047
Travel and Meetings:						
Transportation	32,316	6,938	1,145	10,299	4,306	1,028
Meals and lodging	13,104	1,100	381	5,595	1,499	202
Meetings	13,104	2,437	31	5,318	363	1,716
Auto costs and maintenance	2,077				143	176
Depreciation of automobiles	1,732				1,121	178
Total	91,254	10,468	1,557	18,483	11,037	3,178
Office Operations:						
Books and legal periodicals	14,119	1,532	1,175	1,532	3,641	257
Stationery and office supplies	27,170	3,353	1,090	3,785	3,756	1,659
Printing	21,254	6,884	497	2,921	679	4
Duplication	45,128	1,222	2,533	3,620	4,522	1,929
Postage	13,695	7,654	602	6,511	1,400	811
Telephone and telegraph	64,032	8,334	1,925	8,984	9,586	3,604
Rent and occupancy	79,038		1,932	11,511	5,565	
Depreciation of furniture and equipment	380	1		320		
Miscellaneous office expense	21,640	2,892	967	1,991	692	63
Total	292,456	37,383	8,351	49,023	32,716	8,456
General and Administrative:						
Professional services	24,630	900		9,075	11,807	1,730
Taxes other than payroll	773	11	274	293	413	
Insurance	8,613	602		644	2,133	474
Interest	113			63		
Total	34,130	1,513	274	10,312	16,356	2,311
Grants and Legal Services:						
Court costs and litigation	49,697	2,198	2,216	2,138	16,518	8,416
Contractual legal services	80,533	7,200	36,761	73,480	4,533	
Sub grants	31,013		378	73,420	471	
Total	168,233	9,398	(7,416)	163,740	21,111	8,416
Allocated administrative expenses		19,453		(73,430)		
Total Operating Expenditures	1,728,637	(15,225)	2,018	192,883	111,483	19,282
REVENUES OVER (UNDER) EXPENDITURES	330,751	25,886		35,424	7,646	(13,440)
FUND BALANCE, BEGINNING OF YEAR	168,233			73,420	34,193	9,058
Reimbursement of prior years federal excise tax				(16,912)		
Transfer of fund balance on closed projects		9,092	-0-			
FUND BALANCES, END OF YEAR	$ 325,976	120,571		192,883	124,597	(4,382)

The accompanying notes are an integral part of these financial statements.

LEGAL ASSISTANCE PROJECTS	MANPOWER PROJECT	ELECTION LAW PROJECT	REVENUE SHARING PROJECT	INQUIRY INTO INCARCERATION PROJECT	PUBLIC EMPLOYMENT PROJECT	N.I.E. STATE PROJECT	M.I.E. QUALITY EDUCATION PROJECT	EQUAL EMPLOYMENT OPPORTUNITY COMM. PROJECT	SPECIAL NATIONAL PROJECT	URBAN AREAS CITY PROJECT	OTHER PROJECTS

FELDMAN, SKALER & KANFER

- 7 -

LAWYERS' COMMITTEE FOR CIVIL RIGHTS UNDER LAW

SUPPLEMENTARY INFORMATION

GRANTS AND CONTRACTS RECEIVABLE AND DEFERRED

PROJECT	GRANTOR OR CONTRACTOR	TERM	TOTAL GRANT OR CONTRACT	AMOUNT RECEIVABLE DECEMBER 31, 1974	1973
School Finance Grant 720-0160A	Ford Foundation	8/1/73 - 9/30/75	$387,000	$ 63,505	$ 67,789
Equal Employment Opportunity Contract 71-42	E.E.O.C.	9/26/74 - 1/31/75	104,000	52,000	
N.I.E. Quality Education Contract NIE-C-74-0031	Department of Health, Education & Welfare	10/1/74 - 75	85,117	2,922	
Equal Employment Opportunity Contract 71-42	E.E.O.C.	9/1/73 - 74	315,700		52,633
N.I.E. State Contract NE-G-00-3-0044	Department of Health, Education & Welfare	6/27/73 - 9/30/74	53,337		13,275
TOTAL GRANTS AND CONTRACTS RECEIVABLE				$118,427	$133,297

PROJECT	GRANTOR OR CONTRACTOR	TERM	TOTAL GRANT OR CONTRACT	AMOUNT DEFERRED DECEMBER 31, 1974	1973
Minority Leadership	The Rockefeller Foundation	1/1/75 - 12/31/76	100,000	$ 30,899	
Revenue Sharing	Edna McConnell Clark Foundation	10/1/74 - 75	37,770	28,328	
Prisoners' Defense, Parchman Penitentiary	New York Foundation	7/1/74 - 75	25,000	12,500	
Attorneys' Fees	The New World Foundation	4/16/74 - 75	25,000	7,292	
Attorneys' Fees	The Shalan Foundation	4/16/74 - 75	3,000	875	
Prisoners' Defense	U.S. Catholic Conference Campaign for Human Development	11/20/74 - 75	35,000	5,833	
Public Employment	Rockefeller Brothers Fund, Inc.	12/15/73 - 74	112,100		$107,428
National Headquarters	Andrew W. Mellon Foundation	1/1 - 12/31/74	50,000		50,000
Revenue Sharing	Edna McConnell Clark Foundation	10/1/73 - 74	37,770		28,328
Election Law	Josephine H. McIntosh Foundation	5/1/73 - 74	80,000		26,667
Revenue Sharing	Norman Foundation	12/1/73 - 74	15,000		13,750
National Health & Environmental Law	U.C.L.A.	9/1/73 - 2/28/74	39,710		13,237
African Legal Assistance Grant 730-0040A	Ford Foundation	4/1/73 - 9/30/74	74,278		12,380
National Headquarters	Prospect Hill Foundation, Inc.	1/1/73 - 12/31/74	25,000		10,000
Election Law	The New World Foundation	3/1/73 - 74	25,000		4,167
Jackson, Miss.	Hugh M. Hefner Fund	1/1 - 12/31/74	2,500		2,500
Jackson, Miss.	United Presbyterian Church	1/1 - 12/31/74	2,000		2,000
TOTAL GRANTS AND CONTRACTS DEFERRED				$ 85,727	$270,457

The accompanying notes are an integral part of these financial statements.

INDEX

A

ABA *Bar News* 103

ABA Board of Governors 68, 130, 230, 233, 235

and White House Conference for Lawyers 80

ABA Code of Professional Responsibility 10, 237

ABA House of Delegates 65, 128, 230, 233, 235

ABA *Journal* 19, 48, 107

ABA Section on Individual Rights and Responsibility, formation of 232–37

Abram, Morris B. 112, 158

Adams, John 182

adversarial legal process 1–2

Aelony, Zev 112

African Heritage Studies Association 221, 222

Alabama Act 46

Alabama Bar 52

Alabama Bar Association 89

response to White House Conference 90

Alabama Journal, The 53

Alabama Lawyer, The 53

Alabama, University of, desegregation of 51, 55, 58, 69–70

Alessandroni, Walter 110

Alexandria v. Holmes County, Mississippi 187

Allen, George Edward, Sr. 113

American Bar Association (ABA)

and the civil rights movement in Mississippi 48

and George Wallace 60–86

and the legal aid movement 14–16

Annual Conference, 1963 106

Annual Conference, 1994 153

call to bar associations to support civil rights 123

Committee on Civil Rights and Civil Unrest 80, 95, 128, 153

Committee on Public Relations 20

Committee on the National Defense 18

Committee on War Work 18, 20

defending individual rights 231

formation of 10

Special Committee on Legal Aid 15

Standing Committee on the Federal Judiciary 61, 63

Standing Committee on Lawyer Referral Services 19

Standing Committee on Legal Aid 18, 229

American Civil Liberties Union 17, 27–30, 125

formation of 28–29

American College of Trial Lawyers 68

American Committee on Africa 201, 203, 221, 222, 223

American Friends Service Committee 188, 189

American Jewish Committee 126

American Jewish Congress 125

American Judicature Society 63

American Law Institute 63, 68

American Union Against Militarism 28

Amherst College 113

apartheid policy in South Africa 198–221

Articles of Incorporation of the LCCR 107

Aschenbrenner, Larry 175, 176, 183

J

Jackson, Mississippi, LCCR office of, 134–35, 156, 158–66, 175, 191
chief counsels 175
establishment of 156
funding for 165
staff members 176
Jenkins, Martha Wood 176, 184
Johnson, Lyndon 73, 77
election as president 143
legislative agenda 141–45
request for LCCR involvement in North 162
Johnson, Paul 47
Jones, Thomas Goode 10
Jones, Walter B. 53
judicial legislation 45
judicial review of state legislation 52
Justice and the Poor 14, 16, 21

K

Katzenbach, Nicholas 63, 69, 107, 204, 205
Kennedy Administration
and freedom riders 39
and school desegration 34
desegration of University of Alabama 69
desegregation in Mississippi 48
federal civil rights legislation 70–74
letter of appreciation to LCCR 101
White House Conference for Lawyers 74–86
Kennedy, John F. 102
and George Wallace 56
assassination of 141
desegration of Birmingham, Alabama 57
desegregation of the University of Mississippi 47
election of 34
Kennedy Manifesto 71

Kennedy, Robert F. 48, 55, 101, 171
and formation of LCCR 94
and George Wallace 55
and South Africa 201, 204
assassination of 173
presidential campaign, 1968 172
request for LCCR assistance in the South 122
University of Mississippi desegration 39
Kentridge, Sidney 210
Kerner Commission. *See* National Advisory Commission on Civil Disobedience
Kerner, Otto 168
King, C.B. 112
King, Martin Luther, Jr. 56
assassination of 146, 172
desegration of Birmigham, Alabama 56
emergence as civil rights leader 36
formation of SCLC 36
King, Miller, Anderson, Nash & Yerke 134
Knight, Robert 119
Ku Klux Klan 57
Kuchel, Thomas 153
Kuhn, Edward 236

L

Labour Party 19
Lansden, Robert 183, 184
Law and Lawyers in a Changing World: The President 50
Lawrence, David H. 60
Lawyers' Committee for Civil Rights Under Law. *See* LCCR.
Lawyers Constitutional Defense Committee 114, 124, 140, 161
lawyer's responsibility to the changing law 49
lawyers' statement challenging George Wallace 60–86